Social Science Education in the Elementary School

Social Science Education in the Elementary School

Milton E. Ploghoft
Ohio University

Albert H. Shuster
Ohio University

Charles E. Merrill Publishing Co.
A Bell & Howell Company
Columbus, Ohio

Copyright © 1971, by Charles E. Merrill Publishing Co., Columbus, Ohio. All rights reserved. No part of this book may be reproduced in any form, electronic or mechanical, including photocopy, recording, or any information storage and retrieval system, without permission in writing from the publisher.

International Standard Book Number: 0–675–09239–6

Library of Congress Catalog Card Number: 78–147054

1 2 3 4 5 6 7 8 9 10—76 75 74 73 72 71

Printed in the United States of America

PREFACE

The period following the end of World War Two has been filled with technological and social developments of considerable magnitude, and the implications which these developments hold for the education of children and youth have held the attention of professional educators and concerned laymen since the mid-1950's. Changes in science and mathematics curricula were given vigorous stimulation by the Soviet accomplishments in space, although the mathematics and science educators had been concerned with providing discovery-oriented experiences which were organized in terms of the concepts and structures of the disciplines.

Throughout the decade of the 1960's, there was much ferment and controversy in the curriculum area identified since the early part of the century as the social studies. There are growing indications that new programs are emerging which will place specific emphasis upon the use of rational inquiry into problems in the social domain. Greater attention will be given to the use of facts in the development of concepts that will help the individual understand the situations and institutions of social man and, in the process, identify and clarify his role as a member of a society that aspires to continued freedom.

This book has been developed as a response to a changing situation which calls for the preparation of teachers to meet new responsibilities in social science education in elementary schools. Since we are committed to the use of inquiry in the elementary classroom, this textbook has been designed to involve you *as an inquirer,* both as a student in a professional course and later as a teacher of children. We intend that you will interact with the assumption and inferences that we present and that you will accept only tentatively the conclusions and recommendations which we make.

We have a high degree of confidence in the validity of the observations we make in the overview and chapter one, where we survey the problems and directions of social education in our nation. Our beliefs and values are presented as we develop the rationale for emerging programs; but there are other positions and other points of view, and we urge that you consider them and be alert to any unfounded bias we may have.

The second section of this book deals with dominant values and value conflicts that are of critical importance in shaping the content and process of social education. The value orientations of a society provide direction to the education of children, and the value conflicts provide problems that children encounter in their experiences in the school. Following the consideration of the social science disciplines as sources of concepts in chapter three, the major concepts which underlie informed social behavior are taken up in chapter four. The objectives of social science education are treated in chapter five. This four chapter section is intended to provide the foundations for the curriculum and teaching decisions that you will make.

Following chapter six, which deals with the characteristics of children and their implications for social science education, the third section of the book moves into the areas of inquiry processes, other methods and procedures, and instructional resources. This section is concluded with the consideration of three continuing, but often maltreated or neglected, areas: religion, contemporary affairs, and cross-cultural studies.

Section four includes chapters on the changing role of the teacher in social education and the evaluation of social science education.

There are other elements that set this book apart from social studies methods books. Carefully selected readings are provided as an integrated effort to bridge the gap between the world on the outside and the social education of children and youth. The professional preparation of teachers becomes contemporary and real, as well as interdisciplinary. Throughout the individual chapters and in the Suggested Problems and Projects, students are provided with problems and alternatives which require investigation and decision making. The Related Readings and Suggested Problems and Projects are provided to extend and enrich your study and discussion of each chapter. It is recommended that you direct your attention to them *before* you read each chapter, in order that your outside readings and projects may be integral parts of your course work.

Finally, this book should not be viewed as an attempt to castigate the conventional social studies programs that have predominated in the elementary schools. The changing aspects of modern life, which have put man into new relationships with his fellows, call for new efforts at understanding and objectivity. The advent of space exploration requires that man view his relationship to, and role in, the universe in a new perspective. The intensified problems in intergroup relations, population control, use of the environment, and the place of the individual in highly organized mass societies suggest that new possibilities in the social education of the young are in order.

Acknowledgments

In any effort of this nature, the contributions of many individuals and organizations have made possible the final product. To the authors of the Charles E. Merrill Social Science Seminar Series and to its editors, Raymond H. Muessig and Vincent R. Rogers, we are indebted for the resources drawn from their materials.

The member schools of the Cooperative Center for Social Science Education at Ohio University have provided the operational settings in which ideas were tested with teachers and children. Throughout this book will be found evidences of the contributions made by the Clark County, Nevada, school district, the Cleveland Heights–University Heights, Ohio, school district, the Eugene, Oregon, school district 4 J, and the East Syracuse–Minoa, New York, school district.

The continuing influences of a few persons have motivated us to this effort. To Dr. Julian C. Aldrich, Dr. Lucille Lindberg, Dr. Lindley Stiles, and Dr. Harold Taylor, we express appreciation for the penetration of their ideas, and simultaneously, we absolve them of any responsibility for the shortcomings of our product.

To Mrs. Cheryl Nagle and Mrs. Tate Baird, we offer our appreciation for their patience and perseverance in the preparation of the manuscript for the publisher.

We gratefully acknowledge the courtesy of the Santa Fe Railway for its permission to use the photographs on page 253, the National Aeronautics and Space Administration for its permission to use the photograph on page 257, and the Norfolk, Virginia, Public Schools for their permission to use the photographs on pages 260 and 349.

Credit for the cartoons which appear in the text is given to M. Eugene Ploghoft, an art instructor in the Port Huron, Michigan, School District.

M.E.P.

1971

A.H.S.

Contents

	Section I	1
	An Overview	3
1	Social Science Education—An Emerging Program	19
	Section II	33
2	Values, Issues, and Conflicts in Social Science Education	
	Part I	35
	Part II	65
3	Using Data from the Social Science Disciplines	133
4	Conceptualizing and Generalizing	153
5	Behavioral Objectives in Social Science Education	175
	Section III	**189**
6	The Child and Social Education	191
7	Inquiry Processes for Children and Teachers	207
8	Instructional Methodology and the Teacher	231
9	Instructional Resources for Learning	249
10	Religion and Social Science Education	273
11	Cross-Cultural Studies	289
12	Contemporary Affairs in Social Science Education: An Emerging Role	305

Section IV — 317

13　Teachers in Social Science Education — 319

14　Evaluating Progress in Social Science Education — 347

　　Our Conclusion—Your Beginning — 365

　　Appendixes — 366

　　Index — 405

*For one thing after other will grow clear,
Nor shall the blind night rob thee of the road,
To hinder thy gaze on Nature's Farthest-forth.
Thus things for things shall kindle torches new.*

> Lucretius, *Of the
> Nature of Things*
> First Century B.C.

Social Science Education in the Elementary School

SECTION I

Section one of this book includes two related chapters which deal first with the nature of the social studies through mid-century and with the issues and developments that have given rise to curriculum ferment and change in the direction of "new" social studies or social science education. Second, the characteristics of emerging social science education programs are presented and contrasted with the older social studies.

We are aware of the problems which are involved in the task that we have undertaken. The use of the term "older social studies" may be seen in some quarters as projecting a condescending attitude toward the objectives and efforts of certain persons and programs. However, our intent is to focus upon what we perceive to be the needs and justifications for change in the social education of our children and youth. In the interest of delineating the problem and specifying the differences between emerging programs and traditional programs, we have chosen to use the terms "older social studies" and "social science education."

Social science education will not solve all of the problems of the human condition; it may solve no more than did older social studies, but it is our obvious belief that it offers greater possibilities in that direction.

INTRODUCTION

IN THE REAR VIEW MIRROR

> When did the term social studies appear?
> What are the sources of confusion in social studies?
> What attention has been given to social studies curriculum?
> What are the obstacles to change?

CHARACTERISTICS OF SOCIAL SCIENCE EDUCATION

CHARACTERISTICS OF EMERGING PROGRAMS

> What is the place of behavioral objectives?
> What is the place of inquiry?
> What is the place of conceptualization?
> What will happen to content?

BRIDGING THE GAP

SUGGESTED PROBLEMS AND PROJECTS

RELATED READINGS

An Overview

Introduction

The overview and chapter one attend to the purposes and directions in programs of social education of children in the United States. We recognize that your most pressing concern may be for unit and lesson planning and teaching strategies, and these will be taken up soon. However, we believe that we are obliged to let you know why various assessments of the social studies situation have led to a call for the new programs and new approaches that we choose to call *social science education*.

You may encounter a few terms that will be new to you, at least in the social education context. *Inquiry process* as a way of seeking for valid and extensive meaning is very much like the inquiry that is considered in science education. Inquiry in the social domain moves from problems and concerns to a rational formulation of conclusions and generalizations. Inquiry emphasizes the *use of facts,* rather than coverage of information. In the social context, inquiry has some elements that make it a more difficult task than in the science areas.

Inquiry into problems, issues, and interests in the social realm is aimed at the development of valid concepts which will guide the individual toward more effective, intelligent behavior. The social sciences provide the basic areas of information which can be used to approach the concept development process.

Social Science Education is a term which draws its meaning from those elements just discussed. The investigative methods of scientific inquiry are emphasized in the study of the social nature and condition of man. The end is conceptualization and modified behavior in terms of specific valued outcomes.

Related Readings and Suggested Problems and Projects are provided to extend and enrich your study and discussion of each chapter. It is recommended that you direct your attention to these readings, problems, and projects *before* you read each chapter, in order that your outside readings and projects may be integral parts of your course work.

In the Rear View Mirror

Marshall McLuhan has said that our modern society charges off into the future with its eyes glued to the rear view mirror. The familiar scenes of yesteryear offer a security that is not so readily recognized in the present or in the days ahead.[1] It is probably true that most human beings behave in such a fashion and that the teachers of today's children seek security in the programs and practices of the past, disregarding, to some extent, the realities of the changing world about them.

A look in the rear view mirror at this point is not provided in order to make the reader feel secure in "old things tried and true;" rather, this glance over the shoulder should sharpen the total perspective of the social studies picture as current and emerging programs are considered throughout this book. It may be foolish to look too long in the rear view mirror; it is just as foolish to never look there at all.

One of the interesting characteristics of people is their tendency to believe that things have usually been pretty much as they are now, with exception of some of the technological innovations that have altered man's daily activities. A pertinent example is the widespread notion that, from the beginning, the schools in this country have had as a major responsibility the preparation of competent citizens for democratic life.

A brief review of the educational history of the United States will bring to mind the religious motivations behind the early colonial efforts to teach children to read. It was necessary for every man to be able to read the Bible in order that the "old Deluder Satan" would not find it an easy task to lead people astray. The "three R's" curriculum, which has continued to prevail with strength even into the latter decades of this century, was not created as a vehicle for bringing every young American to the doorway of participatory democracy, although it contained skill areas that were essential to effective citizenship. In an effort to gain an elementary perspective of the role of the school in citizenship education, it should be recalled that one half of the adult population in the United States could not vote until well into the twentieth century. Imagine, if you will, the difficulty you might have in trying to help boys and girls appreciate the privileges and responsibilities of citizenship in a nation where being a female was considered sufficient reason for being denied voting privileges.

Traditional notions of education continued to influence curriculum content, and the early grammar schools of the United States were

---

[1] This is Marshall McLuhan, *The Medium Is the Massage,* a film produced by NBC television and distributed by McGraw Hill (1968).

An Overview

not markedly different from those in England, with the notable exception of courses in American history. After independence from England was attained, the passion of nationalism precluded any general consideration of English and European history in the common schools, and American history soon came to occupy a strong position in the curriculum. To this day, American history has priority in some quarters because of its long standing in the curriculum and because many state legislatures require that it be included.[2] Professor Gifford Doxsee has commented that history provided the means to a nationalistic morality which helped the average American identify with the traditions, legends and myths of his young nation.[3]

The influx of millions of immigrants into the United States in the latter part of the nineteenth century and the first decades of this century quite likely provided strong justification for major attention to American history as a way of bringing the immigrant children into the mainstream of the national heritage. A continuing concern for adequate treatment of the American heritage by organizations, such as, the Daughters of the American Revolution and American Legion, has served to deter questions or modifications of the role of American history in the curriculum, although this may not be their intent.

When did the term social studies appear?

"Social studies," as a term, did not come into use until the 1920's, and it was probably fostered by the 1916 report of the National Education Association, which called for courses at the high school level in "modern problems."[4] This N.E.A. report reflected a shift in educational thinking to the extent that it recommended that real problems and issues of life be studied from a multi-discipline viewpoint, with history being only one of several sources of information.

Deserving of comment is the place of geography in the social studies program. In the common schools of colonial America, geography did not have a place, partly because it was not a popularly studied discipline, and partly because it did not have relevance to the educational goals of the times. After American independence and during the ensuing period of vigorous nationalism, geography was viewed as not being important for young Americans to study. It was the rapid expansion westward across the continent and the rising interest in international affairs in the

---

[2] William H. Cartwright, "The Future of the Social Studies," *Social Education* 30 (February 1966): 79–82.

[3] Professor Gifford Doxsee, in conversations with the writer, Athens, Ohio (March 1968).

[4] The Report of the Committee on the Social Studies (Washington, D.C.: National Education Association, 1916).

latter years of the nineteenth century that gave support to geography as a proper subject for study in the elementary schools.

In the late 1930's and throughout the 1940's and 1950's, attempts were made toward a unified approach to social studies. The textbooks and social studies guides of that period are indicative of the effort. Some of the elementary textbooks included the term "Unified Social Studies" in their titles, although cursory examination often suggests that a geography book and a history book were simply bound together in one cover. The shift to the term social studies appears to have resulted from a growing awareness that the problem of preparing children for life in a changing, complex, multi-ethnic society calls for more than the traditional experiences in history and geography. An additional force was the work of John Dewey, which drew attention to the need for learning experiences that were compatible with the interests and capabilities of children.

What are the sources of confusion in social studies?

The social studies have suffered from a variety of complaints, including an absence of definition as to their specific purposes and, accordingly, their content. The lack of general professional understanding and commitment to the social studies probably arose from this confusion surrounding their objectives and content. Critics, informed and ignorant alike, attacked the social studies as the handiwork of progressive educators, Leftists, un-American intellectuals and questionable persons. Serious scholars of history and geography wondered why their disciplines were being shunned in favor of a thing called social studies, when there was so much confusion regarding the social studies' objectives and content. Classroom teachers, who were faced with the task of planning social studies experiences for children, were often inclined to retreat to a pure textbook approach with an occasional field trip or resource speaker added for good measure.

As recently as 1968, Michaelis wrote, ". . . social studies encompass those aspects of history and the social sciences that are believed to be of greatest value for the general education of students in elementary and secondary schools."[5] As a prospective teacher, you probably would like to know what is meant by "those aspects," and you may be interested to know how it will be decided which aspects of history and the social sciences have "greatest value" for use in the schools.

A 1962 publication of the National Council for the Social Studies stated that the "ultimate goal of education in the social studies is

---

[5] John U. Michaelis, *Social Studies for Children in a Democracy* (Englewood Cliffs, N.J.: Prentice-Hall, 1968), p. 2.

An Overview

the development of desirable socio-civic behavior."[6] Again, the prospective teacher may want to ask whether this is not indeed the ultimate goal of all common education, whether in a free and open society or in a closed authoritarian society. A question that has emerged from the conflicts and confrontations of the 1960's is, "What do we mean by desirable socio-civic behavior?"

The increasing confusion and dissatisfaction with the social studies was summarized by Preston in 1950, when he observed that in many schools the social studies are a body without a spirit, a corpse made of lifeless information to be covered and regurgitated. In other schools, Preston wrote, the social studies program is a "spook," all spirit without body, a thin and chaotic gathering of experiences and materials from any sources for many or no reasons.[7]

In 1965, one writer called the social studies, "curriculum's foggy bottom," and cited the lack of agreement as to the definitions and purposes of the social studies as major causes of confusion.[8] In short, it seems that Alice would be quite at home in the social studies wonderland where words and terms mean just what anyone wants them to mean.

What attention has been given to social studies curriculum?

Following the Soviet Sputnik success, the science and mathematics areas of the curriculum were the recipients of massive federal and foundation funds designed to help the United States catch up in the space race. It may seem unusual that the mounting problems brought on by racial tensions, economic disadvantages, obsolete systems for treating the mentally and socially ill, and continuing failures in coping with international crises did not bring similar financial support for study and strengthening of programs in the social studies. Comparatively meager resources were made available in the 1960's for the support of discipline-oriented social studies projects, on the assumption that better materials for instructional use would help resolve the social studies dilemma.

It was disappointing that the plight of the social studies for elementary children was disregarded in all but a very few federally funded projects, such as, the one directed by Hilda Taba at Contra Costa. Scholars in anthropology, economics, history, political science, geography, and sociology were given funds to develop teaching materials for children. In very few instances were such materials field tested with rep-

---

[6] National Council for the Social Studies, "The Role of the Social Studies," *Social Education* vol. 26 (October 1962).

[7] Ralph C. Preston, *Teaching Social Studies in the Elementary School* (New York: Holt, Rinehart and Winston, Inc., 1950), p. 5.

[8] Milton E. Ploghoft, "Social Studies: Curriculum's Foggy Bottom," *Social Education* vol. 29 (November 1965).

resentative groups of children and teachers; neither were questions considered which dealt with the need for some kind of cooperative efforts by scholars and teachers to develop programs which would relate objectives, learning experiences, and materials to the role (yet undefined) of social studies for elementary children in a free society.

Dr. Ethel Alpenfels, long noted for work as an educational anthropologist, was dismayed that one major anthropology project proposed to introduce the complex concept of "culture" at the second grade level.[9] Dr. Edwin Fenton, one of the early directors of a history project at Carnegie-Mellon, remarked that his own early works on inductive approaches to history were really improperly labelled, and that his later work with young people in the schools had expanded his concepts concerning the role and nature of history in the social studies program.[10]

The candor of scholars in such matters is essential if the prospective teacher is to be aware of the changing views toward various aspects of social studies. Of equal importance is a tentative view of the many social studies projects which have been supported by federal funds beginning in the early 1960's. Frequently, funds were not available to provide for evaluation of social studies curriculum materials, and dissemination of information has been similarly hampered.

No one can predict the nature of the programs in social education that will dominate elementary schools in the latter decades of this century. Nor, for that matter, does there appear to be consensus with regard to what the programs ought to be like. Dorothy McClure Fraser has observed that "the pupils of the seventies and eighties will study their society through vastly different experiences, different both in procedures and in substance. . . ."[11]

Keith, Blake, and Tiedt have identified major criticisms of social studies to include sketchy coverage of too much content, lack of comprehensive evaluation, lack of critical thinking, inappropriate teaching methods, and illogical placement of subject matter. These authors foresee emerging programs that emphasize inquiry, behavioral goals, concept oriented experiences, and content that takes into account psychological factors.[12]

It appears that a new era may be on the horizon, an era that will

---

[9] From comments made by Dr. Alpenfels during an appearance as a Martha Jennings Holden lecturer at Ohio University, Athens, Ohio (April 13, 1968).

[10] From an address by Dr. Fenton, Columbus, Ohio (February 1968).

[11] Dorothy McClure Fraser, "The Changing Scene in Social Studies," *Social Studies Curriculum Development, 39th Yearbook* (Washington, D.C.: National Council for the Social Studies, 1969), p. 1.

[12] Lowell Keith, Paul Blake, and Sidney Tiedt, *Contemporary Curriculum in the Elementary School* (New York: Harper & Row, Publishers, 1968), pp. 189–194.

An Overview

witness the transition from social studies, whatever they have been, to social science education. Persons who enter teaching anytime in the next 30 years will quite likely be involved with the problems of bridging the gap.

What are the obstacles to change?

Curriculum reform in mathematics and science has been, for the most part, content oriented and has depended heavily upon the work in separate disciplines. Accordingly, many educators have waited for similar curriculum development in the social studies area, but the lack of similarity has been overlooked. Changing the mathematics and science curricula did not need to involve a number of disciplines, nor was it necessary to be much concerned with the emotional reactions of teachers and parents. The new mathematics caused some displeasure among teachers who were not convinced of the need for change and who did not wish to reorient their thinking to the new methods and materials. Parental reaction to the new mathematics stemmed from a lack of understanding of the rationale and theory and, to some extent, was related to the inability of parents to help their children with homework.

Changes in the social studies have been, and likely will continue to be, accompanied by highly emotional reactions from special interest groups, parents, and teachers. Some patriotic organizations may respond negatively to proposals that cast doubt upon the relevance of traditional subject matter to the contemporary needs of children and society. The inclusion of the areas of psychology and sociology may be challenged by persons who are skeptical of the validity of behavioral sciences, particularly when the information from these fields questions the accuracy of long revered notions about human behavior. (An example is the conclusive data which shows that capital punishment does not reduce the incidence of homicides. Apparently, some people still *want* to believe that such punishment will control criminal behavior.)

Teachers who have concentrated their studies in one discipline, such as, geography, are understandably inclined to support its major place in the social studies. At the college level, the single discipline specialist may vigorously support the place and status of his field in the social studies. Professor Lawrence Senesh, an economics education specialist, has called for an "orchestration of the disciplines" in the building of new programs, but even so, he concludes that the core of the new social studies should be economics.[13] It is not the intention here to cast the

---

[13] In remarks made by Dr. Senesh in a conference at Ohio University, Athens, Ohio (November 1967).

social science scholar in the role of saboteur of change in the curriculum, but it is necessary to recognize that the multi-disciplinary sources of social studies pose certain challenges to the curriculum makers.

The matter of the preparation of teachers requires careful attention in any consideration of the obstacles to change in social studies. It is common in teacher education programs to require 18 to 27 semester hours of course work in the social sciences. This may include American history and government, which is customarily specified by state certifying agencies. The remaining course work may be distributed among the other social sciences, in which case the experiences of the future teacher may be limited to the introductory level courses.

Professional course work in the teaching of social studies is usually limited to one course which is scheduled prior to the student teaching experience, a course in which you may now be enrolled. Coordination of the professional course work and the social science background appears to be the exception, rather than the rule; hence a disjointed program at the university level may follow the very traditional social studies experiences which you have had in elementary and secondary school. A widespread awareness of the need for change and a commitment to continuing efforts in the years ahead seem to be called for if this obstacle is to be overcome.

Characteristics of Social Science Education

As the term suggests, social science education is directed toward a rational or scientific study of the social aspects of the human condition. Social science education is particularly concerned with the education of the children and youth of the nation to the end that high levels of information and skill will contribute to effective behavior in coping with the complex social problems of the state, nation and world.

Traditionally, the schools and other formal educative agencies of every society have been used to reinforce the cultural image upon the individual, to assist in the acculturation process. This will continue to be the case for many years unless there is a drastic change in human behavior; for, as Frederick the Great said, "What the state desires in its citizens, that will it put into its schools." In the case of modern United States, the issue that has emerged is whether the schools should move to realize the frequently verbalized values of open inquiry for truth, individual responsibility and involvement in the problems of society, and an open, rational approach to public questions.

The extent to which United States society is ready to move toward social science education may be a significant measure of the differences between education in a free and open society and in the closed systems of Mainland China and the Soviet Union. It has become a necessity for nations to encourage and support rational inquiry in the natural sciences or risk lagging behind in the space race. In the social realms, however, the Soviets have not encouraged open inquiry. Indeed, they have insisted upon dogmatic acceptance of the Marxist notion that the communist state is the perfect condition for human life. Open inquiry and confrontation with social, political, and economic ideas is not tolerated, and the young citizen is conditioned to have full faith in the decisions and actions of the Supreme Soviet.

It is not an easy task to examine the educational programs of the United States to determine the degree to which educational objectives here differ from those of the Soviet Union. Much of the content may appear to be the same in some areas, such as, mathematics, sciences, geography, and the like. It is in the role and responsibility of the individual, as an inquirer into the social aspects of life, that the sharp differences are found.

According to one source, Soviet teachers are inclined (obliged?) to stick to a textbook approach in order that they will be on safe ground. Synthesis and interpretation of facts are often delayed until the official viewpoint is well-known. The Soviet teacher is not confronted with the responsibility of dealing with controversial issues and helping students to examine many sides of a problem.[14]

There are those instances in the United States where local communities may overtly, or otherwise, place limits on the school's freedom to inquire. Special interest groups and political pressures may cause the teacher to select a noninquiry course of action in the classroom. When such forces in our society dissuade the development of programs of rational inquiry into sensitive aspects of life, a major difference between education in open and closed societies is lost through timidity and indifference.

At this point, it should be emphasized that the difficulties associated with open inquiry into the traditions, institutions, and values of our society are not the only reasons for the absence of widespread development of programs in social inquiry. The lack of research concerning the readiness of young learners for experiences in social inquiry has probably been a factor, and the traditional approach to the preparation of ele-

---

[14] *Education in the U.S.S.R.* (Washington, D.C.: U.S. Office of Education, 1957), p. 87.

mentary social studies teachers has not anticipated new and developing programs.

It may be helpful to keep this background in mind as characteristics of social science education programs are considered. If you are a typical student, your own elementary and secondary schools social studies experiences were not oriented toward inquiry processes and concept development. As you move ahead in your consideration of more effective ways to enhance the social education of the young, it should not be necessary to feel defensive about your own preparation. The conditions of life that have been modified as a result of technological breakthroughs in communications, travel, and space exploration have posed new questions about the nature and role of youth in our society, about the relations between groups and nations, and about man's place in the universe itself. New ventures in education need not be prefaced with apology to the past.

Characteristics of Emerging Programs

The various aspects of new developments in social science education will be examined in detail in the chapters that follow. In order that you may be oriented to the major characteristics of social science education, a brief overview is provided here.

What is the place of behavioral objectives?

The identification of behavioral objectives is viewed as a necessary part of planning programs in social science education. Although it is common to hear teachers say, "We all know how we want the young people to behave now and as adult citizens," it is seldom that simple when we sit down as a group of students or teachers and draw up a list of behaviors that are appropriate for young people and, at the same time, will have transfer value to adult situations.

Part of the difficulty with behavioral objectives in the social realm lies in the fact that our society prescribes a quite different role for the child from that accepted for an adult. The task is complicated by the fact that we experience considerable divergence of opinion when we try to reach a consensus as to the kind of behavior we desire for adult members of the society. Finally, it is a new and challenging task to formulate statements of behavioral objectives that actually express behavior that can be observed. How can teachers possibly observe children behaving in situations that will lend some evidence that their learning experiences are, in reality, leading to changed behavior?

On the other hand, if the school can do no more than make vague claims that the learning experiences of today will bring acceptable behavior in the distant future when the youngsters are beyond the school, then the public cannot be expected to take us seriously. Of course, there are a certain number of educators who claim that the forces affecting human behavior are so complex that it is futile to even consider behavioral objectives, hence the learning program can be whatever satisfies our own biases.

Social science education is a rational endeavor, hence attention must be given to the kind of behavior that is anticipated as an outcome of the learning experiences planned for children. In those instances where a desired behavior cannot be evaluated in the school, such as, participating in elections as an adult, the responsibility of the school is to provide learning situations which are carefully calculated to develop the attitudes that will lead to the desired behavior.

What is the place of inquiry?

An open inquiry process is an integral part of social science education. Open inquiry requires that the child be given an active role in the sifting and selecting of areas for study, that he be involved in formulating hypotheses, in searching for pertinent information, and in considering alternate solutions to the problem at hand. Open inquiry calls for a participating teacher, rather than one who manipulates the children toward her prescribed tentative conclusions.

It is known that inquiry by the adult member in a free society places great responsibility upon the skills and resources of the individual, that in the resolution of adult problems, there is no teacher available to provide the correct answer. Neither is it envisioned in a free society that there will be a political boss to tell the citizen how to think. The presence today of mass persuasion through mass media has cast open inquiry into a new and urgent role in the education of the young.

What is the place of conceptualization?

One of the major concerns of social science education is the accurate conceptualization of social reality by the child. Conceptualizing is a mental process that cannot be measured directly; the teacher must be satisfied with indirect evidence of the kind and adequacy of the concepts which any child has concerning a specific social phenomenon. A serious weakness of many social studies programs has been the tendency to accept verbal recall of information as evidence of adequate conceptualizing, and since it is quite simple to test children in this manner, the practice is quite common.

With the growing attention being given to concept-centered programs, there may be a tendency to consider the ability of the child to recall a concept statement as sufficient evidence that the child has *conceptualized*. As an illustration, the ability of a child to say that the people in his city are interdependent does not really reveal anything about the completeness of his conceptualizing about the nature and degree of dependency of people upon one another.

The matter of concept development is difficult to deal with because modern education has become accustomed to accepting the recall and recognition of words and statements as the major evidence that learning has taken place. With increased emphasis upon *conceptualizing*, it will be necessary to provide opportunities for children to reveal in additional ways the extent to which they have developed a "mental construction" about specific social phenomena.

At this point, you can sense that the social science education program will not begin with facts to be learned for recall and recognition; it will begin with conceptualizations to be developed through a variety of experiences using many kinds of instructional materials. Information is seen as one means to the end of accurate concept development by children. Evaluation, then, will require new techniques and materials, although it should be emphasized that facts, as such, *have not been left out*. They are put to appropriate and effective use in the concept-centered program.

What will happen to content?

This question has already been answered to some extent, if the traditional meaning of content is synonymous with fact-centered programs. Critics of older social studies programs have complained that the children were given large doses of information capsules to be regurgitated on demand and eventually forgotten. Social science education defines content as the totality of any planned instructional project. The conceptualizations that are anticipated, the problems or topics that are identified for consideration, the types of information that show promise of being helpful, and the inquiry processes to be used form the content of an activity in social science education. The total content of any such undertaking must be justified in terms of its predicted value in the overall curriculum.

Accordingly, it is apparent that social science education does not begin with a set of historical and geographical topics and facts to be learned. Social science education begins with concept areas to be developed in order that valued social behaviors will be supported by open and honest intellectual effort.

What major changes are indicated? After an extensive survey of the literature dealing with the changes that have been called for by a number of social science educators and social studies authorities, David Welton reported the following:

1. An increased emphasis on structural concepts, themes, and generalizations from the social science disciplines
2. A corresponding emphasis on inductive, inquiry-centered teaching approaches and/or methods.
3. The utilization of a wider variety of media and resources in the classroom
4. Less concern for the rote learning of facts with content being viewed as a means rather than as an end in itself
5. A greater emphasis on cross-cultural studies
6. A growing emphasis on the study of the contemporary world at all grade levels
7. Increased concern for the teaching of values and valuing
8. Depth studies of fewer topics as opposed to survey approaches
9. Increased concern for the role of critical thinking skills in social studies programs [15]

Bridging the Gap

There is a predictable assortment of problems that must be dealt with in any major curriculum change in United States schools. Even if we were in general agreement about the need for change (which never happens in a pluralistic society with a decentralized system of education), and if we were at a point of consensus about the type of new curriculum that we wanted, there would remain the complex matters of development of new instructional materials to fit the new program and the appropriate preparation of teachers. So, we are confronted with all of these problems and the obligation to give careful consideration to them.

The elementary school teacher is often a generalist who sees her primary task as one of working with children in their early efforts to understand the world and to behave effectively in it. Social science education is only one of several specific concerns, yet there is a high

---

[15] David A. Welton, "A Study of Characteristics of Social Studies Project Materials and Selected Textbooks" (Doctoral dissertation, Ohio University, 1970).

probability that many of you will be asked to work on social science education committees in the years immediately ahead. Many of you will begin your teaching in the kinds of social studies programs that you experienced as a child, and you may find it a difficult challenge to build experiences in social inquiry and to redirect a single textbook program to make it concept oriented. The writers cannot honestly provide you with recipes, but it is anticipated that your consideration of the ideas, problems, and programs in the remaining chapters will help prepare you for the job ahead.

Suggested Problems and Projects

1. Organize your class to do some sampling of school teachers, college students, and high school and elementary students to gain an idea of the meaning which the term social studies holds for them. Perhaps as few as ten persons from each group in the sample will be sufficient to tell you how the term is seen operationally.

2. Edgar B. Wesley and William Cartwright, well-known social studies specialists and authors, have said that social science denotes advanced studies in college, as contrasted with social studies in high school and elementary school. A committee of your class can test this assumption by analyzing college and high school textbooks in geography, history, and government to see how they differ in content and in the kinds of activities they require students to do. How can you determine the difference in teaching strategies used by elementary, secondary, and college social studies teachers?

3. Arrange for several members of your group to survey the statements of definitions provided in five or six social studies methods textbooks and in the *Encyclopedia of Education*. As a large group activity, examine the collection of statements in terms of their specificity and clarity. Would a layman or a person from another country understand just what the social studies are designed to accomplish and what their content is? What elements of agreement do you find among the several definitions?

4. How would you define the social studies? The authors of this book use the term *social science education* to denote programs that aim for the development of specific social concepts through inquiry into the problems, conflicts, and concerns of man. Social science education is predicated on the belief that the need to know and to act wisely is not limited to scholars, that in a free society all men must join in the quest for meaning. On the basis of these statements, can you identify basic differences between social science education and social studies?

Related Readings

Herman, Wayne L., Jr. *Current Research in Elementary School Social Studies.* New York: The Macmillan Co., 1969.

Kahn, Herman and Weiner, Anthony J. "The Next Thirty Years." *Daedalus* 96 (1967): 718.

Mayer, Martin. *The Schools,* Chapter 16. New York: Harper and Row, 1961.

North, Robert C. "The World of the Forthcoming Decades: A Pessimistic and Optimistic View." *Social Education* 32 (November 1968): 670–672.

Wesley, Edgar. "Let's Abolish History Courses." *Phi Delta Kappan* 49 (September 1967): 3–8.

1

THE STUDY OF SOCIAL MAN
WAYS OF KNOWING
KNOWLEDGE IN PUBLIC AND PRIVATE TRANSACTIONS
HOW MAN HAS STUDIED MAN
WHAT ARE THE SKILLS OF NEW PROGRAMS?
    How do objectives help?
PURPOSES FOR SOCIAL SCIENCE EDUCATION
SUGGESTED PROBLEMS AND PROJECTS
RELATED READINGS

Social Science Education —An Emerging Program

In a way it is surprising that the social studies are "left back" in the mid-twentieth century. If school programs are to be based on objective social needs on the one hand and the state of learning on the other, surely no field can make a stronger claim than the social studies.[1]

When the social education of the young takes up the "we, here and now" aspects of the human condition, a new emphasis must be given to the difficulties and the requirements involved in such studies. The kinds of knowledge that man has relied upon and the ways in which man has used this knowledge become important when the educational purpose is the testing and application of said knowledge to social problems.

Our ways of knowing and our bodies of knowledge have changed as we have been challenged to cope with newly emerging problems. Sometimes, our long-held assumptions about the good life and how to maintain it have not been tested in the light of present conditions. This point is made in the following comment by Robert M. Hutchins:

> Thomas Jefferson based his hopes for American democracy on the proposition that we would not live in cities, that we would all be self-employed, that we would be so well educated that we could meet any new difficulties, and that we would be trained in civic virtue through local government. Now we all live in cities, we are all employed by others, our educational system is partly custodial and partly technical, thus unfitting us to meet new difficulties, and anybody who connected civic virtue with local government would be sent to a psychiatrist.
>
> Few, if any, of the subjects that concern us most today are even referred to in the Constitution of the United States. The Constitu-

---

[1] Bernard Berelson, in the introduction to *The Social Studies and the Social Sciences,* ed., Bernard Berelson (New York: Harcourt, Brace & World, Inc., 1962), p. 7.

tion does not mention cities, bureaucracy, technology, or education. It does not speak of political parties, corporations, labor unions, or judicial review. Its remarks about communications, the common defense, the power of the president to make war, and the relationship of church and state are primitive in the extreme.[2]

The Study of Social Man

The study of man, his behavior, his values, his institutions, and his successes and failures, is most conveniently carried on in the context of history. As years intervene between major events and the people who study those events, a certain degree of detachment becomes possible; objectivity seems more likely to be realized.

The emotions and interests that embroiled so many Americans in the protests of the late 1960's made immediate analysis and interpretation difficult, if not altogether impossible. Only the events of the latter years of the twentieth century will finally tell whether the young people who led the demonstrations at the 1968 Democratic convention were indeed Communist party line followers, as some persons have charged. Only events in time will tell whether Spiro T. Agnew was correct when he observed that the war moratorium demonstrations of 1969 would weaken the United States in its peace negotiations with Hanoi and hence lead to many years of strife and turmoil in Southeast Asia.

Hannah Arendt aptly pointed out that a person's degree of involvement in the events that are taking place around him limits his efforts to assess and understand what is happening.[3] Still, it is a fact of our existence that we must respond to and behave in situations that occur while we are living. It is not particularly helpful to spend our time in the examination and reconstruction of old history merely because we can be more objective and because the facts are "all in."

Newly emerging programs in social science education are concerned with including live people in the study of social man. Part of the job of social science education is to develop *the young person's* awareness of himself as he behaves in a variety of social situations that are part of his life condition. Social science education is, accordingly, committed to helping young people grow in awareness and control of their feelings, while granting that it may be beyond the ability of some youths to understand the origins of their feelings.

---

[2] Robert M. Hutchins, "The Mind Is Its Own Place," reprinted by permission from the March 1968 issue of *The Center Magazine* 1, No. 3, a publication of the Center for the Study of Democratic Institutions, Santa Barbara, Calif.

[3] Hannah Arendt, *The Human Condition* (Chicago: University of Chicago Press, 1958).

"What's all this about teaching children to live in a world of change? Who needs it?"

Social science education is concerned with the ways that man *knows,* or thinks that he knows, for it is here that young people become oriented to the discovery and nature of facts so vital to intelligent inquiry. The involvement of young people in the study of how and why man behaves as he does becomes a much more personal undertaking than does the study of man long ago and far away. This may be a frightening prospect to those of us who have lived most of our lives in the good old days before man walked upon the moon, before the hungry millions in India really touched us, and before the Russians were more than bewhiskered men in funny clothes who looked sad to the tune of the Volga Boatmen.

The years of quiet Negroes and respectful college students were years when it didn't seem so necessary to study the how and why of human behavior. In the days before television we didn't have a constant barrage of persuasive messages coming into the living room. Those were the days when the law of supply and demand seemed to influence the economy. According to economist John K. Galbraith, the industrialists now create consumer *demand* for products which the manufacturer wants to *supply*.

Social science education is concerned with social needs and problems now and in the future. It is concerned with preparing the young people of today to cope with these problems, and that includes understanding that they, too, are part of the social conditions of the time.

Ways of Knowing

How man comes to know anything is a topic for study and discussion that requires far more time than one academic term. It is the purpose here to consider briefly the ways of knowing that have been used by human beings and to examine the implications for social science education.

Myth and legend were depended upon by preliterate man as a way of *knowing* about the natural world and determining his place and relationship to it. It was in myths and legends that man found his early explanations for lightning, thunder, and other natural phenomena. In the scientific era of the twentieth century, myths and legends have continued to exert influence on the lives of men and nations. They are not necessarily related to religious knowledge, although you may find examples of myth and legend that are identified with specific religious groups. An interesting example of this was the action of the Roman Catholic Church in early 1969, when it disclaimed the religious significance of a host of saints, including such useful characters as St. Christopher.

Religious knowledge may include divinely inspired or delivered information about the purpose of life and man's relation to a superior force in the universe, and it may include dogmas that have been pronounced by religious leaders as extensions and interpretations of divine knowledge. Depending upon one's religious persuasion, some religious knowledge may be viewed as mythological, with little reference to historically trustworthy facts.

Philosophical knowledge has been more useful to some groups of people than to others. This type of knowledge is generated by thinkers who usually synthesize a variety of their own observations and beliefs about man and the universe to produce a concept of man as he ought to be. Confucianism, so often regarded by Western men as an Eastern religion, is, in fact, an elaborate philosophic system which for centuries gave the Chinese guidelines for their social organization. Mainland China has brought about the downfall of the social order that was Confucian, but it is interesting to note that the Chinese Communists refer frequently to the teachings of Mao-tse Tung, almost as though they feel it necessary to have a replacement for the great teacher, Confucius.

Mystical knowledge in twentieth-century America is often the source of amusement and is generally rejected verbally. It has yet to be determined if the people in the United States who spend millions of dollars each year on fortune tellers, clairvoyants, palmists, and the like do so just for the sake of amusement. The front page appearance of the predictions of Jeanne Dixon attract the attention and conversation of many people.

Scientific knowledge is usually associated with the natural sciences in which the controlled observations of selected events over a period of time and under a variety of conditions produce information that can be depended upon with a high degree of statistical accuracy. This type of knowledge has been useful in the rise of modern technology because it enables man to predict the outcomes of particular actions based upon his previously observed experiences. In this sense, man develops *empirical* knowledge.

Historically, the question of knowledge, what it is and how it comes to be, is a subject which has received the attention of Plato, Aristotle, Berkeley, Hume, Descartes, Aquinas, and other great philosophers. At issue has been the reliability of human perception in attempting to *know* the real world, and it may be noted that modern science has moved forward mainly through the use of *empirical* knowledge—knowledge derived from controlled observations of physical phenomena. The position of Descartes called for the development of knowledge through the process of reason, since, he argued, the perceptions of men were neither consistent nor compatible, even in cases where only two persons attempted to observe the same thing at the same moment.

It would be highly inaccurate to conclude that modern man, in a society saturated with the products of science and technology, has accepted the empirical theory of knowledge as useful in all of his life situations. The purpose here is to grasp the importance of being aware of the various *sources* of knowledge and of how our failure to do so can only hinder our efforts to identify and to resolve our social problems.

Why should children be concerned with ways of knowing? If we are concerned with the development of people who are competent in making judgments and arriving at decisions, there seem to be few alternatives that are acceptable. However, there are plenty of people who believe that children should not be concerned with ways of knowing because it may lead to a cynical view of life and the world; it may cause them to ask questions that are not appropriate for children; or they may become disrespectful and rude in the face of conventional knowledge. All of these possibilities may become actualities, but they are by no means inevitable.

The characteristics of children's thinking will be taken up in a later chapter where guidelines will be provided for the planning of experiences which will most nearly meet the developmental needs and readiness of various age groups. The point here is that children do acquire their styles of responding to and dealing with situations that require the use of facts in arriving at solutions to problems. Such situations are as much a part of the routine life experiences of children as they are a part of the formal classroom life. The manner in which the teacher structures the search for answers and the way that she helps children become accustomed to a consistent style of meeting problems set the stage for continued extension and growth.

Teachers are not faced with a new problem here. It has bothered many educators for a long time. It is as simple as the question, "If teachers condition children to accept without question or doubt the 'knowledge' that is told to them by teachers and other authority figures, when will the youth be ready to accept the responsibilities of selecting and testing knowledge claims?" When does the process begin?

In the closed systems of communism and fascism, the individual is told which knowledge he should accept; he is not prepared and encouraged to examine it for himself. In an open society, the tendency has been to revere the individual's responsibility for the fact testing job, but many schools have not prepared our youth to use the process.

An objective of social science education is the development of pupil awareness of the different kinds of knowledge that are used by people to deal with various kinds of problems. Related to this is an awareness that feelings and desires enter into the process of *accepting* one kind of knowledge over another. The six-year-old may, indeed, want to continue to accept the legend of Santa Claus and the Tooth Fairy, in spite of his increasing doubts concerning the physical possibilities of such pleasant creatures. Beginning with the primary level child, a *concept of knowledge* will be a developmental concern of social science education. The knowledge concept includes the historical aspect of knowledge, as man has viewed it, and the *process* aspect, as the learner develops his own tools for the identification, application, and testing of his field of knowledge.

Knowledge in Public and Private Transactions

In theocratic states, such as, Saudi Arabia and Pakistan, there are seldom any great tensions within the society as a result of conflict between bodies of religious knowledge. The state religion is Islam in both instances, and divergent views of religious knowledge do not enter into the discussion. Since the church and the state are one, the major problems will usually arise from political differences among the leaders.

In a nation where freedom of religious belief and practice is guaranteed by the Constitution and where public affairs are separated from sectarian affairs, there are many opportunities for tension. It should be recognized that the older social studies programs have failed to identify the crux of the problem that eventually faces the concerned young citizen in this area.

Religious views are private to the person and to his particular denominational group. To the extent that religious knowledge is subject to neither public test nor to the requirements of empirical investigation, it is not appropriate to the discussion and resolution of public issues in an open society.

Many young students can glibly state that separation of church and state is required by the Law of the Land. The unhappy history of religious persecution in other lands and in some of our early colonies can be cited as good and sufficient reasons for the church-state separation. However, there has been a recurring number of instances where usually responsible people have become confused in the application of this principle. Again, it would be helpful in our kind of nation if the children and youth were given opportunities to develop a concept of knowledge and of a problem-solving process which would be suitable for public use. So long as we hold to the value of a government that is free of church domination and interference, it is important that the citizens understand the different kinds of knowledge and the appropriate places for the use of each.

How Man Has Studied Man

In writing about the people who lived far in the interior of the African continent, Herodotus reported that their skins were black from the intense sun and that the semen of the males was also black. Accounts of this nature may be found in histories as old as those of Plutarch and Herodotus or as relatively recent as a 1951 history text [4] which reported that the early Teutonic people "knew hardly more than the American Indians."

Philosophers and religious prophets have, for centuries, commented upon the nature of man, explained the causes of his shortcomings, and speculated upon his destiny. The careful and orderly study of man's social and political behavior has been a development of the last 100 years, with the more recent efforts in social psychology appearing since 1900.

The study of man was a speculative effort for the philosopher, a sifting and compiling job for the historian, and an exercise in folklore for the average man. Within the past 50 or 60 years, much attention has been given to the field of psychology, a one-time branch of philosophy, while sociology is still highly suspected by certain politicians and others who are occasionally unhappy with the information which sociology provides.

Geography is a very old field of study, having been the subject of investigations by the seafaring Greeks as early as the second century B.C. History, as had been noted, is also an old subject of human study, and it was bodies of information from these two fields that dominated the social studies of the schools for so long. It may seem a harsh judgment, but it is accurate to note that neither geography nor history, as known in the schools, brought the learner into contact with the various ways of studying the human condition relative to the student's personal existence. Only at the college level, and not always there, would the student be likely to obtain information about the investigative procedures used by the historian and the geographer. (It continues to be a practice to refer to *teachers* of history and geography at the college level as historians and geographers, although many of them have not applied their investigative tools since completing graduate studies.)

Part of the difficulty experienced in the development of direct, first hand studies of man lies in the dominant views of knowledge and where it comes from. Divinely revealed knowledge, the knowledge that came from respected elders who reported on conditions as they were long ago, and the great body of folk knowledge that came from the shadows of the cultural history have held strong positions, particularly in the study of man as a social being. The behavioral sciences produce knowledge that may be subject to suspicion because the man who

---

[4] T. Walter Wallbank, *Man's Story* (Chicago: Scott Foresman and Company, 1951), p. 142.

Social Science Education—An Emerging Program

generates the knowledge may be rejected for personal reasons. (At the time of Dr. Benjamin Spock's activities with the draft protestors, there were questions raised concerning his competence in the field of child rearing.)

In the realm of the biological and physical sciences, it has been widely accepted that earthly man is able to develop knowledge using his tools of inquiry. In the social realm, where human behavior is the subject of study, there has been much slower progress. The difficulty of controlling the conditions for the study of human behavior is a factor, but this is not the reason for popular skepticism of the behavioral sciences. Consider that society avoids a head-on confrontation with the problems of rehabilitation of criminals, of dealing with illegitimate births, of remedial care for the mentally ill, and of dealing with the variety of handicapped persons, not because of an utter lack of dependable information about ways to proceed, but because people do not wish to acknowledge the problems themselves, their causes, and the requirements of proper treatment.

The man on the street is far more inclined to make knowledge claims about social phenomena than he is about natural scientific phenomena. The only well-publicized disclaimer to the astronauts' first voyage to the moon came from Great Britain, where a group of flat world advocates maintained that the space ship had really gone nowhere. In the social realm, it seems that everyone is an authority on effective teaching practices, how to deal with the hippies, etc. The lack of carefully obtained information does not seem to be a problem here. One well-known state school superintendent proclaimed, in 1969, that "... people who found fault with collegiate football were long-haired beatniks, pseudo-intellectuals, and commies." It is doubtful that any careful study has been made on this topic, but the educational politician in this instance created his own "knowledge" to serve his particular purpose. It is not so easy to do this with knowledge in the biological and physical science areas, nor is it so commonly accepted by the public.

It would seem that United States citizens of the 1970's would be receptive to and supportive of an empirical (scientific) approach to the study of human problems. Our use of science has resulted in enormous attainments in modifying our environments to our desired ends, and our failures to scientifically consider our total condition have resulted in overpopulation, famine, pollution, civil strife, and wars. Can we correctly assume that, since we have witnessed the benefits of science and the catastrophes which result from nonscientific behavior, we are now ready to study social man in a scientific manner?

Social science education places great emphasis upon the careful use of dependable information and upon the tentative application of conclusions that seem to follow. The major concerns are with a high respect for facts that relate to our problems and for the skills necessary to identify and use facts. All of this should not suggest to you that we believe that our fellow citizens have reached general agreement on the proper way to study man, nor would we want to suggest that this is the only way. We believe that scientific inquiry has been neglected in the older social studies and that it will prove to be a valuable element in the education of children and youths.

What Are the Skills of New Programs?

An extensive list of skills that have been viewed as being of importance in newly emerging programs has been compiled by David Welton. As you examine the list below,[5] you should not assume that none of these skills has been attended to in older social studies programs, for it is fair to expect that any program in social science education will provide for the development of these skills. The objectives of social science education, with emphasis on inquiry and conceptualization, seem to call for this. (Welton's listing follows the topical pattern that was used by Helen Carpenter.[6])

Awareness and Identification Stage
1. Identify and define a problem.
2. Recognize the need for additional data.

Data Processing Stage
3. Distinguish between relevant and irrelevant information.
4. Differentiate between objective and subjective evidence.
5. Consider why one source of data is more acceptable.
6. Examine materials for freedom from bias.
7. Recognize propaganda.
8. Locate and evaluate information.
9. Classify data in a sequential or hierarchical structure.
10. Examine materials for consistency.
11. Determine the writer's point of view.
12. Locate key sentences and summary statements.

---

[5] David A. Welton, "A Study of Characteristics of Social Studies Project Materials and Selected Textbooks" (Doctoral dissertation, Ohio University, 1970), pp. 407–412.

[6] Helen McCracken Carpenter, "The Role of Skills in Elementary Social Studies," *Social Education* 31 (March 1967): 221–227.

Analytical-Synthesizing Stage
13. Compare information about a topic drawn from two or more sources to recognize agreement or contradiction.
14. Develop skill in analysis.
15. Examine reasons for contradictions or seeming contradictions in evidence.
16. Develop sensitivity to and demand precision in the definition of words (analyze the linguistics of a communication).
17. Determine the assumptions upon which a position is premised.
18. Subject documents to internal criticism (meaning and accuracy of their contents).
19. Subject documents to external criticism (authenticity).
20. Draw (make, construct) logical inferences from evidence.
21. Structure hypotheses.
22. Reach tentative conclusions.
23. Identify alternative solutions or outcomes.
24. Predict or speculate on the outcomes of situations.

Testing Stage
25. Analyze alternatives in terms of consequences.
26. Structure generalizations from evidence.
27. Evaluate and/or validate hypotheses.
28. Establish criteria for evaluation and judgment.

How do objectives help?

The cynical answers to this question might be, "They don't!" "They help confuse matters." "They tell what is obvious."

In spite of a flood of statements of goals, aims, and objectives in education generally, and in spite of a backlash from students and practicing educators in the past few decades, it remains a fact of rational life that we ought to know where we are heading in order that we may check on our progress and the efficiency of our efforts. This is as essential for social science education as for arithmetic or spelling, but it may present more complexities. We may set as an objective in spelling that a child learn to spell the 100 most frequently misspelled words as shown by a particular research study. We may set as an arithmetic objective, the mastery of a certain set of computational skills. Mastery can be assessed.

In the social studies area, objectives have often included skills in reading, group planning, recognition that every privilege has an accompanying responsibility, respect for ideals of fair play and generous behavior, responsibility for the welfare of others, etc. Some of these objectives are primarily attended to in other parts of the school program, some belong to all school activities, and some sound nice, but are not honest.

Children learn quickly that they must never be so concerned about the welfare of others that they will help another child with a test. Learning has been, and is now, a private, competitive venture where we help ourselves, if need be at the expense of other people, including the teacher. Primary level teachers seem to be more inclined to make learning a cooperative task, but it soon changes. To be helpful, objectives must be at least partially specific for the area; they must be honest and in accord with social and school realities; and they should provide more than a fuzzy notion of direction.

Most of the social studies objectives which have been published in recent years could be used with equal appropriateness in the United States, Mainland China, or anywhere else. Every nation wants its schools to turn out loyal, devoted citizens, properly informed about their proud heritage and concerned with the attainment of the good life in their nation. They will be effective group workers. Respect for law and authority is desired in all nations, but some nations are so concerned that their citizens vote that they fine those who do not.

The vision and possibilities for a human society that are provided within the basic documents of the United States have not been sharply reflected in the social education of young people. There is one objective, stated without qualification, that will differentiate between social education in the free society and the closed society:

To provide for the development of the skills of free and open inquiry into the social existence of man and to nurture the will and spirit to do so.

At a period in our national existence when the adult population receives the majority of its information via television (three major networks and two major news services), the necessity of preparing our youth for inquiry should not require a lengthy defense. If we are serious as a nation of people in our oft stated commitment to a government of the people and by the people, there can be no delay in preparing youth to engage in the affairs of their country.

Purposes for Social Science Education

1. To provide for the development and use of the skills involved in free and open inquiry.
2. To emphasize conceptualizing experiences rather than isolated information-gathering experiences.

3. To provide opportunities for children to become familiar with the types of data which the social and behavioral sciences provide modern man.
4. To provide opportunities for children to become aware of various investigative procedures used to generate knowledge and to recognize their uses in the daily affairs of a democratic nation.
5. To support the development of an attitude of interest and concern in the study of many cultural groups, since this will lead to insights into the areas of international studies, as well as domestic subcultures.
6. To keep the point of contact with human conditions near to the child's own experiences, so that relevance will not be lost and personal involvement not sacrificed.
7. To assist the child in understanding the origins and functions of values in human cultures and to recognize his own responsibilities in the valuing process.
8. To direct the major thrust of the program toward those recurring social and political phenomena which confront modern man and his societies.

Suggested Problems and Projects

1. Develop a statement which tells what you would like to have objectives *do* for you as a prospective teacher. Should statements of objectives tell you what to hope for? What to do?

2. In a synthesizing activity, consider the ideas, issues and problems which have been dealt with in the overview and chapter one. Write a definition for social science education as you understand it at this time.

3. Prepare your own objectives for social science education and submit them to class examination and evaluation.

4. As a follow-up activity, visit an elementary social studies classroom and see whether you can determine what the major objectives are. An examination of the curriculum guide may be helpful, but bear in mind that what goes on in the classroom may not always reflect the objectives of the "official curriculum guide."

5. Arrange to interview a sampling of elementary teachers, 11–12-year-old children, parents, and college students in other fields to discover their views with reference to the question, "Why do we teach social studies in our schools?" After grouping the most frequent responses, compare them with your own objectives. Draw a tentative conclusion from this investigation.

6. In order to obtain information concerning the "growing storm" in the social studies, survey an equal number of issues of *Social Education* for the periods 1955–1960 and 1965–1970 and note the number of articles which dealt with social science education—social studies issues. Your survey should support or reject the idea that the social studies curriculum is in a state of conflict and change.

Related Readings

Griffin, Alan. "Revising the Social Studies." *Social Education* 27 (October 1963): 295.

Hanna, Paul R. "Revising the Social Studies: What Is Needed?" *Social Education* 27 (April 1963): 190–196.

Keller, Charles R. "Needed: Revolution in the Social Studies." *Saturday Review* 44 (September 16, 1961): 60–62.

Kidd, John W. "Social Science or Social Studies." *Social Education* 17 (May 1953): 207–208.

Krug, Mark. *History and the Social Sciences,* chapters 5, 6, 10. Waltham, Mass.: Blaisdell Publishing Co., 1967.

Massialas, Byron and Kazamias, Andreas. *Crucial Issues in the Teaching of Social Studies.* Englewood Cliffs: Prentice-Hall, Inc., 1964.

Massialas, B. G., and Smith, F. J. eds. *New Challenges in the Social Studies.* Belmont, California: Wadsworth Publishing Co., 1965.

Fraser, Dorothy McClure, ed. *Social Studies Curriculum Development: Prospects and Problems, 39th Yearbook.* Washington, D.C.: The National Council for the Social Studies, 1969.

SECTION II

In the four chapters that make up this section of the book, the emphasis is centered on the bases upon which decisions are made with respect to the nature of social science education for children and youth. Accordingly, the place of values and issues; the disciplines as sources of content, concepts, and generalizations; and objectives are explored in detail. Attention is constantly directed to the operational aspects of the ideas that are considered. You are urged to use as your basic question, "What does this mean to teachers who plan to work with boys and girls in our society?"

2

PART I
VALUES IN EDUCATION

    Why is there confusion over values?
    What are universal human values?
    How do values provide structure?
    What is the school's role with respect to values?
    What is the meaning of values?
    What is the problem of changing values in United States society?

THE DEVELOPMENT OF VALUES

    What is the relationship between values and child development?
    How can there be value consciousness in teaching?
    What is the relationship between values and pupil achievement?
    What are the sources of children's values?
    How can we teach for value change?
    How does the teacher work with parents in the matter of values?

ISSUES, CONFLICTS, AND VALUES

    Do the issues and conflicts of childhood contain content and structures suggestive of those of the larger adult society?
    Issues, conflicts, and values in daily affairs
    What is the nature of conflict in the child's life?
    Emerging and continuing issues

PART II

How Could Anything That Feels So Bad Be So Good?, *Richard E. Farson;* **All About Ecology**, *William Murdoch and Joseph Connell;* **The Illusion of Individuality**, *Erich Fromm;* **Dynamite in the Ghetto**, *Stokeley Carmichael and Charles V. Hamilton;* **The Cult of Loyalty**, *Alan Barth;* **The Business Spirit and American Values**, *Max Lerner;* **Social Action for the Primary Schools**, *Bruce R. Joyce;* **A Letter from Death Row**, *Caryl Chessman.*

Values, Issues, and Conflicts in Social Science Education

PART I

This chapter is presented in two parts. Part one explores the function of values in human life and the role that the school plays in the development of value systems that will support the individual as he encounters a variety of problems in real life situations. Part two is a selection of readings which deal with the recurring issues and conflicts in our society.

It is recommended that you begin the reading of the selections in part two as you begin your work on part one. The conflicts and issues of the adult world invade the child's world too, and the arbitrary boundaries that were once thought to separate adult concerns and child concerns have evaporated in the face of mass media. So it is that we have tried to unify the world of reality and the world of the school on this important topic.

We are not proposing special activities for this unit of study. Each of the subdivision titles can provide the cue for lively discussion, because the question of the schools' role in shaping values and dealing with issues is still very much an issue.

Values in Education

There has been a great amount of writing in recent years concerning the place of values and the process of valuing in human societies. With respect to the education of the young, there are those who contend that the school should limit itself to the process of valuing since values are personal and subjective and should not be imposed upon unsuspecting children. An extension of this position suggests that values should originate from family sources and finally be the products of the individual's observations and reflections about the worth of various life conditions. This high degree of concern with the valuing process is essentially psychological; what goes on in the individual as he "values" receives high priority, and the more traditional concern with transmission of values is cast in a lesser light.

At this point, we would like to attempt to persuade you that there are universal human values that exist among men of all cultures across the face of the earth. We believe that an examination of the history of man provides ample evidence that human societies have been possible largely due to the existence of values which have sustained life and cooperative life endeavors. We are not opposed to including the *valuing process* as a proper item of study in the school, but we take vigorous exception to those educators who recommend that the school avoid the teaching of values altogether and focus upon the valuing process.

Why is there confusion over values?

This question cannot be answered on the basis of hard data, but we will draw some inferences from our observations and readings. One source of confusion lies in the tendency to accept gross behavior patterns and life styles as being identical to the value positions of individuals and groups. Accordingly, the emerging nations that have high infant mortality rates, due to the lack of modern medical services, may be accused of placing a low value on human life. Ironically, the high loss of life on U.S. highways and through our continued involvement (since 1941) in international conflicts may be viewed by other people as evidence that a low value is placed on human life in the United States.

The same type of difficulty arises when we view values held by minority ethnic and cultural groups within our nation. The reported tendency of some ethnic groups to keep illegitimate children in the maternal family may be interpreted as a low valuing of chastity, rather than a high valuing of human life and family responsibility.

At the school level, the conflicts between the values of cooperation and competition and honesty and material success are sources of confusion that are more often avoided than examined.

If we were to assume that each person did indeed develop his own set of values, quite apart from the sociological and biological realities of the human condition, perhaps we would accept that each child should be *free* to *value*. The conditions of life as they have been observed and reported have persuaded us that the school has a responsibility to bring the child into an orderly and reasoned acquaintance with the values that have been useful to all men through all ages. It is also necessary to assist the child in his encounters with those many situations where values appear to conflict and to help the child understand that the resolution of value conflicts is an individual responsibility which often carries social consequences.

What are universal human values?

An academic response might be *truth, beauty,* and *good.* A response that is more operational would include the ultimate value of life itself,

Values, Issues, and Conflicts in Social Science Education   Part I   37

Pursuit of the same goal sometimes takes people in opposite directions.

respect, wealth, enlightenment, affection, and power. Immediately you will see that such values are not mutually exclusive; they do not stand alone in any clear sense. Likewise, you may observe that the object or relationship which represents a value may differ from culture to culture. The fact that the expression of a value is culturally influenced should not mislead you into concluding that the values differ. Societies and individuals may assign differing priorities or strengths to a given value, but this neither negates the existence of the value, nor does it say anything about the ultimate wisdom of the priority assigned.

The need for man to be a valuing species may have come either with his entry as a life form or it may have evolved; whichever, the philosophical and psychological ramifications are proper subjects for speculation and research. From an educational viewpoint, we accept *values as realities* which the child will be forced to deal with in his own life situations. Accordingly, we believe that universal values should be introduced as realities, subject to various cultural manifestation, but not as psychological variables which come and go as individual whims.

Value conflicts. We have already stated that conflict may develop when individuals or groups are in competition in the pursuit of a commonly shared value. People who value education (enlightenment) highly may employ devious means to get their children into the desired school, and the pursuit of wealth and power are other values for which humans strive. The conflict that is referred to here is not so much that among adults, but it is to the difficulties which children encounter when they find themselves called upon to choose between two strongly held values.

The child at age six or seven may honor the value of truth as he reports a wrongdoing by his playmates, but by age 14, the value of respect by his peers may outweigh the truth value in actual practice, although the 14-year-old may experience continuing inner conflict and guilt feelings. Another source of confusion is that caused by the changing roles which an individual assumes and the manner in which he rearranges his values. The chief of police who overlooks the illegal gambling activities at a local private club is a case in point. The ten-year-old boy who is chosen to be a playground patrolman will experience the conflict between loyalty to his fellows and a sense of duty in his new role, a role that is transitory at best.

It is from situations such as those just cited that value conflicts arise, both in child life and adult life. Man is a valuing creature and it is this capability that leads him to strive for more favorable conditions of life for himself and his fellow man. Values are not separate and unitary, however, and the complex situations of life provide many opportunities for indecision and conflict in the ordering and honoring of values.

> *Expand the listing of values that you believe to be universal. Do not confuse a practice with a value.*
>
> *What are some of the value and/or role conflicts that you have observed among college students?*
>
> *What value conflicts have you witnessed in elementary school?*
>
> *How would you define the teacher's responsibility and role in helping children deal with value conflicts?*

How do values provide structure?

In any discussion of values, it soon becomes obvious that one may look in many places for evidence concerning the dominant values of the total society and that there are numerous examples of small group and individual deviation from the value patterns that seem to most accurately describe the *goals* and the *means* for attainment of these goals that have high priority throughout the larger society.

Robin Williams has drawn together some thoughts about values, and he suggests that values are "the criteria for deciding what we should want;" that values may be examined as choices and preferences, as points of emphasis and interest, as statements, and as a referent for social sanction (reward and punishment). Williams has identified the following as major American values: [1]

1. Achievement and success
2. Activity and work
3. Moral orientation
4. Humanitarianism
5. Efficiency and practicality
6. Progress
7. Material comfort
8. Equality
9. Freedom
10. External conformity
11. Science and secular rationality

---

[1] Robin J. Williams, *American Society: A Sociological Interpretation* (New York: Alfred A. Knopf, 1960), pp. 400–465.

12. Nationalism—patriotism
13. Democracy

Values provide structure to social science education. It is customary to think of the structure of learning experiences in terms of the structure of a particular discipline or several disciplines. This has been especially true with programs in social studies, where geography, history, government, and economics have often been looked to for structure of the total program. Social science education derives its own unique structure from a concern for and a commitment to certain of the major value orientations of our society. In this sense, the structure of the total program is derived from values, and its activities incorporate features that are intended to strengthen and extend specific values.

Social science education is heavily biased in terms of its commitment to:

1. The use of science and rationality in the study of human problems
2. The freedom of individual inquiry
3. Respect for individual personality and its development
4. Equality of opportunity and access to justice
5. Democratic processes as behavioral goals
6. A humanitarian perspective

This does not mean that all other national value orientations and personal value characteristics are disregarded, but it does mean that these six value orientations provide the central direction for social science education and that other values will be examined against the background of this core group. For example, the achievement-success value must be viewed in the light of equality and humanitarianism. Progress as a value must be qualified in terms of higher order values. External conformity must be carefully examined in terms of its impact upon freedom and democratic processes.

From the major national value orientations, social science education uses six as its clear-cut value core. Social science education is not a valueless approach to social education. Its commitment to inquiry resides in the value given to democratic processes and the use of rational investigation in the study of human affairs. This definitive value orientation of social science education provides a dimension and a thrust that goes beyond a purely academic pursuit of multi-disciplinary or inter-disciplinary studies.

The humanitarian perspective establishes the basis for selection of problems and concerns that have been recurrent and powerful in the social affairs of man. A rational approach to the study of social man calls for inquiry and empirical data. The high value given to the role of the individual person, his freedom to inquire and his access to equality, dictate the nature of the teaching-learning environment that will give a unique quality to the social education of the young in an open society.

Valued behaviors. When teachers discuss values, their considerations are frequently directed toward the valued behaviors that contribute to the smooth running of a school. The typical valued behaviors may relate to the value orientations which have been identified by Williams and others, but this is not always the case. Herein lies one of the reality gaps in many social studies programs. The verbal values and the reward system of the school may be fraught with inconsistencies within themselves and with respect to the major value orientations in the larger society.

Honesty, promptness, diligence, courtesy, and cooperation are frequently listed on report cards, and they express behavior characteristics which the school values. Sometimes, the list is extended to include such items as respects the rights and property of others, obeys rules, and is a good citizen. Such lists are open to criticism when they are used primarily to obtain compliant behavior and when the teacher's behavior does not seem to be subject to the same standards in her relationships with children. It has been argued that these valued behaviors are found in both open and closed societies and hence do not provide for valued behaviors that are unique and essential in a free and democratic society.

> *What evidence can you find to support or reject this statement? The valued behaviors that are commonly emphasized and rewarded by the school are concerned with achievement—success, activity and work, efficiency and practicality, external conformity, and nationalism—patriotism. The value orientations that are often neglected in the school concern equality, freedom, scientific and secular rationality, democracy, and individual personality. These neglected value orientations contain the characteristics that can differentiate the life qualities of a democracy from those of an authoritarian society.*

What is the school's role with respect to values?

There are several different views that are currently held by educators and others concerning the role of the school in supporting and extending certain values. Statements which advance these positions are provided here for your consideration.

Position no 1. The job of the school in the United States has been traditionally concerned with the teaching of basic American values and ideals. Every society expects its institutions of education to support and sustain the way of life that is believed in by the majority of the people. The basic values of a society are an important part of the total culture, and the young people should be taught these values in order that they will be ready to behave appropriately. The elementary school is not the place for the *study* and *comparison* of values. Children need the security of a set of values they can believe in from the start.

Position no. 2. In a multi-ethnic society, such as, the United States, it is not the proper job of the public school to teach any particular set of values. The home and the church are the proper teachers of the child's beginning values. As he matures, he will develop his own set of values from his early teachings and from his wide experiences in school and community. It is true that the teacher will project certain of his own personal values as he works with children, but this does not mean that the teacher has either the right or the responsibility to espouse his values to the children.

Position no. 3. Every teacher has the responsibility to involve the children in the process of valuing and the consideration of how values are used by people to guide their behaviors. The school in the free society should build the child's commitment to the values of the free and democratic society, and this should be done in a rational, rather than a highly emotional, manner. The teacher has no right to *sell* his or anyone else's values to the children. Values are to be examined and understood in light of their functions and consequences. In the final analysis, the child will build his own set of values.

Position no. 4. The school must teach the values that are held by most members of the community as well as the major values of the larger society. Local communities expect this. For this reason the school will reinforce predominant religious values as more general political values. It is unrealistic to expect the school to do anything more than to reflect and amplify major values of the community, and teachers should be prepared to do this.

Position no. 5. Values are of concern to the school only to the extent to which they are factors to be understood and dealt with in the life activities of the larger community. A rational inquiry into the values held by different cultural groups will help the child understand the relationship between values and behavior. Problems which occur as a result of value conflicts are appropriate for study since they are of continuing concern to society and must be handled. The school should teach that values originate from religious beliefs, historical traditions, and life experiences and that values continue to exist only as they are thought to be helpful by the society that holds them. Since values are everywhere, in the life of everyone, there is no need for the school to indoctrinate the child. The job is to help the child understand values as a critical factor in human behavior.

> *Using the small group discussion technique, examine the five positions and identify the one that is nearest to the consensus position of the group.*
>
> *Develop a position that is a group expression on the role of the school in teaching values. Extract any parts of the five positions to use in your own position.*

What is the meaning of values?

Unquestionably, there have been meanings ascribed to the question of values up to this point. Further definitions are in order to give specific meanings and to provide points of references for succeeding discussions.

Whenever a person is stimulated to do something, he acts upon an idea, a need, desire, or an inner compelling force. Figure 2–1 illustrates this point:

```
    The
    Child          MOVES           Goal
    With          ─────────►
    Inner         TOWARD          (Value)
    Desires

  (A Value System)
```

FIGURE 2–1. The Meaning of Values

There is a goal to be attained, and the child moves toward it, whether it happens to be good or bad for him or society. Since he gave priority to that course of action and controls his behavior in deliberate, decisive ways, he must have some sort of inner control or set of values that encouraged him to move when he did, told him why he did so, and even prompted him as to how to carry it out. In this sense, his ideals, objectives, or goals are his values. The family background, the school, church, etc., have helped him to set the stage for his behavior and even furnished him with values. Some of these are transitory and fleeting in nature, or conflictual, but, he has value patterns that do more than impel him in a given direction. He has learned what he thinks he ought to do in specific cases, although he may lack experience and maturity in knowing, deciding, synthesizing, and acting in the best possible ways.

Adults can test their values by determining just what the common, accepted practices and habits of people are. They may even examine what the laws say or look into the past experiences of others. By using rational, common sense comparisons of what is proven and what is unfounded, values can be subjected to appraisal. However, the child may find such processes too complicated, even though he still needs a set of values to guide his behavior. W. E. Martin claims that values exist, even in the unconscious realm of the child's mental life, but, it is only when they act that their affects would be perceived. He agrees that different conditions certainly call for different behavioral manifestations of identical values. Significantly, the child exhibits only that behavior which is consistent with his internal set of values.[2]

The impact of these interpretations of values should be clear. First, the values lead to a philosophical basis which forms the core of a person's ideology and gives him a perspective of life. His very ethical and moral values are sound or poorly defined. Second, the parent, teachers, and others need to be careful in their thinking as to the "kind of child" that is wanted; the nature of life-reality; what kind of society is desired; and what attitudes, abilities, skills, and habits are to be taught in the first place. In summary, the meaning given to values must do more than orient us by telling us what we are doing and where we are; values must suggest a direction and indicate how to go in that direction. For the elementary school child, *values mean his way of believing in and responding to a situation as to what it ought to be or ought to have been and guiding his behavior in such a way that his actions speak of one who has the facts and knows the rules of his culture.* He will make mistakes, but at least his value system is growing and developing in a more orderly fashion because adults are helping him along the way.[3]

---

[2] W. E. Martin, "Learning Theory and Identification: Development of Values in Children," *Journal of Genetic Psychology* 84 (June 1954): 211–217.

[3] H. C. Black, "Values, Philosophy, and Education," *Progressive Education* 32 (July 1955): 109–115, 117.

What is the problem of changing values in United States society?

In a world where traditional values are changing, Getzel [4] believes that the essential problem is not so much a matter of change in itself, but rather the misunderstanding of current values. Equally important, there is a feeling that rapidity of change may result in failure to uncover new values to meet new situations.

There may be some futile efforts by some people in attempting to withstand the changes taking place in jobs, religion, ethnics, etc., but they cannot meet the problem by avoiding the issue itself. The school curriculum that contributes to the solution of this problem may best aid the child by using the process of identification. When a child is able to find a model that is both consistent and in harmony with his personality, he has accomplished the first step. He needs to feel that he is a part of this world of values if he is to be a secure and adjusted person. As values change, or as he moves to a region with different value systems, he must still identify and become a part of this new value world. Through maturation and positive identification, he reaches adulthood with the ability to meet situations with value discrimination and to adjust himself accordingly.

This oversimplified explanation of meeting the problem of changing values needs further consideration. It is believed that succeeding sections of this book will contribute additional insights, but the point of emphasis should be that the child *can* and *must* learn to live in a world of changing values. The following section also sheds some light on this problem by approaching the question of absolute values in United States society.

The Development of Values

It will be seen that both society and the elementary school have undergone a series of changes in terms of values and their relationships to each other. The child grows and develops or progresses through periods or stages. As he changes, it is logical to believe that his values take on new meanings or that new or more mature values are acquired according to his level of maturity.

What is the relationship between values and child development?

There are at least four approaches that aid the teacher in understanding the developmental aspects of values in children. That is to say, children

---

[4] J. W. Getzel, "Stable Identity in a World of Shifting Values," *Educational Leadership* 14 (January 1957): 237–240.

progress through certain stages or periods of development, and values are developed largely through these four avenues. This view is supported by evidence from studies summarized by F. T. Perkins.[5]

The development of values from the genetic approach. The human organism has the basic physical needs and their satisfactions as a matter of determination at the moments of conception and birth. As life begins, a host of influences act upon the person to help create his value system. At about the age of seven, such values as honesty and concern for other persons become interdependent; lying and cheating are usually frowned upon; a value system is gradually becoming significant to the child. Even though he may be highly suggestible, the child generally does not become influenced too significantly unless he has actually identified certain values in light of himself. Some evidence appears to point to the fact that intelligence has some weight in causing a positive acceptance and practicing of certain values in terms of particular traits. In addition, the sex differences seem to suggest that girls tend toward values in honesty, more so than the boys, while the latter favor values in terms of aggressiveness and dominance and are inclined toward the more serious conduct disorders. However, it is believed that children come to possess certain values based upon the kinds of experiences they have had. From the genetic point of view, they have received the capacity for acquiring values, but, by the first grade, the child possesses values based upon feelings of achievement, affection, and acceptance by the group.[6] Therefore, there seems to be no evidence to date to suggest that value possession is primarily a matter acquired from genetics or the hereditary factors associated with the life of the child.

The development of values from social and cultural influences. Even before the child enters school, he has a system of values that has been developed in a variety of ways as a result of his home and neighborhood contacts. Certain roles have been demanded of him, and he has learned, through association and identification with others, ways of action and behavior that are expected to bring results. His class status, whether it is upper, middle, or lower, and where he grew up are influential in shaping his expectancies and demands, both in daily living and in school accomplishment. He is learning to like books, fighting, swearing, etc., by family encouragement. The family helps the child to see his tasks more clearly

---

[5] F. T. Perkins, "Research Relating to the Problem of Values," *California Journal of Elementary Education* 23 (May 1955): 223–242.

[6] C. B. Zachary, "Emotional Needs and Social Development," *Fifteenth Yearbook of Elementary School Principals* (Washington, D.C.: Department of Elementary School Principals, 1936), pp. 259–264.

and gives him his role to play as he internalizes the culture around him. His wide or narrow contacts with a variety of cultural aspects either help him to learn a great deal or restrict his functioning in many ways. Then, there are feelings about society and what are to be his responsibilities; the child expresses his system of values many times in what he wants to be, because he sees the society of which he is a part mainly through the eyes of his parents. Thus, a value system is largely handed to the child, but he is expected to live up to the standards and expectations of the family. In addition, the social group to which he belongs further structures his behavior. In summary, the following factors in the environmental life of the child shape his value system as one regards his family situation: their income and occupational status, parental educational level, neighborhood environment and urban-rural setting, religion, race, and educational expectations of the parents. As the child grows within a varied environment, he is taught certain aggressive ways of behaving and a sex role; these and other roles he begins to model after those that are considered desirable and are expected of him by the family and group. Progress in meeting these tasks varies widely among children and further enhances the individual role differences of the child as he enters the elementary school.

The development of values from personality and ego structuring. The development of a strong ego structure is important to the growth of a sound personality and to good mental health. If there are inconsistencies, undue frustrations, emotional deprivation, fluctuating behavior standards, noncompensating minority group membership, etc., the ego structure and needs may fail to develop certain strengths that can hamper the child's reactions to his total environment. In a study by Brownfain,[7] it is made clearly evident that a child's system of values depends upon the stability of his own self-worth concept. The evidence indicates that the well-adjusted individual has a more stable or higher concept of himself. His value system would include greater self-esteem; more realistic views of his own capabilities and weaknesses as others see him; being known by more people, even as he knows a greater number of individuals; and less compensatory behavior. That is to say, the child who develops a strong ego structure has a more realistic view of himself and gets along better with people. Therefore, his value system includes more positive aspects of his personality and outlook on life by virtue of the fact that he sees life from the healthier, better adjusted personality point of view. These positive aspects of the personality mean that the child is not only more secure as a person, but in every respect,

---

[7] J. J. Brownfain, "Stability of the Self Concept as Dimension of Personality," *Journal of Social Psychology* 47 (July 1952): 597–606.

his view of life is more optimistic and balanced. He tends to have a healthy aggressiveness that carries him forward in a kind of an outgoing rhythm of accomplishment that provides a feeling of well-being. In short, it is clear that the value system of the person is fed by the strong, adjusted personality, and the more defined and adequate the ego structure is, then the more highly developed, realistic, and functional in the life of the child the value system can be expected to be.

The development of values from the school environment. Although the school is only one of the many agencies that contributes to the development of the child, and it properly belongs under the second heading for discussion here, it is believed that particular mention should be made about this influence. The very organization and administration of the school as to its grade standards, reporting practices, the child's placement, and the kind of articulation program of subject matter areas, are contributors (or deterrents) to healthy personality development. There is already considerable evidence in professional literature to suggest that the climate of the school and the classroom affect the personality and the value system of the child, as well as the degree of school success and out-of-school adjustment. The following illustration underscores the tremendous impact that educational activities have upon the development of the child's personality and his values:

> A set of identical twins of pre-school age from a lower socio-economic status were examined and tested psychologically. One child had an I.Q. of around 87, with the other in the area of 78. The higher I.Q. child was the leader. In a pre-school situation conducted under excellent circumstances by professionally trained personnel, the lower I.Q. child was given about a year's experience, while the "leader" remained at home. Re-testing indicated that the school child surpassed the home bound twin both in intelligence and in leadership. In follow-up studies this child continued to make repeated gains, while the other child showed little or no improvement.[8]

It should be stated that this report of a single instance by no means constitutes the only evidence that educational activities can and do influence the child. In this one case, it is clear that the follower became the leader, *viz.,* a value system was acquired that gave direction to a different kind of behavior because certain educational experiences

---

[8] Adapted from a lecture by Dr. Samuel Kirk, visiting lecturer at the University of Arizona, who reported the results of some unpublished research studies at the University of Illinois, July 28, 1958.

had been provided. Credit is given to the educational activities that changed the follower into a leader, although it must be admitted that this child may have eventually acquired this new role in spite of a superiority of educational advantages. It should be pointed out that other cases were cited by Dr. Samuel Kirk to support the theory that children can be given opportunities such as these to change behavior. Specifically, children in these situations are confronted with much the same kind of curriculum as found in any good school, but it should be mentioned that systematic approaches in problem-solving situations, together with orderly acquisition of new facts or knowledge, contribute to growth of the person. In fact, it is not too surprising that the follower becomes a leader in this case, since new skills, attitudes, and understandings are learned by the one child, while the other child, who has not had the benefit of such learnings, may not be expected to make much progress.

How can there be value consciousness in teaching?

At this point the practical question of how the teacher actually concerns herself with the problem of values is asked. Some general approaches are now offered to assist the teacher in becoming a more positive valuer in classroom work, although specific techniques are to be discussed in the final section of this chapter.

Develop insights about values. There is a need to understand what values are held by other people, particularly the family. The teacher must recognize that children have value standards that are in opposition to his in many instances. These must be viewed fairly and impartially.

Be conscious of valuing as a process in itself. The concern for the evolution and development of values helps to clarify meanings and philosophies, as well as to increase understanding of why a particular value set is considered important.

Prepare to go beyond the role of value determiner. Probably one of the most important tasks of the teacher is that of bringing out implied or assumed values that might otherwise go undetected.[9]

Set up genuine value-producing situations. If children are to possess a value consciousness, the teacher must not only make use of their value concepts, but employ varied approaches to build toward addi-

---

[9] H. C. Armstrong, "The Place of Values in American Education," *California Journal of Elementary Education* 23 (February 1955): 141–154.

tional higher values. For example, the show-and-tell activities in the primary grades and other sharing experiences for higher levels are planned activities with value-producing expectations. An optimum school and classroom climate must be present to foster such growth.

Accept the role of leadership in interpreting values. Citizens and parents, as well as the children, may look for leadership from school administrators and teachers in the interpretation and raising of value standards. It is first necessary that school personnel know and appreciate the community values before deciding upon a course of action. Having developed a set of educational policies that reflect community values, both citizens and school people may move toward desired results. The following five categories are suggested by H. G. Shane [10] to provide the teacher with a planning guide in the area of values:

Value guide one: Plan for the value of using intelligence in life. The child is led to use his time and certain freedoms in accordance with foresight and thought. Critical thinking and inquiry are stressed in the solution of classroom problems. Further planning in using intellegence, of course, considers the total life of the child, with special emphasis upon insisting on and providing for meaning in all phases of his work, including drill. If evidence indicates that children are not using what they learn, then research must be employed to determine how more effective utilization or application of knowledge may be gained.

Value guide two: Plan for the value of employing wise use of abilities. There must first be some cooperative appraisal of goal progress, as well as individual help in evaluation of this progress. Through the use of devices, such as, anecdotal records, diaries, conferences, and tests, the value planning may be on a more accurate basis as to the wise use of abilities by the child. The two-fold problem of how well the child is progressing and what abilities he possesses must be considered in planning what particular experiences may be needed to foster better time use of his personal attributes for the development of new skills.

Value guide three: Plan for the value of considering and respecting the other person. Teachers should approach the classroom with the value, as suggested in Figure 2-2. Planning with the child to secure group thinking and purposes can be accomplished only according to maturity level. Through these kinds of experiences the child comes to know and understand his peers in better ways. Through sharing, fair

---

[10] H. G. Shane, "Educational Values as Guides to Planning with Children," *Childhood Education* 31 (October, 1954): 56–60.

Values, Issues, and Conflicts in Social Science Education Part I 51

play in the classroom or on the playground, and in the give and take activities of the daily program, consideration of the other person is learned.

Value guide four: Plan for the value of developing open-mindedness. Classroom experiences can be planned in such a way that daily school living helps the child to see and understand the qualities of open-mindedness. The gradual growth of this value has far reaching effects in the future personal living of the person, who may well make a significant contribution to home and community, or he may be withdrawn and compartmentalized in behavior and thinking.

Value guide five: Plan for the value of acquiring feelings of social responsibility. A child needs to be guided toward growth in social understandings through actual experiences. By seeing his responsibilities associated with planned classroom freedom, he is helped to appreciate them. The development of social responsibility is learned in the home and the school, but it does not happen through chance.

The guides to the planning of value experiences may be thought of as expressions of sound principles of learning, but the emphasis upon these factors is given here to suggest a value consciousness needed for better teaching. As the teacher plans a learning experience, the prime obective may be the acquisition of knowledge or a skill; it is suggested that value planning be made in addition to or in connection with these desired outcomes. If value planning is accomplished, there is a greater likelihood that children will change their behavior patterns of conduct as they reflect those values which give fuller and greater meaning and significance to personality development and to life itself.

What is the relationship between values and pupil achievement?

The classroom teacher may well be perplexed as to the relationship between certain value patterns and school achievement in working with children. Since the acquisition of facts, knowledge, attitudes, and skills are important ends in themselves, the teacher should approach the teaching task in two ways. First, the instructor must formulate a value concept in terms of what is expected of pupils; second, the teacher must strive to develop a similarity of ideals resembling those of the children. Each of these is discussed separately.

Teacher values and student achievement. The teacher is obligated to require high, sensible standards of achievement by all children. The instructor who has a value concept that pupil achievement is important will impart this seriousness of purpose to the students. There is a price to be paid if children are to attain these ends: good planning and classroom management are prime requisites of the teacher.

It is believed that reasonable responsibility should be placed upon the child to develop a desire to achieve, with expectations that he will produce certain results. Achievement pressure often originates from parental sources, with some unfortunate implications for the child who is unable to cope with some unreasonable demands. The teacher needs to assay how much pressure is being exerted from all sources and to reinforce where needed or to assist the child in both understanding the nature of such demands and in meeting successfully his situation. It is felt that when a teacher emphasizes the moral significance of work and consciously strives to develop the work-personality phase of the child, there will be more serious children, who are devoted to definite tasks, in the classroom.

A further value concept that the teacher must keep in mind, in light of student achievement, is that of recognizing the need for producing able, competent people. It is true that the elementary school years are concerned with providing the child with basic tools and skills that prepare him for more advanced education. However, since the child needs goals in order to progress, the teacher is required to have standards and ends toward which motives may be directed.

Relation of teacher values and achievement. Although the teacher has formulated a value approach to teaching that is demanding of good work, commensurate with the child's ability, a second consideration must be made by the teacher. The instructor needs to develop value patterns that are in harmony with those of the children, however, it is impossible, of course, to expect a teacher to have value patterns that are identical with every child. The following diagram illustrates the importance of better teacher-child value concept understandings:

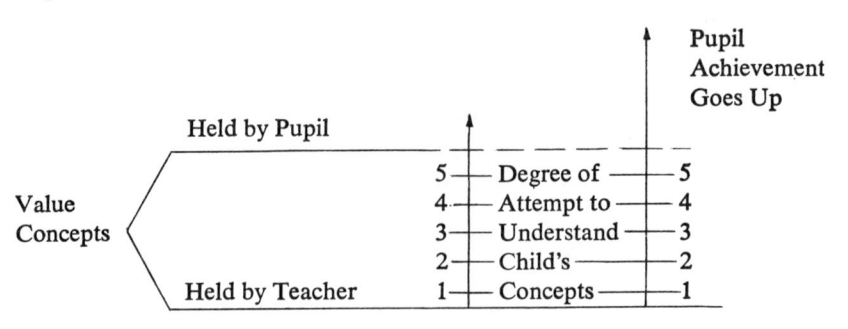

FIGURE 2–2. Similarity of Teacher Ideals and Pupil Values Means a Higher Achievement

Values, Issues, and Conflicts in Social Science Education   Part I   53

It is clear that teacher-pupil value concepts are often different. Yet, there is evidence from a study by H. J. Battle, that value patterns do operate in the interaction of teachers and pupils. Even though these concepts are different, as illustrated in Figure 2–2, the teacher should attempt to understand those patterns held by the child, since there is proof that the degree of similarity of teacher ideal and pupil patterns of values tends to be related directly to the level of pupil achievement according to marks.[11] Therefore, the closer the teacher approaches level five in Figure 2–2 in understanding child's value concepts, the greater expectation there is of pupil achievement. This fact suggests that bias in marking should be avoided; children who differ in value patterns from those of the teacher need learning experiences of a different sort than the teacher may think; and finally, the teacher has an obligation not only to strive for these understandings, but to help the child to develop an optimum value system. The significant fact is that teachers have a greater responsibility for pupil achievement than they may suspect, and when a teacher's value patterns are either identical with those of the child or there is a definite striving to understand them, there is a higher level of pupil achievement. Some suggested techniques and implementations from a curriculum design will be suggested in the next section for the teacher who may use the value approach to teaching.

What are the sources of children's values?

To understand the child's value system is to know him and what forces shaped him. The cultural, subcultural, and psychological influences that contribute to the formulation of the child's value pattern are many and varied. His sex, family, status in the family and other groups, his class, etc., together with his ego concept [12] are sources of values. Sondergaard,[13] Moore,[14] and Wise [15] agree on some value concepts held by the child that can be summarized here to help the elementary teacher in viewing the student more obectively. The values of a child are that he wants:

---

[11] H. J. Battle, "The Relationship Between Personal Values and Scholastic Achievement," *Journal of Experimental Education* 26 (September 1959): 39.

[12] As suggested previously, the ego concept as used here refers to the self-worth or self-esteem the child has of himself. See Mazafer Sherif and Hadley Cantril, *The Psychology of Ego Involvement* (New York: John Wiley & Sons, Inc., 1947), chaps. 2–9.

[13] Arensa Sondergaard, "What a Child Values," *Childhood Education* 32 (February 1956): 255–256.

[14] Bertha M. Moore, "Adults Look at Children's Values," *Childhood Education* 32 (February 1956): 257–261.

[15] William M. Wise, "The Role of Values in Child Guidance," *Educational Leadership* 8 (May 1951): 475–480.

Feelings of togetherness in the home, school, playground, and the like

Freedom to do some of the things he prefers

Some sense of independence, although he needs help in seeing boundaries

Laughter in his daily living

To be listened to by those around him

Experiences of learning new things and having "surprises"

Feelings of growing to be somebody of importance and to be like someone

Time to spend as he wishes, even to be alone

Help in understanding himself and especially his own associates

To love his fellow beings and to be respected

With this partial list of values, teachers may view the child as he learns to be value conscious. These sources of values are also important to the curriculum design in that what a child values, he will seek. Therefore, when learning experiences are based upon realistic values, *viz.,* in light of the child's value system, it is clear that he will be motivated and more deliberately goal seeking in his behavior.

Beck [16] considers the valuing process in terms of mechanisms, or ways by which the child becomes value conscious. Thus, as the teacher comprehends what a child values, he also should know what the process of valuing means to the child.

How can we teach for value change?

It should be clear at this point that teachers and pupils are not always in accord concerning value systems. Evidence has been given to support the claim that pupil achievement is higher when teachers endeavor to understand the values of children.[17] Then, the question arises, how can attitudes really be changed through classroom contact? Many teachers seem to think that children can learn certain facts, skills, and the like, but any deliberate attempts to alter attitudes is quite an impossible task. However, it is extremely important that teachers know

---

[16] Robert Beck, "The Methodology of Decision and Policy Making," *Progressive Education* 27 (April, 1950): 172–176.

[17] A. D. Woodruff and F. J. DiVesta, "The Relationship Between Values, Concepts, and Attitudes," *Educational and Psychological Measurement* 8, no. 4 (1948): 645–659.

Values, Issues, and Conflicts in Social Science Education   Part I   55

how to alter value systems in children in order that they will accept more positive ones which will contribute to improved ways of behaving. Therefore, the specific task of this section is to present ways of working in the classroom that are designed to aid the teacher in altering children's attitudes in a given way.

As a result of an experiment, it was shown that individuals behave in certain ways because they are interested in enhancing or preserving their well-being.[18] That is, one comes to value in a positive way those objects and conditions that he feels will contribute to his personal well-being. Obviously, he will avoid those aspects which interfere with this state of being, and these become negative reactions which, of course, are not desirable. Since values are closely related to behavior, the teacher can arrange certain situations which are designed to alter the child's concept of an object or conditions, as illustrated in Figure 2–3.

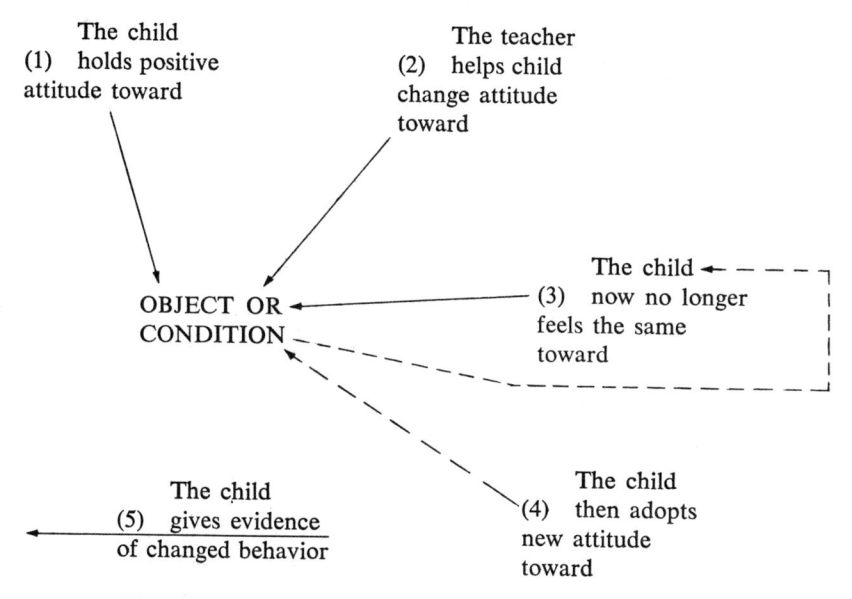

```
The child                      The teacher
(1) holds positive             (2) helps child
    attitude toward                change attitude
                                   toward

                                              The child
              OBJECT OR                 (3)   now no longer
              CONDITION                       feels the same
                                              toward

          The child                    The child
      (5) gives evidence           (4) then adopts
          of changed behavior          new attitude
                                       toward
```

FIGURE 2–3. Changing Children's Attitudes in the Classroom

In the first step in Figure 2–3, the child holds a positive attitude toward the object or condition which evokes a pleasant attitude. However, the teacher (step 2) helps to change the concept that the child has concerning the object and makes the change *known* to the child, who no longer has the same feelings of well-being he once possessed

---

[18] *Ibid.*, pp. 657–659.

(step 3). The way is now open for the child to have a new attitude about the object (step 4), with the result that he alters his behavior because of this new attitude (step 5). Thus, attitudes become favorable in new ways because the change in the situation and the concept of the object can now favor (new) strong positive values, while the unfavorable attitudes are avoided as threats to the strong, positive values. An illustration of a classroom project is given to show how a discerning teacher altered a value system of a group of children.

> Miss Bush was involved in a fifth grade social studies project concerning "How People Vote in Our Community." It was no surprise to her that some of the group held a rather strong, positive attitude that some people should not be allowed to vote because of racial and religious reasons (step 1). She set about to see what changes she could make concerning this narrowed view (step 2). She brought in some films depicting American democracy and how people depend upon each other. Strategic reading matter was given to them that suggested the equality of people in all areas of living. Illustrations, stories, and discussions were pointed in one direction: to change the concept of those who were biased in their feelings about voting privileges. It was no easy task, and Miss Bush learned, to her dismay, that seemingly little headway was being made. After the project was completed, she was still not satisfied that the group had a new concept that would alter behavior. She determined to work on this idea whenever possible during the year. She arranged many situations to get the youngsters to think about this problem and reminded them constantly of the subject they worked upon in this matter of voting in the community. Finally, she saw her opportunity and, after many months, arranged a learning experience that was really needed to bring about the desired results. She had learned that a transfer student was coming to the class, and she was a member of a minority group that the children were so outspoken about in their remarks. She told the group that they were to have a new classmate; the way she described the child, where she lived, and so on impressed the group very much. Then, she asked them to decide how this new girl should be treated. After much discussion it seemed that only the best of treatment should be offered. They then *voted* on it. Almost immediately they saw the point as a result of their own voting. Needless to say the presence of this new student during the succeeding weeks proved to Miss Bush that concepts were changed, (step 4), and the way she was being accepted proved that behavior was changed (step 5). Furthermore, in future discussions it was clear that most of the group had altered their attitudes toward other people of similar backgrounds in more ways than just voting privileges (step 5).

The teacher has a responsibility for changing attitudes, which means a change of behavior in more positive ways. In summary, in order to produce any changes in behavior, the teacher must begin by *changing* the concepts held by the child toward the object or condition. Certainly, the present value patterns must first be considered, since people tend to strive or act for more of the positive values than the negative ones. Thus, the teacher needs to lead the child by meaningful experiences in the areas of desired change, and he will know that the once positive values no longer bring about previously held pleasurable feelings. It is important that there be a tie-in with some previously held values of importance during this process of change, but the primary emphasis must be upon changing the original concept of the object toward which the attitude is expressed. Classroom instruction can change children's concepts and then attitudes can be definitely altered in the desired direction. Whether teachers realize it or not, they can and do set the stage for certain behavior experiences and lead the child to perform accordingly. It is hoped that more deliberate awareness of such learning may prompt the teacher to consider the areas of conflicting values held by teachers and pupils, to know where one's stated values may not be in harmony with what he actually believes, and to be cognizant of how the child may be acquiring certain values (such as honesty) by the ways in which teachers *expect* him to act.

It should be mentioned that changing the child's attitude may be no simple task and could require a considerable amount of time and energy. Individuals will resist making changes for the very reason that their feelings of well-being are being threatened. As already suggested, a series of meaningful experiences, that are designed to give him new ideas or concepts about tthe object, is arranged by the teacher and presented to the child. Thus, he does not feel threatened or insecure, but he can alter his attitude in light of a new concept, particularly when he is aided by expert teaching.

How does the teacher work with parents in the matter of values?

Parents desire that the child achieve happiness, security, and success. They may not express their feelings or even demonstrate outwardly their thinking, but parents do have values for their children which need to be understood by the teacher.

Children and parents are not always in accord with their value thinking. In many instances, some children in upper elementary classes begin to see that their home living standards and ways are not always desirable and agreeable to them. The parents themselves may not understand this and impose controls that produce anxieties within the child. This over emphasis by the parents on certain values may widen the gap between the child and parents and create additional problems. This is not to say that the home should not be the most prominent factor in the development of value systems for the child. Perhaps education may help parents to accept their critical role and enlarge their vision of values by helping them to see the hazards of, as well as to recognize, the better patterns of living. The teacher can work with parents in specific ways in the matter of values by:

> Securing insights and understandings from the parents about the child
>
> Getting the interest of parents in child's welfare, a community or school project, and so on
>
> Reinforcing a parental value system
>
> Reassuring the parent that his values are sound
>
> Getting parents to name values
>
> Suggesting to parents how values may be attained
>
> Helping parents to see how mistakes may be corrected
>
> Encouraging a friendly relationship between school and home
>
> Pointing up creative ways for guiding the child toward higher maturity levels
>
> Showing the parent how daily living situations can become learning experiences to foster value judgments as well as to promote academic skills

As the schools work more closely with parents in the area of values, and as they help children learn the idea of values, the suggested guides offered here should be deliberately cultivated by the teacher if better value relationships with parents are to be secured. It should be clear that no single pattern of working with parents can be followed in that their backgrounds, educations, and experiences will vary even in a given school-community environment. Some parents may be inarticulate and can offer little help to the teacher in expressing their desires and feelings. Other individuals may over verbalize their values and create conflictual problems. However, whatever the situation may be, the teacher should approach each home problem with the framework suggested here and emphasize those aspects that will be apparent in a given case. Improved home-school relationships can enhance the value-learning development of any child.

Issues, Conflicts, and Values

The critical years of childhood, probably ages 3 to 12, constitute a period during which the child formulates a basic "life view," a view that incorporates his conceptions of right and wrong and his attitudes toward an assortment of human relationships and situations. This is not to suggest that little change will occur after age 12 in the basic life view of the child, rather the intent here is to emphasize the enormous potential of the elementary school experience for the development of attitudes that will support constructive behavior in the face of social issues and conflicts which must be parts of life in the free society.

In United States society, as in most contemporary societies, the young are accorded specific roles, and it is not expected that they will be given full status as a member until a particular age has been reached. The age at which a young person may engage in various behaviors differs with respect to the activity. Marriage, driving an automobile, owning property, becoming gainfully employed, voting, these are but a few examples of the rights that are attained at varying ages. It has been assumed that the child's interest and involvement in the wider issues and problems of the larger society are necessarily limited because he cannot be a participant with membership status. A fact that should not be overlooked is that the child is in the middle of the social milieu and that he does develop ideas about issues and conflicts. His attitudes, values, and interests are involved in spite of his disenfranchised condition. (He probably assumes that the attainment of a certain age will provide him with knowledge and skills to participate in the resolution of issues and conflicts.)

It appears that there are several dimensions to the consideration of issues and conflicts in social science education. There is the question of the degree of interest and concern which contemporary problems hold for children at various maturity levels. There is the question of congruency of the genuine child life problems to the problems of contemporary adult life.

Do the issues and conflicts of childhood contain content and structures suggestive of those of the larger adult society?

Should the cognitive elements of issues and conflicts form a part of social science education in the elementary school? Should the concern be mainly for the development of attitudes, awareness of the process of valuing, and the function of values?

How does the teacher perceive and develop her role as an adult mediator who seeks to bring the child to successive stages of effectiveness in dealing with the issues and conflicts of his life environment? We will have more to say on these matters in the latter parts of this chapter, but of greater importance will be the analyzing, valuing, and resolving that will be done by you and your fellow students. We can do no more than urge you to *inquire* with us. We do not assume that you will come to hold the same positions; we trust that you will become more aware of the bases for your positions and decisions as teachers.

Issues, conflicts, and concept development. The inclusion of contemporary issues and conflicts in the social science education of children and youth is justified if we assume that:

> School experiences should provide for the transfer of attitudes, information, and skills into the daily life situations.
>
> Issues and conflicts lie at the core of the inquiry process, since they are sources of the need and the will to inquire.
>
> Issues and conflicts are natural aspects of life in a free and open society and should be encountered at an early stage.

The young member of the democratic society will be neither surprised nor frightened by the emergence of issues and conflicts, but will be inclined to assess his relationship and responsibility to them, to apply inquiry processes to them, and to anticipate solutions that will rarely be final and satisfactory to all parties. You may object at this point that we have suggested a behavioral objective for youngsters that very few adults seem to have accomplished. We are aware of this, but we cannot envision alternatives that are suitable for democratic living. This is not to imply that the objective is easy to attain; rather, our efforts must be in that direction, and our teaching behavior ought to demonstrate that we, as teachers, are skillful in issue and conflict situations.

Issues, conflicts, and values in daily affairs

Now that we have looked at the variety and nature of the issues and conflicts that have moved into the center of the American stage, we hope to consider the content of child experience in order to gain further understanding of the manner in which issues and conflicts enter here. We realize that not all of the issues and conflicts that affect the larger adult society will have concurrent and equal impact on children, but we insist that mass media will bring such matters into the child's realm of awareness and that the adult reactions will provide value and attitude bases for the child.

What is the nature of conflict in the child's life?

Conflict situations are as various as are the children who perceive them, but we can consider those predominant conflict patterns which may be observed in the process of growing up in the United States. With the entry of the child into school, the patterns of behavior that were acceptable to adults and siblings in the home will require some modification and adaptation to the requirements of larger group living. Pressures for approval from schoolmates will generate conflicts with desired normative behavior as projected by school teachers. Behaviors desired by the school personnel are not always compatible with those expressed by parents, and the child, lacking rational bases for understanding such differences between two power groups in his life, perceives such conflict in a largely emotional context. The way in which teachers behave in the face of such home-school conflicts can provide a valuable model. The early concept of conflict may be laden with hostility, suspicion, and emotion, rather than with empathy and a will to negotiate with the other side. Very early in school life, the child will sense the quality of the relationship that exists between teachers and parents. The teacher and parents may compete for the child's respect and loyalty or may seek to assert their respective powers of control, and in so doing they provide a weak and erratic behavior model for the child's reference in future conflict situations.

Another facet of the conflict potential in the child's transition into the wider social membership of the school has to do with the clash between verbal values and action values. Parents and teachers alike may stress the value of achievement in school tasks and frequently the rewards offered at school and home are given for attainment, with little or no payoff for gradual progress. When children learn that reward and recognition are given for getting all of the spelling list correct, rather than for showing progress consistent with their ability, they will soon begin to develop ways of dealing with this inconsistency.

In the school setting, the child is often told by the teacher that he must be careful in dealing with truth; he must not accuse another child of a wrongdoing unless he has clear evidence. Yet at three o'clock on any day, his entire class may be detained because the teacher believes that one of them wrote on the restroom wall. Mutual respect and human dignity are emphasized verbally in many schools, but we let the children know that we do not trust them when we rearrange the seating plan for testing situations. In their first encounter with an agency of the larger society, children may learn that respect is attained with age and power, that trust is something the child is expected to give, rather than to receive.

In the school setting, the child may come into his first contacts with members of other races and ethnic groups. The commonly expressed values of equality and human worth are tested operationally, and within the last few years the school has been sorely put to cope with this problem. Attitudes toward other groups have usually been acquired through family channels, and they may be reinforced by the behavior of the teachers.

Problems arising from open housing, labor-management relations, law enforcement, civil strife, drugs, and poverty will intrude into the lives of most children by way of parents and older family members. Depending upon the outlook of the significant persons around him, the child may learn to accept as inevitable and unchangeable the issues and conflicts of life. The school may administer more of this social anaesthesia or it may promote a sensitivity and an inquiring attitude toward conflict situations. *Unless the school will deal honestly and openly with issues and conflicts that touch children in their relationships with the school, an effective element of social education is lost.*

What are the facts? Can we agree upon the important parts of an issue? How and why do we see the problem differently? How do we feel about the problem? Can we see the other side at all? What can we do to resolve the conflict enough to enable us to move on? These questions have been helpful in dealing with conflict situations involving children in classroom settings. It is essential that the teacher mediate and allow the children time to move toward their own resolutions. The teacher may settle the conflict only to find that no one beyond herself accepted the solution. Of course, the classroom, the crucible of democracy, has seldom been viewed as the proper setting for allowing conflicts to surface; certainly it has not been seen as the place to provide for conflict-resolving opportunities.

Children become involved in conflicts with others who value the same objects. In the school setting it often involves the use of materials, equipment, or space, and such conflict situations are quite like those in the adult domain. The fact that adults regard children's squabbles over the use of a softball diamond *as immature* does not make it less critical to the children involved. From the child's viewpoint, the adult conflicts over international boundaries and political control are pointless, although the young human seems to have little difficulty in accepting violence as a means to conflict resolution. Successive generations have used war and force as adults, a sophisticated response to conflicts that is denied to children!

The means that are acceptable in settling conflicts differ with the situation and the persons involved. The young people of the United States are immersed in the Christian-Judiac religious value system, a system which does not sanction the taking of human life. Yet, violence is an accepted means for the resolution of international conflicts and for the ultimate punishment of criminal behavior in our own society.

Emerging and continuing issues

We do not pretend to present an exhaustive list of contemporary issues, rather, it is our purpose to identify those which have received much public attention in recent years. The fact that these issues persist may suggest that the people of the United States are experiencing value conflicts when they consider how to resolve these and other issues. Some of these issues will certainly be around when your pupils of next year become voting citizens. Some of these issues have already penetrated into the lives of elementary children. Consider this group of issues and add your own to the list:

The environment, its use and modification. This includes problems of pollution, conservation, public and private interest, and control of natural resources, such as, water, oil, timber, and recreational areas.

Population control. Some persons have included "people pollution" as part of the environmental problem, but a more serious aspect is the effect of population control upon the family concept and upon the psychological factors. Marriages may come to be more highly valued when children are not produced. The function of the family and the concept itself may undergo alteration with resultant changes in the lifelong character of marriage. Can we prepare children to attain emotional stability in marriage relationships quite unlike those which they witnessed in their own homes? Should we?

Disadvantaged people. What respect is accorded to human beings who are economically, socially, and politically disadvantaged? How should society deal with such problems in view of the high value that we place upon achievement, success, and independence? The relationships between being disadvantaged and racial and ethnic characteristics may provide the perceptual blinders which help us to disregard the problems.

Individuality and social responsibility. A constant tension exists between individuality and social responsibility; both traits are highly valued in our society. As our society becomes more urbanized, more automated, and even more mobile, individuality will come into conflict with the common will. The mass communication of ideas and values may serve to flatten out individuality in the citizen, to make him subject to more pressure to conform. How may the school prepare young people to encounter situations that call for making a choice of this sort?

Resolution of international conflict. The Vietnam War has seen a vigorous protest made against the use of war as a means to settle human conflicts. The matter of moral and religious objections has been raised, and at least one state has enacted legislation to prevent its citizens from fighting in undeclared wars. This issue cannot be finally settled by only one nation, but should our large, powerful nation take the initiative? How do school experiences condition children for war as a normal phenomenon or as an abnormality to be abandoned?

The role of the young. The late 1960's witnessed the vigorous, sometimes serious, and sometimes rowdy entry of young Americans into the political and social arenas. To be without a vote did not mean to be without a voice. Their voices were heard in many places. Whether the young are to be put down for their brashness and inexperience or accepted on the basis of their commitment, energy, and idealism is not really the question. The question is, how can we accommodate and integrate the young into our society? Age in and of itself cannot be proven to be a discriminating criterion for giving people the right to participate fully in the business of our society. Can we develop new procedures to diminish the alienating effects of arbitrary boundaries that separate the 19-year-old from the 22-year-old? How can we seek to diminish the effects of the natural bio-psychological boundaries between generations? What is the implication for the school and the teacher? When does the school provided by society become the school of the child? How do our ways of working with children build barriers or bridges?

Issues, conflicts, values. The perceptions of human situations, as involving issues and as being conflict laden, differ from person to person, depending upon a number of factors. It is widely held that one's values and the degree of personal interest are strong factors which influence the manner in which any person views issues and conflicts. Later in this chapter, you will have the opportunity to read some carefully chosen articles which deal with the major issues and conflicts of our nation and world. You will become sensitive to the impact of the values held by each writer as he views the current scene, and your own values will provide a personal yardstick which will be applied in your reactions.

Values, Issues, and Conflicts in Social Science Education

PART II

In part two of this chapter, there are a number of carefully selected readings which deal with issues that have confronted our society for a long time. We have reacted to these issues within the framework of our dominant values, but value conflicts have intensified many of the issues. Elementary age children will be aware of these issues through mass media, home discussions, and contact with local problems through which the issues manifest themselves. When will you deal with these issues in the school? What principles will guide you? What will your purpose be?

Richard E. Farson

Richard E. Farson, vice-president for Ecological Affairs and Dean of the School of Design at the California Institute of The Arts in Los Angeles, prefers to view our complex and often frightening problems as the seed beds from which newly conceived solutions will arise.

In addition to analysis of this article by the class, you may want to invite a teacher-parent-administrator group to consider the substantive aspects of Farson's article and to consider what the school's response should be to the suggestions set forth in the last paragraphs of the selection.

How Could Anything That Feels So Bad Be So Good?

Maybe it is time to adopt a new strategy in trying to figure out why life today is so difficult, and what can be done about it. Assume that not only are things often not what they seem, they may be just the opposite of what they seem. When it comes to human affairs, everything is paradoxical.

People are discontented these days, for example, not because things are worse than ever, but because things are better than ever. Take marriage. In California there are about six divorces for every ten marriages—even higher in some of the better communities. One must admit that a good deal of discontent is reflected in those statistics. But the explanation so frequently offered—that the institution of marriage is in a state of collapse—simply does not hold. Marriage has never been more popular and desirable than it is now;

Dean Richard E. Farson, "How Could Anything That Feels So Bad Be So Good?", *Saturday Review* (September 6, 1969).

so appealing in fact, that even those who are in the process of divorce can scarcely wait for the law to allow them to marry again.

The problem is that people have never before entered marriage with the high expectations they now hold. Throughout history, the family has been a vital unit for survival, starting as a defense system for physical survival, and gradually becoming a unit for economic survival. Now, of course, the family has become a physical and economic liability rather than an asset. Having met, as a society, the basic survival and security needs, people simply don't need each other anymore to fight Indians or spin yarn—or wash dishes or repair electrical plugs for that matter. The bonds of marriage and family life are no longer functional, but affectional. People used to come to love each other because they needed each other. Now it's just the other way around. They need each other because they love each other.

Listening to the complaints of those recently divorced, one seldom hears of brutality and desertion, but usually something like, "We just don't communicate very well," "The educational differences between us were simply too great to overcome," "I felt trapped in the relationship," "He won't let me be *me*," "We don't have much in common anymore." These complaints are interesting, because they reflect high-order discontent resulting from the failure of marriage to meet the great expectations held for it. Couples now expect—and demand—communication and understanding, shared values and goals, intellectual companionship, full sexual lives, deep romantic love, great moments of intimacy. By and large, marriage today actually does deliver such moments, but as a result couples have gone on to burden the relationship with even greater demands. To some extent it has been the success of marriage that has created the discontent.

The same appears to be true in the civil rights movement. The gains that have been made have led not to satisfaction but to increased tension and dissatisfaction, particularly among those benefitting from such gains. The discontent is higher in the North than the South, higher in cities than in rural areas.

One could go on—the protests of student activists are greater at the better universities. Demands for freedom and democracy and education and individual liberty and free speech are greatest in the nation which leads the world in these respects. The history of revolutions shows that they come *after* reforms have been made, when people are strong enough to have developed a vision of better things.

The disturbing paradox of social change is that improvement brings the need for more improvement in constantly accelerating demands. So, compared to what *used* to be, society is way ahead; compared to what *might* be, it is way behind. Society is enabled to feel that conditions are rotten, because they are actually so good.

Another problem is that everything is temporary, nothing lasts. We have grown up with the idea that in order to develop personal security we need stability, roots, consistency, and familiarity. Yet we live in a world which in every respect is continually changing. Whether we are talking about skyscrapers or family life, scientific facts or religious values, all are highly temporary and becoming even more so. If one were to plot a curve showing the incidence of invention throughout the history of man, one would see that change is not just increasing but actually accelerating. Changes are coming faster and faster—in a sense change has become a way of life. The only people who will live successfully in tomorrow's world are those who can accept and enjoy temporary systems.

Moments, then, are the most we can expect from the things we create and produce. We are beginning to change their basis of evaluation from the permanent usefulness of things to their ability to create moments of positive experience. Yet with nothing to rely upon except change itself, we find ourselves increasingly disturbed and disrupted as a society.

People are also troubled because of the new participative mood that exists today. It's a do-it-yourself society; every layman wants to get into the act. Emerson's "do your own thing" has become the cliché of the times. People no longer accept being passive members. They now want to be active changers.

This participative phenomenon can be seen in every part of contemporary life—on campus, in the church, in the mass media, in the arts, in business and industry, on ghetto streets, in the family. It is succeeding to the point where people are having to abandon their old concepts of elitism. The myths that wisdom, creativity, and competence are rare, difficult to evoke, and highly desired, are giving way to a view that they are rather common, relatively easy to elicit, and desired only in situations where they are not too disruptive or difficult to manage.

The problem is that modern man seems unable to redesign his institutions fast enough to accommodate the new demands, the new intelligence, the new abilities of segments of society which, heretofore, have not been taken seriously. Consequently, people are frightened by the black revolution, paralyzed by student activism, and now face what may be even more devastating—the women's rebellion.

As if all this weren't enough, society may also be experiencing a reverse transmission of culture. To put it simply, today's young people probably know more than their elders. Wisdom and culture have always been transmitted from the older generation to the younger. Now, perhaps for the first time in history, there is a reversal of that process. Young people used to want to be like their elders; today it's the other way around.

The old, of course, always learned some things from the young. Fashion and dance, for example. But now they are learning from youth about the nature of society, about world affairs, about human relations, about life. The young have much to teach in matters of taste and judgment, in ethics and morals. They are attending school in greater numbers, staying longer, and learning more than former generations did. All kinds of people—advertising executives, futurists, artists, designers, social scientists—now look to youth as the leading edge of contemporary culture. If McLuhan is right, the young are sensing the world in ways never sensed before, and, consequently, they have developed an approach to life which is very different from that of their elders. Margaret Mead describes the plight of the over-thirty generation as being similar to that of the alien trying to learn about a foreign culture. It is small wonder then that the institutions in which leadership is entrusted only to the elders (and what institution isn't?) are so unstable.

Society simply has not had these kinds of problems before, and to meet them it will have to adopt strategies for their solution that are as new, and as different, and as paradoxical as are the problems themselves.

Instead of trying to reduce the discontent felt, try to raise the level or quality of the discontent. Perhaps the most that can be hoped for is to have high-order discontent in today's society, discontent about things that really matter. Rather than evaluating programs in terms of how happy they make people, how satisfied those people become, programs must be evaluated in terms of the quality of the discontent they engender. For example, if a consultant wants to assess whether or not an organization is healthy, he doesn't ask, "Is there an absence of complaints?" but rather, "What kinds of complaints are there?" Psychologist Abraham Maslow suggests that we analyze the *quality* of the complaint being registered. In his terms, a low-level grumble would involve, for instance, a complaint about working conditions; a high-level grumble might have to do with matters beyond one's own selfish interests—a concern for fairness in the treatment of another person, for example—while a meta-grumble would have to do with self-actualization needs, such as feeling that one's talents are not being fully utilized, wanting to be in on things, wanting to make a greater contribution.

As an illustration, instead of trying to negotiate only on the low-order complaints of black students having to do with the number of black teachers on a faculty or the lack of soul food in the school cafeteria, efforts should transcend these problems, meet those demands, and go well beyond them by raising the level of discontent so that black students are complaining about the quality of education and demanding a chance to reinvent the whole system. When such complaints are heard, the situation will be much improved, for then *all* men will be able to engage in a joint effort toward a common goal.

Instead of trying to "cool it" in a crisis, use the time of crisis to make major changes and improvements. Many individuals feel that in a crisis the only thing to do is to try to "hang in there," call everything to a halt, try to maintain previous conditions, let it pass, and hope things will return to normal. Instead, they should capitalize on the momentum that is in the developing mood of people during a crisis to energize the changes that must be made. It is analogous to the jujitsu technique of moving with one's opponent and using his momentum to gain the advantage; of course, in correcting social ills *everyone* gains, nobody loses.

Instead of trying to make gradual changes in small increments, make big changes. After all, big changes are relatively easier to make than are small ones. Some people assume that the way to bring about improvement is to make the change small enough so that nobody will notice it. This approach has never worked, and one can't help but wonder why such thinking continues. Everyone knows how to resist small changes; they do it all the time. If, however, the change is big enough, resistance can't be mobilized against it. Management can make a sweeping organizational change, but just let a manager try to change someone's desk from here to there, and see the great difficulty he encounters. All change is resisted, so the question is how can the changes be made big enough so that they have a chance of succeeding?

Instead of trying to improve people, improve environments. All too often the conclusion is reached that all problems boil down to such people problems as basic attitude differences and personality clashes. And it is believed that work must first be done to change people. But that may not be the best strategy. People, fundamentally, change little in their personalities and attitudes. They can, however, change markedly in their responses to different environments, situations, and conditions.

It is known how to create conditions which will evoke from just about anybody the full range of human behavior. With relative ease, people can be made to lie, cheat, and hurt others. How simple it is to take the nicest kid on the block, send him to Vietnam, and soon have him killing other people. It is comforting also to know that situations can be created in which people become affectionate, honest, helpful, intimate, and cooperative. All this is fairly simple to arrange in the laboratory. The trouble is that society does not have the designs that elicit these aspects in people.

Buckminster Fuller has said that instead of *reforms* society needs new *forms;* e.g., in order to reduce traffic accidents, improve automobiles and highways instead of trying to improve drivers. The same concept should be applied to human relations. There is a need to think in terms of social architecture, and to provide arrangements among people that evoke what they really want to see in themselves. Mankind takes great pains with physical architecture, and is beginning to concern itself with the design of systems in which the human being is a component. But most of these designs are only for safety, efficiency, or productivity. System designs are not made to affect those aspects of life people care most about such as family life, romance, esthetic experiences, and intimate encounter. Social technology as well as physical technology need to be applied in making human arrangements that will transcend anything mankind has yet experienced. People need not be victimized by their environments; they can be fulfilled by them.

Instead of looking to a professional elite for the solution to any social problem, look to the greatest resource available—the very population that has the problem. Many of us tend to have a low opinion of people, those wretched masses who don't understand, don't know what they need or want, who continually make mistakes and foul up their lives, requiring those of us who are professionally trained to come in and correct the situation. But that's not the way it really works. The fact is that some drug addicts are much better able to cure addiction in each other than are psychiatrists; some convicts can run better rehabilitation programs for convicts than do correctional officers; many students tend to learn more from each other than from many professors; some patients in mental hospitals are better for each other than is the staff. Thousands of self-help organizations are doing a good job, perhaps a better job at problem solving than is the profession that is identified with that problem. People who *have* the problems often have a better understanding of their situation and what must be done to change it. What professionals have to do is learn to cooperate with that resource, to design the conditions which evoke that intelligence.

In this way society can be truly self-determining and self-renewing. The special beauty of this formulation is that it fits the democratic goal of enabling the people to make a society for themselves. Mankind can rely on people as a resource for much more than is possible to imagine. It's really quite difficult to find the ceiling of what people can do for themselves and each other, given the opportunity.

The great frontier today is the exploration of the human potential, man's seemingly limitless ability to adapt, to grow, to invent his own destiny. There is much to learn, but we already know this: the future need not happen to us; we can make it happen.

William Murdoch and Joseph Connell

In the book, *Yesterday's People,* Jack Weller wrote about the resistance encountered in one Appalachian village when a community garbage collection plan was proposed. It seemed that a number of the citizens valued their "right" to toss garbage out the back door and into the river which passed through the village.

Issues and conflicts which arise from man's use of his total environment inevitably involve values and the valuing process. In this selection by William Murdoch and Joseph Connell, we are advised that technology alone cannot solve environmental problems which many persons incorrectly believe have been produced by technological developments. As you read "All About Ecology," identify those problems that you believe will require basic changes in prevailing attitudes and values if they are to be resolved. How would you propose to approach such attitude-value changes in the elementary school through very specific learning experiences?

All About Ecology

The public's awakening to the environmental crisis over the past few years has been remarkable. A recent Gallup Poll showed that every other American was concerned about the population problem. A questionnaire sent to about five hundred University of California freshmen asked which of twenty-five topics should be included in a general biology course for non-majors. The top four positions were: Human Population Problems (85%), Pollution (79%), Genetics (71.3%), and Ecology (66%).

The average citizen is at least getting to know the word ecology, even though his basic understanding of it may not be significantly increased. Not more than five years ago, we had to explain at length what an ecologist was. Recently when we have described ourselves as ecologists, we have been met with respectful nods of recognition.

A change has also occurred among ecologists themselves. Until recently the meetings of ecologists we attended were concerned with the esoterica of a "pure science," but now ecologists are haranguing each other on the necessity for ecologists to become involved in the "real world." We can expect that peripatetic "ecological experts" will soon join the ranks of governmental consultants jetting back and forth to the Capitol—thereby adding their quota to the pollution of the atmosphere. However, that will be a small price to pay if they succeed in clearing the air of the political verbiage that still passes for an environmental policy in Washington.

Concern about environment, of course, is not limited to the United States. The ecological crisis, by its nature, is basically an international problem, so it seems likely that the ecologist as "expert" is here to stay. To some extent the present commotion about ecology arises from people climbing on the newest bandwagon. When the limits of ecological expertise become apparent, we must expect to lose a few passengers. But, if only because there is no alternative, the ecologist and the policymakers appear to be stuck with each other for some time to come.

While a growing awareness of the relevance of ecology must be welcomed, there are already misconceptions about it. Further, the traditional role of the expert in Washington predisposes the nation to a misuse of its ecologists. Take an example. A common lament of the socially conscious citizen is that though we have enough science and technology to put a man on the moon we cannot maintain a decent environment in the United States. The implicit premise here seems clear: the solution to our ecological crisis is technological. A logical extension of this argument is that, in this particular case, the ecologist is the appropriate "engineer" to resolve the crisis. This reflects the dominant American philosophy (which is sure to come up after every lecture on the environment) that the answer to most of our problems is technology and, in particular, that the answer to the problems raised by technology is more technology. Perhaps the most astounding example of this blind faith is the recent assurance issued by the government that the SST will not fly over the United States until the sonic boom problem is solved. The sonic boom "problem," of course, cannot be "solved." One job of the ecologist is to dispel this faith in technology.

To illustrate the environmental crisis, let us take two examples of how

---

William Murdoch and Joseph Connell, "All About Ecology," reprinted by permission, from the January 1970 issue of *The Center Magazine,* a publication of the Center for the Study of Democratic Institutions in Santa Barbara, California.

the growth of population, combined with the increasing sophistication of technology, has caused serious problems which planning and foresight could have prevented. Unfortunately, the fact is that no technological solutions applied to problems caused by increased population have ever taken into consideration the consequences to the environment.

The first example is the building of the Aswan High Dam on the upper Nile. Its purposes were laudable—to provide a regular supply of water for irrigation, to prevent disastrous floods, and to provide electrical power for a primitive society. Other effects, however, were simply not taken into account. The annual flood of the Nile had brought a supply of rich nutrients to the eastern Mediterranean Sea, renewing its fertility; fishermen had long depended upon this annual cycle. Since the Aswan Dam put an end to the annual flood with its load of nutrients, the annual bloom of phytoplankton in the eastern Mediterranean no longer occurs. Thus the food chain from phytoplankton to zoöplankton to fish has been broken; and the sardine fishery, once producing eighteen thousand tons per year (about half of the total fish catch), has dropped to about five hundred tons per year.

Another ecological effect of the dam has been the replacement of an intermittent flowing stream with a permanent stable lake. This has allowed aquatic snails to maintain large populations, whereas before the dam was built they had been reduced each year during the dry season. Because irrigation supports larger human populations, there are now many more people living close to these stable bodies of water. The problem here is that the snails serve as intermediate hosts of the larvae of a blood fluke. The larvae leave the snail and bore into humans, infecting the liver and other organs. This causes the disease called schistosomiasis. The species of snail which lives in stable water harbors a more virulent species of fluke than that found in another species of snail in running water. Thus the lake behind the Aswan Dam has increased both the incidence and virulence of schistosomiasis among the people of the upper Nile.

A second example we might cite is the effect of DDT on the environment. DDT is only slightly soluble in water, so is carried mainly on particles in the water for short distances until these settle out. But on tiny particles in the atmosphere it is carried great distances; it may even fall out more heavily in distant places than close to where it was sprayed. DDT is not readily broken down by microörganisms; it therefore persists in the environment for for many years. It is very soluble in fats so that it is quickly taken up by organisms. Herbivores eat many times their own weight of plants; the DDT is not broken down but is accumulated in their bodies and becomes further concentrated when the herbivores are eaten by the carnivores. The result is that the species at the top of the food chain end up with high doses of it in their tissues. Evidence is beginning to show that certain species of predators, such as ospreys, are being wiped out as a result of physiological debilities which lead to reproductive failure, all caused by accumulations of DDT.

Whatever is done to the environment is likely to have repercussions in other places at other times. Because of the characteristic problems of ecology some of the effects are bound to be unpredictable in practice, if not in principle. Furthermore, because of the characteristic time-dependence problem, the effects may not be measurable for years—possibly not for decades.

If man's actions are massive enough, drastic enough, or of the right sort, they will cause changes which are irreversible since the genetic material of extinct species cannot be reconstituted. Even if species are not driven to extinction, changes may occur in the ecosystem which prevent a recurrence of the events which produced the community. Such irreversible changes will almost always produce a simplification of the environment.

The environment is finite and our non-renewable resources are finite. When the stocks run out we will have to recycle what we have used.

The capacity of the environment to act as a sink for our total waste, to absorb it and recycle it so that it does not accumulate as pollution, is limited. In many instances, that limit has already been passed. It seems clear that when limits are passed, fairly gross effects occur, some of which are predictable, some of which are not. These effects result in significant alterations in environmental conditions (global weather, ocean productivity). Such changes are almost always bad since organisms have evolved and ecosystems have developed for existing conditions. We impose rates of change on the environment which are too great for biological systems to cope with.

In such a finite world and under present conditions, an increasing population can only worsen matters. For a stationary population, an increase in standard of living can only mean an increase in the use of limited resources, the destruction of the environment, and the choking of the environmental sinks.

There are two ways of attacking the environmental crisis. The first approach is technology; the second is to reverse the trends which got us into the crisis in the first place and to alter the structure of our society so that an equilibrium between human population and the capacities of the environment can be established.

There are three main dangers in a technological approach to the environmental crisis. The first threatens the environment in the short term, the second concerns ecologists themselves, and the third, which concerns the general public attitude, is a threat to the environment in the long term.

Our basic premise is that, by its nature, technology is a system for manufacturing the need for more technology. When this is combined with an economic system whose major goal is growth, the result is a society in which conspicuous production of garbage is the highest social virtue. If our premise is correct, it is unlikely we can solve our present problems by using technology. As an example, we might consider nuclear power plants as a "clean" alternative to which we can increasingly turn. But nuclear power plants inevitably produce radioactive waste; this problem will grow at an enormous rate, and we are not competent to handle it safely. In addition, a whole new set of problems rises when all these plants produce thermal pollution. Technology merely substitutes one sort of pollution for another.

There is a more subtle danger inherent in the technological approach. The automobile is a blight on Southern California's landscape. It might be thought that ecologists should concern themselves with encouraging the development of technology to cut down the emission of pollutants from the internal combustion engine. Yet that might only serve to give the public the impression that something is being done about the problem and that it can therefore confidently await its solution. Nothing significant could be accomplished in any case because the increasing number of cars ensures an undiminishing smog problem.

Tinkering with technology is essentially equivalent to oiling its wheels. The very act of making minor alterations, in order to placate the public, actually allows the general development of technology to proceed unhindered, only increasing the environmental problems it causes. This is what sociologists have called a "pseudo-event." That is, activities go on which give the appearance of tackling the problem; they will not, of course, solve it but only remove public pressure for a solution.

Tinkering also distracts the ecologist from his real job. It is the ecologist's job, as a general rule, to oppose growth and "progress." He cannot set about convincing the public of the correctness of this position if in the meantime he is putting his shoulder behind the wheel of technology. The political power system has a long tradition of buying off its critics, and the ecologist is liable to wind up perennially compromising his position, thereby merely slowing down slightly or redirecting the onslaught of technology.

The pressures on the ecologist to provide "tinkering" solutions will continue to be quite strong. Pleas for a change of values, for a change to a nongrowth, equilibrium economy seem naive. The government, expecting sophistication from its "experts," will probably receive such advice coolly. Furthermore, ecologists themselves are painfully aware of how immature their science is and generally take every opportunity to cover up this fact with a cloud of obfuscating pseudo-sophistication. They delight in turning prosaic facts and ideas into esoteric jargon. Where possible, they embroider the structure with mathematics and the language of cybernetics and systems analysis, which is sometimes useful but frequently is merely confusing. Such sophistication is easily come by in suggesting technological solutions.

Finally, there is always the danger that in becoming a governmental consultant, the ecologist will aim his sights at the wrong target. The history of the Washington "expert" is that he is called in to make alterations in the model already decided upon by the policymakers. It would be interesting to know what proportion of scientific advice has ever produced a change in ends rather than in means. We suspect it is minute. But the ecologist ought not to concern himself with less than such a change; he must change the model itself.

We should point out that we are not, for example, against substituting a steam-driven car for a gas-driven car. Our contention is that by changing public attitudes the ecologist can do something much more fundamental. In addition, by changing these attitudes he may even make it easier to force the introduction of "cleaner" technology, since this also is largely a *political* decision. This certainly seems to be so in the example of the steam-driven car.

We do not believe that the ecologist has anything really new to say. His task, rather, is to inculcate in the government and the people basic ecological attitudes. The population must come, and very soon, to appreciate certain basic notions. For example: a finite world cannot support or withstand a continually expanding population and technology; there are limits to the capacity of environmental sinks; ecosystems are sets of interacting entities and there is no "treatment" which does not have "side effects" (e.g. the Aswan Dam); we cannot continually simplify systems and expect them to remain stable, and once they do become unstable there is a tendency for instability to increase with time. Each child should grow up knowing and understanding his place in the environment and the possible consequences of his interaction with it.

In short, the ecologist must convince the population that the only solution to the problem of growth is not to grow. This applies to population and, unless the population is declining, to its standard of living. It should be clear by now that "standard of living" is probably beginning to have an inverse relationship to the quality of life. An increase in the gross national product must be construed, from the ecological point of view, as disastrous. (The case of underdeveloped countries, of course, is different.)

We do not minimize the difficulties in changing the main driving force in life. The point of view of the ecologist, however, should be subversive; it has to be subversive or the ecologist will become merely subservient. Such a change in values and structure will have profound consequences. For example, economists, with a few notable exceptions, do not seem to have given any thought to the possibility or desirability of a stationary economy. Businessmen, and most economists, think that growth is good, stagnation or regression is bad. Can an equilibrium be set up with the environment in a system having this philosophy? The problem of converting to non-growth is present in socialist countries too, of course, but we must ask if corporate capitalism, by its nature, can accommodate such a change and still retain its major features. By contrast, if there are any ecological laws at all, we believe the ecologists' notion of the inevitability of an equilibrium between man and the environment is such a law.

We would like to modify some details of this general stand. Especially after the necessary basic changes are put in motion, there *are* things ecologists as "experts" can do: some of them are sophisticated and others, in a very broad sense, may even be technological. Certainly, determining the "optimum" U.S. population will require sophisticated techniques. Ecologists, willy-nilly, will have to take a central role in advising on the management of the environment. They already are beginning to do this. The characteristics of ecology here determine that this advice, to be good, will be to some extent sophisticated to fit particular cases. Thus, good management will depend on long-term studies of *particular* areas, since ecological situations are both time-dependent and locale-dependent. These two features also ensure that there will be a sizeable time-lag between posing the question and receiving the ecological advice, and a major job of the ecologists will be to make the existence of such lags known to policymakers.

Ecologists sometimes will have to apply technology. As one instance, integrated pest control (that is, basically biological control with occasional small-scale use of pesticides) will surely replace chemical control, and integrated pest control can be considered biological technology. In this area there is some promise that sophisticated computer modeling techniques applied to strategies of pest control may help us design better techniques. The banning of DDT, for example, could no doubt be a laudable victory in the war to save the environment, but it would be disastrous to mistake a symbolic victory like this for winning the war itself.

Erich Fromm

Writing in 1941, when the fascism of Germany and Italy seemed to pose the ultimate threat to human freedom, Erich Fromm considered "The Illusion of Individuality" in free societies to be a more serious problem. In the following selection from the book, *Escape from Freedom,* Fromm has examined the impact of the modern industrial system upon individualism and how spontaneity and unique feelings are suppressed from early childhood onward.

Thirty years later, the concerns over individuality and freedom in a modern technocracy are still with us. The external threat posed by Hitler's Nazism has long since passed and "new" internal dangers have appeared. Protesters against the violence of war have taken up violence as an instrument of change, and disenchanted youths have reacted against the cult of middle class conformity. A modern Diogenes might well search for individuality, which seems to be as elusive as honesty. Consider the following questions:

1. Are Fromm's observations valid with respect to conditions in the United States in the 1970's?
2. What is the role, if any, of the school in responding to the threats to individuality?
3. What specific suggestions would you make to teachers who want to foster and sustain individuality within an atmosphere of collective freedom?
4. Read the final paragraph in this selection and then attempt to compile a list of current examples that either support or deny Fromm's positions.

The Illusion of Individuality

In the previous chapters I have tried to show that certain factors in the modern industrial system in general and in its monopolistic phase in particular make for the development of a personality which feels powerless and alone, anxious and insecure. I have discussed the specific conditions in Germany which make part of her population fertile soil for an ideology and political practice that appeal to what I have described as the authoritarian character.

But what about ourselves? Is our own democracy threatened only by Fascism beyond the Atlantic or by the "fifth column" in our own ranks? If that were the case, the situation would be serious but not critical. But although foreign and internal threats of Fascism must be taken seriously, there is no greater mistake and no graver danger than not to see that in our own society we are faced with the same phenomenon that is fertile soil for the rise of Fascism anywhere: insignificance and powerlessness of the individual.

This statement challenges the conventional belief that by freeing the individual from all external restraints modern democracy has achieved true individualism. We are proud that we are not subject to any external authority, that we are free to express our thoughts and feelings, and we take it for granted that this freedom almost automatically guarantees our individuality. The *right to express our thoughts,* however, *means something only if we are able to have thoughts of our own;* freedom from external authority is a lasting gain only if the inner psychological conditions are such that we are able to establish our own individuality. Have we achieved that aim, or are we at least approaching it? This book deals with the human factor; its task, therefore, is to analyze this very question critically. In doing so we take up threads that were dropped in earlier chapters. In discussing the two aspects of freedom for modern man, we have pointed out the economic conditions that make for increasing isolation and powerlessness of the individual in our era; in discussing the psychological results we have shown that this powerlessness leads either to the kind of escape that we find in the authoritarian character, or else to a compulsive conforming in the process of which the isolated individual becomes an automaton, loses his self, and yet at the same time consciously conceives of himself as free and subject only to himself.

It is important to consider how our culture fosters this tendency to conform, even though there is space for only a few outstanding examples. The suppression of spontaneous feelings, and thereby of the development of genuine individuality, starts very early, as a matter of fact with the earliest

---

From *Escape from Freedom* by Erich Fromm. Copyright 1941, © 1969 by Erich Fromm. Reprinted by permission of Holt, Rinehart and Winston, Inc.

training of a child.[1] This is not to say that training must inevitably lead to suppression of spontaneity if the real aim of education is to further the inner independence and individuality of the child, its growth and integrity. The restrictions which such a kind of education may have to impose upon the growing child are only transitory measures that really support the growth and expansion. In our culture, however, education too often results in the elimination of spontaneity and in the substitution of original psychic acts by superimposed feelings, thoughts, and wishes. (By original I do not mean, let me repeat, that an idea has not been thought before by someone else, but that it originates in the individual, that it is the result of his own activity and in this sense is *his* thought.) To choose one illustration somewhat arbitrarily, one of the earliest suppressions of *feelings* concerns hostility and dislike. To start with, most children have a certain measure of hostility and rebelliousness as a result of their conflicts with a surrounding world that tends to block their expansiveness and to which, as the weaker opponent, they usually have to yield. It is one of the essential aims of the educational process to eliminate this antagonistic reaction. The methods are different; they vary from threats and punishments, which frighten the child, to the subtler methods of bribery or "explanations," which confuse the child and make him give up his hostility. The child starts with giving up the expression of his feelings and eventually gives up the very feeling itself. Together with that, he is taught to suppress the awareness of hostility and insincerity in others; sometimes this is not entirely easy, since children have a capacity for noticing such negative qualities in others without being so easily deceived by words as adults usually are. They still dislike somebody "for no good reason"—except the very good one that they feel the hostility, or insincerity, radiating from that person. This reaction is soon discouraged; it does not take long for the child to reach the "maturity" of the average adult and to lose the sense of discrimination between a decent person and a scoundrel, as long as the latter has not committed some flagrant act.

On the other hand, early in his education, the child is taught to have feelings that are not at all "his"; particularly is he taught to like people, to be uncritically friendly to them, and to smile. What education may not have accomplished is usually done by social pressure in later life. If you do not smile you are judged lacking in a "pleasing personality"—and you need to have a pleasing personality if you want to sell your services, whether as a waitress, a salesman, or a physician. Only those at the bottom of the social pyramid, who sell nothing but their physical labor, and those at the very top do not need to be particularly "pleasant." Friendliness, cheerfulness, and

---

[1] According to a communication by Anna Hartoch (from a forthcoming book on case studies of Sarah Lawrence Nursery School children, jointly by M. Gay, A. Hartoch, L. B. Murphy) Rorschach tests of three to five year old children have shown that the attempt to preserve their spontaneity gives rise to the chief conflict between the children and the authoritative adults.

everything that a smile is supposed to express, become automatic responses which one turns on and off like an electric switch.[2]

To be sure, in many instances the person is aware of merely making a gesture; in most cases, however, he loses that awareness and thereby the ability to discriminate between the pseudo feeling and spontaneous friendliness.

It is not only hostility that is directly suppressed and friendliness that is killed by superimposing its counterfeit. A wide range of spontaneous emotions are suppressed and replaced by pseudo feelings. Freud has taken one such suppression and put it in the center of his whole system, namely the suppression of sex. Although I believe that the discouragement of sexual joy is not the only important suppression of spontaneous reactions but one of many, certainly its importance cannot be underrated. Its results are obvious in cases of sexual inhibitions and also in those where sex assumes a compulsive quality and is consumed like liquor or a drug, which has no particular taste but makes you forget yourself. Regardless of the one or the other effect, their suppression, because of the intensity of sexual desires, not only affects the sexual sphere but also weakens the person's courage for spontaneous expression in all other spheres.

In our own society emotions in general are discouraged. While there can be no doubt that any creative thinking—as well as any other creative activity—is inseparably linked with emotion, it has become an ideal to think and to live without emotions. To be "emotional" has become synonymous with being unsound or unbalanced. By the acceptance of this standard the individual has become greatly weakened; his thinking is impoverished and flattened. On the other hand, since emotions cannot be completely killed, they must have their existence totally apart from the intellectual side of the personality; the result is the cheap and insincere sentimentality with which movies and popular songs feed millions of emotion-starved customers.

There is one tabooed emotion that I want to mention in particular, because its suppression touches deeply on the roots of personality: the sense of tragedy. As we saw in an earlier chapter, the awareness of death and of the tragic aspect of life, whether dim or clear, is one of the basic characteristics of man. Each culture has its own way of coping with the problem of death. For those societies in which the process of individuation has progressed but little, the end of individual existence is less of a problem since the experience of individual existence itself is less developed. Death is not yet conceived as being basically different from life. Cultures in which we find

---

[2] As one telling illustration of the commercialization of friendliness I should like to cite *Fortune's* report on "The Howard Johnson Restaurants." (*Fortune,* September, 1940, p. 96.) Johnson employs a force of "shoppers" who go from restaurant to restaurant to watch for lapses. "Since everything is cooked on the premises according to standard recipes and measurements issued by the home office, the inspector knows how large a portion of steak he should receive and how the vegetable should taste. He also knows how long it should take for the dinner to be served and he knows the exact degree of friendliness that should be shown by the hostess and the waitress."

a higher development of individuation have treated death according to their social and psychological structure. The Greeks put all emphasis on life and pictured death as nothing but a shadowy and dreary continuation of life. The Egyptians based their hopes on a belief in the indestructibility of the human body, at least of those whose power during life was indestructible. The Jews admitted the fact of death realistically and were able to reconcile themselves with the idea of the destruction of individual life by the vision of a state of happiness and justice ultimately to be reached by mankind in this world. Christianity has made death unreal and tried to comfort the unhappy individual by promises of a life after death. Our own era simply denies death and with it one fundamental aspect of life. Instead of allowing the awareness of death and suffering to become one of the strongest incentives for life, the basis for human solidarity, and an experience without which joy and enthusiasm lack intensity and depth, the individual is forced to repress it. But, as is always the case with repression, by being removed from sight the repressed elements do not cease to exist. Thus the fear of death lives an illegitimate existence among us. It remains alive in spite of the attempt to deny it, but being repressed it remains sterile. It is one source of the flatness of other experiences, of the restlessness pervading life, and it explains, I would venture to say, the exorbitant amount of money this nation pays for its funerals.

In the process of tabooing emotions modern psychiatry plays an ambiguous role. On the one hand its greatest representative, Freud, has broken through the fiction of the rational, purposeful character of the human mind and opened a path which allows a view into the abyss of human passions. On the other hand psychiatry, enriched by these very achievements of Freud, has made itself an instrument of the general trends in the manipulation of personality. Many psychiatrists, including psychoanalysts, have painted the picture of a "normal" personality which is never too sad, too angry, or too excited. They use words like "infantile" or "neurotic" to denounce traits or types of personalities that do not conform with the conventional pattern of a "normal" individual. This kind of influence is in a way more dangerous than the older and franker forms of name-calling. Then the individual knew at least that there was some person or some doctrine which criticized him and he could fight back. But who can fight back at "science"?

The same distortion happens to original *thinking* as happens to feelings and emotions. From the very start of education original thinking is discouraged and ready-made thoughts are put into people's heads. How this is done with young children is easy enough to see. They are filled with curiosity about the world, they want to grasp it physically as well as intellectually. They want to know the truth, since that is the safest way to orient themselves in a strange and powerful world. Instead, they are not taken seriously, and it does not matter whether this attitude takes the form of open disrespect or of the subtle condescension which is usual towards all who have no power (such as children, aged or sick people). Although this treatment by itself offers strong discouragement to independent thinking, there is a worse handicap: the insincerity—often unintentional—which is typical of the average adult's behavior toward a child. This insincerity consists partly in the fictitious picture of the world which the child is given. It is about as useful as instructions concerning life in the Arctic would be to someone who has asked how to prepare for an expedition to the Sahara Desert. Besides this general misrepresentation of the world there are the many specific lies that tend to conceal facts which, for various personal reasons, adults do not want children to know. From a bad temper, which is rationalized as justified dissatisfaction with the child's behavior, to concealment of the parents' sexual activities and their quarrels, the child is "not supposed to know" and his inquiries meet with hostile or polite discouragement.

The child thus prepared enters school and perhaps college. I want to mention briefly some of the educational methods used today which in effect further discourage original thinking. One is the emphasis on knowledge of facts, or I should rather say on information. The pathetic superstition prevails that by knowing more and more facts one arrives at knowledge of reality. Hundreds of scattered and unrelated facts are dumped into the heads of students; their time and energy are taken up by learning more and more facts so that there is little left for thinking. To be sure, thinking without a knowledge of facts remains empty and fictitious; but "information" alone can be just as much of an obstacle to thinking as the lack of it.

Another closely related way of discouraging original thinking is to regard all truth as relative.[3] Truth is made out to be a metaphysical concept, and if anyone speaks about wanting to discover the truth he is thought backward by the "progressive" thinkers of our age. Truth is declared to be an entirely subjective matter, almost a matter of taste. Scientific endeavor must be detached from subjective factors, and its aim is to look at the world without passion and interest. The scientist has to approach facts with sterilized hands as a surgeon approaches his patient. The result of this relativism, which often presents itself by the name of empiricism or positivism or which recommends itself by its concern for the correct usage of words, is that thinking loses its essential stimulus—the wishes and interests of the person who thinks; instead it becomes a machine to register "facts." Actually, just as thinking in general has developed out of the need for mastery of material life, so the quest for truth is rooted in the interests and needs of individuals and social groups. Without such interest the stimulus for seeking the truth would be lacking. There are always groups whose interest is furthered by truth, and their representatives have been the pioneers of human thought; there are other groups whose interests are furthered by concealing truth. Only in the latter case does interest prove harmful to the cause of truth. The problem, therefore, is not that there is an interest at stake, but which kind of interest is at stake. I might say that

---

[3] Cf. to this whole problem Robert S. Lynd's *Knowledge for What?* Princeton University Press, Princeton, 1939. For its philosophical aspects of cf. M. Horkheimer's *Zum Rationalismusstreit in der Gegenwärtigen Philosophie,* Zeitschmit für Sozialforschung, Vol. 3, 1934, Alcan, Paris.

inasmuch as there is some longing for the truth in every human being, it is because every human being has some need for it.

This holds true in the first place with regard to a person's orientation in the outer world, and it holds especially true for the child. As a child, every human being passes through a state of powerlessness, and truth is one of the strongest weapons of those who have no power. But the truth is in the individual's interest not only with regard to his orientation in the outer world; his own strength depends to a great extent on his knowing the truth about himself. Illusions about oneself can become crutches useful to those who are not able to walk alone; but they increase a person's weakness. The individual's greatest strength is based on the maximum of integration of his personality, and that means also on the maximum of transparence to himself. "Know thyself" is one of the fundamental commands that aim at human strength and happiness.

In addition to the factors just mentioned there are others which actively tend to confuse whatever is left of the capacity for original thinking in the average adult. With regard to all basic questions of individual and social life, with regard to psychological, economic, political, and moral problems, a great sector of our culture has just one function—to befog the issues. One kind of smokescreen is the assertion that the problems are too complicated for the average individual to grasp. On the contrary it would seem that many of the basic issues of individual and social life are very simple, so simple, in fact, that everyone should be expected to understand them. To let them appear to be so enormously complicated that only a "specialist" can understand them, and he only in his own limited field, actually—and often intentionally—tends to discourage people from trusting their own capacity to think about those problems that really matter. The individual feels helplessly caught in a chaotic mass of data and with pathetic patience waits until the specialists have found what to do and where to go.

The result of this kind of influence is a twofold one: one is a scepticism and cynicism towards everything which is said or printed, while the other is a childish belief in anything that a person is told with authority. This combination of cynicism and naïveté is very typical of the modern individual. Its essential result is to discourage him from doing his own thinking and deciding.

Another way of paralyzing the ability to think critically is the destruction of any kind of structuralized picture of the world. Facts lose the specific quality which they can have only as parts of a structuralized whole and retain merely an abstract, quantitative meaning; each fact is just *another* fact and all that matters is whether we know more or less. Radio, moving pictures, and newspapers have a devastating effect on this score. The announcement of the bombing of a city and the death of hundreds of people is shamelessly followed or interrupted by an advertisement for soap or wine. The same speaker with the same suggestive, ingratiating, and authoritative voice, which he has just used to impress you with the seriousness of the political situation, impresses now upon his audience the merits of the particular brand of soap which pays for the news broadcast. Newsreels let pictures of torpedoed ships be followed by those of a fashion show. Newspapers tell us the trite thoughts or breakfast habits of a debutante with the same space and seriousness they use for reporting events of scientific or artistic importance. Because of all this we cease to be genuinely related to what we hear. We cease to be excited, our emotions and our critical judgment become hampered, and eventually our attitude to what is going on in the world assumes a quality of flatness and indifference. In the name of "freedom" life loses all structure; it is composed of many little pieces, each separate from the other and lacking any sense as a whole. The individual is left alone with these pieces like a child with a puzzle; the difference, however, is that the child knows what a house is and therefore can recognize the parts of the house in the little pieces he is playing with, whereas the adult does not see the meaning of the "whole," the pieces of which come into his hands. He is bewildered and afraid and just goes on gazing at his little meaningless pieces.

What has been said about the lack of "originality" in feeling and thinking holds true also of the act of *willing*. To recognize this is particularly difficult; modern man seems, if anything, to have too many wishes and his only problem seems to be that, although he knows what he wants, he cannot have it. All our energy is spent for the purpose of getting what we want, and most people never question the premise of this activity; that they know their true wants. They do not stop to think whether the aims they are pursuing are something they themselves want. In school they want to have good marks, as adults they want to be more and more successful, to make more money, to have more prestige, to buy a better car, to go places, and so on. Yet when they do stop to think in the midst of all this frantic activity, this question may come to their minds: "If I do get this new job, if I get this better car, if I can take this trip—what then? What is the use of it all? Is it really I who wants all this? Am I not running after some goal which is supposed to make me happy and which eludes me as soon as I have reached it?" These questions, when they arise, are frightening, for they question the very basis on which man's whole activity is built, his knowledge of what he wants. People tend, therefore, to get rid as soon as possible of these disturbing thoughts. They feel that they have been bothered by these questions because they were tired or depressed—and they go on in the pursuit of the aims which they believe are their own.

Yet all this bespeaks a dim realization of the truth—the truth that modern man lives under the illusion that he knows what he wants, while he actually wants what he is *supposed* to want. In order to accept this it is necessary to realize that to know what one really wants is not comparatively easy, as most people think, but one of the most difficult problems any human being has to solve. It is a task we frantically try to avoid by accepting ready-made goals as though they were our own. Modern man is ready to take great risks when he tries to achieve the aims which are supposed to be "his"; but he is deeply afraid of taking the risk and the responsibility of giving himself his own aims. Intense activity is often mistaken for evidence of self-determined action, although we know that it may well be no more spontaneous than the behavior of an actor or a person hypnotized. When the general plot of the play is handed out, each actor can act vigorously the role he is assigned and even make up his lines and certain details of the action by himself. Yet he is only playing a role that has been handed over to him.

The particular difficulty in recognizing to what extent our wishes—and our thoughts and feelings as well—are not really our own but put into us from the outside, is closely linked up with the problem of authority and freedom. In the course of modern history the authority of the Church has been replaced by that of the State, that of the State by that of conscience, and in our era, the latter has been replaced by the anonymous authority of common sense and public opinion as instruments of conformity. Because we have freed ourselves of the older overt forms of authority, we do not see that we have become the prey of a new kind of authority. We have become automatons who live under the illusion of being self-willing individuals. This illusion helps the individual to remain unaware of his insecurity, but this is all the help such an illusion can give. Basically the self of the individual is weakened, so that he feels powerless and extremely insecure. He lives in a world to which he has lost genuine relatedness and in which everybody and everything has become instrumentalized, where he has become a part of the machine that his hands have built. He thinks, feels, and wills what he believes he is supposed to think, feel, and will; in this very process he loses his self upon which all genuine security of a free individual must be built.

The loss of the self has increased the necessity to conform, for it results in a profound doubt of one's own identity. If I am nothing but what I believe I am supposed to be—who am "I"? We have seen how the doubt about one's self started with the breakdown of the medieval order in which the individual had had an unquestionable place in a fixed order. The identity of the individual has been a major problem of modern philosophy since Descartes. Today we take for granted that we are we. Yet the doubt about ourselves still exists, or has even grown. In his plays Pirandello has given expression to this feeling of modern man. He starts with the question: Who am I? What proof have I for my own identity other than the continuation of my physical self? His answer is not like Descartes'—the affirmation of the individual self—but its denial: I have no identity, there is no self excepting the one which is the reflex of what others expect me to be: I am "as you desire me."

This loss of identity then makes it still more imperative to conform; it means that one can be sure of oneself only if one lives up to the expectations of others. If we do not live up to this picture we not only risk disapproval and increased isolation, but we risk losing the identity of our personality, which means jeopardizing sanity.

By conforming with the expectations of others, by not being different, these doubts about one's own identity are silenced and a certain security is gained. However, the price paid is high. Giving up spontaneity and individuality results in a thwarting of life. Psychologically the automaton, while being alive biologically, is dead emotionally and mentally. While he goes through the motions of living, his life runs through his hands like sand. Behind a front of satisfaction and optimism modern man is deeply unhappy; as a matter of fact, he is on the verge of desperation. He desparately clings to the notion of individuality; he wants to be "different," and he has no greater recommendation of anything than that "it is different." We are informed of the individual name of the railroad clerk we buy our tickets from; handbags, playing cards, and portable radios are "personalized," by having the initials of the owner put on them. All this indicates the hunger for "difference" and yet these are almost the last vestiges of individuality that are left. Modern man is starved for life. But since, being an automaton, he cannot experience life in the sense of spontaneous activity he takes as surrogate any kind of excitement and thrill: the thrill of drinking, of sports, of vicariously living the excitements of fictitious persons on the screen.

What then is the meaning of freedom for modern man?

He has become free from external bonds that would prevent him from doing and thinking as he sees fit. He would be free to act according to his own will, if he knew what he wanted, thought, and felt. But he does not know. He conforms to anonymous authorities and adopts a self which is not his. The more he does this, the more powerless he feels, the more is he forced to conform. In spite of a veneer of optimism and initiative, modern man is overcome by a profound feeling of powerlessness which makes him gaze toward approaching catastrophes as though he were paralyzed.

Looked at superficially, people appear to function well enough in economic and social life; yet it would be dangerous to overlook the deep-seated unhappiness behind that comforting veneer. If life loses its meaning because it is not lived, man becomes desperate. People do not die quietly from physical starvation; they do not die quietly from psychic starvation either. If we look only at the economic needs as far as the "normal" person is concerned, if we do not see the unconscious suffering of the average automatized person, then we fail to see the danger that threatens our culture from its human basis: the readiness to accept any ideology and any leader, if only he promises excitement and offers a political structure and symbols which allegedly give meaning and order to an individual's life. The despair of the human automation is fertile soil for the political purposes of Fascism.

Stokeley Carmichael and Charles V. Hamilton

As you read "Dynamite in the Ghetto," we suggest that you consider the following questions:

1. How will the situation in the ghettos affect education in the United States in the years immediately ahead?
2. Why does it seem unlikely that the problems will resolve themselves?
3. How might elementary children outside of the ghetto be concerned with any of these problems?
4. Where is there a place in the social science program for consideration of the ghetto conditions? For what purposes?
5. How can you be aware of your biases as you react to the information and interpretations provided in "Dynamite in the Ghetto?" Does your whiteness or blackness provide a base of antagonism or acceptance?
6. What problems *do you see* which call for professional commitment and action in conjunction with, or apart from, political action?

Dynamite in the Ghetto

This country is known by its cities: those amazing aggregations of people and housing, offices and factories, which constitute the heart of our civilization, the nerve center of our collective being. America is increasingly dominated by her cities, as they draw into them the brawn and brains and wealth of the hinterland. Seventy percent of the American people now reside in urban areas —all of which are in a state of crisis. It is estimated that by 1980, an additional fifty-three million people will be living in the cities. By 2000, ninety-five percent of all Americans will be living in urban areas.[1] Millions of these will be black people. For a number of reasons, the city has become the major domestic problem facing this nation in the second half of the twentieth century.

Corporate power has moved its structure and influence to the cities.... No longer do public land grabs and privileged tax structures suffice for corporate power. Instead, they require centralization, intellect and skill for the administration of its productive technology. For these and other reasons, the corporation has come full force to the city. The procession requires favorable opinion to withstand public misgiving. Thus, they have come to control the media, the schools, the press, the university—either by way of ownership, contract, or public service....

Federalism is also moving to the city, through the growth of direct federal-local relations in education, housing, transportation, public welfare, etc. A nation of urban federalism is emerging, while the states gradually become regional administrations of the national government....

Its major interest formation is the new middle class. Technology, corporate consolidation, and public economy are transforming that class from a property to a wage base. It is a college-educated class of salaried administrators, whose primary interest is to secure more objects for service, management, and control. For this purpose the middle class needs a permanently expanding dependent clientele and enough organizational power to protect its function and expanding ranks. Service and expertise are its occupational principles. So the new class seeks to enlarge service programs; refine the qualifications of performance; and control their operation through professional organization....

Correspondingly, the lower class has been transformed from production to permanent unemployment. Its value is no longer labor, but dependency. ... Both groups and allied interests are in daily battle, which is manifested in the recurring disorders that surround housing, education, and welfare administration....

The crucial issue of the public control of technology rests in the city. Here

---

From *Black Power,* By Stokeley Carmichael and Charles V. Hamilton. Copyright © 1967 by Stokeley Carmichael and Charles Hamilton. Reprinted by permission of Random House, Inc.

[1] *Congressional Record,* January 23, 1967.

the felt effects of technology meet the popular power to question, resist, and even possibly, to democratically guide automation to better purpose. Whether democratic decision can prevail over the private control of technology is questionable. But the issue will have to be met in the city.[2]

The problems of the city and of institutional racism are clearly intertwined. Nowhere are people so expendable in the forward march of corporate power as in the ghetto. At the same time, nowhere is the potential political power of black people greater. If the crisis we face in the city is to be dealt with, the problem of the ghetto must be solved first.

Black people now hold the balance of electoral power in some of the nation's largest cities, while population experts predict that, in the next ten to twenty years, black Americans will constitute the majority in a dozen or more of the largest cities. In Washingon, D.C., and Newark, New Jersey, they already are in the majority; in Detroit, Baltimore, Cleveland and St. Louis, they represent one-third or slightly more of the population; in such places as Oakland, Chicago, Philadelphia and Cincinnati, they constitute well over one-fourth. Even at the height of European immigration, no ethnic group has ever multiplied so rapidly in the United States. In order to understand the black ghetto—both its great problems and its capacity to become a key political force in urban America—we should take a brief look at the history of black migration to the North.

Many slaves escaped to the North before emancipation, while some, of course, migrated to Liberia, Haiti and Central America. The Emancipation Proclamation cut many loose from the land and, starting with the end of the Civil War, there developed a steady trickle of freed men from the South. During Reconstruction, this northward migration eased somewhat with the ability of black people to take advantage of the franchise.

Soon after, however, southern racism and fanaticism broke loose. Thousands of black people were killed in the 1870's in an effort by whites to destroy the political power that blacks had gained. This was all capped by the deal of 1876 (mentioned in Chapter IV), whereby the Republicans guaranteed that Mr. Hayes, when he became President, would, by non-interference and the withdrawal of troops, allow the planters—under the name of Democrats—to gain control in the Deep South. The withdrawal of these troops by President Hayes and the appointment of a Kentuckian and a Georgian to the Supreme Court marked the handwriting on the wall.

In *Black Reconstruction,* DuBois portrays the situation clearly:

> Negroes did not surrender the ballot easily or immediately. They continued to hold remnants of political power in South Carolina, Florida, Louisiana, in parts of North Carolina, Texas, Tennessee and Virginia. Black Congressmen came out of the South until 1895

---

[2] Milton Kotler, *Community Foundation Memorandum No. 6, The Urban Polity:* remarks introducing a staff discussion on community foundations at the Center for the Study of Democratic Institutions, Santa Barbara, California, January 8, 1965.

and Black legislators served as late as 1896. But in a losing battle with public opinion, industry and wealth against them ... the decisive influence was the systematic and overwhelming economic pressure. Negroes who wanted work must not dabble in politics. ... From 1880 onward, in order to earn a living, the American Negro was compelled to give up his political power [pp. 692–93].

Black people were therefore looking to move again. About 60,000 went to Kansas, two-thirds of them destitute on arrival. In general, however, migration to escape the new regime in the South did not really get under way until World War I. Business was booming in 1914–15 as this nation became a major supplier of war materials to the Allies. This in turn increased the job market and, with the war cutting off the flow of immigrants from Europe, northern industry went on a massive campaign to recruit black workers. Emigration from the Deep South jumped from 200,000 in the decade 1890–1900 to half a million in 1910–1920. This migration northward did not cease with the conclusion of the war. The Immigration and Exclusion Acts of the early twenties created a great demand by industry for more workers (especially with the new assembly-line concept employed by Ford). As a result, during the twenties and thirties about 1,300,000 black people migrated from the Deep South to the North. By 1940, over 2,000,000 blacks had migrated northward. (However, as late as 1940 more than three out of every four black people still remained in the South.)

World War II intensified black migration out of the Deep South, more so than World War I had done. Black people moved to Los Angeles, Pittsburgh, Akron, Gary, Kansas City, Cincinnati, Philadelphia, Washington, Chicago, New York and many other places. They found work in the steel mills, aircraft factories and shipyards as, for the most part, laborers and domestics. During the forties, roughly 250,000 blacks migrated to the West Coast alone to find work. This migration did not slow down with the end of the war but continued into the sixties.

The United States Census indicates:

Rise in Black Population Outside South

	% of Total	No. of Blacks
1900	10	1,647,377
1910	11	1,899,654
1920	15	2,407,371
1930	21	3,483,746
1940	23	3,986,606
1950	32	5,989,543
1960	40	9,009,470

Today, over sixty-five percent of black people live in urban America. This figure, of course, includes many of the urban areas of the South—Atlanta,

Birmingham, Jackson, etc. Mechanization of southern plantations has been a major reason for the migration. In 1966, over seventy-five percent of all cotton was picked by machines in the seventeen major cotton-growing counties of Mississippi. (A machine can pick one bale of cotton per hour; it takes an able-bodied man one week to pick a bale.)

Census data tell us that the largest percentage increase in black population was in the West, especially California. About 8 percent of the black population lived in the West in 1966, compared with 5.7 percent in 1960. Increases in the Northeast and North Central states were not as sharp, although the overall percentages were greater. (17.9 percent of the black population lived in the Northeast in 1966, compared with 16 percent in 1960, while 20.2 percent lived in the North central states compared with 18.3 percent in 1960.)

What problems did black people face as they moved into these areas? Most of the blacks moving to the North were crowded into the slums of the cities. In the face of bombs and riots, they fought for a place to live and room for relatives and friends who followed them. They also faced a daily fight for jobs. At first, they were refused industrial employment and forced to accept menial work. As we have seen, wartime brought many jobs, but during periods of recession and depression blacks were the first cut from the job market while skill and craft jobs for the most part remained closed to them. Added to the problems of housing and jobs, of course, was that of education. By the early part of the twentieth century, these three issues had become fundamental problems of the ghetto and fundamental issues in the early racial explosions. The city of Chicago offers a classic illustration of this type.

As black people started arriving in Chicago at the turn of the century, they were forced into old ghettos where rents were cheaper and housing poorest. They took over the old, dilapidated shacks near the railroad tracks—and close to the vice areas. The tremendous demand for housing resulted in an immediate skyrocketing of rents in the ghetto. Artificial panics were often created by enterprising realtors who raised the cry: "The niggers are coming," and then proceeded to double the rents after the whites had fled.

The expansion of the ghetto developed so much friction that bombs were often thrown at black-owned homes in the expanding neighborhoods. In Chicago, over a dozen black homes were bombed between July 1, 1917, and July 1, 1919. This sporadic bombing of black homes was but the prelude to a five-day riot in July, 1919, which took at least thirty-eight lives, resulted in over five hundred injuries, destroyed $250,000 worth of property, and left over a thousand persons homeless. In their book, *Black Metropolis,* St. Clair Drake and Horace Cayton describe how the riot was ended on the sixth day by the state militia, belatedly called after the police had shown their inability and, in some instances, their unwillingness, to curb attacks on black people (p. 64).

A non-partisan, interracial Chicago Commission on Race Relations was appointed to investigate and to make recommendations. According to Drake and Cayton, the Commission recommended the correction of gross inequalities in protection on the part of the police and the state's attorney; it also rebuked the courts for facetiousness in dealing with black defendants and the police for discrimination in making arrests. The Board of Education was asked to exercise special care in selecting principals and teachers in ghetto schools (schools at that time were segregated by law, or *de jure,* while today ghetto schools are segregated *de facto*), to alleviate overcrowding and double-shift schools. Employers and labor organizations were admonished in some detail against the use of black workers as strikebreakers and against excluding them from unions and industries. The City Council was asked to condemn all houses unfit for human habitation, of which the Commission found many in the black ghetto. The Commission also affirmed the rights of black people to live anywhere they wanted and could afford to live in the city. It insisted that property depreciation in black areas was often due to factors other than black occupancy; it condemned arbitrary increase of rents and designated the amounts and quality of housing as an all-important factor in Chicago's race problem. Looking at these recommendations, we realized that they are not only similar but almost identical to the demands made by Dr. Martin Luther King's group forty-seven years later in Chicago—not to mention other urban areas in the 1960's.

Such explosions and recommendations were to be heard many more times in urban areas all over the country during the twenties, thirties and forties. But in the fifties a political protest movement was born which had a calming, wait-and-see effect on the attitude of many urban black people. There was the Supreme Court decision of 1954; the Montgomery bus boycott of '55–'57; the dispatch of federal troops to Little Rock, Arkansas, to prevent interference with school desegregation in '57. The student sit-in movement in '60 and '61, the emotional appeal of President Kennedy and the great amount of visibility given to the NAACP, Urban League, CORE, SNCC and other civil rights organizations further contributed to creating a period of relative calm in the ghetto.

Then, in the spring of 1963, the lull was over.

The eruption in Birmingham, Alabama, in the spring of 1963 showed how quickly anger can develop into violence. Black people were angry about the killing of Emmett Till and Charles Mack Parker; the failure of federal, state and city governments to deal honestly with the problems of ghetto life. Now they read in the newspapers, saw on television and watched from the street corners themselves the police dogs and the fire hoses and the policemen beating their friends and relatives. They watched as young high-school students and women were beaten, as Martin Luther King and his co-workers were marched off to jail. The spark was ignited when a black-owned motel in Birmingham and the home of Dr. King's brother were bombed. This incident brought hundreds of angry black people into the street throwing rocks and bottles and sniping at policemen. The echoes were far and wide. In Chicago, a few days later, two black youths assaulted the mayor's eighteen-year-old nephew, shouting: "This is for Birmingham." It was for Birmingham, true, but it was for three hundred and fifty years of history before Birmingham as well. The explosions were soon to be heard in Harlem, Chicago, Philadelphia and Rochester in '64, Watts in '65, Omaha, Atlanta, Dayton and dozens of other places in '66. James Baldwin stated it clearly in 1963: "When a race riot occurs . . . it will not spread merely to Birmingham. . . . The trouble will spread to every metropolitan center in the nation which has a significant Negro population."

This brief scan of history clearly indicates that the disturbances in our cities are not just isolated reactions to the cry of "Black Power," but part of a pattern. The problems of Harlem in the 1960's are not much different from those of Harlem in 1920.

The core problem within the ghetto is the vicious circle created by the lack of decent housing, decent jobs and adequate education. The failure of these three fundamental institutions to work has led to alienation of the ghetto from the rest of the urban area as well as to deep political rifts between the two communities.

In America we judge by American standards, and by this yardstick we find that the black man lives in incredibly inadequate housing, shabby shelters that are dangerous to mental and physical health and to life itself. It has been estimated that twenty million black people put fifteen billion dollars into rents, mortgage payments and housing expenses every year. But because his choice is largely limited to the ghettos and because the black population is increasing at a rate which is 150 percent over that of the increase in the white population, the shelter shortage for the black person is not only acute and perennial, but getting increasingly tighter. Black people are automatically forced to pay top dollar for whatever they get, even a 6 x 6 cold-water flat.

Urban renewal and highway clearance programs have forced black people more and more into congested pockets of the inner city. Since suburban zoning laws have kept out low-income housing, and the Federal Government has failed to pass open-occupancy laws, black people are forced to stay in the deteriorating ghettos. Thus crowding increases, and slum conditions worsen.

In the Mill Creek (East St. Louis), Illinois, urban renewal undertaking, for instance, a Black slum was cleared and in its place rose a middle-income housing development. What happened to those evicted to make way for this great advance? The majority were forced into what remained of the black ghetto; in other words, the crowding was intensified.

Here we begin to understand the pervasive, cyclic implications of institutional racism. Barred from most housing, black people are forced to live in segregated neighborhoods and with this comes de facto segregated schooling, which means poor education, which leads in turn to ill-paying jobs.

It is impossible to talk about the problems of education in the black community without at some point dealing with the issue of desegregation and integration, especially since the Supreme Court decision of May 17, 1954: ". . . In the field of public education the doctrine of separate but equal has no place. Separate education facilities are inherently unequal." However, all the discussion of integration or bussing today seems highly irrelevant; it allows a lot of highly paid school administrators to talk around and never deal with the problem. For example, in Washington, D.C., the schools were supposedly integrated immediately after the 1954 decision, but as a result of the population movements of whites into suburbs and blacks into the inner (ghetto) city, black children attend what are in fact segregated schools. Today, roughly 85 percent of the children in the Washington, D.C. public schools are black. Nor is integration very relevant or meaningful in any of the other major urban areas. In Chicago, 87 percent of the black students in elementary school attend virtually all-black public schools. In Detroit, 45 percent of the black students are in public schools that are overwhelmingly black. In Philadelphia, thirty-eight elementary schools have a black enrollment of 99 percent. In April, 1967, the Rev. Henry Nichols, vice president of the Philadelphia School Board, stated on television that that city had two separate school systems: one for the ghetto, the other for the rest of the city. There was no public denial from any other knowledgeable sources in the city. In Los Angeles, forty-three elementary schools have at least 85 percent black attendance. In the Bourough of Manhattan in New York City, 77 percent of the elementary school students and 72 percent of the junior high school students are black.[3]

Clearly, "integration"—even if it would solve the educational problem—has not proved feasible. The alternative presented is usually the large-scale transfer of black children to schools in white neighborhoods. This too raises several problems, already mentioned in Chapter II. Implicit is the idea that the closer you get to whiteness, the better you are. Another problem is that it makes the majority of black youth expendable. Probably the maximum number of blacks who could transfer from ghetto schools to white schools, given the overcrowded conditions of city schools anyway, is about 20 percent. The 80 percent left behind are therefore expendable.

The real need at present is not integration but quality education.

In Central Harlem, for example, there are twenty elementary schools, four junior high schools and no high schools. A total of 31,469 students—virtually all black—attend these schools. In New York as a whole, only 50.3 percent of the teachers in the black and Puerto Rican elementary schools were fully licensed as compared with 78.2 percent in white schools.[4]

In 1960, in Central Harlem, 21.6 percent of third-grade students were reading above grade level and 30 percent were reading below. By the sixth grade, 11.7 percent are reading above and 80 percent are reading below grade level. The median equivalent grades reading comprehension for Central Harlem, third grade, was a full year behind the city median and the national norm, and by the sixth grade it was two years behind. The same is true of word knowledge. In arithmetic, the students of Central Harlem are one and a half years behind the rest of the city by the sixth grade, and by the time they are in the eighth grade, they are two years behind. The I.Q. scores are 90.6 in the third grade, and by the sixth grade they have gone down to 86.3.[5]

The basic story of education in Central Harlem emerges as one of inefficiency, inferiority and mass deterioration. It is a system which typifies colonialism and the colonist's attitude. Nor is Harlem unique. Rev. Henry

---

[3] Tom Kahn, *The Economics of Equality,* League for Industrial Democracy, 1964, pp. 31–32 .
[4] *Ibid.,* p. 32.
[5] *Youth in the Ghetto,* New York: Harlem Youth Opportunities Unlimited (HARYOU), 1964, pp. 166–80.

Nichols, vice president of the Philadelphia Board of Education, stated in 1967 that 75 percent of the black children who would be graduated that year were "functional illiterates.... The reason for this," he added, "is the attitude of school administrators toward black people." [6]

There can be no doubt that in today's world a thorough and comprehensive education is an absolute necessity. Yet it is obvious from the data that a not even minimum education is being received in most ghetto schools. White decision-makers have been running those schools with injustice, indifference and inadequacy for too long; the result has been an educationally crippled black child turned out onto the labor market equipped to do little more than stand in welfare lines to receive his miserable dole.

It should not be hard to understand why approximately 41 percent of the pupils entering high school from Central Harlem drop out before receiving a diploma, 52 percent of these being boys. When one couples school conditions with the overcrowded and deteriorating housing in which black pupils must live and study, additional factors become clear. Males, in particular, must leave school because of financial pressure. The young drop-out or even high school graduate with an inadequate education, burdened also by the emotional deprivations which are the consequences of poverty, is now on the street looking for a job.

The HARYOU report clearly states: "That the unemployment situation among Negro youth in Central Harlem is explosive can be readily seen in the fact that twice as many young Negroes in the labor force, as compared to their white counterparts, were without employment in 1960. For the girls the disparity was even greater: nearly two and one-half times the unemployment rate for white girls in the labor force. Undoubtedly this situation has worsened since 1960, in view of the report of the New York State Department of Labor indicating that job-hunting was generally tougher in 1963 than in the previous year. Also, it is generally conceded that official statistics on unemployment are considerably understated for black youth since only those persons actively looking for work in the past 60 days are included in census taking... such a situation building up, this mass of unemployed and frustrated Negro youth, is social dynamite. We are presented with a phenomenon that may be compared with the piling up of inflammable material in an empty building in a city block." [7]

The struggle for employment has had a drastic effect on the black community. It perpetuates the breakdown of the black family structure. Many men who are unable to find employment leave their homes so that their wives can qualify for Aid to Dependent Children or welfare. Children growing up in a welfare situation often leave school because of a lack of incentive or because they do not have enough food to eat or clothes to wear. They in turn go out to seek jobs but only find a more negative situation than their fathers faced. So they turn to petty crime, pushing dope, prostitution (joining the Army if possible), and the cycle continues.

---

[6] *The New York Times* (May 4, 1967), p. 23.
[7] *Youth in the Ghetto, op. cit.,* pp. 246–47.

We have not touched on the issue of health and medical care in the ghetto. Whitney Young documented conditions at length in *To Be Equal;* the pattern is predictably dismal. The black infant mortality rate in 1960 exceeded that in the total population by 66 percent; the maternal death rate for black women was four times as high as that for whites in 1960; the life expectancy for non-whites was six years less than for whites; approximately 30 percent more white people have health insurance than blacks; only 2 percent of the nation's physicians are black, which means that in segregated areas one finds such situations as Mississippi with a ratio of one doctor per 18,500 black residents! Those of us who survive must indeed be a tough people.

These are the conditions which create dynamite in the ghettos. And when there are explosions—explosions of frustration, despair and hopelessness—the larger society becomes indignant and utters irrelevant clichés about maintaining law and order. Blue ribbon committees of "experts" and "consultants" are appointed to investigate the "causes of the riot." They then spend hundreds of thousands of dollars on preparing "authoritative" reports. Some token money from the Office of Economic Opportunity may be promised and then everybody either prays for rain to cool off tempers and vacate the streets or for an early autumn.

This country, with its pervasive institutional racism, has itself created socially undesirable conditions; it merely perpetuates those conditions when it lays the blame on people who, through whatever means at their disposal seek to strike out at the conditions. What has to be understood is that thus far there have been virtually no *legitimate* programs to deal with the alienation and the oppressive conditions in the ghettos. On April 9, 1967, a few days after Mayor Daley won an overwhelming, unprecedented fourth-term victory (receiving, incidentally, approximately 85 percent of Chicago's black vote), *The New York Times* editorialized: "Like other big-city mayors, Mr. Daley has no long-range plans for coping with the social dislocation caused by the steady growth of the Negro population. He tries to manage the effects of that dislocation and hopes for the best."

Herein lies the match that will continue to ignite the dynamite in the ghettos: the ineptness of decision-makers, the anachronistic institutions, the inability to think boldly and above all the unwillingness to innovate. The make-shift plans put together every summer by city administrations to avoid rebellions in the ghettos are merely buying time. White America can continue to appropriate millions of dollars to take ghetto teen-agers off the streets and onto nice, green farms during the hot summer months. They can continue to provide mobile swimming pools and hastily built play areas, but there is a point beyond which the steaming ghettos will not be cooled off. It is ludicrous for the society to believe that these temporary measures can long contain the tempers of an oppressed people. And when the dynamite does go off, pious pronouncements of patience should not go forth. Blame should not be placed on "outside agitators" or on "Communist influence" or on advocates of Black Power. That dynamite was placed there by white racism and it was ignited by white racist indifference and unwillingness to act justly.

Alan Barth

In this selection from Alan Barth's *The Loyalty of Free Men,* an unavoidable problem of free societies is examined in detail. Inasmuch as one of the major goals of social science education is the development of knowledge, skills, and attitudes that are the necessary components of effective citizenship in a free society, the prospective teacher must be aware of the complexities of freedom and be familiar with the difficulties involved in educating for life in the free society.

The commonplace assumption made in so many United States communities is that our nation's freedom was "won" in 1776, and it has been defended on various occasions when outside forces threatened. Barth looks at the threats to freedom which always exist within our own society, and in doing so he identifies the forces which give rise to this condition.

As you reflect upon the customary practices of the elementary school in citizenship education and the teaching of loyalty, ask whether the problems identified by Barth appear to be recognized and dealt with in the schools that you know.

When does freedom to dissent become an outright threat to a way of life that guarantees this freedom? When does insistence on loyalty and patriotism become repressive and dictatorial? When should children and teachers become concerned with these problems? How does open inquiry fit into any program which is concerned with the problems of freedom identified by Barth?

In what ways can the educational experiences of the young contribute to the establishment of the attitudes and values which undergird a society of free men? How do teacher attitudes and ways of working with children contribute to the pupil's concept of freedom?

The Cult of Loyalty

The relation of the individual to the State—or of individual liberty to national security—is the crucial issue of our time. The emphasis in this relation marks the essential distinction between a totalitarian society and a free society. A totalitarian society emphasizes the supremacy of the State, seeking national security through rigid governmental control of individual activity and expression. A free society emphasizes the supremacy of the individual, relying for its security upon a democratic adjustment of diverse views and interests and upon the freely accorded devotion of its constituents.

The function of national security in a totalitarian society is to preserve the State, while the function of national security in a free society is to preserve freedom. Those who established the American Republic counted freedom among man's "unalienable" or "natural" rights and believed that it was in order to secure these rights that governments are instituted among men. But there is a looseness about freedom that makes it seem hazardous to security. It involves an inescapable element of risk. There have always been men everywhere who viewed it skeptically as a luxury to be enjoyed only within prescribed limits and when the nation is not subject to any external threat. It is commonly in the name of national security that individual liberty is lost.

The purpose here is to show: (1) that we have accepted, without full awareness of their meaning, piecemeal encroachments on personal freedom that threaten to corrupt our richest inheritance; (2) that the encroachments have been accepted as the result of what are in large part groundless and neurotic fears; (3) that, although accepted in the name of national security, they operate, in fact, to impair the security they are intended to protect; and (4) that whether or not individual liberty is, as the founders of the United States believed it to be, an "unalienable" or "natural" right, it serves vital practical purposes and is an affirmative source of national strength.

This is by no means to suggest that national security can be neglected. The institutions of liberty are under attack. They are threatened by an aggressive totalitarianism abroad, and they need the protection of a strong and resolute government. If that government should fall, the institutions of liberty would fall with it. In some measure, too, the institutions are threatened in novel ways by agents of that totalitarianism at home. They are threatened most of all, however, by well-meaning and patriotic but frightened Americans, who have come to think of liberty as a liability rather than an asset.

The error of these men is that they confuse loyalty with orthodoxy. Acting upon this confusion, they tend to suppress diversity and to insist upon a rigid conformity. But loyalty may take as many forms as religious worship. This much about it seems indisputable: like love, it must be freely given. It can be evoked but it cannot be commanded or coerced. Members of a family are

---

From *The Loyalty of Free Men* by Alan Barth, copyright 1951 by Alan Barth. Reprinted by permission of The Viking Press, Inc.

loyal to one another, not through any oath or compulsion, but as a result of shared experiences, community of interest, and long mutual dependence. A great aggregation of individuals and families becomes and remains a nation, not through geographical propinquity alone, but rather through much this same process of shared experiences—which is to say, a common history—and, above all, through common acceptance of certain fundamental values. The national loyalty of free men is not so much to their government as to the purposes for which their government was created. . . .

The tolerance on which freedom and opportunity must rest was a necessity of early life in America. Conquest of a continental wilderness fostered a tradition of individualism. The opening of successive frontiers widely different in physical conditions and in the problems of settlement encouraged a variety of political forms. Differences of religion, of social background, of economic interest among the settlers required tolerance of diversity. Out of this necessity the early Americans made a virtue. The idea that they had raised a standard to which the lovers of liberty could repair became a source of tremendous pride to them. "This new world," Thomas Paine boasted in *Common Sense,* "hath been the asylum for the persecuted lovers of civil and religious liberty from *every part* of Europe.". . .

Whatever may have been the vices and weaknesses of this country in the past, want of confidence in itself was not one of them. The nation knew that the American dream would inspire all who had a chance to dream it.

But that sublime self-confidence has now disappeared. Aliens are suspect; there is no longer the old certainty that they will be swept into the mainstream of American life. Prospective immigrants must prove that they are not the bearers of contagious opinions, and even transient visitors are feared. In 1950 the State Department denied visas to the Dean of Canterbury and later to twelve members of the Communist-sponsored World Congress of Partisans for Peace, Pablo Picasso among them, because of their political and economic views. The faith of Americans in their own institutions is apparently no longer considered strong enough to withstand Communist propaganda. Eminent artists have been barred merely because their political sympathies were suspect. The German conductor Wilhelm Furtwängler was kept out because he had collaborated with the Nazis. Later Joseph Krips, the conductor of the Vienna State Opera, was forbidden to fill a summer engagement with the Chicago Symphony Orchestra because he had previously conducted performances at Moscow and Leningrad. Tolerance of diversity and faith in the democratic process are giving way to reliance on the quarantine of hostile doctrines.

Indeed, even those born into the American heritage are now only tentatively trusted; they are obliged to affirm and reaffirm their allegiance. And beyond this ritual of affirmation, in the potency of which there is no longer any confidence, they are commonly required before entering upon any post affecting the national interest to deny disloyalty. Anyone who goes to work for the government of the United States today must swear that he does not advocate its overthrow. In point of fact, Congress thought it necessary in 1940 to make it a penal offense for any citizen to teach or advocate the duty or necessity of overthrowing "any government in the United States by force or violence."

A terrible distrust lies behind this shift to negativism. The country's doubts about the loyalty of its citizens are not unlike the doubts of a husband about the fidelity of his wife. The protestations that answer his doubts are never convincing and are likely to dissipate the mutual confidence that is the essence of a marriage. When men lose faith in one another, they lost the substance of what constitutes a community among them. Thus, to a national community, there is nothing that so dangerously corrupts its integrity as such a loss of faith. As in the case of the suspicious husband, this distrust in the expression of a neurotic insecurity.

Such insecurity is perhaps the most pervasive characteristic of our time. The fear of freedom and the difficulties of realizing its potentialities have been illuminatingly treated by the psychiatrists and the social psychologists. They have contributed invaluable insights of which political theorists have as yet made little use. The forces that have led great numbers of Europeans and Asiatics to seek the fellowship of disciplined submission to authority as an escape from the responsibilities and isolation of freedom are at work here too. They exhibit themselves in the exertion of powerful pressures, cultural as well as political, toward conformity and in an attitude novel among Americans that they can neither comprehend nor change the awful tides in which they feel themselves engulfed. The consequence is a stultifying tendency to seek unity through uniformity.

"Loyalty" has become a cult, an obsession, in the United States. But even loyalty is now defined negatively. It is thought of not so much in terms of an affirmative faith in the great purposes for which the American nation was created as in terms of stereotypes the mere questioning of which is deemed "disloyal." The whole postwar accent is on something called "un-Americanism"—a hyphenated synonym for unorthodoxy. Deviations to the Left are regarded as more suspicious or criminal than deviations to the Right; but the tendency is to question all deviations. "Loyalty" consists today in not being un-American, which is to say, in not being different or individualistic. The very diversity which was the wellspring of loyalty in the past is now distrusted.

The term "disloyalty" as it is commonly used today is nothing more or less than a circumlocution for treason. The authors of the Constitution went to a great deal of trouble in dealing with the subject of treason because they knew from experience how readily the term can be twisted to make discontent or dissent, or mere criticism of the government, a major crime, They took care, therefore, to define treason in the narrowest terms. "Treason against the United States," they declared in Article III, Section 3, of the Constitution, "shall consist only in levying war against them or in adhering to their enemies, giving them aid and comfort." No acts other than those specified in the Constitution can be made treasonable by legislation. Congress can neither extend, nor restrict, nor define the crime. Its power over the subject is limited to prescribing the punishment.

The Constitution is no less exacting as to the means by which conviction of treason may be obtained. "No person shall be convicted of treason," Section 3 continues, "unless on the testimony of two witnesses to the same overt act, or on confession in open court."

James Madison explained in Number 43 of *The Federalist*—that brilliant exegesis of the Constitution characterized by Thomas Jefferson as "the best commentary on the principles of government which ever was written"—the reasons that prompted the Constitutional Convention to define treason so narrowly and to make conviction of it so difficult:

> As treason may be committed against the United States, the authority of the United States ought to be enabled to punish it. But as newfangled and artificial treasons have been the great engines by which violent factions, the natural offspring of free government, have usually wreaked their alternate malignity on each other, the convention have, with great judgment, opposed a barrier to this peculiar danger, by inserting a constitutional definition of the crime, fixing the proof necessary for conviction of it, and restraining the Congress, even in punishing it, from extending the consequences of guilt beyond the person of its author.

There is a whole lesson in political science in this paragraph—a lesson peculiarly applicable today. The use of "disloyalty" as a "new-fangled and artificial" form of treason has indeed promoted the rise of violent factions and led to a wreaking of "their alternate malignity on each other." There is no way to measure the impairment of national security that has resulted from this disruption of the sense of national community.

Disloyalty, to be sure, has not officially been held to constitute treason. But when a congressional committee or a quasi-judicial government board says that an individual is disloyal—or that he is un-American, or subversive, or a security risk, or ineligible for employment by the United States, or any of the other circumlocutions of the circumlocution—it is saying in not very euphemistic terms, or at least is encouraging the public to believe, that he is a traitor. The difference is that disloyalty is nowhere to be found detailed as a crime upon the statute books, that nowhere has it been defined, that nowhere has a punishment been prescribed for it by law. This ambiguity merely makes the charge more difficult to avoid and a condemnation less difficult to obtain.

Real disloyalty presents a threat to national security. It might find expression in betrayal of the nation—even in espionage or sabotage. Of course these are statutory crimes, clearly defined and punishable through the normal processes of indictment and trial by jury. The law can easily be used to punish any actual spy or saboteur. But the law can no more be used to punish a potential spy or a potential saboteur than it can be used to punish a potential pickpocket or a potential embezzler. The law punishes specifically prohibited antisocial acts. It does not prohibit and cannot punish antisocial ideas or intentions. The distinction has always been considered basic to a free society.

In a period of international tension, however, a potential spy or saboteur is likely to seem very dangerous—so dangerous that there is enormous temptation to deal with him outside the law. The United States, engaged in a world-wide struggle that has led to armed conflict in Asia, has yielded to this temptation to an alarming degree. It has devised an elaborate system and ritual for punishing men—and punishing them most cruelly—for crimes they have not committed but are suspected of desiring to commit. It punishes them by stigmatizing them as disloyal.

Anyone so stigmatized becomes to some degree an outcast. If he retains any friends, he knows himself to be a menace to them. Any association with them may result in their stigmatization too. Wherever he goes he is marked as a man who would be willing to betray his country. He remains at large but is regarded as a menace to society. He is expatriated without being exiled and denied the opportunity to gain a livelihood without the compensation of being maintained in prison at the community's expense. He and his fellows might come, in time, to constitute something new in American life—a caste of untouchables.

The punishment in such cases is something like that in the old story about the Quaker and his dog Tray. " 'Go to,' said the Quaker to poor Tray, 'I will not kill thee, but I will give thee a bad name,' as he turned him into the streets with the cry of 'mad dog,' and somebody else did kill Tray."

Perhaps the punishments meted out on the ground of disloyalty are not too severe for anyone who clearly and demonstrably intends to serve the interst of a foreign government to the detriment of his own countrymen. The fact is, however, that these penalties are meted out without any of the safeguards embodied in the Anglo-American system of justice for the protection of innocent persons against unjust conviction. They are inflicted on the loyal and the disloyal almost without discrimination.

By the simple stratagem of charging a man with disloyalty, instead of with treason or espionage or sabotage, it is possible to evade the constitutional requirements that he be indicted by a grand jury, that he enjoy a speedy and public trial by an impartial petit jury, that he be informed of the nature and cause of the accusation and confronted with the witnesses against him, that he be accorded the benefit of compulsory process to obtain witnesses in his favor. He is indicted and tried and sentenced by congressional committee or administrative tribunal, with the same men acting as prosecutors, judges, and jury. The presumption of innocence supposed to surround him is ignored. The mere charge of disloyalty is treated as evidence of guilt.

... it is the press which executes, so to speak, the sentences passed by congressional committees or by mere individuals speaking under the immunity from suits for slander or libel afforded by Congress. Newspapers especially tend to make headlines out of accusations and to treat denials less prominently. This stems in large measure from the concept of news as sensation and is scarcely less true of those newspapers that strive for objectivity than of those that deliberately use their news pages to serve editorial biases.

The tradition of objectivity, which is the great virtue of the American press, has operated in this context to make the press an instrument of those seeking to inflict punishment by publicity. Allegations which would otherwise be ignored because they would be recognized as groundless and libelous are blown up on front pages and given a significance out of all relation to their intrinsic merit after they have been made before a committee of Congress. Thus, what is one day properly regarded as unpublishable gossip is treated the next day as news of great moment because it has been uttered under official auspices. Refutation, no matter how compelling, never catches up with charges of disloyalty and never erases their imprint. In addition, of course, many newspapers welcome such charges and inflate them for political reasons or for their commercial value in stimulating street sales....

The short-cut to punishment has an effect on society in other ways as well. The knowledge that men may be accused and found guilty of disloyalty in so summary a manner becomes a restraint on the exercise of constitutional rights. It is no longer safe to talk recklessly or foolishly. If the effect of this were no more than to silence recklessness and folly, perhaps the loss would not be great. But the discouragement of reckless and foolish talk tends inescapably to suppress sound and sensible dissent which may seem unpatriotic because it happens to be unpopular.

The trouble with putting any halter upon individual freedom to talk nonsense—even subversive or seditious nonsense—is that it tends to frustrate the democratic process. That process is one in which nonsense cannot be silenced by authority; it can be silenced, or overcome, only by sense. Since it is often not altogether easy to distinguish between the two, silencing of the one cannot help but result in silencing of the other. What happens, of course, is that unorthodox ideas, whether sensible or not, are suppressed in favor of orthodoxy. And consequently the attention of the society is diverted from its real problems, which call for adaptation and change, and focused instead upon a preservation of things as they are.

The situation should not be overstated. There has been, as yet, no formal or statutory suppression of speech in the United States beyond the prohibition of advocacy of violent overthrow of the government and the punitive restrictions of the McCarran Act. Men may, and fortunately a number of them still do, express nonconformist views liable to be termed treasonable. But as Senator Margaret Chase Smith observed in a speech expressing her revulsion against the name-calling tactics of Senator Joseph McCarthy, "Freedom of speech is not what it used to be in America. It has been so abused by some that it is not exercised by others." Freedom of speech does not mean, to be sure, that a man who says what is unpopular should be protected from the penalties of unpopularity. Heretics and reformers must expect denunciation. The alarming characteristic about what is happening today lies partly in the official source of the denunciation, partly in the easy identification of dissent with disloyalty, partly in the punishment of it by the government itself through extralegal mechanisms.

The cult of loyalty, and its attendant hunt for heresy as a symptom of disloyalty, has generated an intellectually shackled feeling for which terror is too strong a term, but which is marked nevertheless by widespread anxiety. The feeling is most acute, naturally, in Washington, and among government employees.... But outside the capital, the pressures for conformity are mounting to a degree never before experienced by the American people. The Committee on Un-American Activities in the national House of Representatives has spawned imitators in state legislatures; some of them, such as the Tenney Committee in California, the Canwell Committee in Washington, the Broyles Commission in Illinois, have rivaled the tactics of the congressional body. In their role of investigators and with the stated object of protecting national security, they have had the effect of penalizing Americans for exercising the fundamental rights of advocacy and association.

Similarly, the Federal Employee-Loyalty Program has been aped and embellished in states and municipalities—where there is far less warrant for such restrictions. Protective measures designed to keep disloyal persons out of jobs that directly affect the national security become merely punitive when applied indiscriminately to all forms of public employment. In many states extremely repressive legislation, of doubtful constitutionality, has been adopted. These laws are aimed at Communists, but their result is to penalize all forms of heterodoxy. Some of the laws deny a place on the ballot to Communists, thereby revealing a distrust of the democratic process. Some, like the Ober Law in Maryland, drastically restrict the right of citizens to join in voluntary associations if the purpose of these associations is officially regarded as subversive. A number of municipalities, especially in the South, have adopted ordinances banning Communists and Communist *sympathizers* from the city limits. Birmingham, Alabama, for instance, announced that it would jail anyone found guilty of "voluntary association" with a Communist. Other cities have undertaken to require the registration of all Communists. The patent invalidity of such edicts from a constitutional point of view has given no apparent pause to local legislative and law-enforcement bodies. In a number of places, police chiefs have intimated that they mean to apply virtual lynch law to political undesirables. Behind all these measures is a fear of freedom and a panicky willingness to disregard the great procedural safeguards that distinguish a free from a totalitarian society.

The hounding of heterodoxy in the name of loyalty takes an especially ugly and mischievous form in connection with schools and universities. The proliferation of loyalty tests and oaths required of teachers inhibits discussion precisely where it should be most free. But perhaps the gravest consequence of the official cult of loyalty is the inflammation of public opinion to a sometimes hysterical pitch. When political disagreement is branded as disloyalty, when neighbor is invited to look with suspicion on neighbor, the bonds of national unity are strained in a way that is directly injurious to national security. Tragic incidents such as the Peekskill riots in the summer of 1949— when war veterans expressed their devotion to American ideals by behaving like Nazi stormtroopers—flow inevitably from official stimulation of intolerance. No matter how wrong-headed Paul Robeson may be, nothing that he might have said or sung at Peekskill could have injured the credit and the peace of the United States as grievously as the silencing of his voice by violence.

The war in Korea gave a tremendous impetus to this intolerance. In the grip of its excitement, many normally rational and gentle people tended to look upon any association with communism, no matter how remote or tenuous, as evidence of disloyalty and to regard a mere charge of such association as incontrovertible proof of guilt....

Censorship in the name of patriotism occurs on an unorganized basis too. Perhaps the most sensitive example of it was provided by a Hollywood motion-picture studio which, after six months of work, shelved plans to produce a film dealing with the life and exploits of Hiawatha, the Onondaga Indian chief immortalized by Longfellow. Hiawatha had succeeded in establishing peace among the warring Five Nations; and it was felt, according to a studio spokesman, that this might cause the film to be regarded as a message for peace and thus as Communist propaganda.

Political discussion has been debased to a species of fishwifery by shrill and redundant accusations of disloyalty. The immunity from suit for slander afforded by the floor of Congress has been abused over and over again to launch extravagant attacks on the good faith of opponents in every issue of policy....

The point is patently illustrated in connection with events in the Far East. The readiness of the China Lobby to impute disloyalty to every realistic appraisal of the collapse of the Chinese Nationalist government has made a rational China policy impossible. The State Department has been forced to cling to a transparent fiction. In other areas as well, mere anti-communism has taken the place of a reasoned evaluation of American interests, allying this country with discredited regimes abroad. Those who dared to protest or dissent were liable to vilification as Communist sympathizers....

The disloyalty of the Americanists [super-patriots] impairs national security more seriously than the comparable disloyalty of the Communists.... It is more deeply subversive, strikes more injuriously at the real roots of loyalty and of American strength. It would, in fact, meet the threat of communism by the substitution of Communist techniques for the techniques of freedom. If the relatively impotent Communists aim at overthrowing the government of the United States, the Americanists, whether they are aware of it or not, aim at overthrowing the essential values which that government was instituted to secure.

Max Lerner

What is the extent of the impact of the business culture upon American society, and more to the point, how does the spirit of business manifest itself in the schools? Max Lerner, long known and respected for his revealing observations on American civilization, directs his attention to the first part of the preceding question in the selection which follows.

As a group of future educators, it is suggested that you reflect on the second part of the question. What strengths and liabilities do you believe the business spirit brings to the schools? Does it control the school's values? In view of a predominant business culture, what is the school's role in helping the child become effective in the process of valuing? What values should the school reinforce? What kind of success goals should be pursued?

The Business Spirit and American Values

... The reach of the commercial spirit penetrates into every area of American culture. The business principle has sometimes been confused with the machine principle. The latter is used to dispense with human labor and make possible standardized and large-scale production, while the business principle focuses on market sale for profit. It puts the making of money ahead of other craft and civilization values, gives primacy to the cultural and personal traits which lead to that end, and tends to apply money values even to the human personality.

America has often been called a business civilization, but the term is too

---

From Max Lerner, *America as a Civilization*, copyright © 1957, by Max Lerner. Reprinted by permission of Simon and Schuster, Inc., New York.

sweeping. One cannot say that the business principle is the only one operating in American culture. In some areas—religion, education, the arts, the family—it exerts only an incipient influence. But even where it has not become decisive, there has been a creeping imperialism of business over the other domains of life.

The business principle has given a synthetic cohesion to the far-flung diversity of American life. Before the Civil War it could genuinely be said that American culture was a loose collection of principalities—those of politics, of farming and industry, of religion, of literature and art and the press—tied together mainly by a pride of pioneering and a sense of the emerging national strength, and some belief in the democratic idea. The advance of business power and values weakened the hold of the democratic idea, while translating both the pioneering sense and the nationalist pride into the boom terms of growing industrial power and profit. . . .

In America, as everywhere, politics has been vulnerable to bribery. Yet it is a paradox of a business civilization that there has been notably less political corruption in America than in many precapitalist societies such as in Asia, the Middle East, and South America, or even some of the Latin societies of Europe. Perhaps this is exactly because of the importance of business: for those to whom money is all-important there are in America (as in no other culture) more direct channels open to the money-making energies than through the circuitous routes of the political career and political power. Political corruption is most rampant in the cultures where for many men it is the only road to wealth and status; in America it is only one of many.

Yet the business spirit, which directly carries along in its torrential course so many of the talents and energies of men into money-making, also breaks down some of the moral barriers that had been built into the conscience for generations. The big temptation in the era of the expanding frontier was land speculation. In the era of an expanding capitalism the temptations lie less in speculation than in the sale of political influence to businessmen intent on getting some of the Big Money, by crucially placed governmental subalterns who don't see why they too should not get their cut. As in the post-Civil War days of Grant and Conkling, or the post-World War days of Harding and Daugherty, the torrents of fresh business energy which open new opportunities for big profits also carry away with them much of the terrain of social conscience. In this sense, it is not the periods of business decay, but the periods of business expansion and vitality, which play havoc with moral principles, because they fix men's aims at the attainable goals of the Big Money. . . .

Until recently, at least, the appeal of business has been as a way of making money, not as a way of life. Sensitive people have rejected the way of life but then been lured by the money; hence the split in the American attitude toward business, which has been most marked where the tradition of an educated elite has been strongest. The Adams family, for example, showed both a cultivated understanding and a cultivated fear of the new and pushing type of business activity. Writing in *The Education*, Henry Adams expressed the melancholy sense that for all the processes of civilization that had gone to make him, he was unfit to survive in the world that business values were fashioning. Brooks Adams, living as a *rentier* from corporate securities, was able to dissect pitilessly the social sources of his income, all the time ransacking history to explain the emergence of this new form of centralized power to which he owed the leisure he had for ransacking history. The third brother, Charles Francis Adams, was a railroad president who wrote with shriveling contempt for the narrowness of outlook and the niggardliness of spirit of business as a way of life. Henry James, for all his preoccupation with money and what it could buy, always pushed the question of its sources into the background and felt slightly soiled by them. He was most at home with a businessman like the hero of *The Golden Bowl,* spending in Europe the fortune he had made in America, a Maecenas who knew what he wanted and went after it with the practiced assurance that betokened the habitual conqueror. The secret that Sir Joseph Duveen discovered about American businessmen, which made his fortune as an art salesman, was that they gloried in their power over the things that money commanded but hungered for the symbols of the life values that went beyond money. Throughout the history of the business spirit, the monied men have used business first as a way of making the Big Kill, then turned to philanthropy or the lift of the patron, travel, or hobbies as a way of making a life.

The business spirit, then, has not in itself been regarded as a nourishing one, but as a means to bring a good life within reach. For that reason perhaps it has exerted an attraction for the young men of talent who in other civilizations might have gone into government, the Army, or the priesthood, into literature or the arts or the study of philosophy, into science or the professions. Even those in government service have, when successful, been tempted to turn their knowledge to the service of the corporation: if they have worked in the Treasury Department on taxes, or as economists in government bureas, they can command good salaries as consultants or executives in business. If they have been good newspapermen they are eagerly recruited for public-relations jobs in the corporate world. And the corporations have learned to go directly to the colleges in recruiting young men of talent who are rarely able to resist the offer of an immediate job as against the uncertainties of a career in the arts or professions.

Even for those who stay outside business, there is a strong drive to conduct themselves in a "businesslike" way. The trade-union movement in America has been largely, as Hoxie first described it, "business unionism," expressing the competing claims to income of the corporate employees as part of the larger structure of the business economy itself. In education the school administrator and the university president have tended to act as corporate executives. Even in the churches the temptation is to be "practical" in administering vast properties rather than unworldly in pursuing the values of the spirit. In the newspaper and magazine fields the pressure is toward building big power aggregates that can command writing talent and the reader market and get a big share of national advertising: the magazine or big newspaper is likely to make its more blatant public boasts not so much about its newsgathering or its crusading spirit as about its circulation and advertising gains. In radio and television the art forms are subsidiary to the selling of time to the business sponsors. In moviemaking, the final art product has to run the gantlet of box-office appeal, and the Hollywood values of inflated salaries and skyrocketing careers are a kind of caricature of the corporate executives. In literature the emphasis has shifted to the products that can be marketed to a mass audience, notably crime and detection thrillers.

In fact, it may turn out that the business spirit will leave its most enduring imprint on the adjoining provinces of literature and entertainment, government and opinion: for these are the areas in which capital investment counts least and personality and talent still can carve out empires. They are the last Klondikes of venture skills, which are even more important in the history of business than venture capital. The lure of the acquisitive impulse, wedded to talent and ideas, produces a powerful amalgam.

It is customary to speak of this as the "commercializing" of art and opinion. But the process is more complex. The crux of it is that the dominant activity of any civilization colors the prevailing notions of what is effective or futile in the exercise of men's talents. In a business civilization the stamp of effectiveness is placed on whatever can be exchanged in the personality market for money and success; the stamp of ineffectuality is placed on whatever talent is not vendible, whatever cannot move to a maximum degree into the channels where it is capitalized and reaches a mass market with all the accruing rewards. Thus the business spirit, itself incapable of yielding nourishing life values, has become for Americans the prime gateway to a way of life, with few questions asked about what you find when you have gone through the gates.

When one inquires what may account for the "domination effect" of the business spirit, the answer lies partly in the attractiveness of the big rewards and the big market, partly in the admiration felt for the men who have shown that they can run things best, partly in the pragmatic strain of a culture which accepts whatever is practical and successful as the valid and pays it the flattery of mimicry.

The final tribute to the domination effect of the business spirit is the extent to which the phases of the human personality are measured in its terms. In a seminal analysis of types of character structure that bear aptly on American life, Fromm has spoken of the "marketing orientation" as one that is crowding out much else in the business society. There is little question that the marketable personality is becoming the dominant one, even in areas outside business. Courtesy and charm come to be valued not for themselves but because they pay off in salesmanship; clothes must be worn well to make an impression on a propective customer or employer; the "dreamer type" of person is dangerous because he will estrange those who seek alertness. America itself, in the impact it makes on other peoples in the struggle for world leadership, must "sell" itself and its ideas; and the clinching argument used even by liberal intellectuals against the denial of civil rights of Negroes and other minority groups is that it will interfere with such international "selling" and acceptance.

This then is what seems to have happened in the American business economy. The more strictly technical problems of production and scarcity, of income distribution, of bigness in the sense distinct from monopoly, even of the business cycle, are fairly on the way to being resolved. But the bureaucratization of life through the new managerial structures in business, the trade-union, the government, and the corrupting reach of marketing values and the money spirit are being extended through the whole culture. The real problems of the business culture are thus less the technical and strictly economic problems than the moral and psychological ones.

Yet, to say, as some foreign observers and American critics have said, that only money talks in America is to vulgarize the impact of the business spirit. Other values than the acquisitive find a place in American life, and often they triumph; and other qualities than the money-making qualities blossom. But even when they do triumph, it is only after they have been measured and defended against the money values and the vendible qualities. That they survive is the final tribute to their hardihood, and when they do survive—in literature and the arts, in human relations, in religion and education and government, in the armed services, in the professions, perhaps even in business itself—they have a greater strength than in those cultures where they do not have to measure themselves so searchingly against the domination effect of the business spirit.

Bruce R. Joyce

Should young children begin to develop the skills and habits of social action within their school experiences? The answer will vary from one community to another and will be related to the specific social actions proposed. Professor Joyce supports the call for socially active children and offers useful examples of types of activities that are appropriate. As a class activity, you may find it helpful to attempt to expand the list of activities. Will you justify such activities by value of the immediate outcome or in terms of specific concept and skill development?

Social Action for the Primary Schools

Thirty-eight years ago George Counts sounded forth a manifesto that rocked the educational world, "Dare the Schools Build a New Social Order?" Bruce R. Joyce, viewing the serious crisis of values besetting our world, argues that today's answer must be an unreserved "Yes!" Mr. Joyce is professor of Education at Teachers College, Columbia University.

Do the schools have a moral role in the society? Can they espouse a particular direction for human relations? That is, can the school "push" a point of view about the ways children should relate to each other and the kind of society we should create? Let us explore the notion that the answer to these questions

---

Bruce R. Joyce, "Social Action for the Primary Schools," *Childhood Education* 46, no. 5, February 1970. Reprinted by permission of Bruce R. Joyce and the Association for Childhood Education International, 3615 Wisconsin Avenue, N.W., Washington, D.C. Copyright © 1970 by the Association.

is "yes," that the school *should* back an ethical position and begin to teach it from the early years.

THE PROBLEM: A CRISIS IN VALUES

Clearly, our nation is caught in a serious crisis of values these days, and our schools reflect that crisis. You know the forms it takes: alienation of youth, confusion over the United States' role in world affairs, disenchantment by the public with the courses that have led us into foreign wars and domestic riots. It manifests itself in the actions of frustrated blacks and frightened whites, of disenchanted and confused liberals; in the confusion within our churches about their role in society; in the uncertainty throughout all segments of our population over the meaning of civil order, of national solidarity, and of personal life in the public arena.

We all know too that no easy solution awaits us to ease this severe crisis in values. Ending the Asian war will ease certain pressures but will not solve our confusion in the international arena generally. Legal ending of school segregation and unfair employment practices is insufficient, alas, to end our racial crisis or alienation in our cities. Institution of stronger police action might end rioting but not its underlying causes.

What can schools do if they are to play a part in the nursery and primary years of equipping our children to deal with the values crisis haunting their future lives? To explain further one aspect of the task of the schools, let's briefly chronicle some of our past errors in approaching value questions with young children.

MYTHS OF THE VALUING PLACE

The Kids Are Too Young Myth

Watching children from four to eight trot into a classroom or scramble around the playground, we can naturally, easily want to say, "Let them be children; they are only little people and they have enough to do trying to comprehend their child-sized world. Let us stay away from conflict in the wider culture; time enough for that later on." My own heart responds to that statement and yet I know—and you know—that during those years many of the basic outlines of valuing positions are formed. Good evidence tells us that by age nine or ten racial and ethnic prejudices are well established and are already highly resistant to change. And that personal flexiblity and creativity, open-mindedness and tolerance of unfamiliar ideas are formed to a remarkable extent by the interaction of the four- to eight-year-old set with their social environment. The children may be too young to study the intricacies of the issues surrounding the question of whether Communist China should be admitted to the United Nations, but they live in a valuing world and they develop their predisposition toward later growth in valuing during

Values, Issues, and Conflicts in Social Science Education Part II

their early years. Moreover, shielding them from complexity by creating an antiseptic "child's world" not only is liable to risk growth in valuing but is not true to childhood itself. The natural world of childhood is filled with conflict, aggression, interdependence and warmth. To pretend that their world is bland is false.

The Myths of Verbalism

In our primary schools we *talk* about patriotism. We *talk* about interdependence within the family. We *talk* about our rights and duties as citizens toward each other. We *talk* about equality and we *talk* about international cooperation with our "friendly" neighbors in the North, South, East and West. We dramatize conflict situations and then talk about them and analyze them. We get the feeling that we are getting something done when we are able to hold conversation about it. The essence of valuing, however, is affection toward something. To value is to love and cherish, to value country is to love it, and to value your fellow man is to love him. To love is to demonstrate affection through words and *action*. It has been easier for us to talk about values with children than to engage in the demonstrations of positive love that are at its essence. When we have stressed action, we have somehow separated it from the energies of love and affection.

The "It's-Skills-and-Language-Development-That-Counts" Myth

From the nursery school beginnings through the end of the primary years, the burden has fallen upon the schools for preparing children with the language skills and the general language development essential for success in later academic life. The penalties for a failure to achieve language development are so great that teachers are drawn toward the language arts and away from social studies, processes of exploring the sciences, and other sources of curricular activities. The mission of the primary years in school to focus on reading and other aspects of language development is not an irrational choice: the primary teacher who is unable to get children to read is severely criticized and is also filled with guilt, for he knows the hard times that are ahead for them. But as we increasingly give the years of childhood to the language task, there is no time, seemingly, for the development of love when we must get ready for our ascent up the technological ladder.

TURNING THINGS INSIDE OUT

We have tended, then, to avoid some kinds of value issues because they seem premature for the life of the child. We have tended to dilute others with words, substituting conversation for the expression of affection which is at the essence of valuing, and we have let the need for technical proficiency and language development usurp the child's day in the primary school.

Let us dream together about what might happen if valuing were to be the core of our work with young children—if it became the area of priority—the central mission of the primary years. Suppose that we were to express that mission in terms of the following affective goals, so that the resulting activities do not become ends in themselves but serve only as the *means* to positive emotional involvement:

- To develop a commitment toward the betterment of mankind. Included would be involvement and lifelong endeavor to work with others in finding ways of improving social life in one's immediate vicinity, nation, and throughout the world.

- To reach out to all others and to try to make contact with and understand them, to share affection and to grow with them. To be willing also to explore with them the different kinds of problems that keep men apart and—as one matures—engage in a dialogue with them over the problems of mankind. (Even at *this* level, studies of political socialization indicate, children are developing the predisposition for such a dialogue and later adult participation.)

What kinds of means would we employ in the primary school to achieve these objectives? What kind of environment would be likely to move students in those directions? The most appropriate types of activities the children could engage in might best be termed "Social Action on a Child Scale."

Activities to Improve the School Environment

From their earliest encounters in school, children could have animals to raise, plants to tend, toys to take care of and toys to create; and they could be involved by the teachers in working out ways to get those things done. They need to teach each other songs and dances and games. They need to learn how to take care of the record player and how to share it; to show each other films and filmstrips about the wider world. And these activties need to be carried on because they are educational in themselves, not because they enable people to get along quicker to the business of mastering reading and writing. Little children need a corner of the playground that is their own for at least a part of the day. They need to learn how to use it, to divide it up, and to keep it clean—and to work with one another in it. In addition, they need to be taught games that require cooperation, a reaching out toward one another, with conflict and confusion welcomed by the teacher as opportunities for helping the students work out ways of handling their relationships with each other. Conflict between children would not be something swept quickly under the rug so they can get onto the *important* business of *learning*. Learning how to handle conflict and to establish warm relations after a difficulty would be a priority order.

Activities for the Betterment of the Wider Community Outside of School

Perhaps most signifiicantly, children need a corner of the *community* to tend and a social service to render. Sick children await to be visited, sick animals await to be tended. Parties are to be given for one another, for parents and for others in the community. A world is to be made better.

Children need, too, to make positive contact with other people who live far away, both in this country and in other parts of the world.

Some Examples. Quite a few classrooms already exist in which social action is the norm. Here are some of them:

- One third-grade class offers a messenger-shopping service for neighborhood members who are invalids. Each youngster spends one-half hour twice a week fetching things, carrying messages, and shopping for small items for persons who are unable to get out.

- In one nongraded primary unit with teacher cycling, each group of children adopts a classroom in a French or Spanish village at the beginning of the first year and stays "twinned" for three years or until the group leaves the primary unit of the school. Children from the two nations exchange information about their communities and lives. The basic task which the American teacher continually gives her children is to find ways of communicating more fully with the European children, especially ways of exploring values. For instance, the classes exchange experience records that attempt to answer questions asked by the other group. An example of a question that explores values and feelings is, "Tell us all the ways people in your town tell other people that they are friends."

- A first-grade class interviews parents and next-door neighbors to answer the question, "What can six-year-olds do to improve this neighborhood?" The children select some of the recommended activities and carry them out during the years.

- One group of seven-year-olds in a small private school helps a group of five-year-olds learn to read: each week the sevens write a story and illustrate it. The story is copied onto large newsprint sheets and the illustrations are made on brown paper sheets that can be tacked up. Once a week the sevens read and dramatize their story for the fives. They then help the fives to read it (the fives are all beginning readers).

- A third grade studies ways of reaching out to others. The children have made a large "human relating map" of the neighborhood, depicting all the people in the neighborhood whom they contact regularly. They try to figure out how to approach each one in such a way as to make his day a more cheerful and warm one. For example, if one youngster regularly stops at a newsstand and buys a paper for his parents, he and his group will practice ways of saying things and asking for the paper that express goodwill and warmth.

- A New York City teacher of fourth-graders has for many years helped her (usually all white) students try to study the black experience in America.

After a great deal of study she and her children approach the question, "How can we help, *now,* to improve racial relations in America?" Last year they found another class in another school (largely black) that had the same interest. After several meetings they decided they needed to begin with themselves; a long program of activities ensued in which the children carried out small service projects together, exploring their attitudes and reactions as they did so.

In other words, the classroom could be a community of involved young citizens reaching to one another and out to the world, led by a teacher who by his commitment to those activities makes manifest his belief in them. Then in the upper grades and in the junior high and senior high school years, the children would naturally move toward more complex and difficult-to-understand social problems on the local, national and international level. From the middle grades on, each child could regularly engage with his peers in social service work of some nature or other. They could be tending a park or tending younger children; they could be studying the government and the issues that confront it and seeking to find a way to do their bit to serve and to reach their neighbors. Increasingly, they could be brought to reflect on the alternative courses open to mankind and to engage in a philosophical and practical dialogue over the possibilities for mankind, the obstacles to reaching those possibilities. They could begin to form powerful values that operate in interpersonal relations, in the quest for meaning and in commitment to create a better world.

These positive values could take precedence over the traditional role of the primary school, which has been to induct children into certain of the technologies of the culture; e.g., reading and other language skills. The school, in short, could be devoted to the fundamentals of American life—to the values of love—to the rich emotional life that ties us together by giving us the basis for meaningful contact and a loving life on our one earth.

Caryl Chessman
(1922-1960)

The problems of crime and punishment remain among the most compelling, often the most avoided, of all the concerns of society. In the following letter from death row, Caryl Chessman commented at length on the complex implications to society and to the individual which the use of the death penalty poses. Chessman was executed in 1960, insisting to the end that he was innocent of the crime for which he finally died.

How does adult society explain capital punishment to young people? Or is it possible that they do not notice? When should the school allow such issues to come into the classroom? What interpretations can be given to such problems that seem to raise value conflicts? Christian-Judaic values require that "man shalt not kill." Society appears to say that such a religious value must stand aside at certain times. What guidelines can you suggest for the teacher in the face of such issues?

A Letter from Death Row

Name: Caryl Chessman
Box 66565, San Quentin, Calif.
Date: February 26, 1960

The Hon. Edmund G. Brown
Governor of the State of California
State Capitol
Sacramento, California

Dear Governor Brown:

As you know, at approximately 4:45 P.M. on Thursday, February 18, 1960, I was removed from the Death Row Unit located on the fifth floor of the North Block here at San Quentin and locked in the small holding cell, just a few feet from the State's lethal gas chamber, where California's condemned spend their last night on earth. The death watch began. So far as I knew, I would be put to death at ten o'clock in the morning.

I was permitted to see an early edition of a Friday newspaper. Its headlines were large and black: CHESSMAN MUST DIE, BROWN SAYS. Again, only an hour earlier, the members of the California Supreme Court had voted 4 to 3 against a recommendation to you for clemency. Thus, by a simple vote, you were foreclosed from exercising your commutation powers. The court had made its order "final forthwith." I had been notified of that action a few hours before being taken downstairs to the holding cell. In anticipation of it, I had put my affairs in order and executed a new will. . . .

And death appeared inevitable. I held out no feverish, desperate hope for a life-sparing miracle. On the contrary, what sustained me, what made it possible for me to await the morning and oblivion with a detached, almost clinical calm was hope of an entirely different sort: the burning hope that my execution would lead to an objective reappraisal of the social validity or invalidity of capital punishment, and that such a reexamination would lead, in turn, to an awareness on the part of all Californians that Death Rows, and death chambers and executioners were unworthy of our society, that the former, in fact, were gross obscenities, solving nothing but rather confounding solution.

The minutes passed, the hours. The prison's Catholic Chaplain, Father Edward Dingberg, visited me. Associate Wardens Walter D. Achuff and Louis S. Nelson saw me for a few minutes. Dr. David G. Schmidt, San Quentin's chief psychiatrist, came in. Attorney George Davis conferred with me hurriedly, intending to return later. Warden Fred R. Dickson dropped by for a talk.

A copy of a letter to Governor Edmund G. Brown of California from Caryl Chessman in death row at San Quentin, February 26, 1960. The letter previously appeared in *Contemporary Moral Issues,* Harry Girvetz, ed. Belmont, California: Wadsworth Publishing Co., 1963.

Contrary to published accounts that I consumed the condemned man's traditional hearty meal of "fried chicken, French fried potatoes, vegetable salad, coffee and two kinds of pie—apple and chocolate cream," I am compelled to confess these reports, seemingly attesting to my capacity as a trencherman, are somewhat exaggerated. Actually, my wants were more modest. I had a hamburger and a coke about 7:30, and during the course of the evening I drank three cups of coffee. I also puffed on a cigar, although I normally do not smoke.

I waited. Midnight came. All my visitors had left but Warden Dickson. Then the telephone rang mutedly, and one of the death watch officers said, "It's for you, Warden." I watched Mr. Dickson disappear around a bend in the hallway. I paced the floor, my steps reduced to almost soundlessness by the cloth slippers. The radio outside the cell played quietly. Over it I had listened to a succession of newscasts. The news was all negative. One commentator reported Miss Asher [1] had been unable to see you but, in vain, had talked with two members of your staff. A second commentator solemnly quoted you as having said, "Only an act of God can save Caryl Chessman now."

My eyes fell on the newspaper I had been allowed whose stark headline I quoted above. One of its front-paged lead paragraphs read: "The world was disturbed last night as the hour for Caryl Chessman's execution drew near. Protests echoed from continent to continent." This San Francisco daily also reported: "There was little question that the Governor . . . was undergoing great emotional stress as Chessman's last hours ticked away," and: "The mail—most of it running about three to one for clemency—continued to pour in. So did the telegrams and the zero-hour telephone calls. . . ."

On page two were pictures of the gas chamber and this account of how I would die in less than ten hours:

". . . He'll get a physical examination from the prison's chief physician, Dr. Herman H. Gross, at 9 A.M. and undoubtedly will once again be found to be in perfect condition.

"At 9:45 A.M. come the last, formal visits from Warden Dickson and his aide to hear any last requests. Once again the chaplains will wait silently.

"Over a carpeted floor, his stockinged feet should take the last walk at 10 A.M. on the dot.

"There have been 164 people in the gas chamber before him, and experience gives the prison staff an almost split-second foretelling of the rest.

"By 10:01 A.M. he should be in one of the two death chairs—chair B. in his case.

"Two straps for each arm and leg, one across the chest and another for the waist. That, and the final slamming of the great iron door—less than three minutes.

"At 10:03½, by schedule, Warden Dickson would nod at a guard and a lever will send the cyanide pellets into the sulphuric acid basins."

---

[1] Chessman's attorney.

I smiled, grimly, I'm sure. I knew how it felt to be a dead man. Only the ritualized formalities of physically extinguishing my life with hydrocyanic acid gas remained.

"Has the Warden gone?" I asked one of the death watch. "No," I was told, "he's still on the phone."

I gave no thought to the significance of the call. Then, audibly, I heard Warden Dickson say, "All right, Governor." A few seconds later the Warden reappeared. I'd glanced up from the paper I was reading. As he approached the cell, the Warden's face was a thoughtful mask.

"I have some news for you, Caryl." Mr. Dickson paused. "Oh?" I responded. He nodded, smiled. "The Governor has just granted you a 60-day reprieve."

The words had been spoken softly—but they crashed and reverberated in my mind like thunder in an echo chamber. Except possibly in a mocking, sadistic nightmare, they were words I truly never had expected to hear up to the instant of their utterance. I had been prepared to die; now I must be ready to go on living, I realized, for at least another 60 days."

I drew a deep breath as my thoughts raced. My words have been reported in the press: "Thank you. This is a great surprise. I really didn't expect it. Tell the Governor I thank him. I am surprised and grateful.

The Warden said he would see me again later in the morning. We said goodnight. Swiftly I was taken back upstairs in the elevator to Death Row. Swiftly, in the office, I changed into my regular clothing. Accompanied by the officers, I was passed through the "Bird Cage"—with its double doors and multiplicity of bolts and bars and locks—into the Row proper. From most of the occupied cells, yellow light spilled out into the corridor. The condemned were awake, listening to their earphones, silent, waiting—for what? Somehow, even better than I, they had sensed their fate was tied to mine, and mine to a pressing social issue of far greater significance than what might, individually or collectively, happen to any or all of us. They had heard me say repeatedly that obviously the greatest hope for abolition of the death penalty lay with my death. They—even the tortured and troubled ones—knew this to be true. Their obvious course was to accept this fact and hope it might lead them out from the cold shadow of the gas chamber. But, as I later learned, they had sent you a telegram, urging your intercession in my behalf. They had refused to believe that death—even another's—was a solution. I don't know whether that telegram ever came to your attention in the flood of messages you were receiving. I do know it had a profound effect on me. . . .

I continued along the corridor, stopping for a moment or two to speak to the occupant of each cell. The reaction was the same. Here was a genuine and spontaneous expression of brotherhood, commingled for them with a miracle. And make no mistake, Governor, I was for my doomed fellows no arrogant, swaggering hero returned after breathing defiance into the teeth of the cosmos. On the contrary, since they had come to know the man rather than the counterfeit black criminal legend, I was a flesh and blood human being whose appointment with man-imposed death had come to symbolize the critical and yet unresolved basic struggle of social man to rise above wrath and vengeance, to trust not the executioner, but their—mankind's—own reason and humanity in building a saner world for their children and their children's children. These men had been accused and convicted of homicidal violence, and so, better than any, they knew the futility of such violence. Now, after a bitter contest, life in my case had claimed at least a temporary victory. . . .

We got the word [that] you had granted the reprieve because, since the people of California were sharply divided on the issue, you wanted "to give the people . . . an opportunity, through the Legislature, to express themselves once more on capital punishment.". . .

And then, as well as in the hectic days to come, before there were calmer reflections and clearer analysis, the paradoxical evidence mounted: While the Chessman case had made evident the urgent need for a calm, careful and objective reexamination of the question whether capital punishment should not be discarded as a barbarous anachronism, productive finally of nothing but division and uneasy doubt among us, my continued existence, if only for another few weeks, and the fearful Chessman legend, which portrayed me as a cunning, fiendish, Cataline-like mocker of justice, threatened to throttle such a reexamination and reevaluation at the outset.

I remain haunted by that paradox. Beyond the descriptive power of words, these have been troubled and difficult days for me. I do not resort to hyperbole when I say they have been hell, even more than the past 11½ years have been hell. I cannot escape the fact I owe you my life for whatever days remain to me. I cannot forget that literally millions of people from nations around the world spoke out for me. In terms of the larger social good that is your goal, my obligation is a heavy one, and I refuse to try to rationalize it away. Over and over I have asked myself the questions. What possibly can I do, if anything, to divorce the ugly, emotion-inflaming image of Caryl Chessman from the grave social issue of capital punishment? What can I say—and mean, and demonstrate?

. . . I decided I can and I do, without theatrics, offer them my life. If the hysteria and the mob wrath that surrounds the problem only can be propitiated by my death and if otherwise they agree that the death penalty should be abolished, then I earnestly urge the members of our Legislature to frame their bill in such a way as to exclude me. This can be done readily—for example, by a declaration in the law that anyone convicted of a capital offense during or subsequent to the year 1950, whose sentence of death remains in force and unexecuted, shall be treated as though serving a sentence of life imprisonment. I give my solemn word before the world that I will never challenge such a law in the courts and I will disavow any attempt by any attorney purporting to act in my behalf.

. . . If the legislators do not necessarily demand my death but do believe the final question of my fate, under the California Constitution, should be resolved by yourself and the majority opinion of the State Supreme Court, then I urge them so to indicate. This way, by the passage of the type of bill mentioned above, they can sever the two problems. . . .

Except for the days I was out to court, I have occupied a death cell continuously since Saturday morning, July 3, 1948. I have had eight dates for execution in California's lethal gas chamber fixed and then canceled, some in the very last hours. A ninth date soon will be set. Ninety-odd men have taken that last, grim walk by my cell to their deaths since I came to Death Row. If it gives them any satisfaction, Californians may be assured my prolonged half-life in the shadow of the gas chamber has been an indescribably punishing ordeal. The shock of it, I think, has brought me to maturity; it has forced upon me keen social awareness of the problem that, in exaggerated form, I am said to typify.

I am now 38 years of age. I was 26 when arrested. Behind me is a long record of arrest. I am a graduate of California reform schools and prisons. I have been called a "criminal psychopath." Certainly, as a young man, I was a violent, rebellious, monumental damn fool. I was at odds with my society; I resisted authority. I am ashamed of that past but I cannot change it. However, with my writings, I have tried to salvage something of larger significance from it. Without shifting responsibility for my conduct, I endeavored in my first book to tell the story of my life and hence to explain how young men like myself got that way. I realized that Death Rows made sense only because people like Caryl Chessman didn't.

After being brought to the death house, the change in me and my outlook came slowly and painfully. Defiantly, I stood and fought in the courts for survival, asking no quarter and expecting none. But, ironically, to have any chance for survival, I had to turn to the law; I had to invoke the protections of the Constitution; I had to study, often as much as 18 to 20 hours a day; I had to learn to impose upon myself a harsh self-discipline; I had to think and to be ruthlessly honest with myself; in time, I forced myself to admit, "Chessman, you have been, and to some degree still are, an irrational, impossible fool. What are you going to do about it?"

At that juncture, the traditional thing, the conventional response almost certainly would have been for me to confess my past folly and to beg for mercy. But I hesitated, not out of pride or false pride. I couldn't escape the fact that such a response on my part would, in practical effect, amount to affirmation that gas chambers and a system of justice ultimately based upon retribution possessed a genuine—rather than a mistakenly conceived and defended—social validity. I knew they did not possess such a validity. Without mock heroics, I became aware then that the greatest contribution I could make was to cause people, all people, to become angrily aware of places like Death Row and the administration of criminal justice in general. This, in my own way, I did: by continued total resistance. I was told I could not write another line for publication and I wrote anyway. When concerted efforts were made to suppress my manuscripts, I found a way to smuggle them from the prison. I intensified my court fight, winning some battles, losing others. Vituperation was heaped upon me. I became known as a mocker of justice. Editorial writers and public officials roundly denounced me. The public clamored for "this cunning fiend's" execution. Often I was half-mad with doubt; often I was ready to collapse with a brutal fatigue; often I sardonically sneered at myself and my goal. But I kept on somehow. A remorseless voice within told me, "This is your penance, fool—to be reviled and hated. This, if you call yourself a man, is the price you must pay."

I had certain advantages, and almost impossible handicaps. Among others I had been convicted of unsavory sex offenses, sordid acts that, when recounted, inflamed the mind of the listener. They had inflamed the judge, the prosecutor, the jury. A Red Light Bandit—so-called because the bandit had operated, according to trial testimony, with a car equipped with a red spotlight such as those on police cars. He had accosted couples in lonely lovers' lanes. Armed with a gun, he would sometimes rob the couples, if they had any money. On two occasions testified to at my trial, he took the woman to his car. In one of these instances, under threat of death, he compelled her, the victim, to commit an unnatural sex act before letting her out and driving off. On a second occasion, he drove off with a 17-year-old girl to another secluded area, compelled her, too, to commit a perverted sexual act and attempted to rape her. Then he let her off near her home. (This tragic young woman, who had a history of serious mental disturbance, was committed to a mental hospital some 19 months after her traumatic experience. "Today," the wire services have quoted her mother as saying, "she just sits and stares"— lost in the withdrawn unreal world of the schizophrenic.)

It is no wonder, then, that the Red Light Bandit crimes so aroused judge, jury and prosecutor and antagonized them against the man accused of their commission. They angered and outraged me to an equal or greater degree, to an extent where in a red haze of emotion, I was unable to defend myself as effectively as otherwise I might. Stupidly and stubbornly, as well, I had withheld certain vital facts about my involvement in a violent internecine struggle for control of an illegal but police protected bookmaking syndicate. The convict's code said I shouldn't talk, or name names. I didn't. Then, not by myself, other critical evidence got suppressed. Witnesses disappeared. And a damning net was drawn around me. The jury returned verdicts of guilty, doomed me. I was brought to Death Row, twice sentenced to death and to 15 consecutive prison terms. The question of guilt or innocence was closed unless I could convince an appellate court I had been convicted illegally. Otherwise, branded a loathsome sex predator, I would die. I would have no chance to establish California had convicted the wrong man. It would make no difference that the description furnished the police of the bandit didn't remotely fit me; that the 17-year-old girl said her attacker had been "shorter than the usual man" and had weighed nearly 50 pounds less than the evidence showed I did, while I was six feet tall; or that she said the bandit had spoken with a slight accent, had appeared to be Italian and had a linear cut scar extending back from his right ear; or that this bandit usually gave his victims a look at his face before pulling up a handkerchief mask, while I had been released from prison on parole and knew that my photographs almost certainly would be the first shown robbery victims; or that I had absolutely no history as a sex offender; or that I had been refused the right to produce witnesses at the trial who would testify to my reputation for sexual normality as well as to produce expert psychiatric evidence that I did not possess the psychological disposition to commit sexual crimes, particularly those involving force or violence, and that I was not a sexual psychopath.

All this made no difference. In the eyes of the law, I was guilty and would remain guilty unless I could win a new trial and acquittal. This galled but it also drove and sustained me. . . .

I wait to die. I remain locked in a death cell. More than 12 years have passed since my arrest. The State has spent nearly a million dollars in trying to kill me.

Now, in a few days, the California Legislature will be called into special session to consider abolition of capital punishment. Disturbed that a vote against the death penalty will be a vote for me, the man they believe has embarrassed their State and made a mockery of their laws, many legislators have vowed publicly to see that capital punishment is retained. I do not presume to tell them what to do; I do pray they will reconsider and reevaluate. . . . I am more than willing that they separate me decisively from the greater issue. I am quite willing to die if that will bring about this desperately needed social reform. I do suggest that if our positions were reversed and they had found themselves occupying a death cell under the conditions I have they too, and honorably, would have done as I have done, even though it meant bringing the wrath of the State down upon them. Happily, they will never know what it means to be doomed, to be within hours and minutes of execution, to feel the full, terrible impact of mob wrath, to have a claim of innocence brushed impatiently aside, to be called a "monster" and vilified, to seek redemption, not through hypocritical groveling, but by a harder, perhaps impossible road to win friends and want desperately to justify their friendship and their faith, to want to live and to believe, humbly, that within them is a gift for words that can enrich our literature and, their own case aside, contribute significantly to the pressing social problems of our day.

I do not overstate when I say I gladly would die ten thousand gas chamber deaths if that would bring these truths into the hearts and minds of those who make our laws: A vote for either abolition or a moratorium is not an indication of approval of murder or other capital crimes, for the death penalty does not deter; it does not protect society. On the contrary, it leaves it defenseless, since as long as we have an executioner and a gas chamber, we will be content to believe that we can bury the problem with the offender. We will think that revenge is enough. It isn't. We must find why men kill and we must learn to prevent killing. We must become as intensely concerned with tomorrow's prospective victims as yesterday's actual ones. We must learn how to save lives and to salvage lives.

As long as the death penalty is on our statute books, there will be too much emotionality and circus atmosphere tainting our administration of justice. And for those who doubt this, there is a ready and rational test at hand: Let a moratorium be ordered on the supreme penalty for a period of, say, five years. I am certain during that period there will be no rise in the per capita crimes. Rather, I am convinced the crime rate will drop appreciably, and that justice will function in a far more even-handed and fair way. The sensationalism inevitably attending capital cases will vanish. The citizen will be reassured.

He will know that the man who has killed has been isolated. The accused is more likely, if he is guilty, to plead guilty. Our courts thus will be able to perform their duties more efficiently. And if an innocent man is later found to have been mistakenly convicted, it will not be too late to correct the error.

Unfortunately, as investigation will confirm, too often it is the friendless and the fundless upon whom the death penalty is imposed. The man with means or who knows the angles does not come to Death Row. As well, under our outmoded tests for legal sanity or insanity, too often the man who is executed is one who, while not legally insane, suffers from some serious mental disability. It needlessly demeans our society to engage in killing the mentally ill. Still further, among this group, as psychiatrists and penologists will attest, is the type of personality who is inflamed by the thought and threat of the gas chamber. His response to it, his overt expression of defiance, is to strike out homicidally. In effect, he gets his revenge in advance, and we in turn get ours after the tragedy.

That is why so many thoughtful citizens advocate abolition or a moratorium. They feel, as I do, a sense of guilty responsibility at a lethal act that is both more than futile and less than futile when the States takes a life. They want their laws to express humanity's ideal of nobility, compassion, understanding and social awareness. They know that our laws can do so without endangering the citizens of California. The basis for their opposition to man's government killing man is thus, in the highest sense, ethical, social, practical and religious. They do not want to see their society needlessly degraded, their system of justice compromised.

I must close, and in closing I again earnestly urge you to ask the Legislature to consider the question of capital punishment apart from Caryl Chessman and the Chessman case. I urge you to request that they consider framing their bill as suggested above, to exclude me. You can do this honorably by taking my life back into your hands alone. You can let me die. Indeed, as the matter now stands, you are powerless to do otherwise because of the present 4–3 vote against me in the California Supreme Court. But, at the same time, you can give your proposal to the Legislature a chance.

It deserves that chance. It deserves your forceful leadership. You are right in the position you have taken. It is time to speak out, for too seldom does enlightened humanity in this age of fear and awesome nuclear devices have a spokesman with the courage to advocate that death and hate are not and never can be an answer to the problems that beset our civilization. Mankind and future generations ever will remain in your debt and ever will honor your name.

Yours respectfully,
/s/ Caryl Chessman

3

SOCIAL SCIENCE DISCIPLINES AND THEIR STRUCTURES
    History
    Geography
    Sociology
    Anthropology
    Economics
    Political science

SUMMARY

SUGGESTED PROBLEMS AND PROJECTS

RELATED READINGS

Using Data from the Social Science Disciplines

There is little doubt today that the importance of the social sciences will be even greater in the years ahead than during the past century. Complex decisions, which must be made by citizens in all facets of life during the difficult years ahead, call for a vigorous social science program that will have a positive impact on the learner. The social studies curriculum of the past relied heavily upon too few of the social sciences. It is our belief that the social science curriculum should reflect all of the social science areas from which the program has evolved. There has been developed, during the last half of the century, a large fund of scholarly and scientific material in the social and behavioral sciences which must find its way into the elementary social science education program.

In current times, as in the past, there has been some conflict between what different authorities believe to be the aim of the social studies curriculum. Some believe the basic purpose is to produce good citizens, while others feel the aim is to make pupils knowledgeable in certain of the social sciences (history and geography making up most of the traditional social studies curriculum). Your authors do not believe this is an either/or issue, inasmuch as we see the aim of modern social science education to be (1) to produce dynamic citizens, (2) to provide the learner with tools and procedures essential to inquiry, and (3) to make persons knowledgeable about the social sciences in order to draw upon them in problem solving. We view the social sciences as reservoirs of information to be used as needed to help develop understandings of human situations.

Social Science Disciplines and Their Structures [1]

History

Perhaps no other social science has had as much time devoted to it in the elementary school as history. Children have been taught the names of persons and places and the dates of important events and happenings, but in far too many cases only to the dislike of the learners. In this old, traditional approach we haven't taught children to question history or to make effective use of it as a tool in problem solving. History would exist without the history book—the past is there and things happened even if they were not recorded by historians. Children should learn that things did not happen because of the historian, but that the past has its own existence and, therefore, its own influence in the present and future. However, children should learn that the historians have made it possible for us to know something of the past; thus history is the memory of the past.[2]

The learner also needs to know that history, at best, has serious limitations. The historian can only collect and record facts which are available and relevant and try to organize them for presentation. Since in many instances the records are fragmentary, we must accept this without becoming too disturbed. Obviously, the older the data being collected, the more fragmented and incomplete it will be. In addition, only when a happening was recorded and preserved can we know of that particular incident of the past. Certainly, since the invention of the Gutenberg press, the records of man's events have been more accurate; but even at that, the particular bias of the writer, as well as his imagination, may produce inaccuracies or distortions. Also, disastrous fires, wars, and other calamities destroy valuable documents which provide us with records of the past. On the subject of bias, Commager states:

> Let us admit at once that history is neither scientific nor mechanical, that the historian is human and therefore fallible, and that the ideal history, completely objective and dispassionate, is an illusion. There is bias in the choice of a subject, bias in the selection of material, bias in its organization and presentation, and, inevitably, bias in its interpretation. Consciously, or unconsciously, all historians are

---

[1] The authors have, for much of this chapter, drawn on the writings of the Charles E. Merrill Social Science Seminar Series, Raymond H. Muessig and Vincent R. Rogers, eds. (Columbus, Ohio: Charles E. Merrill Publishing Company, 1965).

[2] For a complete treatise of history see Henry Steele Commager, *The Nature and the Study of History* (Columbus, Ohio: Charles E. Merrill Publishing Company, 1965).

Using Data from the Social Science Disciplines 135

biased; they are creatures of their time, their race, their faith, their class, their country—creatures and even prisoners.[3]

It becomes readily apparent that for the historian to be objective in recording the past is virtually impossible. Certainly we recognize the integrity of the historian, but even here standards of integrity are not universal, and honest men differ on the nature of truth in history.[4]

"Running Fox, one of these days a great white explorer will come and discover our land.*"*

Efforts to locate data to fill in the gaps between two significant dates or events might have been in vain; consequently, interpretations may be mere "educated" guesses, rather than accurate recordings. Perhaps the best we can hope for is that no historian will consciously distort evidence in presenting his interpretation. The point made here is that the teacher needs to be aware of the problems of recording history, as well as the positive force it can have when children use history as a source of information in problem solving.

[3] *Ibid.,* p. 53.
[4] *Ibid.,* p. 37.

Helping children discover history. As the teacher seeks to help history come alive for children, she might start with a study of the local community. The children might attempt to collect facts from old newspapers or from tombstones in local cemeteries; senior citizens, who have spent a lifetime in the area, can relate stories of the past (although the accuracy of these may also be in question). As the students attempt to develop the history of their community, they can learn the procedures and techniques of the historian. They can make the necessary decisions in writing the account and determine the accuracy of their interpretations. Through this procedure, children will gain a better understanding of the historian at work and the tools of his profession.

Perhaps one of the best learning experiences for children of elementary school age is for them to discover who they are. That is, a nine-year-old child might start the study of a time line with his own age, showing his birthday and his present age. He then could add other important events to his time line as shown in Figure 3–1. Such dates as the child's first day in school, the last presidential election, etc., could be added to his individual wall chart, thus helping him to record facts as they have occurred, as well as facts of other events that he can verify. This can be the beginning of his understanding of himself and his place in time. As he extends this understanding he can examine the things in his society which he has inherited, eg., his language and culture, as well as those values held by his society. Thus, as he broadens his understanding of time and space, he moves into the study of history through

| Mother's birthday May 1939 | Older brother's birthday Oct. 1961 | John's birthday December 1963 | First Moon Landing 1969 | John will be 10 years old in 1973 |

FIGURE 3–1. Time Line

recognizing how facts are collected, how they are related, and how conclusions are drawn from these facts. Using his newly learned skills of inquiry, he seeks answers to relevant questions, and he puts this information to work. The child must learn that when he forms a generalization it should be based upon the best-known information available to him to date, and that it is possible for new information to come to light which might change his conclusions.

Reference was made above to the biases in historical writings. Certainly, the elementary school child, as he reads history books, can start to examine problems of interpretation. As the children use the methods of historians, they should gain understanding and recognition of the efforts historians have exerted to provide us with an accurate picture of the past. Perhaps the most difficult task the teacher has is determining whether the material being read by the children is appropriate for their levels of understanding. Because of the complexity of the nature of human problems, the level of maturity necessary to understand the issues involved must not be oversimplified. Therefore, it must be best for some children to deal with less complex learnings. (If individual differences are to be considered, there is no more justification for all children to be learning the same concepts in history than there is in any other elementary school curriculum area.)

Geography

Geography is the study of man and his relationship to the physical environment. Stated differently, Jan Broek says, "Geography is orderly knowledge of the diversity of the earth as the world of man." [5] If the teacher envisions geography as the learning of the names of capitals, rivers, states, countries, and continents, then she cannot assume that the above conceptualization will take place. This kind of teaching has destroyed the interest and enthusiasm some children might have had for geography. Like the other social sciences, geography has a definite body of knowledge and requires the learning of certain skills to make its use effective. Geographical knowledge and skills are important to the study of our depressed areas in this country and to the study of underdeveloped countries, as well as to the understanding of the way of life of any group of humans and their interconnections with material resources.

The late President Kennedy was one of the first national figures to use a wall map when appearing on television. He effectively used the map to point out the strategic importance of Laos and Vietnam in Southeast Asia and the significance of this area to world affairs. This method serves to help us see the geographic concepts of location and interrelationship between parts of the earth.

Geography helps us to find relationships among various categories, such as, climate, crops, and settlements. Such relationships as climate and vegetation are well established, but we might look at the relation of per capita income and longevity of life or climate and production, for example, to better understand problems which are revelant. Certainly, in working with children, we can help them become better observers as they look at the surroundings in their home towns. The location of the

---

[5] Jan O. M. Broek, *Geography: Its Scope and Spirit* (Columbus, Ohio: Charles E. Merrill Publishing Company, 1965), p. 4.

railroad and why it was placed there, the river or creek beds, the rock quarry and/or other geographic factors of import might well serve as points of departure for studying social problems with geographic data impact.

As important as the physical features of our surroundings are, we must not lose sight of the fact that geography is man centered. That is, the physical geography of any given location is a determiner of man's behavior. The diet of the Eskimos is related to their environment. In man's exploration of the moon, he found that he had to transport the necessities of life with him, and because of the problem of gravity, he had to adjust his behavior to traverse the moon's surface. Man puts the environment to his use. Little or no change has taken place in the physical environmental boundaries in continental United States since 1607, but we have put our energies to work in finding different uses for it, which have affected our behavior. To be sure, we have depleted much of the nation's formerly rich soil and virgin forests, and we have polluted its beautiful streams and clear air, the results of which may drastically alter our way of life unless we reverse this trend.

A study of geography in the elementary school suggests that the emphasis be placed upon social or cultural geography—the interaction of human groups with their natural environment. This doesn't mean that physical geography is to be avoided or neglected, since certain knowledge and skills in that area are essential to the understanding of cultural geography. It does, however, raise the question as to when the skills of physical geography should be taught.

The teacher should keep in mind that geography, like the other social sciences, has certain methods and procedures for its study. The basic or inherently geographic approach to the study of geography is the regional, or as it is sometimes called, the cartographic method.[6] In this approach, "the focus is on a specific area which has some kind of homogeneity resulting from the association of areally related features." [7] Certain features selected as criteria are identified in marking out the region. Irrelevant details are ignored, but the dominant features which characterize the area are learned. These features must delimit it from other regions. Whether you select regional factors, such as, climate, main economic activities, or major relief features, the important point is that some mental judgment must enter into the selection so that understandings of the region characterize the learnings. In using the regional approach, you must recognize that a region is of no set size. The size can range from a small trading area or valley to a vast area the size of Southeast Asia. However, regardless of the size of the region which the

---

[6] *Ibid.*, p. 58.
[7] *Ibid.*

Using Data from the Social Science Disciplines

class is studying, the teacher must bear in mind the fact that *geography is man centered*. She must not become so engrossed in the physical aspects of geography that she fails to recognize that geography is primarily concerned with the earth as the home of man.

Maps are the tools of geographers, and every child can learn to use these tools. Each kind of map requires special techniques to convey a true and accurate picture of its contents. There is a wide range of map-making and map-reading concepts, techniques, and devices that will have to be learned if children are to use geography as a source of data in solving problems. These concepts range from the simple to the more complex, and their mastery cannot be expected by all children at any given grade level. The teacher will have to help children to move from one level of understanding to the other only as the concept required for mastery is grasped. An individual approach to learning these concepts and skills will be needed.

If teachers use the following generalizations to plan geographical learnings, it is important to recognize that these are not all inclusive. They have been generalized from writings of Broek: [8]

1. The natural conditions of land govern how man uses it; in turn, the use determines his behavior.
2. Man has moved from an independent, primitive way of life to an interdependent, megalopolis with vast systems of communication and transportation resulting in an "open world" concept.
3. Man's problems differ depending upon the physical environment and the way he uses it to meet his needs.
4. Certain regions of the earth have been delimited from other regions according to some predetermined criteria established through man's intellectual judgment.
5. Physical, chemical, and biological processes have interacted over the ages and continue to do so in various combinations, changing the natural features of the earth in a variety of forms.

Helping children discover geography. Geographical knowledge and skills can be taught in many interesting and creative ways. At any grade level, units which have been developed with the children will often involve information drawn from many disciplines. Of importance for the child, however, is that the curriculum provide for some sequence which is commensurate with the child's learning rate and maturity in dealing with the concepts required to understand the information. Geographical concepts do require certain levels of maturity in acquiring

---

[8] *Ibid.*, chaps. 1–6.

skills, as well as knowledge that will be meaningful if the knowledge and skills are taught in isolation. At the primary level, units can be developed around such topics as "How Men and Animals Provide Homes for Themselves;" "How Animals Care for Themselves;" and "What Physical Features of the Earth Did Man Have to Overcome to First Move to Our Community." These and other topics could be developed with the children and would prove to have high interest levels. It is easy to see that certain data related to geography would need to be collected and certain skills would have to be learned. From the data collected and the concepts learned, generalizations could be developed in many different situations. These generalizations take on increased meaning when applied in different situations; at the same time, they assist in relating one activity to another, thus developing the power of the individual to act with deeper understanding.

In the units cited above, geographical terms and concepts would come into play. Valleys, rivers, creeks, habitats, hills, weather, seasons, natural behavior, and innumerable other ideas would develop as the children progressed in their study of the topic. Map skills would be further developed as locations were investigated and terrain studied. The task would become one of helping children to see and understand the relationships that exist—the animals which live and survive in their community and their environment, the conditions which seem essential to sustain life in their community, and those which make it impossible for other animals to live there.

It is not the purpose of this section to isolate the many kinds of experiences which teachers might provide for children in geography, but to present a few ideas which might stimulate thinking. The school districts' curriculum guides may have many suggestions for each grade for teaching geographical knowledge and skills. Of importance here is the fact that geography, like the other social sciences, has a method of study which serves as a vehicle for data collecting and leads to seeking solutions to everyday problems. If, for instance, children learn to grasp the idea that they—man—have it within their power either to destroy all of mankind and leave the world to itself or to find ways to clean up our rivers and streams, clear the air of pollution, and restore the forests to hills and valleys, then life can become richer and more meaningful.

Sociology

This social science makes its contribution to the social education program through its emphasis on group life. Sociology shares many common interests with the other social sciences, but it dwells upon the study of groups—families, tribes, races, rural and city dwellers, etc. It seeks to answer questions about the effects of groups on the individual and why a group forms and stays together. Sociologists divide groups into at least five categories for analysis and study of their relationships.

Institutions: relatively permanent groups, present in almost all societies, like the family, the army, a school or an industry.

Small voluntary groups: groups more ephemeral than others, like the PTA's, bridge clubs, or political parties.

Stratified groups: groups, like castes and classes, whose members have differential amounts of whatever the society values and which, as a result, have differential amounts of power.

Relationships within and among groups: relationships such as conflicts within a political party or between political parties, or the accommodation that results when union and industry representatives sign a contract.

Relationships within and among groups as they are affected by the environment: as the effect of a rural or suburban environment on the family or the school system.[9]

As the teacher works with children in the sociological realm, she must help them to recognize that social behavior is not the result of one powerful determining force, but is the product of a complexity of forces interacting on the group. Some groups come together because of the mutual dependence which is fundamental in modern society. There is a multiplicity of occupational groups in modern society, each dependent upon the other—teachers, doctors, civil servants, garbage collectors, etc.

The sociologist at work. Since the sociologist is interested in social behavior, he must first delimit the area of human behavior he wishes to study. After delimiting the problem area, he will write what he knows about the area to be studied. This information may come from previous studies, in addition to data generally accepted by sociologists. After compiling this information, he will form his hypothesis or tentative prediction. His next step will be to locate a group or an area where groups reside that fit his hypothesis. Of course, he would prefer to locate two such areas, for in this way he could determine if certain local conditions affected his expected outcomes.

The next step for the sociologist will be to develop the instruments he will need to collect the data. This might be a questionnaire, interview form, field observation log, projective tests, etc. After collecting the

---

[9] Caroline B. Rose, *Sociology, the Study of Man in Society* (Columbus, Ohio: Charles E. Merrill Publishing Company, 1965), pp. 4, 5.

data, the task of analysis and interpretation becomes all important. The sociologist might call on the historian for help in finding out if comparative studies based on historical materials substantiate his theory. Remember, the sociologist is interested in being as objective as possible; he uses statistical techniques to check out objective data.

The case study procedure is another important research technique for the sociologist. When the person or group studied is representative of the group, then a reasonably generalized statement can be made concerning the whole category. Case studies are useful in tracing changes over periods of time, and they make it easier to compare phenomena.

Controlled laboratory experiments are used occasionally by the sociologist, but there are more risks in generalizing from such experiments than from case studies, since too many other factors may enter into laboratory experiments. The group in the laboratory may not be representative of the group outside the laboratory, so there are inherent dangers in such experimental efforts. Perhaps two of the more important points which you need to be aware of are that new research techniques and new ways of refining predictive techniques are being sought. The task is to put order into observed human behavior, so that an understanding of how it was caused can become clear.

The sociologist is concerned with both the individual and groups. He continues to seek ways to understand what goes on in the mind of the individual through observation of his external behavior. *A culture consists of the shared meanings and values that the members of any group hold in common;* it is the result of the interaction and communication that goes on among its members. One of our concerns here is that as children undergo the socialization process, they become aware of the techniques used to collect data and form generalizations. It is in this realm that sociology serves the individual. It is easy for us to accept or reject a value without any analysis; we react emotionally. Conflicting values within a group must be reconciled. Therefore, a country which has many groups, each with its own values and learnings, can expect that social change will be inevitable.

Helping children discover sociology. Whether consciously or unconsciously, children and teachers deal with sociology in the elementary school curriculum. While there is no graded sequence of sociological curriculum defined for use in elementary schools, there are certain concepts and generalizations which are useful in forming a basis for study. Such topics for study by primary children have been found in many curriculum guides. As early as 1943, the Virginia "Course of Study for Elementary Schools" pointed out for study such topics as

"The Families of a Community Can Improve Living Conditions by Cooperating;" "Members of Our Community Depend Upon Each Other for Many Things;" and "Discovery and Invention Change the Forms of Social Life." Such topics help the child to become aware of the sociologist and how he works. Community and school groups, organized for helping other groups, can be studied and analyzed for the values these groups hold and the reasons why the groups stay together. Children can explore the values held by some of these groups and suggest what happens when there is conflict between individuals in the groups concerning values. The point here is that as the teacher approaches the new social science program, she helps the children to know the procedures for study available to them and the contributions of the sociologist, as a social scientist, to improving our way of life.

Certainly, many areas of study for each grade level can be derived from the five major statements presented here:

1. Man is a social animal who lives always in groups. He may belong to a variety of groups, each of which can be differentiated by its structure.
2. Society exists in the minds of its members and occurs only when there is communication or interaction among those members. The mere groups or aggregating of people does not produce a society.
3. Man is a flexible, becoming creature. Through the socialization process, he can learn approved ways of behaving in a variety of societies.
4. The interdependence of groups in a complex contemporary society serves as a bond which holds that society together.
5. Every group is a complex of roles. Group members perform given roles and have some understanding of the expectations associated with those roles. As a member of various groups, a person may learn and assume different roles during a particular period in his life and at various stages in his development and maturation.[10]

As the elementary schools make more use of sociological materials, it is hoped that children will gain deeper insights into the problems they face in their society. As they acquire skills and knowledge relevant to social living, it is hoped that they will work toward the alleviation of social problems which are a blight on our culture.

---

[10] Muessig and Rogers, "Suggested Methods for Teachers," in *Sociology, the Study of Man in Society*, by Caroline B. Rose (Columbus, Ohio: Charles E. Merrill Publishing Company, 1965), pp. 63–93.

Anthropology

A relatively new social science, anthropology, has been defined in a broad sense as "the study of man and his works." [11] Anthropologists are are interested in the similarities, biological and social, of various human groups. They seek to find how modern man became the creature he is. The anthropologist has proven that men are physically more alike than different, regardless of the different continents and regions they inhabit. This science has generally two main divisions, physical and cultural (or social).

Since the eighteenth century, man has classified animals and plants and listed himself among the animals. This resulted in the study of the physical aspects of man as a branch of natural science. Man then was studied as one aspect of biological anthropology. Recent developments in the science of genetics have changed the study of racial classifications from the cataloging of traits to an exciting search for patterns in genetic inheritance of blood types, resistance to diseases, and biological adaptation to world climates.[12]

Cultural anthropology is concerned with the human pattern of life or socially learned patterns of behavior based on symbolic processes. A study of the whole range of human behavior patterns is the source of discovering principles of culture and social systems. Very early in life, children become fascinated by some of the books they read about Indian culture, lost continents, explorations in Africa, and the exotic South Sea islands people. Such interests in the different and unusual among people and cultures have led to scientific study by the anthropologists.

The very interests of the anthropologist in the culture and subculture of man takes him into the field to seek information. Since he must collect data firsthand, travel to the sources of the data becomes a favorite activity. The data he collects from the field and the work he does in the library then require vast amounts of time for analyzing and writing the findings. Observation becomes a very important research technique. In addition, the anthropologist uses interviewing as a means of gathering data. These two techniques must be carefully developed in order to render objective data. In more recent research, such aides as recording devices, photography, X-ray, and sound spectrographs have all assisted in the accuracy of the research. The point here is that efforts are being made by anthropologists to become more scientific, thus adding more validity to their findings.

---

[11] Pertti J. Pelto, *The Study of Anthropology* (Columbus, Ohio: Charles E. Merrill Publishing Company, 1965), p. 1.
[12] *Ibid.*, p. 2.

Helping children discover anthropology. The interest of children in folklore, strange customs, exotic people, etc., makes it relatively easy to use this behavioral science as a means of helping children understand the world. Perhaps children might study man around the world to determine if his needs are similar, even though his culture is different. That is, as problems in the immediate environment are studied, the work and techniques of the anthropologists become known to the children.

Muessig and Rogers point out eight teachable ideas about anthropology which might be considered as guides for curriculum:

1. It appears that humans everywhere shape their behavior in response to the same fundamental human problems and needs.
2. Practically all important differences in human behavior are understandable as variations in learned patterns of social behavior —not differences in biological apparatus, type of blood, or any other genetically inherited mechanism.
3. Every society has regular patterns of behavior that make it possible for individuals to predict each other's behavior and to act accordingly.
4. Man's perceptions of his experiences are strongly influenced by his cultural heritage; and he tends to view his own way of life as the most reasonable and natural.
5. Every human cultural system is logical and coherent in its own terms, given the basic assumptions and knowledge available to the specific community.
6. Man has the capacity to adopt, adapt, and reconstitute present and past ideas, beliefs, and inventions of others who are living or dead.
7. Every cultural system is composed of an interconnected network of behavioral patterns; no system is ever completely static: changes in one area generally lead to alterations in other segments of the system.
8. Personal perceptions, predispositions, and values complicate man's study of man.[13]

Using the above guides as a means of shaping the social science curriculum should lead to opening the doors for children to gain a better understanding of man and all of his complexities.

Economics

There are numerous definitions of economics, but the one preferred here is "...the science which studies behavior as the relationship

---

[13] Muessig and Rogers, "Suggested Methods for Teaching," in *The Study of Anthropology,* by Pertti J. Pelto (Columbus, Ohio: Charles E. Merrill Publishing Company, 1965), pp. 81–111.

between ends and scarce means with alternative uses." [14] This definition takes into consideration that when a thing is scarce, whether it be goods or services, then man is faced with making alternative decisions. Thus, in the act of choice that is economizing, Richard Martin and Reuben Miller point out that if life were just a matter of staying alive on bare subsistence, then no economizing would be required.[15] Man's wants are not limited to his physical needs alone. In this civilization, science has been harnessed to control and improve the conditions under which we live, and new wants have been generated faster than we can satisfy them. Only if Americans were willing to live on the same level of life as simple peasantry could all our wants be satisfied with about one hour of labor per day.

However, under conditions of scarcity we satisfy our wants through income, because the things we want must be paid for. Thus, the real cost of the goods is not the money we spend for them, but doing without the alternative goods and services the money could have purchased. Such alternatives include leisure time, which is paid for by reduced money incomes. So, it is easy to see that the choices which must be made in earning and spending money determine the amounts of resources used as well as the specific goods consumed.

In many fundamental respects, all economic systems have common elements. Men who make their livings together must establish and maintain a set of man-made arrangements to supply answers to the basic questions posed by the problem of scarcity. Every economy must supply answers to basic questions, in terms of which the system is organized.

1. What commodities shall be produced and in what quantities?
2. How shall the goods be produced?
3. For whom shall the goods be produced?

Answers to these and still other questions are part of a pattern system that is adopted by the society; thus, each economic system produces its own answers to these questions.

Helping children discover economics. Obviously, the brief discussion about the study of economics must have at its base the decision-making process. A system based on selecting alternatives leaves much responsi-

---

[14] Lionel Robbins, *An Essay on the Nature and Significance of Economic Science,* 2nd ed. (London: The Macmillan Company, 1937), p. 16.
[15] Richard J. Martin and Reuben G. Miller, *Economics and Its Significance* (Columbus, Ohio: Charles E. Merrill Publishing Company, 1965), p. 6.

Using Data from the Social Science Disciplines 147

bility to its citizens. Children must examine the values involved in selecting alternatives to the act of choice when wants and needs are related to scarcity.

Much has been done in the field of economic education to provide curriculum concepts for children in the elementary school. In the past decade, materials have been developed at virtually every grade level for use with children in helping them to understand our nation's economic system. But the emphasis is the same here as it has been throughout this book: children must experience inquiry-oriented learnings if the learnings become a part of the learner. It is easy for a child to memorize a generalization, such as, "Machine production tends to increase the interdependence of groups." But does the child understand all the implications of such a generalization? This area of study needs to have the child collect data concerning machine production and its affect on various groups. As data are collected and as the child forms his own generalization, the learning becomes a part of him. Of importance to the teacher's activities is the ability to help the child secure data and to know the limitations of forming generalizations without sufficient data.

In the realm of values, children could study the whole area of family income. They could examine the premise that prices help families decide which goods and services to buy and which to do without. Such a study might raise questions concerning how people spend their incomes. What families' differences are, as when grocery shopping. What are bad choices? What are good choices? Why are choices considered good or bad? A study of the family also brings into play the concept of division of labor. Here it is easy to see the need for a division of labor, as well as a need for specialization.

The elementary school, at all levels, provides excellent opportunities for including economics with science, health, or many other curriculum areas. For example, when studying natural resources, we cannot avoid discussing their scarcity. In addition, the interrelationship of resource allocation and the processes of production, distribution, and consumption becomes an important subject for inquiry. Many topics, such as, competition and cooperation, provide an opportunity to introduce and to have children explore economics; the private enterprise system; social systems within our system, as well as those outside; savings and investments; functions of supply and demand; etc. While it is not the purpose here to delineate an economics curriculum, the area is pregnant with ideas. Economics must become a vital aspect of the social inquiry process and an important aspect of the social science education program.

Five generalizations have been drawn by Muessig and Rogers which seem appropriate here as guides in examining the economic aspects of the social science curriculum:

1. Every society has some kind of economic system. This pattern of arrangements involves the production, distribution, and use of goods and services and reflects the values and objectives of the particular society.
2. All economic systems are confronted by the problem of relative scarcity of unlimited wants and limited resources.
3. Economic conditions and systems change over a period of time.
4. Every economic system possesses regularities which make certain forms of prediction possible.
5. In a modern complex economic system, individuals are dependent upon others for the satisfaction of many of their needs and wants.[16]

It should be kept in mind that in the final analysis it is the teacher who is the curriculum maker and that the suggestions here are for her use in formulating some very basic concepts concerning economics and the part it plays in the total social science education program.

Political science

Perhaps no area of the curriculum is more misunderstood than that of political science. The basic connotation most teachers would denote is, "It is fine for the high school or college student, but we can't deal with political science concepts in the elementary school." Either consciously or unconsciously, we do deal with many of these concepts at all levels of formal education. The goals or policies carried out by our neighbors in Canada and South America or the attitudes and policies of the developing nations of Africa affect political decisions of the United States, as well as the feelings or emotions of the citizens of this country. A study of political science provides us the opportunity to understand the fundamental nature of the political processes which become even more significant in a world which is facing rapid changes leading to increasing interdependence.[17]

There are many approaches to political science. Some authorities approach it as a study of the complex processes and institutions which make "the authoritative allocations of values in society,"[18] while for others, this allocative system can be better understood by examining

---

[16] Muessig and Rogers, "Suggested Methods for Teachers," in *Economics and Its Significance* by Richard S. Martin and Reuben G. Miller (Columbus, Ohio: Charles E. Merrill Publishing Company), chap. 7.

[17] Francis J. Sorauf, *Political Science: An Informal Overview* (Columbus, Ohio: Charles E. Merrill Publishing Company, 1965), p. vii.

[18] David Easton, *The Political System* (New York: Alfred A. Knopf, Inc., 1953), chap. 5.

Using Data from the Social Science Disciplines

the power and influence of participants in it, by examining the ability of people to affect the allocation.[19]

The concern of this aspect of social science ranges from the individual's political interest and awareness to the complex operation of the large political institutions. Decision making in the specific political system and the processes and influences which bring about decisions made by the elected are major concerns. Political science, as practiced and professed in this country, studies the political system of the U.S. and examines it from the following four perspectives:

1. It studies the processes of behavior and institutions of political systems in order to make systematic generalizations and explanations about the political.
2. It seeks generalizations about relations among political systems, especially the politics of nations in the international system.
3. It studies the end products, the public policies, of the political processes.
4. It studies, finally, ideas and doctrines about government and the political, ideas such as the concepts of and justifications for democracy, justice, and equity.[20]

Political science can readily be classified among the behavioral sciences. It draws from the concepts and techniques found in psychology and sociology, and its new concern evolves around the individual and small group behavior. The tools of political science are similar to those of other behavioral sciences; thus, they are of importance to teachers as they involve children in the inquiry process to seek knowledge about political problems. These methods and techniques of collecting data are drawn from sources such as newspapers, government reports, personal accounts, correspondence, diaries, memoirs, official state papers, etc. But, on the other hand, certain data must be collected from observation, interviews, questionnaires, etc. Thus, the kind of data one wants dictates the method or technique of collecting it. Since raw data is of little value and since the political scientist is interested in the development of generalizations and theories about political behavior and political systems, plans for careful analyses of data become extremely important. Relationships between two sets of data must be established; thus the political scientist uses statistics to become more precise in analyzing data.

---

[19] Harold Lasswell, *Politics: Who Gets What, When and How* (New York: McGraw-Hill Book Company, 1963), p. 39.

[20] Sorauf, p. 7.

Making children aware of political science. Children often come to school with notions of their family politics, just as they do their church preference. For example, they might say, "My father is a Democrat," but have little or no understanding of the meaning of this statement. Children can become involved in issues with such questions as "What might our community be like without any laws?" Inquiry might be approached from simple research questions which can be conducted in the community, but which will lead to providing insights to the decision-making process (or the lack of it) of citizens in operation.

As you look for the place of political science in the schools, you might want to look at the following statements developed by Muessig and Rogers; they could help to bring about a more meaningful approach to the subject:

1. As minimum conditions for its existence, a society establishes authoritative institutions that can make decisions which are binding on all the people, provide for the resolution of dissent, and effectively enforce basic rules.
2. The larger society is, the more an individual must rely upon group membership and representation to achieve his aims. By working with others he is able to increase his strength of his voice and improve the chances that his wishes will be made known to those in decision-making positions.
3. The nature of a given society's political system and the nature of its political behavior are closely related to the fundamental system of values to which the society adheres.
4. Political ideals, values, attitudes, and institutions develop and change over time.
5. In every society, individuals and groups disagree over some societal goals and directions, over how aims will be achieved, and over the enforcement of standards of behavior.[21]

Summary

It becomes apparent that each discipline within the social sciences plays an important role in the elementary school and in helping to achieve the objectives of a modern social science education program. The modes of data collecting, the techniques and methods of studying the disciplines, and the skills and competencies needed to fulfill citizenship in a democracy become more complex as the world "shrinks" in size and as

---

[21] Muessig and Rogers, "Suggested Methods for Teachers," in *Political Science* by Francis J. Sorauf (Columbus, Ohio: Charles E. Merrill Publishing Company, 1965), pp. 75–109.

the population continues to expand. Decision making is one important aspect of active citizenry, but decisions must be based in the best available data, and this we must help children to find through acquiring competency in the inquiry process.

Suggested Problems and Projects

1. Examine at least six series of elementary school social science textbooks in grades 4–6 to determine through an analysis the percentage of concepts dealing with history, economics, geography, sociology, anthropology, and political science. Discuss with your classmates the imbalances found in time and space devoted to the various social sciences. Why do these imbalances exist? What can the teacher do to correct this situation in the elementary school?

2. Each discipline purports to have its own research techniques. After pursuing study in basic references for each of the social sciences, can you develop, in general form, research techniques that could be used by primary children? By intermediate grade children? Compare your research form with those developed by other members of your class. Form groups and see how many usable forms of research procedures emerge which can be justified for elementary school use.

3. What safeguards must a teacher use to see that children value each of the social sciences, even though they are not exact sciences? Form teams and debate this issue.

Related Readings

Easton, David, *The Political System,* chapters 1, 2, 3. New York: Alfred Knopf, Inc., 1953.

Muessig, Raymond H. and Rogers, Vincent R. *Charles Merrill Social Science Seminar Series* (Anthropology, Economics, Georgraphy, History, Political Science, and Sociology). Columbus, Ohio: Charles E. Merrill Publishing Company, 1965.

The American Council of Learned Societies and the National Council for the Social Studies. *The Social Studies and the Social Sciences.* New York: Harcourt, Brace & World, Inc., 1962.

4

CONCEPTS
    Where are concepts found?
    What is the relationship between overt behavior and concept development?
    How do conceptualization and content relate?
    Are there several types of concepts?
    Which concepts should be developed?

GENERALIZATIONS
    How are generalizations useful?

TEACHING FOR CONCEPT DEVELOPMENT
    Taba Curriculum
    Clark County Guide Generalization Statements
    The Eugene, Oregon, Guide and Generalizations?

FACTORS OF PLACEMENT
    Are there levels of concepts and generalizations?
    What is a developmental view?
    A suggested approach to the concept of economic system
    Political science concepts and generalizations
    Early experiences with history concepts
    What is the place of map concepts and skills?
    Guidelines for developing map concepts and skills
    Special considerations in map work

SUGGESTED PROBLEMS AND PROJECTS

RELATED READINGS

Conceptualizing and Generalizing

"I wanted to be certain that the pupils had mastery of the important economic concepts, so I had them memorize them all."

"Thank goodness, we are finished with the concept of culture. I thought the children never would get it. I'm not even sure that I do."

"I really don't worry too much about all these concepts. What it really boils down to is teaching the facts anyway. If the pupils know the facts I figure that the concepts will take care of themselves."

Concepts

Now would be a good time to suggest that you retrieve your psychology textbook and refresh your concept of concept, but, to save time, and because we fear that you might not follow our suggestion, we shall attempt a brief review. A concept is, from an educational and psychological point of view, a mental construct, the organization of our perceptions to such an extent that we establish relationships and explanations for the phenomena and objects of our perception. Needless to say, the concepts that we develop may be near to a correct representation of the phenomena that we have perceived or our concepts may be weak or completely at odds with reality. The ancient tale of the three blind men attempting to arrive at a concept of elephant points up a very common problem which results from limited perceptions where only one part of a reality is experienced. The manners in which the blind men attempted to verbalize their concepts of elephants are examples of the way in which "new" concepts are shaped by concepts already possessed.

At this very moment, we are faced with a basic difficulty in dealing with concepts, since we are forced to rely on printed symbols to communicate to you our concepts. This is the difficulty which may lead us to ask children to list three economic concepts as evidence that they have conceptualized about certain economic phenomena. It would seem a plausible hypothesis that centuries of educational practice, which considered verbal recall of words and phrases as evidence of learning, have left us reluctant to change our teaching practices to coincide with the principles of learning suggested by psychology.

In the social realm, the concepts which we hope to develop frequently deal with abstract social relationship, attitudes, and institutions. It is one thing to deal with the concept of water, with respect to its chemical properties, and quite another matter to deal with the concept of water as a cause of human conflict.

Where are concepts found?

They really aren't found anywhere. They are completely personal, the property of the individual who formulates his own endless array of concepts. It is, of course, incorrect to believe that you will find concepts in a book or even in the world of things and actions. However, you will find the symbols which give rise to recall of perceptions and to your organization of percepts into the mental property that is called concept.

Inasmuch as we are concerned with a rational approach to social education, it is necessary to direct our attention to those situations in human society which we believe are deserving of conceptual development by the child. It is our judgment that there are certain conditions and possibilities in human affairs that deserve careful investigation as part of a calculated educational effort to promote concept development. As is the case with any measurement of intelligence, we can only draw inference from an assortment of pupil behaviors to indicate how accurately and extensively the child is conceptualizing. The child cannot write a concept on paper. A word or phrase that suggests a concept to you is not the best evidence that you can get concerning the child's conceptualization.

The fact that concept development is an abstract process should not deter us from our concern for this mental function which seems to separate man from other animals. It does require that we not succumb to verbalism in an effort to satisfy our desire for some kind of definite evidence that the child is learning. After all, you might think, you would prefer to have a child show you that he can write *scarcity* and *demand* when asked to name two economic concepts. To determine that he has conceptualized about these real phenomena of human life may be an overwhelming challenge.

What is the relationship between overt behavior and concept development?

The behavior of conscious, sane people is thought to rise from their concepts about a given situation, and their actions are in accord with the way they understand a situation and their relation to it. At a cocktail

Conceptualizing and Generalizing 155

party, people may express themselves with respect to the low level of concern that one man holds for another, yet when one of these persons perceives a person lying helpless on a city sidewalk, his concept of human responsibility may or may not lead him to give assistance to the victim. Competing concepts about personal safety and about people who lie on sidewalks may direct the person's behavior in this situation.

Visible behaviors are believed to offer evidence of the conceptualization that has occurred about a specific thing or situation. The appropriateness of the child's behavior in a particular situation will offer clues as to the adequacy of his concept and, in the teaching situation, may suggest that the child needs to have more experiences to extend the concept that he appears to possess.

Verbalizing behavior, as an avenue to evaluating the nature and extent of concept development, should not be disregarded, but the one word or one phrase expression of the symbol that is used to *talk* about a concept should be avoided in favor of analytic and interpretive discourse about situations which involve certain concepts. More will be said about behaviors and evaluation in a later chapter.

Conceptualization is open-ended. Concept development is an ongoing process by which the individual continues to modify and extend his concepts. To the extent that new experiences suggest new relationships between things and situations, a particular concept is changed. Viewed in this light, the teacher will not plan to *cover* a given number of concepts in a school year, nor will the sixth level teacher assume that any specific concepts have been dispensed with by the fifth level teacher. The tendency of teachers and parents to seek absolute results is out of place where concept development is concerned. Rather, the aim should be toward the refinement of the perceiving process, which would enable the individual to be active and effective in a lifelong quest for the rich meanings that life and the universe holds.

How do conceptualization and content relate?

You may be inclined to believe that we have overplayed the abstract, highly personal nature of the conceptualizing process, but our experience has led us to err on the side of too much attention, rather than too little. Now, with respect to the relationships between concept development and the use of content, it is again considered necessary to emphasize the obvious.

The content of any planned learning experience includes the teaching strategies and the pupil activities, as well as the data which have been selected because of their potential for fostering concept development by the children. Content, which traditionally has been used to mean textbook material, has been the focal point of older social studies programs, although it was difficult to see direct relationships between the content taught and the variety of aims that were held for social studies. Social science education requires that a serious effort be made to select concept development experiences which are, indeed, related to our objectives and to direct, accordingly, our investigative activities to bodies of information that hold good prospects for concept development. It is not reasonable to guide the child through masses of information which have been assembled with no reference in mind other than chronology or location on the earth.

If we believe that accurate conceptualization about a variety of recurring problems and conditions will support intelligent behavior, then it seems grossly negligent to leave the child to roam through reams of subject matter in quest of some related meanings. Content is essential, but it is essential only as one part of the concept development process, and it must be organized to suit the needs of the learning experience. It is not self-justifying. (Should children read about George Washington's boyhood in order that they may learn what it means to be a good citizen; in attempting to extend a concept of citizenship, do we consider the way in which historical material can be useful?)

Are there several types of concepts?

If by this we wonder if the human "intellect" proceeds in various ways in its conceptualizing efforts, we cannot offer an answer. Several suggestions have been made about *concepts,* but they are, in reality, suggestions about information and situations which seem to differ. For example, John Mallan has found it helpful to use the terms *descriptive concept* and *process concept,*[1] while Joyce and others have used the term *organizing concepts.*[2] Herbert Blumer has referred to *common sense concepts* and *scientific concepts.*[3] It is the opinion of the authors that Blumer was really referring to the likely limitations of concepts which are formulated as an outcome of random perceptions of events, a defect in the search for meaning, and a miscarriage of the inquiry process.

Mallan uses *descriptive concept* to denote what we may call facts, which, in and of themselves, take you nowhere. He cites July 4, 1776, as an example, maintaining that it has no transfer value to other human situations in time and space. *Revolution,* on the other hand, is a cue

---

[1] John T. Mallan, *Conceptual Frameworks for Social Science Education* (Athens, Ohio: Cooperative Center for Social Science Education, Ohio University, 1967).

[2] Bruce Joyce, *Strategies for Elementary Social Science Education* (Chicago: Science Research Associates, Inc., 1965).

[3] Herbert Blumer, "Science Without Concepts," *American Journal of Sociology* 36 (January 1931).

Conceptualizing and Generalizing 157

word to a *process concept;* it has possibilities for extension and application in human affairs over the years and from one society to another. Names of people and dates are not promising data from which to build process concepts, according to Mallan.

Which concepts should be developed?

The selection of specific aspects of human activities for formal study is determined by the nature of the conceptualizing that you hope will occur. If your choices and those of the local curriculum development groups are designed to bring the child into contact with a broad range of human experiences which have been of continuing concern and are filled with relevance, the prospects for the development of many related concepts are enhanced.

Roy Price and others at Syracuse University extracted 34 concepts from the several social science disciplines. Their selections were based upon *scope* and *uniqueness*. By scope, they meant the extent to which a particular concept was useful in more than one discipline, and by uniqueness, they meant the position of a concept in only one discipline. So it was that Price and his colleagues identified the following list of concepts. Let us look at those that may be helpful in thinking about concept development:

1. Sovereignty of the nation-state
2. Conflict
3. Industrialization-urbanization
4. Secularization
5. Compromise
6. Comparative advantage
7. Power
8. Morality and choice
9. Scarcity
10. Input and output
11. Saving
12. Modified market economy
13. Habitat
14. Institution
15. Culture
16. Social change
17. Social control
18. Interaction [4]

---

[4] Roy Price, Warren Hickman and Gerald Smith, *Major Concepts for Social Studies* (Syracuse, New York: Syracuse University, 1965).

At this point, it is suggested that the class organize into groups of four or five for the purpose of identifying some of the human problems, relationships, and experiences which you and your fellow students believe should be considered by children sometime during the elementary school years. Then, refer back to the Syracuse list to see whether your choices seem to relate to the concepts included in that list.

Critical observation. It should be stated that the Syracuse project involved specialists from several of the social sciences and that each of them may have had a number of additional items that are included in any one discipline. There was no effort made to identify the Syracuse list as a basis for a total curriculum, nor to arrange the items for sequential study at various age levels. Professor Price has observed that the discipline specialists have not arrived at the point of developing a structure for social studies. His implication that the discipline scholars *should* do this is inappropriate, we believe. It is our position that people who study children and who work with the problems of education at the school level must, of necessity, be heavily involved in decisions as to the structuring and organizing of social education for children and youth.[5] Professor Price's position is somewhat like Lawrence Senesh's call for a "grand orchestration" of the social science disciplines with an array of "soloists" from the disciplines moving across the curricular stage.[6] In the last analysis, however, the teacher(s) with the children provide the interdisciplinary orchestration, and in the task of curriculum planning and development, the educator-teacher is an essential member of the team.

Generalizations

How are generalizations useful?

It is not uncommon to find some authors and teachers using the terms *concept* and *generalization* interchangeably, as though they were synonymous. *Generalizations* are derived from concepts and suggest the develment of relationship among several concepts and the transfer and application of concepts to new situations. Generalizations are, according to David H. Russell, verbal formulations and expressions of the relationships that one sees among concepts, and they may be used as rules, principles, and conclusions.[7] Let us consider several generalizations:

---

[5] *Ibid.*
[6] From an address by Lawrence Senesh at Ohio University (November 1967).
[7] David H. Russell, *Children's Thinking* (New York: Ginn and Company, 1956).

Conceptualizing and Generalizing

All social groups develop ways of dealing with strife and dissension.

Customs of a social group will be modified as the group members come into close contact with members of other groups.

People migrate from one situation to another, not to find a new way of life, but to find an environment where they can pursue their most highly valued group goals.

Refer to the Syracuse list and see which concepts are being related in each of these generalizations. Keep in mind that *generalizations,* like *concepts,* are personal to each individual. Although *generalizations* may be verbalized, they come from organizing and relating what you think (conceptualize) about your percepts. It is not particularly helpful to have children repeat or write down the generalizations that you are concerned with as you plan a learning activity. In fact, the ability to quickly memorize a list of generalizations probably cuts short the child's thought processes. If your goal for children is conceptualizing and generalizing, you must not allow rote learning to be the basis for evaluation and reward of the pupils.

Generalizations and statements about concepts are primarily useful to the teacher in her planning. Children should be encouraged to say what *they* think about the topic they study. Their verbal statements will provide evidence of their conceptualizing-generalizing processes, but this will not be true if the name of the game is, "Say it just the way the teacher would say it herself."

How many generalizations are there? How many generalizations will be drawn by the pupils in your room next year? How will you ever know? A number of efforts have been made to identify the "important generalizations" which should receive the attention of teachers. Neal Billings compiled a list of 880 generalizations drawn from a number of books by recognized social scientists.[8] In a later study directed by Paul Hanna, a myriad of generalizations and values within ten categories of behavior common to all cultures was identified:

1. Production of goods and services
2. Distribution of goods and services
4. Consuming and using
5. Communication
6. Conserving human and natural resources
7. Education
8. Recreation

---

[8] Neal A. Billings, *A Determination of Generalizations Basic to the Social Studies Curriculum* (Baltimore: Warwick and York, 1929).

9. Government
10. Esthetics and religion [9]

Social Science Seminar Series. A recent useful reference set is provided in the Merrill Social Science Seminar Series, which devotes one book to each of the social science disciplines. In this series, generalizations are identified by discipline area, although many of them could be related to several disciplines. The generalizations from this series were presented in the preceding chapter; it is suggested that you examine them in connection with your work on this chapter.

Generalizations as focal points. Generalizations are useful in providing focal points for the organization, implementation, and evaluation of learning activities. At the outset, a particular generalization or set of related generalizations is selected because it suggests the nature and kind of *conceptualizing* activity that you want to promote. Accordingly, generalizations suggest the vehicles that will be most appropriate, that is, the materials and activities that will be valuable in eliciting conceptualizing processes from the children. In evaluation of child progress, as well as in assessment of the strength of the selected vehicles and teaching strategies, generalizations provide points of reference and emphasis.

Teaching for Concept Development

The practice of putting old wine in new bottles is not limited to the grape industry. Teachers who are asked to use curriculum guides that focus upon concept development and generalizing skills may continue to teach for the memorization and recall of isolated bits of information. We mention this before we provide examples from curriculum guides to show the contrast between information- and concept-centered approaches.

Taba Curriculum

The Contra Costa Social Studies Project materials, developed under the leadership of the late Hilda Taba, organized the learning program around "main ideas," which are, in fact, statements of generalizations. Some examples follow:

---

[9] Paul R. Hanna, "Generalizations and Universal Values—Their Implications for The Social Studies Program," *Social Studies in the Elementary School,* 56th Yearbook of the National Society for the Study of Education, Part II (Chicago: University of Chicago Press 1957), p. 46.

GRADE I UNIT I

MAIN IDEA: THE SOCIALIZATION OF CHILDREN TAKES PLACE PRIMARILY WITHIN FAMILY, EDUCATIONAL, AND RELIGIOUS INSTITUTIONS.

Organizing Idea:	Children learn from their parents, friends, teachers, and ministers (or priest, rabbi, guru, etc.).

Contributing Idea:
Content Samples:
	1. Children learn in a variety of ways.
	Observing a child:
	  Being told
	  Being rewarded and punished

Contributing Idea: Content Samples:	2. Children differ in their feelings about what they are being taught. What is hard or easy? What do children expect to learn at school?
Contributing Idea: Content Samples:	3. Children learn rules of behavior for different times and places from a variety of people. At church or in the synagogue On the playground In the classroom During fire drill
Contributing Idea: Content Samples:	4. Children learn a variety of skills and knowledge from a variety of people. Symbols for rules—from teachers and parents or other adults Symbols of the country—from teachers and parents or other adults How to make friends—from boys and girls How to read, etc.—from teachers How to talk, walk, etc.—from parents or other adults

GRADE II UNIT I

MAIN IDEA: COMMUNITY NEEDS ARE MET BY GROUPS OF PEOPLE ENGAGED IN MANY RELATED ACTIVITIES.

Organizing Idea:	Some groups of workers make goods people need; others do work that is needed by other workers or by the people who live in the community

Contributing Idea:	1.	Services generally require a place, workers, equipment, and other services.
Content Samples:		Workers at the supermarket Truck drivers Gas station attendants Etc.
Contributing Idea:	2.	Most workers are members of a team of workers.
Content Samples:		Workers at the supermarket Truck drivers Gas station attendants Etc.
Contributing Idea:	3.	People who produce goods require raw materials, workers, a place, equipment, and other services.
Content Samples:		Baker Dairy worker Etc.
Contributing Idea:	4.	Change takes place in the kinds of goods and services that are produced and in the way they are produced.
Content Samples:		Fire Department Food processing Etc.

GRADE VI UNIT V

MAIN IDEA: CHANGES THAT OCCUR IN ONE PART OF A SOCIETY OFTEN PRODUCE CHANGES IN OTHER PARTS OF THE SOCIETY.

Organizing Ideas:		Technological changes in Middle and South America have brought about many changes in other aspects of the society.
Contributing Idea:	1.	Change in the economy may affect change in other institutions.
Content Samples:		Industry Farming Education
Contributing Idea:	2.	Change may be both planned and unplanned.
Content Samples:		Growth of the middle class Organizations dealing with health, education, food. Changes in Puerto Rico—Mexican Revolution

Conceptualizing and Generalizing

Contributing Ideas: 3. Many people in a society oppose change.[10]

Clark County Guide Generalization Statements

In this excerpt from the Clark County, Nevada, Guide for Social Science Education, you can see how each statement is related to concepts, sub-concepts, and behavioral objectives:

1. *Generalization*
   Each culture tends to view its physical habitat differently. A society's values, goals, organization, and level of development determine which elements of the land are prized and used.
2. *Concepts*
   Habitat and its significance
   Empathy
   Causation
3. *Sub-concepts*
   Man affects and is affected by his natural environment.
   Habitat is the resource of man's society.
   Habitat is the resource base of man's society.
   Rituals and ceremonies may be related to physical environment.
4. *Behavioral Objectives*
   The student will draw a sketch of the kind of shelter he would build for himself in a windy climate.
   The student will describe the causes of the dust bowl of the American plains and tell what was done to remedy the situation.[11]

Can you differentiate readily between the statement of generalization and the sub-concepts? Bear in mind that one definition of generalization is that it is a statement which expresses the application of a concept in actual social operations.

The Eugene, Oregon, Guide and Generalizations

Another example of the use of generalization statements in curriculum guides is provided from the Eugene, Oregon, Guide.[12] Notice the relationship between generalization, theme, teaching strategies, and objectives.

---

[10] *The Taba Curriculum Development Project in Social Studies,* final report of project number 5–1314, Office of Education grant number 6–10–182 (Menlo Park, Calif.: Addison-Wesley Publishing Co., 1969).

[11] Used by permission of Clark County, Nevada, Public Schools, 1970.

[12] Used by permission of Eugene, Oregon, Public Schools, District No. 4J, Lane County, 1968.

CHART 4-1. Eugene, Oregon, Guide

Theme: Social problems and social change.
Generalization: Man is a social animal who lives in groups. He may belong to several groups, each of which can be differentiated by its structure.

Objectives	Teaching Strategies
Concept to develop—Intergroup relation may be complicated by prejudice.	Suggested approaches to developing understanding of prejudice which may lead to discrimination.
	Read the story, "The Stranger Who Came to Town."
	1. Why was the Duvitch family not accepted on Syringa Street?
The student formulates an hypothesis to explain a problem.	2. List the ways in which they are different.
	3. What tie did the mother see between herself and Mrs. Duvitch?
	4. Why did the boys sabotage the Duvitch family fishing trip?
The student makes critical judgments to test hypothesis.	Extended discussion:
	1. What uncomplimentary names have you been called which indicate that members of a group did not like you?
	2. What was your reaction?
	3. What other expression of unfounded dislike or prejudice have you suffered?
The student examines social attitudes and data.	4. What prejudices have you? Are they based on differences in social values or lack of communication?

164

Factors of Placement

Although Jerome Bruner's observation that any concept can be developed at any age level, if the elements are projected within a context that is familiar to the learner, is often quoted, the fact remains that decisions must be made with respect to the placement of certain learning activities. Since our ultimate concerns are with conceptualizing and generalizing, we must consider which concepts and generalizations are nearest to the child's life reference and, consequently, hold highest potential for development and extension.

Are there levels of concepts and generalizations?

One needs only to observe and listen to children to establish that conceptualizing and generalizing occur from a very early age. We are also aware that factors of experience and maturity contribute to the complexity of the conceptualizing and generalizing process. If we follow the suggestion that concepts that have concrete representations in the real world are dealt with most readily by the child, we have a guide that can be helpful in planning for the early levels. Generalizations that can be seen in operational situations would, accordingly, be appropriate for development.

An example of this can be found in the early consideration of the concept of man as a social being. The simple question, "How does man differ from other animals?" will generate some hypotheses that can be tested in the experiences of children. The generalizations, "Man always lives in groups," and "He may belong to a variety of groups, each of which will have a different structure," are generalizations that can be developed inductively in the primary grades, without the verbal baggage.

Let us consider other sociological generalizations and ask you at what age level you would seek to develop and extend them. "A society exists in the minds of its members and occurs only when communication or interaction occurs." "Man learns to become what he is." It seems to us that these generalizations may be most readily developed at the middle levels of elementary school in conjunction with the cross-cultural learning experiences that will reveal the learned differences among men.

Interdependence as a concept has been approached typically in the early grades with admonitions to be a good group member and to help the group benefit from cooperation of its members. The examples within the scope of a child's experience seem to have the most power in establishing the concept as a basis for all kinds of generalizations in real life. How can you see this concept being approached within the ongoing classroom activity? What possible dangers do you see? Does a classroom group have its own legitimate purposes for holding itself together? What are the penalties for independence at the expense of interdependence?

The concept of *role* and its generalization into various social groups where the individual is a member may be approached at the awareness level in the primary grades. We behave in various specified ways as we assume different roles in different groups. The generalizations of the concept of role can be more richly developed in the middle and upper levels when youngsters have become active in various groups and can draw on their own experiences to extend the concept and its generalization. This will serve as a tool for understanding as they engage in cross-cultural studies.

What is a developmental view?

Let us draw from the commonly considered concepts and generalizations of economics for an example. The generalization, "Every society has some kind of economic system, with a pattern of arrangements that involves production, distribution, and use of goods and services reflective of the values and objectives of the society." Examine the preceding statement carefully and see how many separate concepts have been related in the statement. This complex statement represents a generalization of a high order, and we doubt that it will be generated below the upper elementary level. It represents a goal toward which simpler concept development moves at a deliberate pace.

Consider the concept *economic system* and how the child comes to be aware of it and finally knowledgeable about some of its aspects. Do not confuse the words that suggest the concept with the concept. In what settings is the child likely to encounter this concept in operation? How will he integrate its many features and finally generalize it to other societies and other situations?

A suggested approach to the concept of economic system

This plan for dealing with learning experiences that are designed to promote conceptualization takes as its guides the general characteristics of child development and child experience, if indeed one can generalize about either! In addition, the complexity of the concept and its generalizations are considered. What examples of learning experiences inside or outside of school will relate to this scheme?

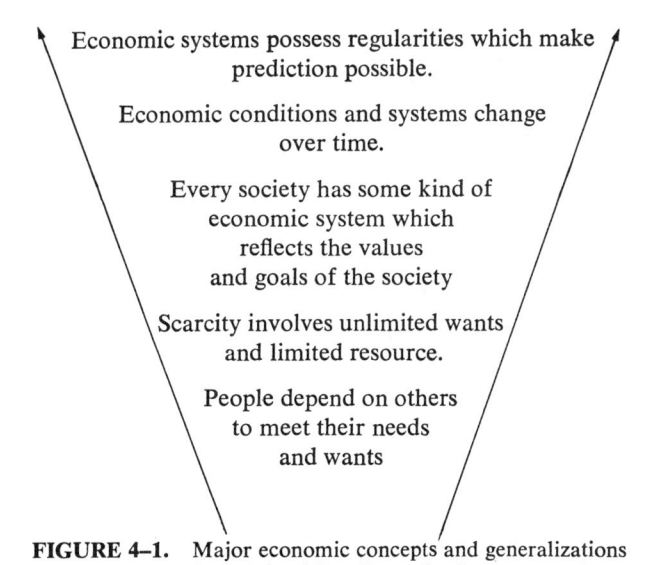

Conceptualizing and Generalizing

```
    Economic systems possess regularities which make
                  prediction possible.
        Economic conditions and systems change
                     over time.
           Every society has some kind of
             economic system which
               reflects the values
             and goals of the society
          Scarcity involves unlimited wants
                and limited resource.
             People depend on others
                to meet their needs
                    and wants
```

FIGURE 4–1. Major economic concepts and generalizations from "simple" to "complex."

Political science concepts and generalizations

Now we will present some key concept and generalization statements drawn from the political science field, ask that you consider the relative complexity of each, and that you suggest learning experiences and child life situations that provide bases for further development.

> In order to exist, every society provides for the control of its people, for the settling of conflicts and for the support of special institutions to do these things.
>
> As a society becomes larger, the individual must depend upon his membership in groups to make his wishes known to those who make decisions for the total society.
>
> The political system of every society is related to the values that the society holds concerning the role of the individual in the decision making process.
>
> Political ideals, values, attitudes, and institutions change over time.
>
> In every society, people disagree over goals, aims, and over the enforcement of behavior.[13]

---

[13] Raymond H. Muessig and Vincent R. Rogers, "Suggested Methods for Teachers," in *Political Science: An Informal Overview* by Francis J. Sorauf (Columbus, Ohio: Charles E. Merrill Publishing Company, 1965).

Early experiences with history concepts

Historical experience begins in the family setting with the awareness by the young child that some persons, who were important to his father and mother, lived at another time; that his parents were children at some point which preceded his own existence. There were events which occurred before the child joined his family, and although his stake in such events is minimal, he does come to accept them as significant forerunners of the life conditions of which he is now a part.

Senesh has suggested that the young child may be aided in conceptualizing about the time factor in history if we locate events in terms of how many "grandfathers ago" that happened, rather than referring to years, centuries, and the like. There is no evidence to support this idea, but it does have an element of familiarity denied to terms such as years. At the elementary level, it is doubtful that the child needs to be concerned with specific dates as much as with the changing circumstances of life conditions and how people dealt with the new possibilities and problems of their time.

The family-school-community base for early experiences with history offers a rich setting that is physically and psychologically near to the child. Consider the kinds of questions that may be raised to channel children's interest in the history of family, school, and community. How old is our town, village, city? When our town was very young, how did people travel about? What were the main ways of making a living in our town when it was young? What were the houses like? The stores? Has our town grown larger, remained about the same, or become smaller since it was "born?" Can we find out why? What important things have happened in our town? Did they have lasting effect on life in our town? Have any of the town's citizens become well known to the state, nation or world? When was our school built? How is it different from the first schools in our town? What was a school day like 50 years ago, or when our parents were in elementary school? How are our books different from those used long ago? How has our school been affected by recent inventions? What per cent of the town population goes to school today? How can we find out how this compares to attendance in our schools 50 years ago? How were children punished in the schools of some years ago?

Obviously, the list can be extended into many aspects of school-community life, and the types of inquiry activities are numerous. The resources are likewise unlimited if the teacher is primarily concerned with developing a base of interest in things historical. The possibility of conflicting accounts about a particular event need not be disturbing, in fact, such discrepancies provide excellent opportunities for children to encounter one of the real problems of historiography—conflicting evidence and conflicting interpretations of the meaning and significance of certain events.

One might well ask, "Why has history become so depersonalized?" "In our efforts to provide mass education, factory style, have our textbooks led us away from that part of our heritage that is local and personal toward a much more distant and abstract generalization of the American experience?" "In our age of specialization have we come to view important history and accurate history as reposing between the covers of textbooks?" The use of local resources to help the child begin to relate to the past seems to be commonly overlooked. The need for each human individual to locate his existence with reference to people and events before him has been discarded in favor of historical experiences aimed at developing a national identity. It is doubtful that a choice between one or the other needs to be made. At the elementary level, the emphasis ought to be, it seems to us, upon the personal and local dimensions of historical experience.

History Professor Robert Koehl once shocked a group of elementary teachers when he said, "The major purpose of early experiences with history should be to build and sustain the child's interest in things that happened before now—that is all—nothing more." We agree with Professor Koehl and urge that efforts be made with experiences that hold promise as interest builders and question raisers. With a background of early encounters with history, we predict a continuing interest into the high school years where inquiry will be more vigorous and genuine than we have known it to be.

What is the place of map concepts and skills?

Concept and skill are interrelated—each supports the other; the interplay is the source of continuing development of both. The understanding and ability to use maps is an excellent example of the concept—skill relationship, for without a concept of what maps are and what can be done with maps, the skill in construction and use of maps can be no more than a mimicking exercise.

In addition to the value of map concepts and skills in aiding the child in *thinking about* the physical space in which he lives and its relation to the earth environment of human beings, maps are a part of the scheme of communication whereby vast amounts of socially important information are presented to the public. Maps are used to locate physical phenomena and characteristics just as frequently they are used to show the location of social phenomena, such as, economic activity, political groupings, population density, intergroup conflicts, and anything where we are as concerned with the *where* as well as with the *what*.

Until recent years, man has been concerned with the surface aspects of space on the earth and the activities that took place on this surface. Maps are concerned with surface representations. Now, with the extension of human activity into the space around the earth and within the solar system, there will doubtless come a time (perhaps it is now) when we will be concerned about the location of space stations with respect to our own location on the surface of the earth.

Guidelines for developing map concepts and skills

At the outset, we would present a case for a relaxed, developmental approach which will move from the child's own familiar world and eventually involve considerations outside of his personal realm. Remember at all times that the major objective is concept development by the child concerning the manner in which his existence and activity relate to location and how this can be shown to others through the use of maps. This is an experience with symbolism, just as is the use of numerals, numbers, and signs of mathematics. If your objective, as a teacher, is to get the child into the symbolic world of maps in a predetermined period of time, then you may be certain from the outset that the *conceptualizing* process will suffer.

As early as the second year in school, teachers have introduced developmental experiences which lead to understanding and skill in using maps. Some of the initial activities may involve the following:

> Draw a floor plan of the house or apartment where the child lives. There is no attention placed on scale, but rather on the matter of the position of one thing as related to another. The different sizes of the rooms can provide an opportunity for children to observe that a "map" of the place they live may tell other people which room is the largest, etc.

> Lay on the floor a large paper grid (wrapping paper will do, especially if the children can remove their shoes for the activity) with the school represented in the center. Use a large block or picture of a school to represent the building.

> Compass directions should be shown on each side of the grid as well as posted on each wall of the classroom. Each square on the grid should represent one block, although in some modern neighborhoods, the street layout may not correspond. Go outside with the children to the entrance frequently used by the group and ask them to notice carefully which way they travel when they go directly home from the school. Back in the classroom, have each child step onto the paper grid and show how he walks away from school to

Conceptualizing and Generalizing

his home. Using smaller grids on 8½' x 11' paper, the children should be asked to show the location of their homes with reference to the school and then to locate several familiar stores, friend's homes, etc.

An important consideration is the allowance of time and experience in the development of the concept concerning maps to show real things. If it appears that your group is bewildered, do not force any particular activity. Use the floor grid for children to show many things—where I go to help my parents shop, where I go to play. Teachers of older children may believe, mistakenly, that such simple experiences are not appropriate, that their 10-to-12-year-olds should be concerned with longitude and latitude! The same type of grid may be used to represent the larger area of the community or county, with children showing relative locations of home, school, football stadium, swimming pool, a relative's residence, state park, nearby cities, and a host of such items within their experience.

Special considerations in map work

Wherever possible, make use of familiar and local phenomena before involving children with maps which show space use, routes of travel, and demographic distributions in far away places. Older elementary school children can develop local maps which show where their class or school population lives in the area served by the school. They can begin to grasp the relationship of business and industrial areas to major highways, railroads, housing developments, rivers, and dominant land features, such as, formidable mountains or hills.

The mechanics of map reading and map making were outcomes of man's need to represent natural and social phenomena and their relative locations. Maps and globes were not invented by an ancient Ben Franklin who then searched for an application. A considerable educational advantage is possible where teachers will work from a concept-oriented base rather than moving from manipulations in the hope that some day the child will conceptualize.

Experiences with a variety of points of reference will provide foundations for later use of world maps and globes which use the Equator and the Prime Meridian as basic points of reference. The child's home and school are familiar points of reference which are used by five-and six-year-olds to determine their surface positions. A main city street, highway or landmark building may be another.

Provide children, throughout the elementary years, with opportunities to explain how to locate the town where their grandparents live, how to find a favored picnic spot, etc. Have children deductively work out the details of the map of their own city to discover what points of reference have been used in the plan for numbering streets and houses.

The concepts of rotation and revolution and the designation of the Equator as a reference point for map and globe construction involve information usually developed in the physical sciences. The curriculum in science should be considered in order that the pupils will be helped to see the interactions between man's needs for directional and positional references as he moves about the earth.

It is the position of the writers that the work of the cartographer and his science need not be studied in any detail. Basic concepts are the concern of elementary experiences with maps.

A developmental approach to the use of maps will provide a sensible foundation for the child's later use with other graphic representations of physical and social phenomena, such as, tables, charts and graphs.

Move from the familiar and the concrete toward the symbolic. Do not begin with maps. Be sensitive to difficulties that children have when the grid on the chalkboard or wall replaces the one on the floor. It is simple for you to say, "The top is North," on a map, but it can be confusing if the map is on the south wall of the room.

There are many opportunities for children to refer to maps of their city, state, and nation when they discuss interesting events. Such use of the map should be seen as building awareness to maps in early grades, rather than as a direct approach to the development of concepts relating to locations in space.

Once the children understand map development and use, they can make effective use of maps which they encounter in their school work and elsewhere.

Conceptualizing about maps and map skill development are not viewed as parts of geographic study, as has so long been the case. The personal identification by the child with the whole system of symbolic representations of real things is seen as opening a rich vehicle for social communication, understanding, and action.

Suggested Problems and Projects

As a class project, work in groups of three or four for the following purposes.

Conceptualizing and Generalizing

1. Examine the unit in Appendix A and make a list of the concepts and generalizations for which you think specific provisions are made.
2. Observe a classroom or view a videotape of a classroom discussion. Jot down those statements that are generalizing in nature. This task may seem difficult, but continued experience with it, followed by analytical discussions with your colleagues, will assist you in becoming operational.
3. Familiarize yourself with at least one curriculum guide to learn how concepts and generalizations are presented there.
4. Analyze a chapter, unit or section of an elementary social science textbook and list the concepts and generalizations that are presented.
5. After reading the Quillen article (see Related Readings), which was written in the 1940's, consider whether the concepts set forth then are still appropriate and relevant. What would you add, delete or modify?

Related Readings

Brownell, W. A., and Hendrickson, G. "How Children Learn Information, Concepts and Generalization." *Learning and Instruction,* 49th Yearbook of the National Society for the Study of Education, pp. 92–128. Chicago: The University of Chicago Press, 1950.

Carroll, John B. "Words, Meanings and Concepts," *Harvard Educational Review* (Spring 1964), pp. 178–202.

Dimond, Stanley E. "The Role of Generalization in Teaching Social Studies." *Social Education 22* (May 1958): 232–234.

Fancett, Verna S. et al. *Social Science Concepts and the Classroom.* Syracuse, New York: Social Studies Curriculum Center, Syracuse University, 1968.

Preston, Ralph C. "Implications of Children's Concepts of Time and Space." *Social Studies* 36 (May 1945): 219–220.

Quillen, I. James, "What Are the Basic Concepts to Be Developed in Children?" *Childhood Education* 23 (1947): 405–406.

5

HISTORICAL PERSPECTIVES ON OBJECTIVES

COGNITIVE GOALS OR KNOWLEDGE
    Cognitive domain

METHODOLOGY—PROBLEM-SOLVING PROCESSES, INQUIRY, DECISION MAKING

AFFECTIVE GOALS
    Affective domain

BEHAVIORAL OBJECTIVES

SELECTION OF BEHAVIOR TO BE DEVELOPED
    What is the teacher's role in identifying cognitive and affective objectives?
    How can *The Taxonomy* be useful?

SUMMARY

EXAMPLES OF BEHAVIORAL OBJECTIVES FOR THIS COURSE

SUGGESTED PROBLEMS AND PROJECTS

RELATED READINGS

Behavioral Objectives in Social Science Education

Few, if any, societies leave the perpetuation of the modification of their way of life to chance. United States democracy is based on the belief that the social organization is open and uncoerced, but its success or failure depends upon the willingness of its citizens to understand and act on certain basic concepts. If the dynamics of a free society are to unfold, citizens must be willing to: recognize the role of the individual as an informed, thinking being; cooperate with others; know when to protest and demonstrate and when to conform. Thus, social science education through the school organization becomes the vehicle for developing knowledge, skills, attitudes, and appreciations for the further development of a way of life.

Some research efforts tend to indicate that past social studies programs have not been held in high esteem by parents or lay citizens. Graduates of high schools have ranked social science education low on interest inventories. You, as a college student in preparation to become an elementary teacher, should spend some time thinking in retrospect about the experiences you had in the conventional social studies program. Were you aware of the objectives of the third-grade program or of those of any other grade? Did you have any idea of what was expected of you? Were your learnings relevant to your needs? Were the objectives subject oriented? Objectives have become like dirty words to some teachers because they have been discussed so much and the teachers have been coerced to learn them, but the objectives have not become meaningful enough to give direction to act upon. Objectives are the guides to our actions. They give direction to where we are going, both specifically and in a general way. Objectives are the only bases upon which we can determine the effectiveness of our instruction. Without them we do not really know what we must teach nor do we know what we have taught. In addition, we don't know which materials and procedures will work best to achieve that to be learned.[1] Suffice it to say, at

---

[1] See Robert F. Mager, *Preparing Instructional Objectives* (Palo Alto: Fearon Publishers, 1962).

this point, that teachers must become skilled in writing useful, meaningful objectives if social science learning is to be evaluated.

Historical Perspectives on Objectives

Since the beginning of the twentieth century, numerous committees and commissions related to the social sciences have prepared vast lists of objectives. From the Committee of Seven of the American Historical Association to a recent effort of the Exploratory Committee on Assessing the Progress of Education, attempts have been made to list and to clarify the goals or objectives of social science education. Some of the early objectives emphasized moral and religious values, citizenship education, and social literary education, but were gradually expanded to include the development of the individual and the social arrangements for enhancing his life. During the past several decades, resulting from some attempts to systematize social science objectives, most writers have defined objectives in terms of knowledge, skills, and attitudes. There appears to be more agreement today, than previously, that the goals of social science education fall into three categories:

1. Cognitive goals or knowledge—facts, concepts, generalizations, principles
2. Methodology—problem-solving processes, modes of inquiry, decision making, cognitive skills
3. Affective goals—attitudes, values [2]

Cognitive Goals or Knowledge

Perhaps this objective of social science education has been one of the basic reasons for conventional social studies programs having little or no impact on elementary school pupils. This is not an indictment against elementary school teachers, but against their preparations. While teachers have devoted large blocks of time in their preparation programs to social science (sometimes to meet state certification requirements), this has not resulted in their achieving the above stated objectives. Instruction in social science at the college level has often resulted in reinforcement of the negative attitudes formed about these disciplines at the

---

[2] Dorothy McClure Fraser, ed., *Social Studies Curriculum Development: Prospects and Problems, 39th Yearbook* (Washington, D.C.: National Council for the Social Studies, 1969), p. 42.

elementary and secondary levels. Students tend to see a discipline in terms of the instructor's evaluation procedures. Knowledge facts have been the bases of evaluation used by teachers in the traditional social studies program. Since it was important to recall facts to be successful, learning often was a meaningless rote-type memorization process. It is not uncommon for middle grade teachers to resort to some type of teaching situation emphasizing the memorization of isolated facts. This writer observed a teacher reviewing a sixth grade class for a test in which specific population figures were placed on the chalkboard for provinces in Australia, along with names of rivers and their lengths. This teacher actually thought she was fulfilling the cognitive objective by having the pupils acquire facts, concepts, and generalizations in a rote fashion.

You must put yourself in this sixth grade teacher's place and determine how the pupils could accomplish this cognitive goal and still maintain relevance and acquire a future source of useful information at the same time. Such useful information should broaden the knowledge of the learner and provide him with new general ideas or principles which are transferable to a given situation.

There seems to be little or no conflict on the need for structure in the cognitive learning of a discipline. But, there is conflict in how learners should acquire facts, concepts, and generalizations. Some persons look at a discipline as an end in itself, while others look at each discipline as a resource to call upon in seeking solutions to problems.

Cognitive domain

Because so many elements of the cognitive domain can be dealt with by conventional means and pencil-paper activities can be used, many teachers tend to restrict their attention to this category of objectives. (Apparently they value cognitive processes more than affective processes.) Perhaps education in the past has relied almost solely on the use of certain aspects of the knowledge level since it lends itself to a form of measurement. This becomes readily apparent when you examine the following elements of the cognitive processes. Note particularly those elements which you have seen teachers use to test for learning, but also be cognizant of the other elements presented:

1. The knowledge level, often regarded incorrectly as the lowest level, includes the following elements: terminology, specific facts, conventions, trends and sequences, classifications and categories, methodology, principles, theories, and structures. At the knowledge level, the teacher may deal with no more than recall and recognition of events, dates, and people; but

the other elements of knowledge are essential to an inquiry program.
2. Comprehension includes translation, interpretation, extrapolation, and interpolation. In a social science context, a child may examine a graph which shows the number of television sets and the percentage of literate persons in two different nations and translate this into a statement of the facts given. The child might *interpret* the graphic representation into a statement about the relationship between literacy and incidence of television sets; if the child could assume that the literacy rate in any underdeveloped nation was to be improved from 20 per cent to 80 per cent in the next ten years, he could extrapolate a trend in the use of television.
3. Application involves applying a principle to an actual situation. An elementary child, who is informed about the principle of decisions made according to the desires of the majority who will be affected, would apply this to a situation where 20 pupils wanted to hold a class picnic on Wednesday at 4:30 p.m., while 15 wanted to hold the picnic on Tuesday at 5:00 p.m.
4. Analysis includes the identification of the various elements of a problem or situation, the identification of relationships, and the identification of organizing principles. In an account of any happening, the child would identify those elements that were central to the problem or issue as contrasted to the peripheral elements. "The big, black car raced through the red light and struck the delivery truck. Bill Jones reported that he was watching television in his home nearby when he heard the crash, so he was not sure who was at fault. A policeman, who was standing on the corner, saw the accident. It was a hot afternoon and it rained soon after the crash. The policeman remembered this because he said the heat had caused him to feel dizzy and things had looked hazy to him."
5. Synthesis includes three types of operations: the drawing together of separate parts into a whole; the producing of a plan or operation; and the development of an abstraction from several related concrete elements.

"It has been reported that the Australian Bushmen roast the grub worms which they find in old tree trunks, and that some West Africans eat the chicken bones, as well as the flesh. American children often find these food preferences to be unappealing. On the other hand, the West African is puzzled at the food choices of Americans who eat raw oysters and rare beef, and they wonder why a popular sandwich would be called a hot dog."

Given this kind of information the child, usually by the middle grade level, will be able to formulate an abstract statement that will synthesize the elements into a unifying idea.[3]

Methodology—Problem-solving Processes, Inquiry, Decision Making

The conventional social studies programs have been too concerned with the acquisition of facts and the "covering" of material to the detriment of process. No one can look into a crystal ball and foretell what information a child of today will need twenty-five years hence. But, perhaps there are a few guideposts along the way that can give direction. We do know that with the population increasing, the complications of human beings working out social arrangements for meeting their needs, skills of inquiry, and even greater technological advancements will become increasingly important. You, as a teacher in training, must become skillful in using this process to facilitate decision making. Unless you make this process a part of your "nervous" system, then, to the extent that you rely on this skill, it will become an academic exercise for your students. We need to know how to identify a problem and how to determine priorities of time and relevance in seeking solutions if citizens are to be active participants in the democratic processes at all levels of development and stages of life.

Curriculum guides, social science education textbooks, and other sources of objectives for education in general, and social science education in particular, point to the need of teaching problem-solving skills. But, the truth of the matter is that it's too time consuming for teachers to get more than a little involved. Pressure to complete the textbook takes precedence over the actual learning of knowledge or a skill. In fact, the affective goals of wanting the pupil to continue to learn on his own after the course is over may actually be lost. You see, it becomes important for you to know how to make decisions as a teacher, because you control the curriculum; you determine whether something will be thoroughly learned or merely glossed over for the learner. How do you make such decisions? Do you develop an analytical question, form an

---

[3] See Benjamin S. Bloom, ed., *Taxonomy of Educational Objectives: The Classification of Educational Goals, Handbook I: Cognitive Domain* (New York: David McKay Company, Inc., 1956), pp. 96.

hypothesis, collect the data or gather evidence, test its credibility before taking action? What alternatives do you have under such conditions?

Affective Goals

The question must be posed, "Are affective goals a part of the methodology objective?" Certainly the direction of social science education in the future is toward a more scientific method or an inquiry approach. The emphasis on empirical data, structured cognitive skills in the disciplines, and developing skills used by the social scientists may detract from the awareness of the affective objectives. If the new social science education is to succeed and if learners are going to be taught skills of inquiry and use this process, then is there danger that some learners might question why we do things in a given way, and might they change their ways of thinking and feeling about some things, as they presently are to the way they believe they "ought to be?" Such results might be very disturbing to "closed" teachers or to persons in society in general. But, the real hope, perhaps, for individual improvement and broad social change, as well as for the extension of democracy to a way of life, might well be found in this process. Yet, there is real danger if the process is not thoroughly understood and the means of selecting alternative choices is not consciously developed. That is, how do we reconcile a fact from a value, and how do we act on each? This discussion of the current general objectives of elementary social science education recognizes the need for teachers, lay people, and social scientists to continue to collaborate in reviewing, modifying, and developing said broad general objectives.

Affective domain

1. Receiving or attending, including the aspects of awareness, willingness to receive stimuli, and controlled or selected attention
2. Responding, which includes a willingness to be attentive and to respond, and satisfaction in responding to stimuli, verbal and otherwise
3. Valuing, which includes dimensions ranging from acceptance through preference for a value to commitment to a value
4. Organization of values into those which are related and are not contradictory
5. Characterization, by a value, of problems and issues to the

end that the context of a situation does not cause the individual to abandon his value system [4]

How can these be useful to the teacher who is concerned with behavioral objectives? At the *receiving* level, the child usually gives his attention to the situation at hand, and the strength of his attention can be observed according to the ease with which he is diverted and the types of stimuli which serve to divert him. It is wise to take into account maturational factors and the normative behavior of the group before concluding on any one child. Either the child listens to the teacher or the person speaking and attends to the content of a task at hand, or he does not. The child either responds with enthusiasm and pleasure, or he is compliant, possibly refusing to respond. The response is an indicator of attitude and feeling toward the teacher and/or the total setting.

Valuing can be observed as the child pursues goals which are deemed to be socially necessary or as he pursues goals that are often contrary to valid social goals. His acceptance and commitment to the value of respect can be observed, and in crisis situations, his commitment to a consistent set of values can be observed. If the child persists in defense of an opinion in the face of evidence that denies his opinion, his valuing of objective inquiry may be viewed as only a conditional commitment.

While it is of urgent importance, according to our own value system, that the teacher be constantly concerned and observant of behavior which reveals the development of values, it is equally important that she be aware of value conflicts and of the need to support youngsters in the face of conflicts. (Lying is sometimes valued by the child if it will help him avoid an unpleasant consequence.)

Behavioral Objectives

The previous topic dealt with global or long range objectives. These become the overall goals for, in this case, social education. But, there should be long range objectives not only for each grade level, but also for the total educational program, K-12. Some of these have been stated on pages 30–31 in this book; therefore they will not be repeated here, but we will use one of them as a learning experience. You may recall that

---

[4] David R. Krathwohl, Benjamin S. Bloom and Bertram B. Masia, *Taxonomy of Educational Objectives: The Classification of Educational Goals, Handbook II: The Affective Domain* (New York: David McKay Co., 1964), pp. 191–192.

we said above that objectives tell us what we are to teach. Therefore, long range objectives give us some clues as to where we are going during any given year in our curriculum, recognizing that there will be deviations along the way for some children. We are not only cognizant of pupil learning differences, but we are responsible for providing for them. Now, long range objectives indicate an overall outcome for a large block of teaching time extended over a long period of time. We might be able to measure or determine some *general* evidence of achieving the outcome, but we cannot determine the *specific* knowledge, skills or attitudes acquired, nor would it be fair to the learner to hold him responsible unless the specific objectives have been mutually agreed upon by himself and you.

On page 30, you will note this general objective for social science education: "To provide for the development and use of the skills involved in free and open inquiry." Now for a general objective, this can serve as an outcome of some type of instruction since it does give direction to a destination or a product that we want the learners to acquire, perhaps by the time they complete 12 grades of school or perhaps by the time they reach adulthood. Thus, we may never really know if the general or long range objective was achieved. But, this objective does not tell the learner specifically what skills to develop or what skills he will be called upon to use in inquiry. In addition, it does not tell him what is meant by "free and open inquiry." So, from this general objective, specific or short term objectives must be developed. Let's assume that some type of curriculum committee, representative of the school district, developed and agreed upon the general or long range objective. It then becomes the responsibility of the teacher to work with the learners in developing common specific objectives which will lead to the achievement of the general objectives.

What then might be a specific objective related to achieving the long range objective stated above? The teacher will first have to spend time, as a member of the class, determining what is meant by free and open inquiry. After the pupils reach agreement on this concept, then we can proceed to develop our specific objective relative to the needed skills of inquiry. It should be understood, however, that there can be no fixed boundaries when seeking truth, which is what we are seeking through inquiry. Our specific objective, leading to the broad general objective, might be: "To develop the skill of inquiry by using a variety of procedures for data collecting." Now, let's see if this objective meets the criteria of acceptability. *First* of all, does the objective communicate to the learner what we want it to impart? That is, could the learner misinterpret what he is trying to achieve? *Second,* does it give direction to that which is to be taught or learned? *Third,* does it result in any visible activity by the learner? *Fourth,* will the objective result in the kind of behavior performance that will continue when the learning period is over? *Fifth,* can the achievement of the objective be determined?

The objective we are examining suggests that more than one procedure for collecting data must be learned. For example, can data be collected through firsthand observations? What is raw, uninterpreted data? Are statistics data? Are charts, maps and globes sources of data? The point here is that the learner can determine just what he has acquired relative to the objective to be achieved. The teacher can evaluate the learning against the objective and assist the learner as he needs help or faces an obstacle to further learning. It should be kept in mind that the very essence of inquiry is the willingness of the teacher to permit the learner to interpret the data and determine its significance.

Selection of Behavior to Be Developed

Perhaps two of the more difficult tasks teachers, as a group, have is the selection of behaviors to be developed and the content with which to interact. This involves making judgments concerning what is valuable in the conduction of human affairs. Our way of life has given prominence to the concept of the worth and dignity of the individual, and social science education has accepted a large share of the responsibility for fostering the development of the potential of each individual toward total fulfillment. Although the purpose of fulfillment is directed toward the individual, it is twofold since the individual's fulfillment is also directly related to his responsibility and commitment to society at large.

Surely we cannot predict the circumstances under which the next generation will live, but we do have some notions on the development of large, complex metropolitan areas stretching from New York to Chicago and in other locations in America. We have only touched the surface in technology. The extent to which this vast technological revolution will alter the lives of mankind, resulting in changes in our social institutions, longevity of life, and the great economic complex, is difficult to predict. But, it seems clear that life in the United States will be urbanized for nearly all of its citizens; that as transportation, communication, nuclear energy and the computer are further developed, man's quest for purpose of life will become more complex and elusive.[5]

If, as Mager has stated, an "objective is an intent communicated by a statement describing a proposed change in a learner—a statement of what the learner is to be like when he has successfully completed a

---

[5] Fraser, p. 34.

learning experience,"[6] then the task of the teacher is to identify specific behavioral objectives for her teaching. Only when the objectives have been clearly stated can you have a basis for evaluating the effectiveness of the learning. Teachers often function with some objective in mind, but for the learners it becomes a guessing game to try to figure out what the teacher wants him to do. Unless the child knows what he is attempting to achieve, he cannot know what kinds of experiences and materials will be of help to him in accomplishing the task. Remember, the objectives are to the teacher what the blueprint is to the builder. When the objectives have been clearly defined, then the teacher has a sound basis for identifying teaching strategies. The recommending of appropriate materials, the selection of initial subject matter to be read, and the suggesting of a filmstrip or other learning aid are made to facilitate learning.

What is the teacher's role in identifying cognitive and affective objectives?

It has been stated that the teacher works within the framework of the school district's broad general objectives for the social science curriculum. The curriculum guide may or may not state the many specific behavioral objectives to be achieved, but it is the teacher's responsibility to share with the learners the experiences of identifying and selecting the specific objectives for any given learning experience. The teacher could put on the chalkboard the broad general objectives for discussion purposes. One such an objective might be, "We are dependent upon many people in different places for the variety of goods which we need in our community." After a discussion of this general objective by the third grade class, with the teacher submerging herself within the group and serving only to see that the many ramifications of the objective are brought into the open, the group then might cooperatively plan some specific behavioral goals to be achieved. The success of the learning experiences related to this objective may depend upon the extent to which the children have shared in developing the objectives. The teacher's role is vital in this respect, since she must refrain from being in a "telling" situation. She must see that each child has a chance to be heard in shaping the objectives. She has a particular responsibility to recognize constantly the need to clarify issues as she helps the children to develop critical thinking and to sharpen each issue with additional insights. The entire climate of the classroom must be conducive to producing sound thinking through group decision making.

---

[6] Mager, *Preparing Instructional Objectives*, p. 24.

Behavioral Objectives in Social Science Education 185

After careful consideration of the general objective, the third grade class has agreed that the following are some specific objectives to be learned:

1. To be able to name at least seven different foods that we eat in our community, but do not grow in our region of the country.
2. To be able to name at least three raw materials which we are dependent upon other countries for and the names of countries from which they come.
3. To be able to demonstrate, by drawing a graph, the average rainfall and the average temperature in this region of the country and to compare it with another region of our country.
4. To understand the influences of climate on growing plants.

Now, let us take a look at these four specific behaviors that were finally agreed upon by the class. We must ask ourselves whether or not each objective indicates some kind of performance which can be evaluated to determine if the learner has achieved the objective. The first objective seems to fulfill this requirement since the behavior of the learner can be determined in at least two ways. The learner can supply verbally or in writing the names of at least seven different foods consumed in the community, but grown out of the region. The second objective also meets the criteria for a specific behavior to be acquired. Now, what do you think about the third objective? Can the specific behavior be determined? What would be required of the learners to achieve this objective? How does the fourth objective differ from the first three? What does it mean "to understand?" Can our college class agree on what is to be understood in relation to the fourth objective? You see that this doesn't really tell the learner what he is to understand or how you will ask him to describe or demonstrate his understandings. He will need to know if you want him to understand the effects of a hot, humid climate on plants; the effects of a hot arrid climate on plants; the effects of the length of the growing season on plants in each type of climate; the effects of the climate on the workers who grow the plants, and many other understandings which could be added here. You will need to become skillful in writing the kinds of behaviors you and your class agree are important learning outcomes from the problems studied.

The development of specific objectives in behavioral terms becomes a major responsibility of the teachers. This task must be done for each problem studied, and as the teacher involves the children, they will become more skillful in setting their own goals. Such objectives or goals help the learner to be aware of his achievements as they are accomplished. Thus, the setting of goals or the establishing of behaviors to be learned facilitates the evaluation process, both self-evaluation and evaluation by the teacher.

In the realm of affective objectives, the teacher plays a vital role in helping children to recognize the importance of developing desirable pupil behavior. These goals "... emphasize a feeling tone, an emotion, or a degree of acceptance or rejection."[7] It is apparent that objectives dealing with attitudes and appreciations are desirable, but you will find them elusive in trying to describe them in behavioral terms which will meet the criteria listed above. But, if you will write these objectives separate from the objectives in the cognitive domain, then you can describe the kind of evidence you will accept as an outcome of learnings in the affective domain. These descriptive evidences will then serve as the bases of the instructional program as it effects the affective goals.

How can "The Taxonomy" be useful?

The *Taxonomy of Educational Objectives*[8] is compatible with the goals of social science education and is a useful tool for the teacher as she organizes learning activities. It should be pointed out that *The Taxonomy* was arranged in such a manner that the cognitive domain was presented first and the affective domain second, whereas the justification of national social education arises largely from a *value* for objective inquiry into the human realm and for an awareness of our biases, attitudes, and values.

Summary

The modern elementary social science program is developed around relevant needs of the individual, as well as those of the democratic society. Teachers must become skilled at helping pupils to identify their specific skills, knowledge or attitudes in determining their learnings. In addition, the teacher needs to be competent in writing behavioral objectives for her own use in evaluating her instruction.

Examples of Behavioral Objectives for this Course

1. When given a concept statement, the student will formulate at least three questions which will provide direction to inquiry

---

[7] Krathwohl, Bloom, and Masia, *Taxonomy of Educational Objectives, Handbook II: Affective Domain*, p. 98.
[8] *Ibid.*

into the concept area; formulate at least three generalizations of the concept into life situations; and suggest one learning activity that can be developed for extension of the concept at a particular age level.
2. When given a statement of a generalization, the student will identify the concept or concepts which are related in the generalizations.
3. When auditing a discussion by his peers (and by elementary pupils), the student will select sample statements and classify them according to the type of "truth claim" which supports them.
4. The student will write five behavioral objectives for social science education for the age-grade level that he plans to teach.
5. The student will classify as social studies- or social science education-oriented, sample curriculum guides, textbooks, and project materials given to him for analysis.
6. When presented with statements of instructional objectives, the student will identify those which are stated in behavioral terms.
7. During observation of an elementary social science education activity, the student will classify the components of the activity, using Bloom's *Taxonomy of Educational Objectives as a guide.*
8. The student will select five stories or books suitable for use by intermediate level pupils in the development of the concept of cultural diversity.
9. The student will write a simple episode dealing with the conflicting values of cooperation—competition in a life experience of an 8- or 9-year-old child—and prepare a plan for its use with children to get them involved in the valuing process.
10. The student will name two references to which he can turn for assistance in selecting and planning for the development of specific social science concepts; he will support his choices with a descriptive statement of each.

Suggested Problems and Projects

1. A helpful activity would be to organize your class in several small teams of two or three students to develop objectives for each level of *The Taxonomy*. These could be tested against the criteria established by such writers as Bloom, Mager, and others.

2. Refer to the examples on pages 178–179, items 4 and 5, and try your hand at analyzing and synthesizing them. Compare your results with others in your class.

3. Organize into groups of three or four and have each group develop one item for each classification of *The Taxonomy* that could be used with elementary children to give them experience with the various objectives.

4. As a group, or as an individual assignment, make a list of short term and long term behavioral objectives that you would recommend for social science education.

Related Readings

Bloom, Benjamin S., ed. *Taxonomy of Educational Objectives: The Classification of Educational Goals, Handbook I: Cognitive Doman.* New York: York: David McKay Company, Inc., 1956.

Douglass, Malcolm P. *Social Studies from Theory to Practice in Elementary Education,* p. 10. New York: J. B. Lippincott Company, 1967.

Fraser, Dorothy McClure, ed. *Social Studies Curriculum Development: Prospects and Problems, 39th Yearbook,* chapter 2. Washington, D.C.: The National Council for the Social Studies, 1969.

Joyce, Bruce R. *Strategies for Elementary Social Science Education.* Chicago: Science Research Associates, 1964.

Krathwohl, David, Bloom, Benjamin S., and Masia, Bertram B. *Taxonomy of Educational Objectives: The Classification of Educational Goals, Handbook II: Affective Domain.* New York: David McKay Company, Inc., 1956.

Mager, Robert F. *Preparing Instructional Objectives.* Palo Alto, California: Fearon Publishers, Inc., 1962.

Preston, Ralph C. *Teaching Social Studies in the Elementary School,* pp. 8–13. New York: Holt, Rinehart, and Winston, 1968.

Servey, Richard. *Social Studies Instruction in the Elementary School,* p. 10. San Francisco: Chandler Publishing Company, 1967.

SECTION III

In this section, the stage is set for selecting and implementing the learning experiences of children and youth. The developmental characteristics of children are considered in chapter six, with particular attention to their implications for social education. Inquiry processes, other methodologies, and instructional resources are considered in chapters eight, nine, and ten. Finally, in the remaining chapters of this section, three continuing concerns—religion, cross-cultural studies, and contemporary affairs—are highlighted and considered in their relationship to the overall structure of social science education.

6

INTRODUCTION
    What is the expanding-environment approach?
    What is an organic-experiential approach?
    What are the social concerns of children?

CHILD DEVELOPMENT AND SOCIAL EDUCATION
    What are the findings of psychologists?
    What are universal developmental tasks?
    How do the disadvantaged differ?
    What is the relationship between language and social education?

SUGGESTED PROBLEMS AND PROJECTS

RELATED READINGS

The Child and Social Education

Introduction

"The task of teaching a subject to a child at any particular age is one of representing the structure of that subject in terms of the child's way of viewing things." [1] This statement of Bruner's concerning the use of structure in teaching and his further comment that "any idea can be represented honestly and usefully in the thought forms of children of school age . . ." [2] require careful thought and testing. Especially in the social domain of child experience, it is proper to ask to what extent, if any, children have begun to conceptualize about certain social phenomena and processes. A number of educators and specialists in various academic fields have accepted Bruner's hypotheses and assumptions as statements of fact and may have disregarded the developmental aspects of human learning and the individual variability among children. In some instances, they seem to have accepted the notion that any learning that is *possible* is, accordingly, *feasible*.

At this point, it is necessary to emphasize the characteristics that are commonly found in the social development of most children in our society. We can assume that these are produced by the various experiences which the child has had in his home-neighborhood-school setting and that these characteristics must be taken into account as we consider the readiness of children to engage in a productive manner in selected learning experiences in social science education.

One authority in the field of child growth and development has concluded that social development progresses as follows:

1. Child is essentially ego-centric, self-assertive, quick to protect his own interests, and somewhat negativistic.
2. Child avoids injuring others, respects their property, and endeavors to avert open conflicts.

---

[1] Jerome Bruner, *The Process of Education* (Cambridge, Mass.: The Harvard University Press), p. 33.
[2] *Ibid.*

3. Child tolerates other peoples' views, conforms to their wishes, obeys elders, and joins in gregarious activities.
4. Child considers rights of others, is cooperative, is interested in social betterment movements, respects individual personalities, and is concerned with social skills designed to promote harmonious relationships.[3]

It is true that descriptions, such as, this one from Thorpe, do not tell us what is possible or feasible in regard to the *kinds* of intellectual activities that children may engage in with respect to social phenomena and problems. The seven-year-old child may *learn* about the concept of change in political institutions, but it would appear that the typical pattern of social development and his own experiential background would make such a learning task a questionable undertaking. We would do Bruner an injustice if we were to suggest that he would approve such an approach, but some teachers and social scientists have interpreted his views as being supportive of teaching anything at any age level without regard to developmental factors.

What is the expanding-environment approach?

This is essentially a plan for organizing social studies learnings to correspond with the problems and interests that the child encounters as his life expands outward from the home and community to the nation and world. Assumptions were made that the study of family and home could be carried on in the primary years since the child was concerned with those institutions and processes in his immediate environment, and the erroneous assumption was made that the problems of the expanded environment of state and nation were more complex, hence they were studied at higher grade levels.

From a "human condition" point of view, the same fundamental processes and problems are present in the life affairs of a school community as in the nation state. The child does not first encounter the idea of "differences among people" when he studies the Eskimo in grade four or five; he has encountered it in his own school and home, but the encounter may have been avoided as a learning experience.

Generally, the expanded-environment approach led to the following scope and sequence in social studies programs:

First Grade: Home and Family
Second Grade: School

---

[3] Louis P. Thorpe, *Child Psychology and Development* (New York: The Ronald Press, 1955), pp. 468–469.

Third Grade: Community
Fourth Grade: World Communities
Fifth Grade: Our State and Nation
Sixth Grade: The Western Hemisphere

The content was generally descriptive in nature, providing an assortment of historical and geographical information. The psychological dimensions involved in the child's growing awareness of the culture to which he belongs, to his roles in his life situations, and to the dynamics of the human condition were usually overlooked in the expanding-environment approach.

What is an organic-experiential approach?

Having presented critical comments concerning the expanded-environment approach and having remarked on the limitations of Bruner's subject structure approach, we intend to suggest an approach that will be realistic in terms of the learner's interests and characteristics, one which will make use of the structures of human experience. Wentworth Clarke has called this broader conception an "organic-experiential" approach.[4] The term may at first seem to obfuscate, but it means what it says. The predominant life *experiences* of children are used as the bases for development and extension of concepts and skills which constitute the organic makeup of human society. The structural approach of Bruner is utilized in a more lively fashion here. It is not the *structure of a subject*, rather, it is the structure of human experience that is the focal point. It is not the expanding space of the child's physical environment that is the key concern, rather, it is the dimensions, psychological and sociological, of the child's experiences that offer the guidelines for planning the social science education of all children.

What are the social concerns of children?

When and in what manner does the child become an economic, political, and social being? At birth? When does the child become aware of and concerned with the social processes of human life? Does the child usually become involved with some aspects of social process before other aspects? Can these become the stepping stones to social science learnings that will involve a structural approach?

Children come to the elementary school with an infinite assortment

---

[4] Wentworth Clarke, "An Organic-Experiential Curriculum" (materials developed for inservice purpose, Public Schools, Cedar Rapids, Iowa, 1967).

of concepts about people and the things people do. They come to school with well-developed coping skills that have been effective in helping them get along with adults and other persons in the home and neighborhood environment. Children have done a great deal of social studying in the informal, but very meaningful, arena of their daily lives. Let us consider the social content of a child's daily life; he is becoming increasingly cognizant of this, although he may not be able to verbalize its meanings:

1. Family membership and other human groups
2. Social roles filled by people near to him
3. Social control within the family and in the nearby community
4. Scarcity and desire for things that he and others want
5. Dependence of human beings on other individuals
6. Special institutions in society: religion, education, family
7. Conflict with others over valued objects and activities
8. System of values, sensed but not specific or clear
9. Territoriality, man's use of boundaries.
10. Time as a controlling factor in human activity
11. Space in its psychological and physical dimensions

You may question whether such a beginning list is relevant for the rural child, the ghetto child, the wealthy and the poor child. We think that these are universal aspects of every child's life experience. The experiences of one child with his family may be traumatic and barren, while another child's family experiences may be secure and enriching. Similar differences may be expected across the spectrum of human social existence, but the spectrum is there; few will escape it. There are many implications for the teacher of children.

It should be helpful to consider the social content of the child's life experiences as forming the real structural framework for the educational efforts of the school. Social science education builds from this foundation of experience and provides the child with the vehicles and skills that will finally take him into effective contact with the variability of the human condition of his world. In this regard it seems that social studies should be the most exciting and meaningful area of the curriculum for the majority of boys and girls. Instead, research has indicated that the conventional programs have resulted in rapidly declining interests and enthusiasm as the youngsters moved up the educational ladder. How could any youngster, possessed of normal perceptual abilities, come to the school with few or no working concepts about man's social condition? Why did the conventional program abandon reality?

Child Development and Social Education

In the preceding paragraphs we have presented informal information dealing with the social content of the child's life experiences. We have assumed that interaction between the child and his total environment has occurred, but we have not been able to suggest in any specific manner the range and precision of the child's conceptualizing behavior. Implications for teaching must be drawn from the general understandings taken from psychological investigations, rather than from specific knowledge applicable to all children.

What are the findings of psychologists?

At the outset, we would do well to remember that careful studies of children are recent additions to the concerns of scientists. For many centuries, conventional knowledge or mystical and mythical wisdom provided the bases for understanding human growth and development. Philosophers, of course, speculated on the several stages of human life, but hardly from a biological-psychological point of view.

It should not surprise you that there are conflicting ideas as to the most appropriate and dependable methods for studying human growth and development. There are difficulties in obtaining large numbers of children of preschool age, the matter of determining the nature and extent of family-neighborhood influence is still a concern, and there is a need for testing and measuring devices of high validity and reliability. In spite of these real limitations, we can gain from a consideration of growth and development factors in the social education of the child, taking care to remain receptive to further information and new points of view.

Intellectual development. If we accept Jean Piaget's ideas concerning the "stages" of intellectual development of the child, we would be inclined to defer learning tasks of an abstract nature until the age of 11 or 12 years. Piaget's investigations have suggested that the child's intellectual development will be of the "concrete operations" type until the age of 11 or 12, after which time the thought processes become more nearly like those of the adult.[5] After age 11 or 12, the youngster is generally more capable of dealing with abstract problems and is able to hypothesize beyond the problems and situations which are immediately familiar to him.

In summarizing a vast amount of research on the topic of children's concept development, David Russell states that "the growth of knowl-

---

[5] Phillip Muller, *The Tasks of Childhood* (New York: McGraw-Hill, 1969), p. 61.

edge of concepts is orderly, (but) any group of children of the same chronological age shows a wide range in their understandings, and overlapping between grades and the range of achievement within any one grade is considerable. The range usually increases as children grow older." [6]

Piaget has viewed intellectual development as resulting from "the interaction of things mental and the environment," a view which does not mean that mental development takes place in a void, but rather insists that it is an outcome of the interaction of many forces.[7]

Traditionally, the social studies programs have taken children into the "reading about" type of learning experience. Although the primary level programs claimed to focus upon the social content of the child's environment (home, school, community), the use of a social studies textbook required that the six-, seven-, and eight-year-old child think about a rather mythical family, home, school, and community that was somehow built to fit the idealized versions. In essence, the study of someone else's family, school, etc., does not insure that the child's immediate environment is being tapped for the content of relevant learning experiences, nor does it offer opportunities for the child to deal with the concrete elements of his social milieu.

Marian Breckenridge and Lee Vincent, among others, have questioned the validity of Piaget's views with respect to the development of reasoning ability in the child, and they have offered experimental evidence that children in the three-to-seven-year age group exhibit ability to generalize and to take exception to a given principle.[8] Breckenridge and Vincent believe that the school must provide experiences based on the assumption that young children are capable of reasoning and that the learning program must be oriented toward problem-solving experiences that involve reasoning processes.[9]

If we were forced to implement pure Piagetan views in the social science education of six-, seven-, and eight-year-olds, would we limit the experiences to observations and discussions of the socially significant objects around school and home? Would we include descriptive studies of other children, other schools, and other communities, so long as we dealt with the concrete elements rather than abstract analysis of relationships, functions, and the like? These are the kinds of questions that the teacher must ultimately consider.

---

[6] David H. Russell, *Children's Thinking* (New York: Ginn and Company, 1956), pp. 162–163.
[7] Muller, *The Tasks of Childhood*, pp. 63–65.
[8] Marian E. Breckenridge and E. Lee Vincent, *Child Development* (Philadelphia: W. B. Saunders & Co., 1950), p. 421.
[9] *Ibid.*, p. 422.

The Child and Social Education

Authors' comment. In working with seven groups of six-year-old children on the concept of family, we found that the typical idea that was verbalized was that a family must have a father, mother, and children. However, in all of the groups, there were children who would insist that a picture of a woman and a child, or a man and a child, could be a family. A picture of a man, a woman, and three children, one of whom was a Negro, was seen, by at least one child in each group, as being a family because white parents could adopt children that were not the same color. It seemed to us that these six-year-olds differed widely in their readiness to "hypothesize" about family, but that in each group hypothesizing was initiated by some children. It is the opinion of the writers that an open inquiry approach provides a situation which invites natural intellectual activity by the children and that the interaction of children operating at different levels provides a healthy environment for concept development.

Does the authors' experience mentioned above confirm or reject Piaget's view? Does it agree with Russell's position? What does it suggest about learning activities for children?

Principles of learning. In view of conflicting theories and principles regarding the learning process, Thorpe has chosen to offer guiding principles which should be helpful to the teacher as she plans and supports learning situations for boys and girls. *Motivation through the use of children's interests, adjustment to maturation levels, discernment of meaningful relationships, directing learning through evaluation, and broad integrated development* are five principles which apply to effective learning conditions for any group of human beings.[10] The problem for the teacher has not been one of understanding and accepting these principles; the difficulty has come about when the interests of the children diverged too widely from the school's prescribed program. Teachers generally subscribe to the principle that effective learning occurs when the task is geared to maturity levels, but they have not been able to ascertain maturity with respect to readiness for certain social learnings, nor has the problem of individualizing the instructional program been solved.

We believe that the first two principles continue to provide the most difficult challenge to education, and that the remaining three principles can be attended to with relative ease. Teachers have it within their capability to involve children in the assessment of their progress in any learning activity; the climate of the total school can be supportive and

---

[10] Thorpe, *Child Psychology and Development*, pp. 554–560.

optimistic if teachers and principals desire, and the relationships between the learning activities and real life can be established if teachers wish it to be so. It is not an easy task to obtain information about those pupil interests that will also satisfy some measure of social significance. Information about the maturation levels of children is often limited to their reading levels, and we then make inferences about the readiness of children to deal with other learning tasks. In the social science education area, how shall we decide that a group of nine-year-olds are ready to inquire into the family organization of a non-Western society?

Perhaps one of the most frustrating realizations of the young teacher is that these principles of learning continue to operate in spite of our shortcomings in taking them into account as we work with boys and girls. We may have good reasons or poor excuses, such as, following a rigid curriculum guide or requiring that the class cover a textbook, for ignoring these principles, but the damage to the learning situation is not lessened by such reasons or excuses.

> *What can you say about the relationships which exist among the five principles listed by Thorpe? Do you believe that you can observe any one and continue to overlook or minimize any of the others?*

What are universal developmental tasks?

It may seem risky to refer to "universal developmental characteristics" in view of the diverse forms in which various cultures have shaped acceptable human conduct. Yet, the common element of humanness requires that all men cope with certain developmental tasks. Muller regards these tasks as:

1. The growth of self-awareness
2. The attainment of physiological stability
3. The formation of simple concepts related to physical and social reality
4. The formation of the concepts of good and evil, appearance of the conscience [11]

These four tasks, Muller believes, begin to receive the attention and energy of the child from the age of three years into the middle elementary school years, by which time other developmental tasks are being confronted. These later developmental tasks include:

---

[11] Muller, *The Tasks of Childhood,* p. 184.

1. Learning social communication in the peer group
2. Learning the appropriate sexual role
3. Achieving a healthy attitude toward his own development
4. Mastery of the physical skills necessary in games
5. Learning reading, writing, and arithmetic
6. Acquiring the concepts necessary in everyday life [12]

It is common to find treatment of developmental tasks in books dealing with the problem of learning the basic language skills, and it seems that the social education of the child demands at least this much attention to the broader developmental factors that affect the learning of attitudes, thinking skills, and information. The child comes to school with a well-defined self-concept. Not only is he aware of self, possessing the "I-you" concept, but he has a further concept of self as a member of a particular human group. One of the first tasks that school life will present is that of identity in a group of peers who have been brought together for the very special purposes of education. Although the informal play contacts of home and neighborhood have introduced the need to work out his role identity with siblings and peers, the learning regimen of the school imposes new criteria by which the child will come to know himself and others as successful or unsuccessful, energetic or lazy, good or bad, important or unimportant.

The basis for building social concern and civic responsibility must lie beneath the cognitive level, since it is a complex mixture of certain attitudes about the relationship between self and others. Unless the teachers are sensitive to the role that self-concept plays in the development of constructive social behaviors, the massive efforts of the junior and senior high schools to politically socialize children are likely to be pointless. Consider that the parents may send to school a child who is in the process of developing a self-concept that is supportive of his efforts to communicate with people, to do the approved things, to get along. Does this mean that an adequate self-concept is established to the point that it need not be the concern of teachers? The early contacts that the child has with the other powerful adults (teachers) provide a base from which he will generalize his feelings about school and about other adults who are called teachers.

An overriding concern for the mastery of the three R's has led many teachers to modify, in a negative manner, the self-concept which the child has brought to school. There are classic studies which have identified the profound effect which a failure concept can have upon the total school experience of a child. In this respect, the teacher is needed as a

---

[12] *Ibid.*, p. 185.

helping adult, one who will support each child through his difficulties and weaknesses. This is simple to say, but it is apparently difficult for those teachers who are as success oriented as the larger society and who see their own successes only in the attainment and perfection of their pupils.

How do the disadvantaged differ?

The term "disadvantaged" has come to replace the term "deprived," largely because it has been recognized that few children are deprived of culture or deprived of life experiences. The circumstances of race and economic condition seem to be two of the prime factors which produce disadvantaged environments. Children may be at a disadvantage in school and in the larger society because of childhood experiences that do not relate to the learning expectations of the school program.

It is inaccurate to generalize about the characteristics of so called disadvantaged children because there is great variability here. The quiet, retiring, submissive child from a poverty stricken home may be quite unready for the highly verbal learning program of the school, but he is not so quickly identified as the ghetto youngster who may bring with him aggressive behavior and "bad" language. The accepted means of dealing with conflict may vary from one disadvantaged community to another or from one home to another.

A number of comprehensive treatments of the disadvantaged and their education are available and your attention is directed to them. From the viewpoint of social science education, we will emphasize one vital characteristic that appears to be present in many disadvantaged children—the alienation which they feel with respect to other people outside their family-neighborhood circle. A self-concept that is not adequate to support the child in his relations with the people in the outside world may be the product of his limited social environment, but the school must not reinforce the notion of inadequacy and unacceptability.

Alienation is built by family inputs, the child's early contacts provide him with the idea that he is different, that his people are different from those on the outside. The language that the child brings to school may serve as a barrier to the establishment of effective relationships with other children and with teachers. Substandard language and an outward appearance of poverty frequently lead to the classification of the child as one who will undoubtedly do poor academic work. Teachers' behavior toward such children may make the self-fulfilling prophecy complete. The teacher may be a key person in helping the disadvantaged child begin to move away from his alienated position. The teacher usually appears to be one of those persons from the other world, a person who is not like the people at home. The respect which the disadvantaged child receives from the teacher may be a critical factor; we have reason to

The Child and Social Education

believe that teacher hostility and rejection are definitely not helpful! Let us consider a brief report of an elementary principal:

> Raymond came into the office with a look of good natured defiance. We had met before.
>
> "What is it, Raymond?" I asked
>
> "Teacher sent me here. I called Rosanna a fat ass." Raymond regarded me closely, a hint of humor on his face. For an eight-year-old, he knew how to "put on" a white principal.
>
> "I guess we should talk to Rosanna. I think she is the one who has been hurt. I haven't been." I asked the clerk to bring Rosanna.
>
> As Rosanna entered I could not refrain from noticing that she was plump.
>
> "Rosanna, I understand that Raymond called you by another name. Is that right?"
>
> "Yes, Mr. ———, he done called me a fat ass."
>
> "What do you think I should do?" I asked.
>
> "Give him a couple of whacks," Rosanna advised.
>
> "What do you think, Raymond?"
>
> "Okay with me." He knew I didn't paddle as hard as his mom.
>
> "You can't call people by other names, you know. They just won't stand for it. Well, let's get this paddling over with so you can both get back to class."

There is little evidence to support the notion that the school alone can bring about major positive changes in the motivation which children have for academic achievement. Wilbur Brookover's investigation of self-concept and school achievement deserves our attention, although it involves "slow achievers," rather than children who were identified as disadvantaged. Brookover reports that teachers and others in the school have very little effect upon any change in the child's self-concept as a learner; he states that parents are the most significant persons in this respect. More than 90 per cent of the students in the Brookover study saw parents as being of academic significance, a fact which should direct our efforts to the problem of regularized parent-teacher-child relationships.[13]

In light of findings such as those of Brookover, teachers may be inclined to adopt a hopeless attitude toward the disadvantaged child who

---

[13] Wilbur B. Brookover, "Self Concept of Ability and School Achievement," Cooperative Research Project #1636 (East Lansing: Bureau of Educational Research, Michigan State University, October 1965), pp. 203–209.

has low motivation for school achievement. Such inclinations toward hopelessness are supported by the untested assumption that disadvantaged children do not have parents or other significant adults who have an interest in their success. If the school can have little impact generally on raising motivational levels of children and if we assume the parents to be disinterested, then, can we not justify *our lack of hope* for the school success of disadvantaged?

> *If the school cannot alone change a pupil's self-concept toward academic tasks, does it follow that the neglect of disadvantaged pupils will have no negative effects either? If we cannot bring about significant positive changes in self-concept, it follows that we can do little damage to self-concept, doesn't it?*
>
> *What errors, if any, do you see in this line of reasoning? What new efforts would you recommend in the event that teachers really want to do something about helping the disadvantaged child?*

Reward systems. Olympia P. Lowe has raised pertinent questions about the "reward system" of the school and its relevance to many disadvantaged youngsters in the city ghettos. Professor Lowe views the use of stars, grade marks, and other symbols of achievement as rewards for desired responses which often hold little value for the ghetto child. The ability to make four or five dollars shining shoes after school will be praised in the ghetto home, according to Lowe, and the achievement will be held up before other children in the home. By contrast, the gold star for spelling performance will buy nothing, at least not in the near future. Lowe concluded that the school would do well to try out tangible rewards, such as, coupons that will buy oranges, since the disadvantaged world is one of concrete needs and tangible values.[14] On the spur of the moment, Lowe's analysis seems to be accurate, but his reward suggestion may strike the typical teacher as wrong and impossible. What do you think?

What is the relationship between language and social education?

In a specialized book of this nature, it is not feasible to attempt to exhaust the implications which language development and patterns have

---

[14] Taken from a video tape by Olympia P. Lowe prepared at Ohio University (August 1968).

The Child and Social Education 203

for the social educaton of the child. Beyond the fact, often overlooked, that the emotional power of certain words may interfere with the communication so essential to social science education, is the more mundane problem posed by the use of special terms that have no broad common meanings for children. The humorous anecdotes which have been told of garbled pledges of allegiance are actually testimonials to poor communication in the teaching process.

A fantastic amount of verbalism has been generated in the social science education field, due in part to the contributions of the specialized disciplines which constitute the field of social and behavioral sciences. Several decades ago, the elementary school child would encounter the usual history and geography terms; today additional terminology from sociology, anthropology, political science, and economics may be encountered in the instructional materials.

Consider the following terms and ask in what life context the elementary school child would be likely to encounter either the term or the concept it is expected to elicit:

1.	Landforms	13.	Extended family
2.	Latitude	14.	Services and goods
3.	Longitude	15.	Immigration
4.	Meridian	16.	Mobility
5.	Equator	17.	Wealth
6.	Poles	18.	Scarcity
7.	Erosion	19.	Equality
8.	Altitude	20.	Democracy
9.	Delta	21.	Republic
10.	Peninsula	22.	Bill of Rights
11.	Legislative	23.	Compromise
12.	Roles	24.	Racial groups

This is by no means an exhaustive list, and we do not suggest that you seek to teach the dictionary meanings to your pupils next year. However, we do suggest that you identify how the ideas or processes which are projected by these words and terms enter into the life of the elementary school child. Can you develop an operational definition for each?

Terms are used to designate things, ideas, and processes that exist (or once existed) in actual life situations. Special terms were not invented before they were needed to help people communicate about a particular phenomenon. In your work with young people, verbalism will be avoided and communication enhanced if new processes and concepts can be considered in vocabulary that is familiar to the group. This will take more time, but the meaning will be sustained when the brief, more specific term is introduced.

Social science education is concerned with the development and extension of meaning. Special terms are not used either to challenge or to confuse children. Asking questions about terms that are strange or vague is an indication of pupil growth and teacher effectiveness.

Suggested Problems and Projects

1. It is customary in many schools to teach the children "The Pledge of Allegiance" and "The Star Spangled Banner" during their first year. What reason can you give for not teaching to six-year-olds the meanings of all of the words in the pledge and the national anthem? On what grounds can you justify having the children memorize these selections?

2. If you were to follow the stages of growth suggested by Muller, what would be the nature of the content and activities of social education in the primary grades?

3. Examine several textbooks and *social science* curriculum guides for each of the elementary levels and draw some conclusions with respect to how they follow or deviate from the pattern of learning experiences suggested by authorities in human growth and development.

4. Develop your own summary of the chapter, giving special emphasis to the implications which you see for the social education of children.

5. Organize for analysis and discussion of Olympia Lowe's comments on effective rewards. What are the implications of an individualized approach to rewarding children for desired behavior changes?

6. How would you handle the problem of Raymond and Rosanna? If conditions permit, it would be helpful for the class to collect some data from principal's and teachers concerning the way they deal with such problems.

Related Readings

Ausubel, D. P. "Effects of Cultural Deprivation on Learning Patterns." *Audiovisual Instruction* 10 (January 1965): 10–12.

Beiser, Morton. "Poverty, Social Disintegration and Personality." *Journal of Social Issues,* January 1965.

Bowerman, C. E. and Kinch, J. W. "Changes in Family and Peer Orientation Between the Fourth and Tenth Grades." *Social Forces* 37 (1959): 206–211.

Davie, J. S. "Social Class Factors and School Attendance." *Educational Review* 23 (1953): 178.

Deutsch, M., and Brown, B. "Social Influences in Negro-White Intelligence Differences." *Journal of Social Issues* 20 (1964): 24–35.

Easton, David and Dennis, Jack. "The Child's Image of Government." *The Annals of the American Academy of Political and Social Science* 361 (September 1965): 40–47.

Elkin, Frederick. *The Child and Society, The Process of Socialization.* New York: Random House, 1963.

Friedman, K. C. "Time Concepts of Elementary School Children." *Elementary School Journal* 44 (1944): 337–442.

Gordon, I. J. *Children's Views of Themselves.* Washington, D.C.: Association for Childhood Education International, 1959.

Hartley, E. L., Rosenbaum, M., and Schwartz, S. "Children's Perceptions of Ethnic-Group Membership." *Journal of Psychology* 26 (1948): 387–398.

Horowitz, F. D. "The Relationship of Anxiety, Self-concept, and Sociometric Status Among Fourth, Fifth, and Sixth Grade Children." *Journal of Abnormal and Social Psychology* 65 (1962): 212–214.

Parten, M. B. "Social Play Among Preschool Children." *Journal of Abnormal and Social Psychology* 28 (1933): 136–147.

Sears, P. S., and Levin, H. "Levels of Aspiration of Preschool Children." *Child Development* 28 (1957): 317–326.

7

INQUIRY IN THE SCHOOLS OF A DEMOCRACY
Elements in the inquiry process
What is the teacher's role in inquiry?
What are suitable areas for inquiry?
What are some common problems?
What is a developmental approach to inquiry?
What strategies and techniques are most helpful?

A PERSPECTIVE ON INQUIRY

SUGGESTED PROBLEMS AND PROJECTS

RELATED READINGS

Inquiry Processes for Children and Teachers

I think teaching is primarily the business of listening to the pupil and responding to whatever happens in the pupil with further questions, and it could be that the questions are statements. Statements, as I said before, can be questions if you understand them properly—they are proposals to entertain something. A statement is saying, "Well, what do you think of this?" Then, when you hear what they think of this, you try some more. Jacques Martain's book on education is one of the best statements I've ever read about what a teacher does in this respect. Martain thinks of a teacher as knowing more than the pupil does, yet in some sense not conveying it, but seeing that it is made available to the pupil. The great use of superior knowledge is to understand what the pupil is learning as it is learned. It takes great wisdom to be able to follow a learning pupil sensitively enough to know what the next step is for him, and you don't press the next step. You watch it happen. If it sticks, you help it a bit, but it's not a transmission, or an imposition, or a filling of a vessel, or any of those things. Those are all bad images of the real teaching function; the real one is this penetration of one intelligence by another.[1]

It is difficult to find a teacher who will say that she is not concerned with inquiry in her classroom. In its loosest sense, some form of inquiry goes on whenever anyone seeks to resolve a question or a problem situation, regardless of his identification with the problem, his motivation, or his efficiency in carrying out the inquiry process. We want to direct our attention here to the nature and place of inquiry as a deliberately conceived process of efficient problem solving. In the older types of social studies programs, where information gathering and recall were major objectives, inquiry was simple, and its transfer value to real life situations was low.

---

[1] "The Constant Questioner—An Interview with Scott Buchanan," reprinted, by permission, from the January 1970 issue of *The Center Magazine,* a publication of the Center for the Study of Democratic Institutions in Santa Barbara, California.

Inquiry in the Schools of a Democracy

If we believe that skill in inquiry is essential to effective participation in the affairs of a democratic society, the place and the nature of inquiry in social education is defined. Open inquiry becomes a developmental task that occupies a central position in the rational program of social science education. Such inquiry will be directed, more often than not, to the problems and situations of the here and now that are representative of recurring human concerns and that are within the conceptual grasp of the maturity level of any given group of youngsters.

Open inquiry is considered an essential developmental task that must be initiated in elementary school and extended and refined in succeeding years, hopefully carrying into the adult life of each individual. Open inquiry requires that the individual be involved in the valuing of the problem or issue to be investigated and in the identification of several alternative solutions; this is in contrast to a carefully manipulated, closed inquiry which conducts the learner through a carefully structured situation leading inevitably to the conclusions that the teacher had anticipated. Closed inquiry will seek to limit the scope of investigation in order that predetermined positions will be reached. This type of inquiry is, of course, safe in most classrooms and safe in most societies, whether they be democratic or authoritarian.

In the adult life of a citizen in the United States, there are problems and issues, public and private, which call for prudent use of inquiry skills. In these adult situations, the problem elements will not always appear in crystal clear fashion; a benevolent wise man will not be present to suggest various hypotheses, to direct the adult to pertinent data, nor to tell him whether he has sorted fact from fiction. The validity of the conclusions that the adult draws in his own problem-solving process will be tested as he moves to act. Open inquiry is a valued behavior in United States society, but a behavior that has been neglected in many classrooms for an assortment of reasons.

It is folly to believe that skills in inquiry will suddenly emerge in young people at age 21, if their formal experiences with investigative procedures have been limited to reading, recall, and closed inquiry. Social science education experiences provide the pupil with opportunities to inquire during the school years with the teacher acting as an adult participant. The barrage of persuasive messages that the individual receives daily via the mass media dictates that the school be very much concerned with the development of the skill involved in open inquiry.

Elements in the inquiry process

In everyday life, inquiry is generated by a *conflict,* an *interest,* or a *problem* that commands the attention of the individual. In the school setting, this element may be almost totally lacking to the extent that the problem, conflict, or interest may be perceived as such by no one except the teacher. In such situations, the pupil problem is one of doing the thing that the teacher wants done and the inquiry is psychologically closed.

Hypothesizing is logically the next step, although in real life situations it may be given scant attention. The development of *questions of fact* that will aid in checking the hypotheses is another step in the investigation. The identification of likely sources of relevant information follows, and finally the *testing* of hypotheses is carried out in light of available data. Hypotheses will be *retained* or *rejected,* but always with a tentative attitude which will be related to the confidence one has in the data which was used.

Attitudes and inquiry. At the outset, the inquiry process depends upon an attitude or a value for a particular way of trying to resolve questions in a manner that makes use of the higher mental processes. A considerable degree of self-discipline is required if one is to proceed to inquire into a problem about which his feelings or emotions have already suggested an answer. An example can be drawn from the problem of draft evasion during the late 1960's and early 1970's. The cause of the draft evasions has often been viewed as stemming from overpermissiveness on college campuses and the effects of draft counselors. Yet, data, apparently unchecked by people who moved quickly from hypotheses to conclusions, reveals that the number of draft evaders has been proportionately lower during the years of the Vietnam controversy than for several other major war periods when campus activities were not viewed as cases of youth rebellion.

Emotions are vital factors which operate in the selection of problems to be studied (or in their recognition as deserving study). The reluctance to include certain kinds of data may be based on strong attitudes which limit rational investigation. When Margaret Mead testified before a senate committee looking into the marijuana problem, she observed that it was probably less harmful than the popular adult stimulants of alcohol and tobacco. The following day, a U.S. senator concluded that Margaret Mead was a nasty old woman!

Other public issues, such as, birth control, air and water pollution, and highway safety, evoke emotional positions that often preclude careful inquiry. Such issues and problems will not go away merely because a vested interest builds an emotional obstacle to inquiry or because of long standing biases. The school must find the means, with community understanding and support, to bring contemporary problems into the inquiry activities of youngsters. Dealing with the emotional aspect of inquiry is as crucial as any other part of the inquiry process.

What is the teacher's role in inquiry?

If we can agree that the teacher's major responsibility is that of planning opportunities and coordinating children's activities in order to attain desired goals, we can move directly to the teacher's role in inquiry. You will want to keep in mind that an important characteristic of social science education is its concern for the inquiring-conceptualizing-behaving relationships. Information, facts, data—these are used to assist the child in his pursuit of meaning—the end in view is conceptualizing-behavior, rather than the display of a body of assorted facts. How will the teacher's role be modified when she is especially concerned that the child will develop his inquiry skills and the concepts that support specific behaviors? Wentworth Clarke views her role as a senior team member.

Senior team member. Clarke has used this term to describe the teacher's relationship with children (not other teachers) in activities that are inquiry oriented. This represents an important point of difference from the teacher as a leader in this particular type of learning situation. Do not confuse this with the overall role of the teacher as the designated adult who is responsible for pupil welfare and management in addition to her role in specific learning activities. It should be understood that children and teachers have different qualifications for the role expectations assigned them by the larger society, but it is equally obvious that open inquiry cannot flourish in a classroom dominated by an adult whose sheer authority pervades the atmosphere throughout the day.[2]

The inquiry teacher is a senior team member because she is skilled in facilitating individual and group efforts. She has a wider experience background than children, and she has a broader acquaintance generally with the issues, problems, and organized information about human activities. Her skills are essential in *organizing, planning,* and *facilitating inquiry,* and her familiarity with sources of information provides guidelines to the pupils in their search for data. The senior team member does not provide the lists of right and wrong answers, she is more concerned with the ways in which the pupil arrives at a conclusion and what kinds of evidence satisfy the search for meaning.

The senior team member will be, more often than not, caught up in the inquiry process with the children, and this need not be an artificial involvement. The recurring problems that confront people all around the world are by no means solved, and man has barely made a beginning in his efforts to understand his own behavior and the nature of his role and relationship to his total environment. The teacher who feels

---

[2] Wentworth Clarke, "Changing Teacher Roles," Cedar Rapids City Schools, Cedar Rapids, Iowa (1969).

smugly superior and uninvolved in the efforts "to understand" of even the youngest pupil should let the whole adult world in on her secrets! Let us examine the following comparison:

Teacher-leader	Senior team member
Talks more than pupils	Talks less than pupils
Tells pupils the important questions	Develops questions with the children
Restates the pupils' questions and comments	Examines and selects material with children
Is the focal point for pupil discussion	May ask for restatement, may permit "poor" questions to be pursued
Is critic and judge of pupils' ideas	Is a facilitator, not a focal point
Invites convergent thinking	Evaluates with the children, the total effort
Desires closure, finality	Invites divergent thinking
Is knowledge and fact oriented	Will identify, with pupils, points of consensus, positions and reasons for continuing doubt and further inquiry
Is failure avoidance oriented	Is concept, skill and behavior oriented

Use of time. Teaching strategies are often controlled by the teacher's concern for covering a certain amount of material and for doing so in a specified span of time. The involvement of pupils in inquiry requires a flexible schedule for the learning activities. If the inquiry is highly structured and closed, the teacher-leader can, indeed, "take the class through" an area of study; in an open inquiry program, the children will move through a problem investigation and the senior team member will be sensitive to the development of concepts, use of skills, and degree of commitment and energy levels which the children exhibit as they work. There is nothing wrong with the interruption of a task that, in the teacher's view, is incomplete, if teaching-learning factors seem to indicate that such an interruption is needed. This is possible and feasible where both children and teacher understand that all inquiry into human affairs is ongoing and that we—as students and as adults—expect to return many times to an issue or a topic.

Since coverage of material has been supplanted by the development of concepts and skill building, the allocation of time must be geared to the progress of the pupils in conceptualizing and using skills. Display of a storehouse of facts is not reasonable evidence of such progress, although many of us in college teaching continue to pretend that it is.

Evaluation. The teacher's role as an evaluator of pupil growth in the inquiry process requires modification. The realities of adult life in a democracy call for the skillful inquiry into human problems by all citizens. It is ludicrous for the teacher to view a child's growth in inquiry on a pass-fail basis, when it is a fact that, at age 18 or 21, he will have the full privileges and responsibilities of citizenship. Failing social education in a democracy would be nothing more than humorous were it not for the negative affects that it has on the child's continuing interest and participation in the affairs of his society. The "failure" will be called upon to defend democracy in time of war, to support his schools with tax money, and to vote on people and issues at election time.

In social science education, there are no acceptable alternatives to growth and progress unless we are to deny licenses to practice! In our own peculiar way, we have failed to differentiate between preparing a person to be a mechanic or a doctor, a role for which he might not qualify, and preparing people to be citizens, a role for which they will "qualify," regardless of the quality of their preparation. Accordingly, emphasis is currently upon development rather than perfection.

What are suitable areas for inquiry?

This question leads back to a consideration of the behavioral objectives of social science education and to the concepts which support the desired behaviors. The inquiry process calls for children to conceptualize about knowledge and the rational processes for gaining and developing knowledge. Beyond that, the inquiry process becomes a set of tools that is useful in the development of concepts about a number of human problems, conditions, and situations. In the formal school program, the crucial or highly functional concept areas will receive priority for investigation. These areas are presented in the chapter which deals with *concepts*.

Individualization of inquiry. Concept areas that are selected for inquiry are highly relevant in terms of their persistent and universal importance in the continuing effort to understand and deal with human existence. They have high relevance from an adult point of view; their inclusion in the school program depends upon the manner in which their relevance is perceived by children on their own terms.

The social science education program does not limit the child in his own individual efforts at inquiry. So, beyond the concept areas

Inquiry Processes for Children and Teachers 213

"*This year, boys and girls, there is a new thing called inquiry in social studies.*"

which are considered very important, the inquiry-oriented teacher encourages and assists the individual child in his private search for meaning. This type of inquiry takes on the elements of the inquiry process, which is the investigative model in the classroom program, and it goes beyond the usual limits of outside reading. Individual inquiry may involve the teacher conferring with the child about an area of concern to him and developing, with the child, a working plan for investigation of the problem or topic, including hypotheses and questions that are formulated to guide the inquiry. Subsequent individual conferences between child and teacher may be held as needed. There follow a few words of caution concerning the teacher's role in this type of individualized inquiry.

> The child is the controller of the inquiry effort, he may stop short if his motivation wanes.
>
> The child is the final judge of his interest in the problem, although it may arise with either teacher or child.
>
> The teacher is not "judgmental" about the outcome or duration of the individual inquiry, she is a consultant to the child as he reviews his own interest, processes, and outcomes.
>
> Individualized inquiry sets the behavioral stage for the kind of inquiry the person will do as an adult when he will not have group support and guidance.

What are some common problems?

It has been the rule, rather than the exception, that children are conditioned to a particular pattern of classroom behavior, which consists, for the most part, of teacher cues and pupil responses. As the emphasis is shifted to pupil participation in developmental inquiry, the behaviors of the children will be modified to accommodate their expanded role in the learning experience. Teachers will encounter some frustrating moments, particularly as they work with older children who have become comfortable with the "teacher question—pupil answer" relationship.

Problem identification. This has typically been a task of the teacher. Children who have perceived the experience as something that has to be accepted and tolerated do not consider the identification and selection of problems to be studied as an appropriate pupil responsibility, even on a shared basis with teachers. Nor do some teachers!

Until children become accustomed to cooperative teacher-pupil inquiry, they will be inclined to spend as much time trying to figure out what response the teacher is fishing for as they devote to considering the situation that contains many possible problems. In the conventional social studies programs, it is customary to tell the child what the problem is, just as we are now telling you.

A sixth grade teacher posted a display of magazine and newspaper articles and pictures which told about airplane hijacking from the United States to Cuba, and in one instance, to Italy. She included, also, items which dealt with the presence in Canada and Sweden of deserters from the United States Armed Forces. She asked the pupils to read the articles and to think how they all contained the same kind of problem. The following day they compared their ideas.

Among the problems identified were:

1. People violate our laws and then go to another country, and we cannot punish them.
2. It is bad when one country protects the criminals from another country.
3. When people know they can break a law and then escape to another country, it just causes a lot of law breaking.
4. All countries ought to have agreements to return all law breakers to their own country for trial.
5. The different countries do not seem to agree about what is serious lawbreaking.

There were, also, a variety of ideas concerning what the United States should do to force other nations to return law violators to stand trial. As you examine the five items in the example, you will notice some statements that express a value judgement and at least one statement which suggests an hypothesis. During this phase of inquiry activity, it is recommended that all statements be listed, except obvious duplicates, and that the final list be considered to sort out hypotheses and value statements. These can be placed in a separate list for later use.

What reason do you see for accepting all pupil statements at this stage of inquiry?

In this particular case, the teacher was concerned with concept development in that aspect of government that has to do with the jurisdictional characteristics of man-made laws. At a later date, the teacher introduced information about seizures of United States property by certain foreign countries and the problem of fishing boats intruding into our territorial waters. We are including this information in order that the inquiry process will be seen in its relationship to the development of concepts.

Hypothesizing. It is not necessary to dwell on the terminology, and children should have considerable experience with educated guessing before they are told that they are making hypotheses. The major consideration is with development of a way of thinking about problems and a way of proceeding, not with the memorization of terms.

We have observed that students are often concerned that their hypotheses be correct, when it would be more helpful if they would be concerned with making an honest statement of what they think *might* be true about a situation. Again, the teacher will want to list all statements offered by the pupils and then examine, with the class the final list to sort out statements that are not hypothetical in nature.

The problem that had been introduced concerning the airplane hijackings and military deserters produced some hypotheses that were not easily checked out by sixth graders because of a lack of available information. Others were subject to investigation. Some of the hypotheses are included here:

1. People hijack airplanes because they want to get away; they do not want to steal an airplane.
2. If all countries would make the same laws, then the offenders could be punished in any country.
3. If all countries would send back anybody wanted in his home country, there would be no hijacking.
4. We should tell anybody that wants to leave our country that we will help him leave, then no one would hijack planes.
5. Never let those people come back home, and they would not go.
6. Tell Cuba and Canada that we will keep their lawbreakers unless they send ours back, and I'll bet they will.
7. It would help if countries would cooperate.

Remember that the teacher had intended that the children would conceptualize about the limits of law enforcement depending upon where a person was located, particularly in regard to national boundaries and law enforcement. The hypotheses could, in some instances, become focused on a sociological problem dealing with nonconforming behavior. However, in this case, the teacher suggested that the pupils think about questions they would need to answer if they were to find out if their assumptions were in keeping with reality. Some of the questions were:

1. Why do people want to leave their country?
2. Don't any countries work together on catching people who break laws?
3. How can we force other countries to send people back to us?
4. Do we send lawbreakers back to other countries?
5. Don't we ever send the F.B.I. after guys who do these things?
6. Do we tell the family they better get the person to come back or else?
7. Does the United Nations help?

The teacher suggested that they ought to think about *where* the answers could be found. She urged them to be sure that the answer probably existed. This group of sixth graders struggled with the fact that the third question would require experimenting with different ways of getting people back unless it could be reworded. Finally, it was put into past tense, and it was agreed that some kind of answer could be found. Some children objected to the sixth question because they thought our government should not do this kind of thing and that the answer could not be obtained.

Do all of the questions relate to the problem of the limits upon a nation's laws? Teacher involvement at this point is frequently necessary in order to help youngsters focus upon the heart of the problem, rather than get a confusing assortment of questions that relate to other problems. This particular teacher moved back into the hypotheses after the session on questions, and she asked the class to decide which hypotheses were closest to the problem and seemed to be most manageable. She asked the pupils to see which questions would help check each hypothesis. Only one hypothesis was kept after the pupils identified four questions that might help them check it out. From the standpoint of teaching strategy, it should be emphasized that the teacher suggested that each pupil keep his own pet hypothesis and question even though the class effort was being focused on one problem area.

> *As you review the way in which the class and teacher worked up to this point, what kinds of questions do you want to raise with other students and the instructor? (Do not worry about the materials that the children will use. That will come later.)*
>
> *Which hypothesis do you think the class chose for further study?*
>
> *Which four questions?*

Use of information. The search for pertinent information provides the setting in which the usual research and study skills are applied with purpose. The sources of information should not be limited to those which the teacher suggests. Pupils should be given opportunities to use information obtained outside of classroom materials.

A constant concern of teachers is the lack of variety of materials they would like to have in the classroom for pupil use, and we will neither pretend that most teachers have maximum resources, nor tell you that the good teacher will develop her own resource packets and adapt much of the material from other sources. Time, energy, and individual teacher ingenuity are not without limits.

There are some bright spots in the picture, however. With the advent of mass media—more books, magazines, and other printed material are now consumed on a per capita basis than ever before in our history—there are opportunities for locating valuable learning materials outside of the classroom. It cannot be argued that the school of today houses the major materials for learning, rather it brings together resources in an environment which is supportive of learning. Our long held views about educational materials and where they are located must be modified to allow the pupils to extend their search for information beyond the classroom, certainly at the middle and upper levels.

In schools where a commitment has been made to inquiry-oriented programs, social science resource areas in the classroom and in the building library become highly desirable. A team effort involving teachers and children from several classrooms can result in a resource area that will serve the basic needs of social science education. (Materials, such as, newspaper clippings, pictures, graphs, booklets, and the like, should be outcomes of inquiry activities by children rather than a busy work assignment.) A daily newspaper and current publications prepared especially for children should be available.

As more textbook materials, kits, and modules become available, the teacher can use these as base materials, but the search for current information on the outside will continue to be a vital aspect of the inquiry process. The individual citizen needs to be able to locate information long after he is out of school; the habit must be formulated in the school years. Children need assistance and guidance in the location of pertinent information, in assessing its validity, and in applying it to the question at hand. The crucial need is for teachers to look upon this as a developmental part of inquiry skill and to provide opportunities for children to search for and assess a variety of materials in their inquiring activities.

> In an attempt to sensitize a fourth grade group to the difficulties involved in assessing the validity of a piece of information, Miss Irwin presented a news item to the pupils concerning a U.S. troop retreat in South Vietnam. She asked the class if they believed it to be true. Most of the children said that it probably was true. Then Miss Irwin told them that the news item had been published by a Soviet newspaper. Did this make any difference? More than one half of the class then

said that they had doubts about its truth. A few said that they would believe it if it was also reported by the U.S. government.

Miss Irwin asked the children if we should never believe information that is reported by a foreign nation. Should we always believe U.S. sources? Should we try to check more than one account of an important event or situation? She did not believe it timely to press the problem further with ten-year-olds.

> *What other directions would you follow on this problem with 12-year-old children?*

The confidence that we have in any piece of information will involve many factors, but in the final analysis, it is an individual matter. The task in inquiry is to help children become as objective as possible, defending their evaluative processes, rather than the data itself. In adult situations, there will not be a teacher to say what is accurate or false.

What is a developmental approach to inquiry?

If human beings were naturally aware of the processes and problems of inquiry and were inclined by instinct to objectivism, the instructional task would be much simpler. Humans acquire their problem-solving habits from their cultural environment, and since our experience with scientific-rational approaches to human problems is so recent and limited, many children and teachers will continue to use mythical and mystical approaches. We are particularly inclined to abandon rational inquiry when we really want to avoid a problem, when we do not want to change our ideas about a set of social phenomena.

A realistic approach to inquiry in the classroom requires that the difficulties be recognized, not avoided. A developmental approach is concerned with growth and change, not with instant perfection. Children are not automatically proficient in posing hypotheses, formulating questions, locating and selecting data, and forming and testing conclusions; nor are teachers. Adults continue to be limited in their application of inquiry in certain problem areas, probably because the weight of social pressure or long held values causes avoidance. Developmental inquiry is, then, an appropriate activity for both teachers and children.

A beginning. A major objective of social science education is the efficient use of the open inquiry process. A realistic beginning usually calls for a modest, non-threatening approach. Most children depend upon the subjective, emotional sources of ego support which come from authority figures and beliefs and values which have not been doubted. Classroom inquiry into a problem that calls for high levels of awareness of self-interest and emotional bias may be disturbing and destructive. A developmental approach is designed to assist the individual in the acquisition of skills that are essential in coping with human situations and problems —skills that will move the individual's perception of reality to higher levels of accuracy and objectivity. This process is not accomplished by destruction of the child's conceptualizations of social reality through abrupt interventions. After all, the modification of the pupils' inquiring attitudes and skills should result from an internalization of experiences resulting in the emergence of more adequate concepts of knowledge, process, and problems.

Over long periods of time, man has reshaped his concepts of the world and of man, he has refined the processes which have led to new knowledge and new skills. The child should be helped to feel comfortable in his quest for understanding. Early experiences in inquiry should be directed into cognitive areas that are low in emotional content. Inquiry into values and traditions close to the child may be delayed. Structured, closed inquiry will provide opportunities for children to develop the skills of inquiry and to acquire a problem-solving habit or set of behaviors. The developmental goal of open, self-directed inquiry remains, but we do not expect to accomplish it with seven-year-olds.

> A group of seven-year-old pupils worked with the question, what is a family? They talked about it for 15 minutes, presenting their ideas. On another day, the teacher had a variety of pictures of groups of people which she had placed on a tack board. The children examined the pictures and tried to decide which groups *could* be families and which could not be. All of the children except one believed that there had to be a father and a mother in the group if it were to be a family group. One little girl said that her father was dead, but that she and her mother were a family. One picture contained an elderly couple with a younger couple and children. There was disagreement as to whether grandparents were part of the family. A picture of a multi-racial family caused the children to wonder how white parents could have a black child in their family, and one youngster said that you could adopt a family. A picture of a young couple alone led the children to say that a family has to have children!
>
> At this level, the teacher was not concerned with the abstract legal and sociological concepts of family as a social unit. She wanted to begin the development of an awareness of the family concept and to entertain some of the problems in definition. Certainly, she did not wish to involve

the children in deciding whether each of them belonged to a particular kind of family. Family is a psychological entity too.

Another phase of the inquiry dealt with the question, "What do families do?"

At later levels of this social science education program, children will compare a family in the U.S. with a family of another culture. It seems likely that the problem of family disintegration and impact on society and youth should be deferred as a group activity until later adolescence, when other group attachments can support the youngster whose family experience has been distressing.

A concept of inquiry. Just as the child is provided with planned opportunities that will enhance specific conceptualizations about human situations and relationships; likewise, the inquiry process is developed as a concept and also as a tool. A concept of inquiry will be derived from the individual fundamental concepts of knowledge and ways of knowing and from a self-concept that includes the "need to know" as an accepted part of personal goals. Inquiry is not a recipe for problem-solving that can be memorized and then used in the manner of a psycho-motor skill. The inquirer needs to be aware of the process and to understand it as a normal aspect of intelligent human behavior.

The consideration of inquiry as a concept tool is helpful in understanding the pitfalls that await us if we attempt to use the process as a regular problem-solving method. Rarely do we have access to even a majority of the facts which should be considered in making a decision. In real life, and in school too, we arrive at conclusions in order to proceed to action, in spite of the fact that we know that further information may cause us to change our conclusion, even to regret an action. Our concept of inquiry includes the belief that it is a more reliable way of understanding and resolving problems than any other that man has used thus far.

At the problem identification and clarification stage, our intense desires about a solution may lead us to avoid the real problem; we may see only those facts that will support our premature conclusion. The inquiry process cannot be correctly conceptualized as devoid of human feeling and value, but an adequate concept of inquiry requires that we recognize these factors.

Children, particularly younger age levels, are impatient with their problems; they want to get to a comfortable answer and move on. Their experiences in inquiry may seem simple, though they are often intense for the children, but this is the setting in which the inquiry concept is initiated. The day to day behavior model of the teacher as she interacts with children on problems of knowing can have a strong influence on the development of the inquiry concept. The hidden persuaders of the teacher's language are worth considering. How often do we use these expressions:

> "Now, boys and girls, we all know..."
>
> "Let's look in our books now to find the right answer."
>
> "I don't know why people act that way—just human nature, I guess."
>
> "Don't answer unless you are absolutely sure you are right."
>
> "Let's get all the facts."
>
> "We can't waste time with questions about that."
>
> "I realize you would like to spend more time on this, but this is all we need to know now."
>
> "I don't believe we should question the book—the author knows more than we do about it."

> *In what ways do you believe such comments, made day after day, may shape the child's concept of inquiry?*
>
> *How would you restate some of these expressions in order that you could give guidance without shutting off children?*

What strategies and techniques are most helpful?

By this time you will recognize this question as one that suggests a problem which will be of considerable concern to you when you begin your work with boys and girls. The discussion which we present may be viewed as a great deal of hypothesizing with some offering of evidence. We make a strong plea to you to test the strategies and techniques with groups of children and in peer teaching situations.

Use of questions. We have mentioned earlier that the inquiry teacher must make a conscious effort to move away from the old role of answer giver. Likewise, the inquiry teacher is no longer the major questioner in the classroom since the inquiry process requires that children grow in the skills of identifying and formulating questions about a problem situation.

Byron Massialas and his associates at the University of Michigan have suggested four question categories as being helpful in calling for certain cognitive responses.[3] Although these categories are developed

---

[3] Byron Massialas, "Inquiry Into Social Issues," Office of Education Contract 3-7-061678-2942 (Ann Arbor: University of Michigan, July 1969).

Inquiry Processes for Children and Teachers

in conjunction with a secondary school project, they appear to be valid in elementary situations also. The question categories are as follows:

1. Question calling for expository responses.
   What is the capitol of Iowa?
2. Question calling for definition and clarification.
   What does "cheating" mean?
   Were you fighting or playing?
3. Question calling for position or hypothesis.
   Do you think that a cousin is part of your family?
   What are the reasons for so many auto accidents?
4. Question calling for grounding.
   Why were so many children absent the last day of school?
   Why do we use report cards?

For our purpose, we want to point out the importance of the teacher's being aware of the kind of question that will provide appropriate guidance to the child at a particular point in his inquiry. The teacher should also be aware of the importance of assisting the child in formulating his own questions. An example referred to earlier in this chapter dealt with the concept of family. The writers worked with many groups of six-year-olds on this concept and observed that a father, a mother, and children are a family, but some youngsters will include grandparents, while others will not. Some six-year-olds will include their pets in their family (we have been criticized by some first grade teachers when we did not tell the children that a pet is not part of a family).

What kinds of defining questions would you ask first graders, or older children, to extend the definition of family?

As you examine the four question types, which do you believe will most often call for higher thinking processes?

Develop four or five questions of each type and have a colleague react to them in terms of their appropriateness and clarity.

You will notice the flow of relationship among the question types in this cognitive category. Observe that the grounding type question may call for responses that are based on clear evidence (30 children were absent on the last day of school because their families left on vacation trips) or on an untested assumption. (We used report cards to make children study.) A grounding question may lead to a definition or to a clarifying question—what number do you believe is *many* children?

Keep in mind that most adults make tentative decisions on less than complete and perfect evidence, and sometimes they have defined the problem incorrectly. Children will become frustrated if you trap them in an endless circle of questioning that prevents tentative decisions. The objective is to develop the questioning habit as an essential part of inquiry and to view the task as developmental. No one can tell another person *when* to be satisfied with his questioning and inquiring activities—only the testing of his conclusions in real experiences will tell the individual this much.

It has been commonly observed that children quickly become conditioned to a pattern of response which rarely goes beyond the question asked. "Why do so many children lose their mittens?" A question such as this will produce a number of grounding responses beginning with, "Because," and followed by some kind of reason which may not be based on evidence at all. Seldom will children turn the question to one of clarification of the term "many." Skillful teaching technique will include moving from one type of question to another if the original question includes fuzzy terms or questionable hypotheses.

In adult life, we can witness the operation of this closed pattern of question-response in many current issues. A vice-president says that television news should ignore the activities of "kooks," and few persons bother to press for a definition of "kooks" or to question the consequences of such action if it were to become a reality. Skillful use of questions, careful use of expository statements, and an honest use of hypothesizing statements are critical parts of teaching behavior. Expository statements are most likely to terminate or limit further questioning by children, while hypothesizing statements tend to keep the problem open for continued attack by the children and teacher.

Initiating inquiry problems. The use of data at the initial stages of an inquiry activity may serve to engage the pupils in the complex tasks of sorting out important problems and sensing conflicts or disagreements between sets of data. In this regard, data may be pictorial, audible or printed matter; data is not necessarily found between the covers of a textbook.

To begin an investigation of the types of groups to which people in our society belong, one teacher used a collection of pictures which showed many formal and informal groups of people of various ages. Children were asked to identify the groups to which they could belong now, which groups were carefully organized and which were loosely formed, and finally to make observations about the functions of the several groups. In this case, the children generated an array of questions which led them into an investigation of the groups in their community and the reasons why these groups were formed and continued, in addition to the involvement of self and family in various groups. Questions raised by the children gave impetus to the deepening of the study. Data in the form of pictures led to questioning and to the search for further data that would help children learn about the human groups in their own community.

A sixth grade teacher used slides to provide the children with a means to reveal their conceptions of Africa. The questions raised were then the bases for launching their study. Fifteen slides were used, ten of them having been taken in west Africa and the other five elsewhere. The children were asked to identify each slide as being Africa (A) or other (O), and their responses (hypotheses about the slides) were tabulated and compared. On many slides the class was nearly evenly divided, some seeing Africa, others seeing a non-African setting. Pupil reasons for identifying a slide as African were explored (a grounding operation), and the problems of individual expectation and perceptions were finally recognized.

Some children expected Africa to be mostly jungle and grass huts, with few or no modern cities, television, railroads or deserts. The general conception was that African people are black, scantily clad, and savage. Such ideas were rephrased as questions that required further evidence. Then a series of 30 slides was shown to illustrate the diversity of the African continent from Egypt in the north to Capetown in the south, and two questions were raised: "How can we answer our questions about Africa?" "Where can we find information that will help us to answer our questions?" In the case just mentioned, the conflict in expectations and perceptions was used as a jumping off point. In other cases, the conflict or problem may appear in printed information and further study may be needed to clarify the issue.

The important experience for you is that of working with several kinds of data in setting the stage for inquiry activities. The problem area is not nearly so critical as your need to work with data in developing inquiry questions and procedures.

A Perspective on Inquiry

Problem solving, critical thinking, creative thinking, and general thinking ability have been the subject of recurring concern and study throughout most of the twentieth century. The emphasis that has been given recently to the inquiry processes in the social realm may mislead the young professional into the belief that a new field of investigation has been uncovered, when indeed, the current concerns are with extending and refining the inquiry processes in the study of social man.

"Where will all this inquiry lead us?"

As long as school people (and society) viewed the educative process as one of assimilation of basic facts, the place of inquiry processes was not an urgent problem. Eventually, the growing demands of our scientific-technological environment and the Soviet advances in space combined to force the attention of society and the educators to the nature and role of inquiry and discovery in the programs of science education. It is appropriate to recall that John Dewey authored a book, *How We Think* (1910), in which he suggested a five step problem-solving process and that John S. Gray, Cyril Burt, Benjamin Bloom, and William Vinacke made subsequent contributions to this area. It is interesting to note that

Bloom (1950) and Vinacke (1952) appear to be among the first to include, as explicit components in a problem-solving activity, attitude toward the solution of problems and emotional responses to problem situations.

David Russell, in an excellent and extensive treatment of problem solving, has offered some conclusions based upon the research available:

1. Problem solving is a complex of a number of abilities. Analysis of test results suggests that there is a reasoning or problem-solving factor somewhat *independent of general intelligence and of factual knowledge in the field tested.* (Italics added)

2. Most problem solving involves awareness of the problem (or the set or attitude of the solver), search for solution materials, and critical judgment of the hypotheses produced. In many types of problem situations, of course, children and adults seldom attain this nearly idealized pattern of problem-solving behavior.

3. Problem-solving activities do not seem to vary because of age or general intelligence so much as they vary because of the nature of the problem and because of the motivation and set of the solver. There is some evidence,... that children faced with a problem go about solving it in much the same way as do adolescents or adults.

4. In most human problem solving, personality factors have great influence over the methods used and the outcomes achieved. Confidence and a suitable level of aspiration affect problem solving favorably.

5. In comparison with the individual, the group can provide more possible solutions to a problem with more effective criticism of the solutions proposed.[4]

The fact that inquiry processes, problem solving, and the like have been subjects of comment and study for many years (when did Socrates live?) need not cause us to believe that the place of inquiry in the school experiences of our children is well-defined and secure. To know something of the psychological nature of inquiring behavior is not synonymous with broad social acceptance of such behavior, nor does it mean that teachers have devised and tested a variety of strategies and techniques which will assist youngsters in their development of the inquiry processes.

It appears that for the past 40 to 50 years, U.S. education has had dependable research information concerning the inquiry area which has not been generally implemented in the classroom. For many decades the typical classroom program has been oriented heavily toward information

---

[4] David H. Russell, *Children's Thinking* (New York: Ginn and Co., 1956), pp. 269–270.

assimilation and recall, in spite of the fact that there is hard information on the high rate of forgetting and the low correlations between knowledge possession and problem-solving skills. It would seem that we do not need reasons for those things that we want to do, and we shall never recognize as valid that evidence which points us in an undesired direction.

1. Identify the implications for working with boys and girls that are contained in the five point summary from Russell.

2. Do you see the author's closing remarks as cynical or hopeful? Consider with your colleagues in class whether you hold an optimistic outlook or a pessimistic view.

Suggested Problems and Projects

1. Arrange to observe one or more sessions of an elementary class during your consideration of inquiry. Look for evidence of the inquiry process being used by children and teachers. Does it appear that inquiry is being used in a planned and deliberate manner? Two or more students should visit the same classes in order that you may compare your observations.

2. Arrange to visit a class where the teacher has specifically planned for an inquiry oriented activity. It is desirable that you observe inquiry at different levels in order that you will become aware of differences that may be due to maturation and experience.

3. As a synthesizing activity, plan an inquiry-oriented project for any level of the elementary school. It is suggested that you work in teams of three or four. Use a concept or generalization statement as a point of departure. Include activities that you would use as well as materials. How will you evaluate pupil growth during your proposed activity?

4. In conjunction with the above activity, arrange to peer teach at least part of the project.

Related Readings

Beyer, Barry K. *Inquiry in the Social Studies Classroom: A Strategy for Teaching.* Columbus, Ohio: Charles E. Merrill Publishing Co., 1971.

Crabtree, Charlotte. "Inquiry Approaches to Learning Concepts and Generalizations in Social Studies." *Social Education* 30 (October 1966): 407–411.

Edgerton, Stephanie G. "Learning By Induction." *Social Education* 31 (May 1967): 373–376.

Ellsworth, Ruth. "Critical Thinking—Its Encouragement." *National Elementary Principal* 42 (May 1963): 24–29.

Getzels, J. W. "Creative Thinking, Problem Solving, and Instruction." *Theories of Learning and Instruction,* 63rd Yearbook, Part I of the National Society for the Study of Education, pp. 240–267. Chicago: The University of Chicago Press, 1964.

Joyce, Bruce R. "The Modes of Inquiry Problems." *Social Education* 30 (March 1966): 181–183.

Russell, David H. *Children's Thinking,* chapters 9 and 10. Boston: Ginn and Company, 1956.

8

EARLY METHODS OF TEACHING SOCIAL STUDIES
    Teacher-centered methods
    Pupil-centered methods

GOALS TO BE ACHIEVED THROUGH THE SOCIAL SCIENCES

PLANNING FOR CONCEPT-CENTERED LEARNING ACTIVITIES

SUMMARY

SUGGESTED PROBLEMS AND PROJECTS

RELATED READINGS

Instructional Methodology and the Teacher

The process of teaching has a long history dating back to the beginning of time. The Socratic method is used effectively by some college instructors and public school teachers, the aim being to bring the pupil to the place where he will be able to acquire the attitude of a "true learner." Modern education, including social science education, holds this same principle of teaching. Throughout the history of U.S. education, some teachers and most educators have been concerned about the effectiveness of the instructional methods they were using. Schools in the early period of our history were known for their read-recite-test plan for organized instruction. Local examining committees would appear at the school to determine the effectiveness of the instruction (or the teacher). However, in 1873, the Quincy, Massachusetts, Board of Education, under the persuasion of Charles Francis Adams and Colonel Francis Parker, examined the children to determine if their learnings could be applied to problems of everyday life. This committee was astounded to find that the children were badly lacking in ability to apply their rote learnings to real life problems.

Each generation has had its critics of pedagogical practices. Educators and psychologists have continuously conducted investigations to find better ways of teaching. The purpose of this chapter is to furnish teachers of social science education in the elementary school with some practical guides for the improvement of their methods of instruction. The teaching process will be traced from the teacher-dominated instructional organization to the present movement toward placing the responsibility for learning on the learner. The writers purport that teachers emerge as master teachers through a conscious effort to evaluate and modify their procedures. But they also recognize that, for the most part, these changes come about slowly and deliberately.

Early Methods of Teaching Social Studies

Early efforts at teaching geography, citizenship, and history were largely carried out through the assign-read-recite-test method. In fact, this method of teaching has dominated the social studies well into the twentieth century. The mechanical nature of this method of instruction has led to much criticism of teacher training. But, this criticism led to concerted efforts to produce methods of teaching more compatible with the cooperative principles of democratic living. The basic movement in teaching has been from teacher-centered or centric methods toward pupil-centered methods as a means of achieving the fundamental goals of education.

Teacher-centered methods

Teacher-centered methods in social science teaching are those procedures which focus a major portion of the attention upon the teacher as the controlling factor in the organization of learning. Usually these methods are characterized by patterns of instruction that are based upon an approach to learning in which the results are evaluated in terms of the number of correct responses the children can write or recite back to the teacher. Thus, this concept of learning is one based on memory.

The recitation method. This method emerged with the use of the textbook as the basic determiner of the curriculum. By providing drill exercises at the end of the chapter, the child was led to memorize the list of important dates in history or a list of important events. His success in mastering these lists had much to do with his success in school. The authors recognize that some teachers would change their teaching strategy if they had some guides to go by. But, supervisors and educators frequently expect the teacher to change from a basically traditional teacher to a modern teacher by using the latest developments for learning, which is sheer fallacy. For the teacher to be effective in changing, she must develop a sound psychological and philosophical basis for learning and teaching. If the primary purpose of learning is to change the behavior pattern of the learner, the teacher must keep in mind that this change in behavior can produce negative, as well as positive, results. The supervisor or principal should recognize that this also holds true for the teacher.

The methods thus used by the teacher might result in verbal learning only, or the learning might be dictatorial if carried out in an authoritative environment and lead to false concepts of the whole process. Children may fail to develop an appreciation and understanding of certain races, socio-economic groups, or religious groups because poor inter-group relations result from the ineffective methods of the teacher. The quality and quantity of learning in any given classroom depend upon the understanding the teacher has of method, since her concepts of method are indicative of her understandings of the major factors in learning situations. The recitation then becomes the focal point of the method used. Although this method is rapidly fading out of elementary classrooms, far too many children are still subjected to it in learning the social sciences. Of importance here are some guides which will aid the teacher in improving this pattern of teaching:

1. Differentiate assignments to provide for enrichment of the more able pupils; set minimum requirements for slow learners.
2. Provide questions or guides to aid the student in getting the most from his assignments.
3. Supplement assignments with films, field trips, and presentations from resource persons.
4. Plan questions that will relate the assignment to meaningful situations.
5. Relate assignments to contemporary times—cause, effect, current usage, etc.
6. Permit pupils to share in making a list of questions to be used during every recitation period.
7. Relate previous assignments to current recitation to provide continuity in learning.

The interested teacher should carefully analyze these guides in terms of the demand made upon the teacher and pupils in order to determine the degree of reorganization of teaching required to improve pupil learning. Modern elementary school textbooks do provide many helpful suggestions which teachers at this stage of development might find useful.

What is the developmental approach to teaching? Changing a pattern of operation to a new design which affects tradition or custom is a gradual process because people are so closely related to their environment. We have lagged behind in social progress while technology has moved ahead. There were ample volunteers to take a first airplane ride or ride a rocket to the moon, but when it comes to breaking down barriers of social customs, which have hampered human progress in solving significant social problems, we find it difficult to change.

Teachers who are interested in self-improvement can improve if they will take one step at a time. On the other hand, the training of preservice teachers should involve only the best practices since the perspective teachers are not indoctrinated with philosophical or psychological principles which hamper change. A teacher who is doing a good job of being a textbook teacher can learn some techniques for supplementing the textbook with appropriate materials, as well as learning to understand, philosophically and psychologically, the learner's need for these resources. Thus, the teacher can grow toward utilizing more acceptable principles of teaching, which are consistent with psychological principles of learning, yet can maintain personal security. This step in the development of the teacher then requires her to:

1. Plan a topic or theme based on textbook content.
2. Stimulate the interests of children in a study of the topic.
3. Identify purposes for learning (pupil questions).
4. Provide a wide variety of resource materials.
5. Use appropriate audio-visual materials—films, filmstrips, pictures, etc.
6. Use individual and group reports.
7. Evaluate learning.

The teacher who has been using this pattern of social science instruction needs only to appraise carefully her procedures in the light of the objectives of modern social science education. That is, the entire procedure is a definite breakthrough for the textbook-limited teacher. But, even this step doesn't provide for the vital decision-making process which is essential in building democratic skills. In addition, it presupposes that the teacher can judge what segment of knowledge the learners need at their particular stage of development. But, significant learning can result from the pattern of instruction discussed above; the content to be learned may meet a practical need as the children relate their readings about the Middle East, for example, to some vital and persistent problem in their own community. The point is, that the teacher at this stage of development is now ready to initiate learning experiences with children beyond the points enumerated above. Thus, she is ready to move to a higher instructional level.

The discussion method. This method of instruction is probably the most widely used teaching strategy in social science instruction. It provides the opportunity for individuals to interchange ideas and to ask questions. The teacher usually serves as a moderator, but her ability to see that all children participate in the discussion is an important skill, which is essential for the success of the method. This method is an extension of the recitation approach and follows some of the same procedures. Of importance here is the fact that the method usually is pupil-centered, but it can become teacher-centered if the teacher controls the discussion. Some guides for improving the discussion method follow:

1. Seek to develop the ability to ask questions which stimulate reflective thinking and which require the pupil to:
    A. Compare or contrast
    B. Make decisions for or against
    C. Classify data

      D. Show cause and effect relations
      E. Cite examples or illustrations
2. Release the children from trying to give the answer they feel the teacher wants:
      A. Discourage fragmentary answers
      B. Make application to new situations

Perhaps one of the weaknesses of the discussion method is the lack of skills possessed by the teacher in working with small groups. The discussion method should involve 15 or fewer students, thus providing for good interaction. But, the problem is that teachers tend to use the same techniques with ten pupils as they do with 30. That is, they are accustomed to accepting one word answers with 30 pupils and are inclined to accept the same in small groups. By applying the guides stated above to small group situations, teachers can develop skills which will lead to improved instruction.

Pupil-centered methods

Early leaders in educational reform, such as, Friedrich Froebel, Johann Pestalozzi, John Dewey, William Kilpatrick, and others, have led the way for an attack against the teacher dominated classroom. This attack was based upon a social utility philosophy which relates the learner to his needs and interests. The methods or procedures used in pupil-centered teaching are problem-solving techniques with the teacher serving as a guide.

Teacher-pupil planning. The modern social science program, with its accent on self-learning and inquiry, sets the stage for cooperative planning. Teacher-pupil planning offers the following advantages consistent with the modern approach to social science instruction: 1) it is consistent with democratic principles; 2) individual, as well as group, welfare is considered; 3) group skills essential to cooperative living are fostered; 4) sound principles of learning are utilized; and 5) learning is meaningful when its application becomes an instructional goal.

The teacher-pupil planning method gives impetus to the unit approach, which found widespread acceptance in the field of social studies instruction in the 1940's and 1950's. The following diagram shows how cooperative planning, which establishes goals or objectives, gives direction to solving problems which have been agreed upon by the learner and the teacher as being worthy of study. This graph presentation shows the sequence of learning activities.[1]

---

   [1] Albert H. Shuster and Milton E. Ploghoft, *The Emerging Elementary Curriculum*, 2nd edition (Columbus, Ohio: Charles E. Merrill Publishing Company, Inc., 1970), p. 108.

236   *Section III*

```
              ⎧ Purposing    See reasons for ⎫
              ⎪                                ⎫
              ⎪ Planning     How to reach      ⎪
Teacher ⎫     ⎪                                ⎪    Objectives
 and    ⎬ →  ⎨ Executing    Carrying out      ⎬    or Goals
Pupil   ⎭     ⎪                                ⎪
              ⎪ Evaluating   How well these were reached ⎪
              ⎪                                ⎪
              ⎩ Modifying    Means of improving ⎭
```

FIGURE 8–1. Teacher-Pupil Planning

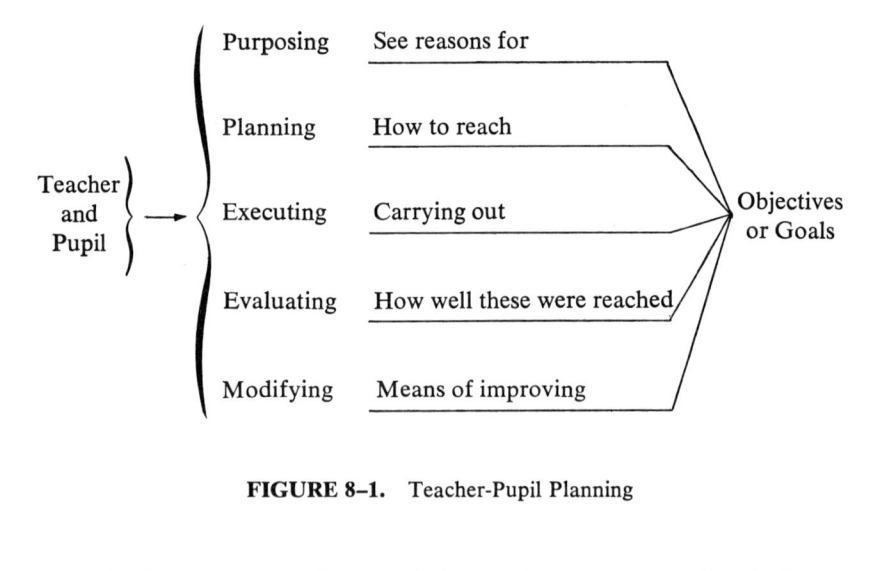

Teachers need to identify their own levels of growth relative to such facets of the instructional program as planning. There are many levels of planning which move along a hierarchy or continuum from least to most desirable. Such a self-evaluation device can be developed for all aspects of instruction. Presented here is one part of a self-evaluation instrument on planning. The teacher can then determine "where she is" and what she needs to do to progress to the next higher level.

CHART 8–1. Classroom Procedures [2]

Level I *Planning*	Level II *Planning*	Level III *Planning*	Level IV *Planning*
The teacher has little understanding of cooperative planning.	The pupils are given little opportunity to participate in planning. The teacher plans the selection and use of materials as they are related to topics.	The suggestions of children are recorded by the teacher and used as they seem helpful.	Teachers and pupils work together with each accepting the contributions of all members as worthy of consideration by the group.

The unit. A unit of learning as used here means "a series of related learning experiences which are developed around the interests, needs,

---

[2] Adapted from "A Guide to Teacher Growth Through Self-Evaluation," Norfolk, Virginia Public Schools.

and problems of children, are socially significant and produce purposeful activities resulting in a modified behavior of the learner." The unit [3] usually is subject oriented, but the subject may grow out of interests or experiences of the learners or it may be a topic in a textbook. However, Dewey pointed out that "providing an experience for children is not in itself a self sufficient event," and he further stated that experiencing has an existence apart from subject matter.[4] This was basically the problem with the early efforts of the activity schools—the lack of selection and organization of subject matter to facilitate learning, as well as failure to supplement the activity itself. In the unit approach to teaching, knowledge is acquired in an ongoing effort to satisfy the need or desire as the individual matures. The typical unit would be organized around the following headings:

I. Topic or theme
II. Development of purposes
   A. Specific
   B. General
III. Overview
   A. Nature of problem
   B. Scope of problem
   C. Generalizations involved
IV. Initiatory or approach
   A. Ongoing interest
   B. Prearranged to stimulate interest
V. Working period
   A. Length of time per day
   B. Particular time in school day
VI. Culminating the unit
   A. Summary of learning
   B. Accentuate activities or projects
   C. Identify related interests resulting from unit
VII. Evaluation
   A. Determine extent to which objectives were achieved
   B. Pupil self-evaluation
   C. Use variety of evaluation techniques
VIII. Instructional materials
   A. Reference books, pamphlets, etc.
   B. Films, filmstrips, recordings, tapes, etc.
   C. Maps, globes, charts, pictures, etc.

It should become obvious that the unit can be developed cooperatively with the children, and it can provide for meeting individual differences of children. Teachers, who have not had experience in teaching a unit, usually begin by structuring it in order to maintain a feeling of security and self-confidence. But, as the teacher gains experience, she

---

[3] See sample unit in Appendix C.
[4] John Dewey, *Philosophy and Civilization* (New York: C. P. Putnam's Sons, 1931), p. 261.

will soon see how the children can become more and more involved in carrying out the complete unit from the planning stage to the final evaluation.

Inquiry process. Chapter seven has been devoted to the inquiry approach to instruction, but it should be pointed out that this approach is a natural outgrowth of the unit approach, which is research oriented. In the inquiry process, however, it is possible for an individual, a small group or a class to be developing their learnings around the same social problem, each investigating the topic which most interests him and following through with the essential research to reach a conclusion. Suffice it to say here that this approach does place the responsibility for learning on the learner, and it is directed at making the learner knowledgeable about the decision-making process as he progresses in developing skills essential in using the elements of inquiry.

Individually guided education. When the teacher and the school have a definable commitment to serving the individual, the lockstep method of instruction will be broken. Children grow, mature, comprehend, and learn at different rates of time. Thus, the teacher must understand each child as she plans instructional strategies. The child who is learning at his own level will then be matched with the appropriate materials, the right instructional procedure, and the time will be varied for each child to achieve or master the task to be learned.

The inquiry approach will be planned to allow children to function at different levels. Some problems may not be recognized by children who are less mature than others in the same classroom, thus, children might be working individually at different levels of sophistication on the same broad social problem. The levels of conceptualization will be different, the materials used will vary in difficulty, and the generalizations reached and the applications made might all be at different knowledge levels.

Taking the following list of objectives for children to achieve in the social science program, differences in attainment will vary widely. But, these differences will be largely those of time required to learn or of the ability to comprehend at a given period in the child's schooling.

Goals to Be Achieved Through the Social Sciences

1. Students should be presented with opportunities to identify and define a problem.
2. Students should be provided with opportunities wherein they recognize the need for additional data.

3. Students should be presented with opportunities to identify pertinent information.
4. Students should be presented with opportunities to develop the ability of distinguishing between relevant and irrelevant information.
5. Students should be provided with opportunities to differentiate between objective and subjective evidence.
6. Students should be provided with opportunities to consider why one source of data is more acceptable (than another).
7. Students should be presented with opportunities to examine materials for freedom from bias.
8. Students should be presented with opportunities to recognize propaganda.
9. Students should be presented with opportunities to locate and evaluate information.
10. Students should be presented with opportunities to classify data in a sequential or hierarchical structure.
11. Students should be provided with opportunities to examine materials for consistency.
12. Students should be provided with opportunities to determine a writer's point of view.
13. Students should be provided with opportunities to locate key sentences and summary statements.
14. Students should be provided with opportunities to compare information about a topic drawn from two or more sources to recognize agreement or contradiction.
15. Students should be provided with opportunities to develop skill in analysis.
16. Students should be provided with opportunities to examine reasons for contradictions or seeming contradictions in evidence.
17. Students should develop sensitivity to and demand precision in the definition of words (analyze the linguistics of a communication).
18. Students should be provided with opportunities to determine the assumptions upon which a position is premised.
19. Students should be provided with opportunities to subject documents to internal criticism.
20. Students should be provided with opportunities to subject documents to external criticism.
21. Students should be provided with opportunities to draw (make, construct) logical inferences from evidence.
22. Students should be provided with opportunities to structure hypotheses.
23. Students should be provided with opportunities to reach tentative conclusions.
24. Students should be provided with opportunities to identify alternative solutions or outcomes.

25. Students should be provided with opportunities to speculate or predict outcomes of situations.
26. Students should be provided with opportunities to analyze alternatives in terms of their consequences.
27. Students should be provided with opportunities to structure generalizations from evidence.
28. Students should be provided with opportunities to validate hypotheses.
29. Students should be provided with opportunities to evaluate hypotheses.
30. Students should be provided with opportunities to establish criteria for evaluation and judgment.[5]

After a look at item number eight in the above list, "Students should be presented with opportunities to recognize propaganda," it can be readily recognized that all children won't achieve this goal at the same time. For some children this might conceivably be accomplished in the fourth grade; for many others this will be achieved at some variable time throughout their school years. However, many people in today's society have not yet achieved this skill and are subject to making decisions based upon propaganda. It is important that the teacher become cognizant of the differences in pupils as they encounter problems in social education. We need to work toward finding teaching procedures or strategies which will promote the fullest development of the individual.

Planning for Concept-Centered Learning Activities

Following are three unit outlines, each of which is based upon a primary concept. These outlines are designed as practical guides for teachers interested in using concept-centered methods.

MAJOR CONCEPT: INTERDEPENDENCE

Levels of development and key questions to guide inquiry

Primary children—sociological orientation—What do other people do for us, around the house, neighborhood, school, and city? Why don't we do all of these things for ourselves? Could we do all, most, or some of these things for ourselves (classifying activity)? How would

---

[5] David A. Welton, "A Study of Characteristics of Social Studies Project Materials and Selected Textbooks" (doctoral dissertation, Ohio University, 1970).

Instructional Methodology and the Teacher

our lives probably change if we did not have other people to do many things for us? Why do people do important things for us?

What kinds of things do we do for other people in our homes, schools, etc.? What do you think you want to do when you are older? Will other people benefit?

Middle and upper levels—economic and historical orientations—How do we depend upon people in other parts of our nation (or world) for things (goods and services) that we use in our daily lives? What is produced or manufactured in our city (or region) for use by people in other parts of our nation or world? How do we communicate with other people (near at hand and far away) so they will know of our needs? Why is transportation so important in helping people satisfy their needs and wants? How have we made use of ideas of people who lived in other decades or other centuries (contributions to scientific thought, technological breakthroughs, such as, those of Galileo, Watt, Guttenberg, Edison, and Marconi)?

Hypothetical statement

The United States depends upon the people of Latin America for some important products. Good relations among the nations of Latin America and the United States are important.

Questions to guide inquiry

1. What products does the United States buy from Latin America nations?
2. Which Latin American nations sell the most in dollar value to the U.S.?
3. Which Latin American nations would be hurt most if the United States stopped buying from them? (How could we estimate this?)
4. Which Latin American nations are the biggest customers of the U.S.? What items do they buy from us? What would be the effect upon the U.S. if these Latin American nations stopped buying from us?

Sources of information

Export graphs in the Carls, Sorenson, and McAulay text [6]
World Almanac
Most recent yearbook of the Encyclopaedia Britannica for information on export-import situation for the various nations

---

[6] Norman E. Carls, Frank E. Sorenson, and John D. McAulay, *Knowing Our Neighbors in Latin America* (New York: Holt, Rinehart and Winston, Inc., 1966).

MAJOR CONCEPT: MIGRATION

Related concepts

Interaction, culture, needs and wants, conflict

Generalizations

People move from place to place in an effort to satisfy needs and wants. Such movement leads to interaction and conflict.

Questions to guide inquiry

1. Who were the first (early) settlers of our town, city, community?
2. Why did they come here?
3. Where did they come from? In the U.S.? Other countries?
4. When did our families migrate to our present place of residence? Why did they come? How long ago did they come?
5. When did our ancestors first come to the "New World?"
6. What ways of life did they bring—religion, food choices, clothing, house designs, language? Can we find evidences of these influences today?
7. Did the various groups of people have any trouble in getting settled?

Teaching procedures

1. On a large United States map, ask children to place pins or dots to show where they lived before coming to this city or community
2. Develop with the children a list of reasons why people move. Then ask the children to place a mark after the reason for their move to this community (Avoid listing of sensitive personal reasons, such as, "Moved here to live with grandparents because father is in prison." Have one category labelled "other reasons."
3. Do the same things as in (1) and (2) for family members who came from another country. Place approximate date by each marker.
4. If possible, in order to gain first hand data on the reasons for modern day migration, use as resource persons some of those individuals in the community who migrated from another country.

Using textbook resources for concept development

The Carls, Sorenson, and McAuley textbook provides an extensive survey of the Latin American countries with a major orientation toward "human geography." The authors of this textbook suggest that it may be used to serve a variety of instructional strategies. Teachers who follow an inquiry-concept approach could plan for an in depth study of one country which has experienced immigration from many other countries of the world. Chile affords an excellent case for comparison of migration to the United States and to another country. In this instance, children should be referred to several sources for information about the many ethnic groups that have settled in Chile. Many of the same questions that are raised concerning migration to the U.S. may be used to guide inquiry in this study topic.

The children may be grouped for the purpose of investigating the migration question in five or six Latin American countries. Such small group investigations should focus on well-defined targets, such as, the production of a map of a particular country showing the breakdown by ethnic groups, the periods of major immigration, and some hypotheses concerning the reasons why the immigrants came. Some of the hypotheses may be tested when information is attainable, but there is no reason why children and teachers should feel that all hypotheses must be retained or rejected as a result of a unit of study. Some hypotheses may very well be held as unresolvable by the class at this particular time. Such unresolved issues provide excellent topics for continuing investigation by highly motivated individual pupils.

Note:—Affect of migration—In any consideration of human migration, the tendency is to look for attractive features in the country to which people have moved and to focus upon the negative aspects in the land of emigration. A good many people do not leave their land for another. Some people who migrate to another land later decide to go back to their homelands.

MAJOR CONCEPT: SOCIAL CONTROL

Related concepts
Customs, mores, folkways, and laws

Generalizations

All human groups control the behaviors of their members. The degree and strength of control differs according to the value which the group places on a particular behavior, with the most powerful controls being laws that are made concerning behavior about which the society has very strong feelings.

Levels of development

Primary Levels—The purpose here may be simply that of developing awareness to certain folkways, such as, dress, eating practices, ways of greeting other people, and an understanding of the ways by which the home and school control certain behavior of young children in our society.

Comparison with other societal practices, as shown in pictures, films, and stories, is an effective approach. The teacher may develop the concept through questions such as:

> Why do we have a school rule that all children should be in school at ———— o'clock?
>
> What would you expect the children in this picture (display a picture of children in dress that is very different from ours) to do differently if they came to live in our town?

Middle levels—Experiences designed to develop concepts of law and justice are appropriately included for children age nine and above. A growing concern for fairness, for following the rules of the game, and for equitable treatment of individuals are characteristics of later childhood that make the study of men and the law both timely and fruitful. Generalizations concerning law are of value in refining the major concept of social control and are intended to provide the child with a realistic introduction to an area that becomes increasingly important with entry into adult life. Some examples of such generalizations follow:

> Rules about very critical areas of behavior are often written by (legislative) special groups of people and become laws that bind all members of the larger social group.
>
> Laws often apply only to the people who belong to a certain group or who live within certain boundaries, such as, those for a county, state or nation.
>
> Laws change with time and in keeping with the changing attitudes that people hold toward the behavior that is controlled.
>
> Enforcement of a law may be applied more or less severely depending upon circumstances.
>
> Determination of innocence or guilt under a law is based upon facts rather than on opinions.

Teaching approaches

We would suggest the use of contemporary situations to present what appears to be contradictory aspects of law and its application. For example, in Florida, a man was found guilty of the murder of his wife, and he was sentenced to 20 years in prison. Because the man was a manager of a business that recruited laborers for the fruit and vegetable farms in the area, the judge decided that the guilty man could spend just three months of each year in jail since his services were too valuable to take away from the farmers for 20 years. In another case reported in the newspapers, a Texas man was sent to jail for the rest of his life because he stole 75 cents. This was the third crime that he had committed, and he was judged to be a criminal by habit, not fit to live in free society.

Other examples may include the person who is wanted by authorities in one state because they believe he committed a crime, but he has fled to another state where the officials will not return him for trial. Young men who have gone to Canada to avoid the draft are not returned to the United States, although our laws state they should be brought to trial for draft evasion.

In some states and cities it is against the law to go to a movie on Sunday, to meet a horse and rider on the road without stopping your car, and for a lady to smoke a cigarette in a public place.

Newspaper and news magazines probably provide the most readily available sources of problem situations which can be adopted for classroom use. Textbook materials tend to afford only the most generalized and often idealized versions of the legal characteristics of social control. At the middle grade levels, the aim is one of developing awareness of law as an institutionalized form of social control and of its variable characteristics. It is suggested that you examine several intermediate level textbooks to determine the way that law, as a social control, is treated. How would you build from the textbook material to extend conceptualization in this area? Section seven of *The Social Sciences: Concepts and Values* [7] will provide a textbook example for this purpose.

Summary

Learning is an intricate process which must involve each learner personally in that which is to be learned. A teacher can grow in her utilization of good teaching strategies, but she always must be conscious of the need for improvement. As she evaluates her present stage of development, the next steps she should take in utilizing improved methods will become obvious. Newer teaching techniques take into consideration the basic and fundamental knowledge, skills, attitudes, and understandings needed by pupils in a democratic society.

Suggested Problems and Projects

1. Social science education is concept and inquiry oriented, hence teaching strategies call for careful attention to problem identification and the

---

[7] Paul F. Brandwein, et al., *The Social Sciences: Concepts and Values,* Section Seven (New York: © 1970 by Harcourt Brace Jovanovich, Inc.).

development of questions that will provide direction to pupil investigations. We have selected some of the major concept areas that we believe deserve high priority in elementary programs and recommend that you work in groups to develop an overall unit outline and specific teaching procedures for development of these concepts through inquiry:

Social control	Social groups
Conflict	Interaction
Interdependence	Migration
Needs and wants	Values

Refer to examples given in this chapter. If at all possible, you should work with children, or as a second alternative, peer teach the activity.

2. After reading this chapter, form teams of three or four students each and develop a check list to determine what level of teacher-growth a specified teacher is operating on in the classroom. Have a representative from each group form a new group to develop a final check list from those developed by the initial groups. Make a copy available and observe three different elementary social science teachers. Do not identify the teachers by name, but discuss your results with the class. Did you find observable operational differences in teaching procedures?

3. After reading research in elementary teaching methodology, support or refute this statement, "New teaching procedures have not produced evidence to justify their use."

4. Examine at least three elementary school social science textbooks and indicate how they facilitate or discourage teaching procedures fostered in this textbook. What is the teacher's responsibility in methodology as related to your examination of social science textbooks?

Related Readings

Anderson, Robert H. *Teaching in a World of Change*. New York: Harcourt, Brace and World, Inc., 1966.

Bloom, Benjamin S. "Learning for Mastery." *Evaluation Comment*, No. 2 (May 1966). Los Angeles, California: Los Angeles Center for the Study of Instructional Programs, University of California.

Bruner, Jerome S. *The Process of Education*. Cambridge: The Harvard University Press, 1961.

Hanna, LaVonne A., Potter, Gladys L., and Hagerman, Neva. *Unit Teaching in the Elementary School*. New York: Holt, Rinehart and Winston, Inc., 1955.

Michaelis, John U. *Social Studies for Children in a Democracy*. Englewood Cliffs, N.J.: Prentice-Hall, Inc., 1968.

Shuster, Albert H. and Ploghoft, Milton E. *The Emerging Elementary Curriculum,* 2nd edition, chapter 4. Columbus, Ohio: Charles Merrill Publishing Company, 1970.
Shumsky, Abram. *In Search of Teaching Style,* chapters 5 and 6. New York: Appleton-Century-Crofts, 1965.
Thomas, George I. and Crescimbeni, Joseph. *Individualizing Instruction in the Elementary School.* New York: Random House, Inc., 1967.

9

INSTRUCTIONAL RESOURCES
    Reading materials
    Still pictures
    Radio and television
    Motion films
    Tapes and records
    Maps and graphic representations
    Simulation games
    Programmed materials and teaching machines
    Educational resources of the community
    Guideposts for using audio-visual aids

THE USE OF THE ELEMENTARY SCHOOL LIBRARY IN THE SOCIAL SCIENCES

EVALUATING LEARNING MATERIALS FOR THE SOCIAL SCIENCES

SUMMARY

SUGGESTED PROBLEMS AND PROJECTS

RELATED READINGS

Instructional Resources for Learning

At no time in the history of U.S. education have the schools had access to so many communication aids. Teaching strategies are closely aligned with a knowledge of effective use and skillful employment of instructional aids. Certainly, an understanding of the learning processes and the requirements of the learner for efficient learning demands that each teacher have a thorough understanding of the media of communication. There can be no doubt that the type of media selected by the teacher for instructional use in the social science education program has a tremendous influence on how the course is presented to the students. The use of various aids tends to reinforce and add effectiveness to the teaching-learning process.

In the social science program, media resources play a vital role in extending experiences beyond the physical limitations of the classroom. Social studies laboratories, where not only books are available, but also magazines, newspapers, filmstrips, globes, maps, films, videotapes, television viewers, records, tapes, games, and simulations, should be established in the elementary schools.

Instructional Resources

Reading materials

Traditionally, the textbook has been the basis of the social studies curriculum, particularly at the intermediate grade level. It simplifies the instructional organization for the teacher, since each child has the same book. Although teacher committees generally examine the textbooks available and select the ones to be used by the local school district, it should be pointed out that some states screen the available textbooks and make available to the local school districts an approved list from which they make their local adoptions. It is assumed here that textbooks will continue to be used in most classrooms until teachers are trained in the techniques suggested throughout this text. The indictment here is that textbooks cannot do the whole job, nor should they be expected to provide the entire curriculum for the social science education program. For the teacher who feels "hung-up" on the textbook approach to teaching, a few suggestive guides to improve the effectiveness of the textbook procedures are made here:

1. Differentiate assignments to provide for enrichment of the bright children and minimum reading requirements for slow learners.
2. Provide questions or guides to aid the student in getting the most from his reading assignment.
3. Enrich assignments by providing films, filmstrips, field trips, and the like to supplement the textbook.
4. Plan questions that will relate assignments to meaningful situations.
5. Inquiry can begin with conflict found between textbook statements and student differences.
6. Relate assignments to contemporary times—cause, effect, current problems, etc.
7. Encourage students to make a list of questions to be used for discussions.

The above list of guides for improving the use of the textbook as the basis of curriculum in the social science program should assist the teacher in making the learning more meaningful, but stark dangers will still exist if the teacher is not alert to the needs of a good social science program. For example, a textbook might be lacking in presenting a "real" view of American life as it exists. The American Indian might be pictured as the enemy in the Old West, and the Negro as a slave with little or no treatment of the contributions which the black race has made to the American way of life. An over-emphasis on history, to the detriment of other social sciences, might be another danger in the single textbook approach. As early as 1916, the Social Studies Commission of the National Education Association suggested that greater attention should be given to social sciences other than pure history.

Teachers must seek out and direct children to use a variety of reading materials. Reference materials, such as, atlases, encyclopedias, and almanacs should be accessible. Supplementary materials, such as, leaflets, pamphlets and bulletins of various kinds should be made available for pupil use. Many of these are found in lists of free and inexpensive materials. The social science program can also be enhanced by children's newspapers and magazines which report on current issues and events, in addition to adult magazines such as *Life, Look, Harpers* and others. Children's literature carefully selected as representative of a wide variety of folklore, fiction, autobiography, biography, historical

Instructional Resources for Learning

Resources for independent study are important.

materials, stories of minority groups and about other lands should be available for instructional use. Research skills related to using the printed work can be acquired by children soon after they gain independence in reading. They can learn to locate information for themselves, which leads to independence in learning.

Still pictures

Still pictures make up the largest number of single instructional aids used in the elementary schools. This group consists of flat pictures, photographs, and filmstrips, with each having a certain function if used with careful preparation.

The filmstrip is one of the easiest to handle and saves instructional time. It can be used by one child alone or by a group of children with or without direct assistance from the teacher. The filmstrip may be used to an advantage because it is so well adapted for discussion during its actual use. It is particularly useful in providing for individual differences, since it helps to clarify meanings through the visual media. The new single concept filmstrips can be used with individuals as they indicate a readiness to move to a higher level of learning.

Sister M. J. Flattery,[1] in an interesting experiment, compared the effectiveness in teaching informational and conceptual social studies material to 442 fifth grade pupils. She used three methods of presenting material to be learned: 1) sound motion pictures; 2) filmstrips without participation; and 3) filmstrips with pupil participation. The results reported that the filmstrip, with or without participation, was significantly superior to the motion picture, and there were equal results at various intelligence levels. The filmstrip with participation resulted in a significant increase over the one without participation.

In addition to the use of filmstrips in the still picture category, the overhead projector and the opaque projector serve a very useful purpose. Teachers and certain intermediate grade children can learn to make transparencies or overlays for use with the overhead projector. The overhead can be used most effectively for student or teacher presentation of data to a class or to a group. Historical, geographical, and statistical data, to name a few, can be put on an overlay for comparison purposes or be used for small group discussion; pages from reference sources can be shown by the opaque projector or reproduced for use with the overhead. It will not be the purpose of this chapter to delineate the advantages and disadvantages of each, but the opaque projector does require a darkened room for reproduction. Pupils do need to be able to see without eye strain. Suffice it to say that once teachers find the versatility of these two pieces of equipment (in the flat picture category), they will find how important these tools are for good instruction and individual learning.[2]

Flat pictures can be valuable sources of data and can serve to help pupils improve their skills of observation. There are more excellent

---

[1] Sister M. J. Flattery, "An Appraisal of the Effectiveness of Selected Instructional Sound Motion Pictures and Silent Filmstrips in Elementary School Instruction" (Washington, D.C.: Catholic University of America, 1953), p. 67.

[2] See Morton J. Schultz, *The Teacher and Overhead Projection* (Englewood Cliffs, N.J.: Prentice-Hall, Inc., 1965), for a complete discussion.

Carefully selected flat pictures can be used to initiate and support important social science concepts.

pictures available today than ever before, and these pictures depict modes of transportation, communication, conservation, cultural differences, and innumerable other topics which contribute to building concepts and understandings.

Radio and television

Although radio and television have been with us for a long time, they are still used largely for special events. Yet, these aids to learning should play a very important role in the school education of pupils. Instruction in the social sciences could be enhanced by the use of these aids, if careful planning for their use were made. Where television is not available, a radio could be used for up-to-the-minute news events.

The gamut of television's value in instruction has yet to be realized. One of the major drawbacks at this time is the unfortunate timing of certain events for school use. Commercial programming restricts the use of this medium for the classroom. Even the scheduling of educational television limits the desired flexibility. But, as the costs keep coming down, more schools will be able to take advantage of videotape recorders for events which are not copyrighted by the commercial networks.

The teacher who plans to take advantage of television teaching will find the *T.V. Guide* and other pre-telecasting literature valuable in planning school use of scheduled programs. Homework or out-of-school assignments might well be related to using this medium of communication, and such assignments can help to make the classroom discussions meaningful. Many programs on race relations, international understandings, and other pertinent issues are presented at hours when the child is at home, and these programs can be taken advantage of through outside assignments. But, a word of caution—no child should be penalized because he didn't see the program. Keep in mind that some parents have their priorities during the evening hours.

Most of the research on television supports the fact that television has a high motivating value, but far too often the medium is used for talk fests or, as the *39th Yearbook of the National Council for Social Studies* points out, television teaching dwindles into "talking textbooks."

We should not be doing things on television that we can do without it, just to have children looking into a "box." Perhaps one of the basic misuses of television is the use of it for all children at the same time. Televised instruction requires certain learning prerequisites, as does using the same textbook; both methods assume that all children are ready at the same time for the same learning experiences. The problem with using educational television, which is scheduled daily, is one of pacing or trying to have all fifth graders, for instance, ready for the next lesson the following day. Under such circumstances, children lose interest and get behind, just as they do in trying to stay abreast of the textbook. The time is past when teachers can focus instruction on the average pupil in the class. Thus, it is strongly suggested that the teacher differentiate her use of television as she would other instructional aids. Some children may be lacking readiness for certain concepts and understandings which are essential if they are to gain from the viewing of certain programs. This and other problems will be solved as we recognize pupil differences and plan our instruction for them.

One of the major areas involving television instruction, which needs to be attacked by the classroom teacher, is that of the use of this medium for propaganda or public influence. Little or no research is available to help us know the extent to which children are influenced by this medium. Although we have not set up television viewing for the purpose of helping children to collect data and analyze its meanings, they can and should learn to use the inquiry process to analyze for themselves the extent to which television is attempting to influence them by both commercials and by newscasters who analyze and interpret, as well as present, the news. This medium must be recognized as having vast influence on people's actions, and in a democracy, individuals must arrive at their own decisions based upon an analysis of many sources of data. Certainly, no area in the social sciences is more challenging than that of developing instructional guidelines for helping children to become astute televiewers and to understand that viewing can be limited to what the programmer wants one to see. This is a basic and fundamental area of instruction for the social science education program and should be coordinated with the communications curriculum program.

Motion films

Good motion films have been used for many years in the social sciences. They can help to make the past alive for children if the quality of the film is good and if the content it authentic. They bring to the classroom social, economic, and cultural reality. Even though most of the materials available are expository in nature, the way the teacher prepares for the film and the follow-up activities of the viewing might add some balance to the learning process if the plans call for inductive teaching.

Tapes and records

Just as children are taught to be careful observers in the collection of data, they need to learn the art of careful listening. Often this needs to be taught. Some authorities point out that listening becomes effective when it involves participation. When primary children have been permitted to respond to rhythmic records by doing what the music tells them, it becomes evidence of the quality of listening taking place.

Many uses of tape recorders have been found for the classroom. Teachers can put materials on tape for individual or group reactions. Pupils can also put their own ideas about certain issues or problems on tape for other pupils to react to and analyze. Pupils can interview each other or resource persons on tape for later use. The point to be made here is that, for the creative teacher, the tape recorder can have many valuable uses in the social science education program.

Maps and graphic representations

Perhaps at no other time has there been such an abundance of commmercially produced graphic aids. These are essential in every classroom. Primary teachers spend much time working with children and producing large neighborhood maps and keys, showing the way to school and locating important places in the community to the child. Such experiences build skills and understandings for the child as he learns early concepts of cartography. These pictorial maps give meaning to the child's understanding of space, distance, and direction—essential parts of the program of social science education.

Recent materials, such as, the photograph on page 257 and maps, such as, the three of the state of Oregon [3] shown on pages 258, 259, and 260, might be used to help children learn to interpret maps through the use of keys and to determine the physical features, such as climate and density of population. A comparison of density of population with the average rainfall in various regions of the state might be studied. Comparisons with maps of other states might be made to determine if generalizations can be drawn concerning the relationship of population density and the temperature and humidity of specific regions. Here again, however, teachers will need to recognize that children will differ in their abilities to comprehend such data and to use the keys effectively. All children should not be expected to achieve these skills and understandings at the same time.

Charts and graphs, which show natural resources, raw materials, major commercially produced products, and other characteristics of an area, contribute to the child's developing skills and supplement his concepts of a particular state or region. As each child reaches the point where he can move beyond this stage of skill development, he is ready

---

[3] "The Community Structure," *Third-Grade, Eugene Social Studies Curriculum,* 1968, a publication of the Instruction Department, courtesy of the Eugene, Oregon, Public Schools.

Recent materials enhance map study by visually depicting a new dimension through which children can conceptualize about their ever-changing world.

to master maps which depict physical features, such as, boundaries, continents, rivers, arid land, fertile land, etc. By the time the child reaches the upper elementary grades, he should learn to handle latitude and longitude by locating positions both on flat maps and on globes. These skills become important tools to inquiry and should be thoroughly developed and mastered by each child. But, keep it in mind that children will differ in terms of their rate and time in achieving these skills. Provision must be made for these differences; children should not be overlooked because they are not ready at any given time to move ahead in developing these skills.

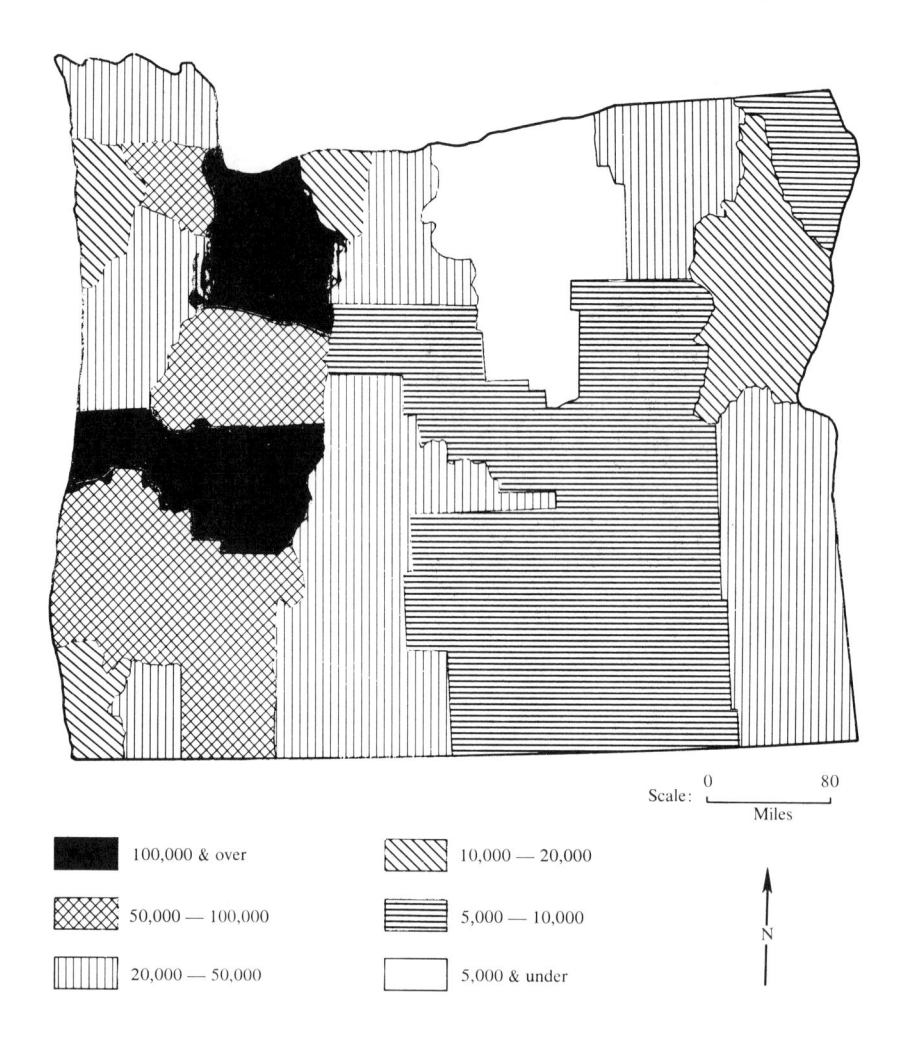

FIGURE 9–1. Oregon's Population Density

Tables, charts, and graphs become important means of utilizing data to depict such things as average rainfall or average temperature, where statistics can be graphically read. In all these experiences, it becomes essential that pupils see relationships between the skills to be learned and the usefulness of the learning. Children might be asked to construct their own tables from keeping daily records of temperature. As they record the temperature at 9:00 a.m. and at 3:00 p.m. each day for the month of January, for instance, they would have a series of figures representing temperature in degrees taken twice a day. An example

Instructional Resources for Learning 259

might be:

January	9:00 a.m.	3:00 p.m.
2	27°	39°
3	18°	30°
4	26°	34°

With a series of recordings, the children might be asked to make a table showing the temperature for each school day. The table should also indicate the days with the widest and the closest range of degrees, the average temperature for 9:00 a.m. and 3:00 p.m. respectively, and the month's lowest and highest temperatures. This experience would provide

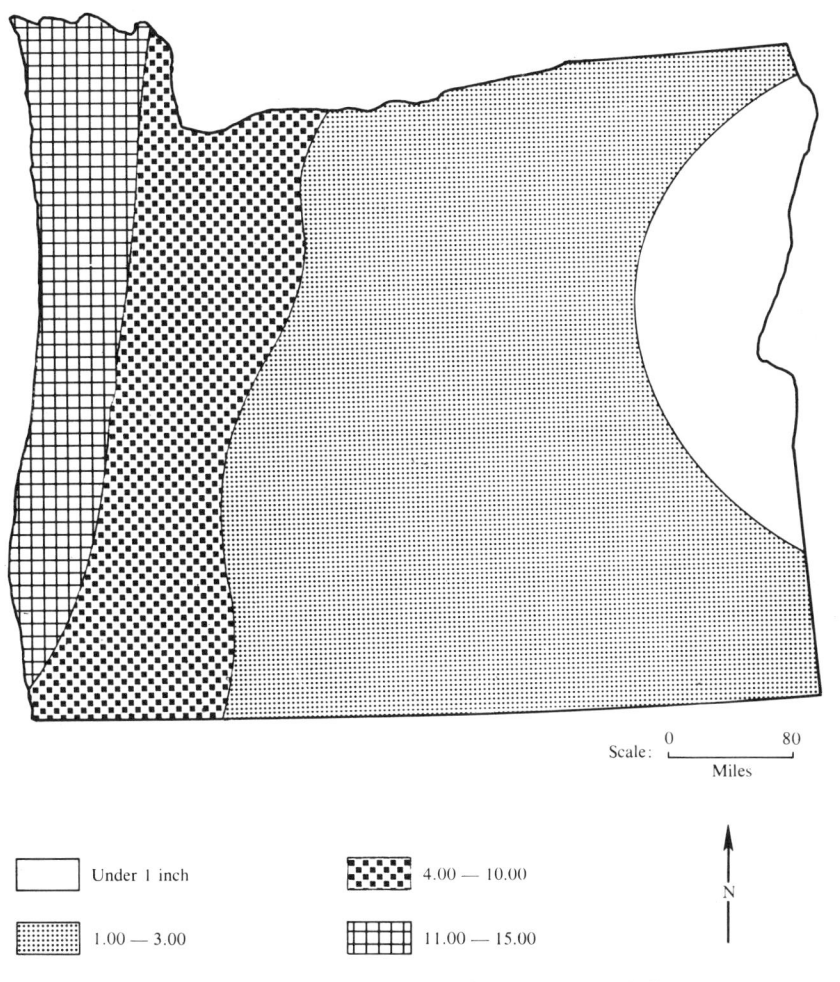

FIGURE 9–2. Oregon's Rainfall in January 1967

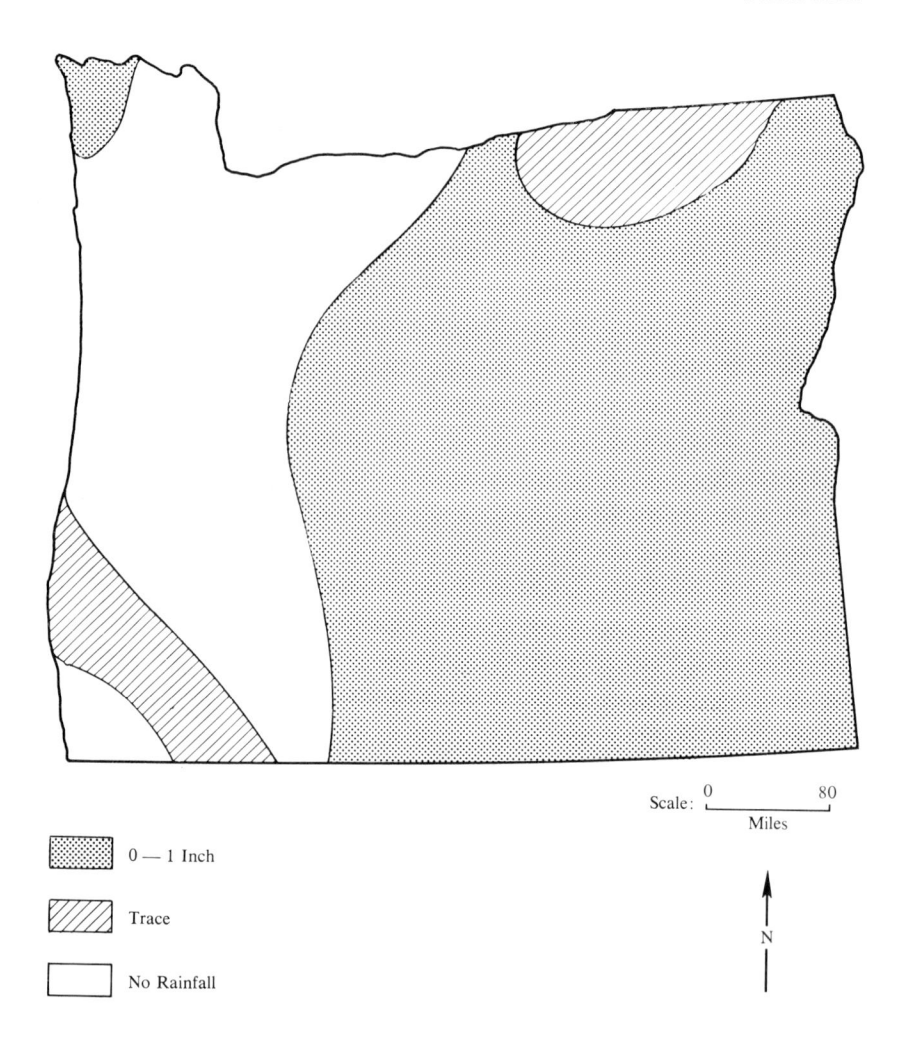

FIGURE 9-3. Oregon's Rainfall in July 1967

them with the knowledge of how tables are constructed, which would also help them to interpret tables which they might want to use in seeking data. Similar exercises could be used for making and interpreting graphs and charts.

Simulation games

Among the many innovations which have been gaining favor with teachers are simulation games. Educational journals during the past several years indicate that the use of games in the classroom is gaining some attention. Children become highly motivated, which provides a readiness for learning, when the term "game" is mentioned. The basic idea of simulation games is to provide the learners with a simplified system for understanding some significant life situations. Most of the simulation games which are being introduced into the schools are dealing with topics appropriate for the social science education program. These games tend to place the pupil in a decision-making situation.

For the teacher who uses simulation games, certain changes in classroom management become important. Children do not normally play games in dead silence, and the playing of games stimulates them to activity, which, in sedentary activities, will often be vocal. When such is the case, the teacher has to change her concept of the learning environment, despite the fact that most of us have learned to think of the ideal learning environment as being a quiet room without physical activity. In addition, the concept of game itself might be repugnant to the teacher's understanding of instruction. Games are fun and children can and do learn from activities which they enjoy. So, if you plan to use games, you should develop, with the children, a suitable environment and the essential controls.

Before you use a game as a learning experience with children, you should play the game yourself. This will help you to determine some of the concepts which can be learned and their levels of difficulty. You need to determine the value of the game as it relates to the social science curriculum. If the simulation game is to be a part of the instructional program, then the value of it needs to be determined, just as you would evaluate any other teaching-learning aid or experience. You will need to keep in mind, in forming your judgments, the length of time it takes to play the game and the number of pupils who can participate at one time. The time required to play the games currently on the market varies considerably; some games may be completed in only a few hours, while others will require the entire social studies period for several days. Some games provide for only two pupils to participate, while others can involve as many as thirty pupils.

A brief description here of a few of the games on the market will serve as a basis for understanding the topics covered: [4]

Name	*Description*
Caribou Hunting (for upper elementary)	A board game in which students simulate some of the difficulties Eskimos experience in acquiring an adequate

---

[4] *Invitation to Feedback* 3, no. 1 (Athens, Ohio: the Cooperative Center for Social Science Education, College of Education, Ohio University, January 1969).

food supply from their harsh environment and learn the advantages of a cooperative strategy. (Under development at Education Development Center, 15 Mifflin Place, Cambridge, Mass. 02138.)

Consumer
(for elementary-junior high)

Designed to teach something about the problems and economics of installment buying. (Available from the Johns Hopkins University, Department of Social Relations, Attention: Mrs. Trowbridge.)

Githaka
(for upper elementary)

By assuming the roles of tribesmen, children simulate the Kekuyu system of land use on large estates held by a clan. (Available as part of a unit on Kekuyus from Learning Center, Social Studies Department, Princeton, N.J. 08540.)

Market
(for elementary)

A game designed as part of a sixth grade unit on exchange. (Industrial Relations Center, University of Chicago, Chicago, Illinois. This center is working on other games, including "Economy," but they are not available as yet.)

The Sumerian Game
(for elementary)

An experimental computer-based game in which a player assumes the role of ruler of Sumeria. The country has an agricultural economy, and he must improve the lot of his people by making decisions. (Board of Cooperative Educational Services, Westchester County, Yorktown Heights, New York 10598.)

These are but a few of the simulation games in the social science area for elementary school use. However, even though quite a few have been produced, there is still a scarcity of good simulation games available for the elementary school and even fewer games for the primary grades. Adequate research has to be completed in determining the value of games in helping children achieve their objectives. Yet, action research might well justify their use in the meantime, if teachers observe and evaluate the resultant learnings carefully.

Do-it-yourself games. One area which could prove to be very beneficial for teachers would be to develop their own games. Workshops or inservice meetings might be utilized for such an activity, with several teachers brainstorming to come up with some creative games constructed around social, economic, religious or political learnings. Such games could be tested with the children to determine the level of difficulty, the motivation to play the game, and other criteria for a good game. Some steps which could be used in inventing games are:

1. Decide on an economic, sociological or psychological problem area in which there are dilemmas in life decisions. Set a problem appropriate to the curriculum for the class.
2. Determine the participants needed to simulate the problem and construct a simplified model of the process necessary to deal with it.
3. Allot resources to participants and establish goals that lead them into the dilemmas.
4. Plan for sequences of stages of play and for a culmination of the game. Make rules appropriate for those who will use the game.
5. Plan a debriefing.[5]

Follow-up on games' results. The devotion of instructional time to game playing is important, if the teacher recognizes the many values which can accrue. But, one of the crucial elements in this instructional strategy is the follow-up activity which originates in the game. Many devices can be used to insure maximum learning from this instructional innovation. Pupils can plan a panel on key issues in the game and relate these to real life situations. Some teacher-directed discussion can follow to see what concepts were obtained and what generalizations or principles might be stated. Data can be collected to substantiate or refute the facts of the game. Suffice it to say that the follow-up activity can and should serve as a reinforcement of the learnings, but this will not occur without teacher planning.

Programmed materials and teaching machines

The social sciences, like other curriculum areas, have seen a variety of programmed learning materials, both for machine use and in textbook form, made available by various commercial companies. Most of these serve a purpose when the memorization of factual material is the goal of the social science teacher. Although some authorities indicate that materials are being developed which facilitate the use of problem-

---

[5] Dorothy McClure Fraser, ed., *Social Studies Curriculum Development: Prospects and Problems, 39th Yearbook* (Washington, D.C.: National Council for the Social Studies, 1969), p. 164.

solving skills, such materials have not yet reached the market. However, some programs have been developed which are useful for learning geography skills. These are some sound psychological principles for the use of programmed materials:

1. They recognize individual differences and take the learner "where he is" and let him proceed at his own rate of learning.
2. The materials require the learner to be active in the learning process and thus bring into play the learning-by-doing principle.
3. They provide for immediate feedback of the results of the learning. Knowledge of immediate feedback of the results of learning has long been advocated both by psychologists and educationists from the point of view that this provides reinforcement and immediate reward in cognitive learning.
4. They require that the materials be carefully organized and sequenced so that concept development will proceed from the easiest to the more difficult.
5. They must provide for review proportionately spaced throughout the learning in order to insure a high order of success.
6. Programmed learning reduces anxiety because the learner is not threatened by the task. He knows that he can learn; and he is learning; and he can see here the immediate results of his success, which brings satisfaction to him.[6]

Teachers need to be aware of the many programmed materials available, some of which might fulfill the requirements for helping a learner acquire the knowledge or skills essential to some particular activity. Frequently time can be saved for both the teacher and pupil if the material meets the specified need of the learner. It becomes apparent that teachers are not encouraged to make indiscriminate use of programmed materials. Much research is needed in both the development of newer materials and in the types and kinds of materials needed. Although programmed materials are very effective in helping to develop certain skills, they are of little value in directing learning in inquiry.

Educational resources of the community

The better and the sooner the teacher understands the community in which she teaches, the less time will be wasted in getting effective teaching underway. It cannot be assumed that communities are all alike. They differ in many respects; the teacher will discover this and will want to read available materials and visit the community and its major

---

[6] Ernest R. Hilgard, "What Support from the Psychology of Learning," *National Education Journal* 50, no. 20 (November 1961).

Instructional Resources for Learning 265

social institutions in order to build initial understandings and gain early concepts about available resources—human, natural, and material.

Most school systems have developed some policies governing field trips and the use of community resources. The teacher should acquaint herself with these policies. In using community resources, it is apparent that the resources must either be brought to the school or the children taken to the resources.

Human resources have much to contribute, and there is no limit to the variety of resources available. Many persons who have special talents, skills or experiences (being a native of another country, possessing a unique collection of certain items or having a trade or profession, to name a few) can make significant contributions to the social science program. Resources which require field experiences are those where a particular industry is being studied or a visit to a section of the community—a park, a lake or an agency—is required for data collection.

Important to the utilization of community resources are the specific purposes for their use. Purposes should be identified and thoroughly understood by the teacher and the group in cooperative endeavor. Some suggested guides which will facilitate the use of human resources in the classroom are:

1. To develop a purpose for the visit so that the learners will be aware of the purpose
2. To know your visitor in terms of the specific contributions he is able to make
3. To inform the visitor in advance of the problems which led to his invitation and of special or particular situations which may arise
4. To plan with the children ways in which they can acquire the most from the visit; this should be done prior to the visit
5. To plan for follow-up activities to clarify concepts, clear up misconceptions, and appraise the visit with the children in terms of the purpose [7]

Guideposts for using audio-visual aids

It is not the purpose of this chapter to deal with all the possible audio-visual aids available to teachers, since there are numerous other aids which could be added. But, teachers should recognize the large number of instructional aids available to them, including the kinds which teach-

---

[7] Albert H. Shuster and Milton E. Ploghoft, *The Emerging Elementary Curriculum*, 2nd edition (Columbus, Ohio: Charles Merrill Publishing Company, 1970), p. 159.

ers can make for their own purposes and uses. The point here is that there are important psychological concepts for learning based upon the use of audio-visual aids. Too often teachers feel apprehensive about using aids or they don't want to go to the trouble required to prepare for their use. Some guides are presented here which should be kept in mind before abandoning the idea of using an audio-visual aid:

1. They have a strong motivating factor which increases and sustains attention.
2. They help to bridge the gap between abstract learning and meaningfulness in the development of concepts.
3. They can result in the learner's moving out on his own in further learning.
4. They can be used by the learner alone or in small or large groups.
5. They change the type of communication from strictly verbal to a combination of systems.
6. They span the time gap by bringing to the classroom remote events in either space or time.

The Use of the Elementary School Library in the Social Sciences

The inquiry processes rely heavily upon the learner's ability to use a vast array of materials. Educators and the public alike are beginning to recognize the need for a good elementary library—adequately staffed and well equipped—with a wide range of reading materials. In addition, the library's name is being changed to imply that it houses a broader range of materials and aids for learning. Modern buildings are being constructed with the educational resources learning centers serving as the hub of the instructional program.

The basic tools of research are among the many skills children learn in the elementary school. They learn skills that assist them in locating materials, but often the library is not a place where children are encouraged to go on their own. Tradition has it that children still visit most elementary libraries in classroom groups where they are herded in to select a book and then taken back to the classroom. Teachers must free children to use the library in a normal, natural way; when the need for further research arises and the information is available only in the library, children should be free to go to the library. Social science instruction cannot be improved or carried on without the full use of resources available, and most of these might well be in the educational resources center.

Instructional Resources for Learning 267

Look at Chart 9–1 to see the many skills which can be developed through the library. The teacher and librarian then should work as a team to insure that these skills are developed to facilitate independence of learning on the part of the pupil.

CHART 9–1. Skills to Be Developed Through Use of the School Library [8]

Grade I	Grade II	Grade III
(1) *Library Citizenship*	(1) Library Citizenship	(1) Library Citizenship
(2) *Care and appreciation of materials*	(2) Care and appreciation of materials	(2) Care and appreciation of materials
(3) Locating library materials	(3) *Locating library materials*	(3) Locating library materials
(4) Borrowing materials from school library	(4) *Borrowing materials from school library*	(4) Borrowing materials from school library
		(5) Discussing books
		(6) *Reporting on books*
		(7) *Using an index and a table of contents*

Grade IV	Grade V	Grade VI
(1) Library Citizenship	(1) Library Citizenship	(1) Library Citizenship
(2) Care and appreciation of materials	(2) Care and appreciation of materials	(2) Care and appreciation of materials
(3) Locating library materials	(3) Locating library materials	(3) Locating library materials
(4) Borrowing materials from school library	(4) Borrowing materials from school library	(4) Borrowing materials from school library
(5) Discussing books	(5) Discussing books	(5) Discussing books
(6) Reporting on books	(6) Reporting on books	(6) Reporting on books
(7) Using an index and a table of contents	(7) Using an index and a table of contents	(7) Using an index and a table of contents
(8) *Using a juvenile encyclopedia*	(8) Using a juvenile encyclopedia	(8) Using a juvenile encyclopedia
(9) *Using a card catalog*	(9) Using a card catalog	(9) Using a card catalog
(10) Borrowing books from public libraries	(10) *Borrowing books from public libraries*	(10) Borrowing books from public libraries
(11) Taking notes	(11) Taking notes	(11) Taking notes
(12) Using pamphlet and picture materials	(12) Using pamphlet and picture materials	(12) *Using pamphlet and picture materials*
	(13) *Using an atlas and a globe*	(13) Using an atlas and a globe
	(14) *Using an unabridged dictionary*	(14) Using an unabridged dictionary
		(15) Using *WORLD ALMANAC*

[8] *School Library Guide* 38, Virginia State Board of Education (September 1955): p. 57.

Evaluating Learning Materials for the Social Sciences

Evaluation of social studies materials has been largely limited to an examination of the subject matter. Textbooks have been examined to determine the amount of space devoted to the various social sciences. Subject matter has been investigated to determine the levels of difficulty of the concepts presented. Free and inexpensive materials have been investigated from many areas of interest. But, there has not been a widespread effort (as there was in the elementary science curriculum areas) to develop social science materials and test them in a school setting.

The *39th Yearbook of the National Council of Social Studies* points out that the only "major generalization that can be made about present practices in selecting instructional materials for social studies programs is that they are varied, often haphazard, and too frequently lacking in a professional approach." [9] However, it is a fact that more materials for the social science curriculum are available today than ever before. These materials do place a difficult burden on the teacher in terms of deciding which ones to use. Therefore, some guides are presented here for the evaluation of materials to be used in the social science education program:

1. Is the level of material appropriate for the children it is to serve?
2. Does the material serve the instructional purpose?
3. Is the material accurate in content?
4. Does it present more than one side of an issue or problem?
5. Will its use result in a high degree of interest?
6. Does it supply a concrete basis for conceptual thinking?
7. Will its use provide experiences in learning which would be difficult to obtain through other material?
8. Will its use enhance growth and meaning in vocabulary development?

In using the suggested guides above, the teacher should keep in mind that these are not all-inclusive and that she must use her judgment in reviewing materials as to whether they will contribute to the general and specific objectives in terms of the behaviors she hopes to develop. Perhaps one activity which might prove valuable would be to develop

---

[9] Fraser, *Social Studies Curriculum Development: Prospects and Problems*, p. 200.

similar guides with the children and have them critically examine materials in terms of the criteria they develop for use in their learning. The goal is to introduce children to as wide a variety of learning aids as possible so that they will know there are many sources from which to secure data and to check the validity of their sources.

Summary

The social science education program is dependent upon the use of a wide variety of resource materials and learning aids if it is to be process oriented. Materials help to promote critical thinking and serve to reinforce, as well as to add to, the effectiveness of the instruction. However, teacher judgment is an important factor in the selecting of materials and audio-visual aids, and the differences of individuals and of teaching strategies play an important part in selecting the appropriate resources for the learner. Research has supported the thesis that learning is improved and greater efficiency is gained from wise use of audio-visual aids. But, much is yet to be accomplished in researching social science education materials.

Suggested Problems and Projects

1. Through peer teaching, use at least three different instructional media which might be effective in presenting certain data or concepts. Have the class discuss the pros and cons of each medium in terms of its instructional value for the task you have selected for it to accomplish. To what extent does this help you to see that the application of instructional media is involved with individual differences in learning style?
2. Use various printed media to present some concept, from abstract to concrete, to a fourth-grade class. Evaluate your success in using each type of media. What does this tell you about how children learn and about how instructional media should be used?
3. Form groups in your classroom and develop criteria for distinguishing between facts and propaganda in viewing television. After each group has developed its criteria, discuss these in class and arrive at a common set of criteria. Each class member should then view the same programs independently and evaluate it according to the criteria agreed upon. Discuss the results in class.

Related Readings

Brown, James W., Lewis, Richard B., and Harceleroad, Fred F. *A-V Instruction: Materials and Methods.* New York: McGraw-Hill Book Company, Inc., 1964.

Phillips, Lewis. "Instructional Technology." *New Curriculum Developments,* pp. 85–95. Washington, D.C.: Association for Supervision and Curriculum Development, N.E.A., 1965.

Sand, Lester B. *Audio-Visual Procedures in Teaching.* New York: The Ronald Press, 1965.

Schultz, Morton J. *The Teacher and Overhead Projection.* Englewood Cliffs, N.J.: Prentice-Hall, Inc., 1965.

Skinner, B. J. *The Technology of Teaching.* New York: Appleton-Century-Crofts, 1968.

10

WHY CONSIDER RELIGION AT ALL?

HOW DOES RELIGIOUS EXPERIENCE RELATE TO THE HUMAN CONDITION?

IS THERE A PLACE FOR TEACHING ABOUT RELIGION?

A FIFTH-GRADE UNIT, WHEATON, ILLINOIS, DISTRICT 36

SUGGESTED SCOPE AND SEQUENCE
    Primary levels
    Middle levels
    Upper levels

SUGGESTED GUIDELINES FOR THE STUDY OF RELIGION

OTHER ASPECTS OF RELIGION

SUGGESTED PROBLEMS AND PROJECTS

RELATED READINGS

Religion and Social Science Education

In recent years, opinions by the U.S. Supreme Court have clarified the First Amendment with respect to its implications for prayer and other religious activities sponsored by public schools. At the time of this writing, it is generally agreed that required group prayer and religious instruction are not in accordance with the supreme law of the land. The expressions of the Supreme Court on this matter have emphasized that the public schools should not be hostile to religion, but that the responsibility to protect the individual's right to the "free exercise thereof" necessarily precludes religious instruction and required prayer in the classroom.

It is not difficult to visit schools where group prayers are still required by the teachers, and, in some instances, by school board policy. So long as no one brings legal action in such situations, these apparently illegal practices may continue. Occasional attacks are leveled against the Supreme Court because of its decisions in this area, and not infrequently, the schools are labelled "Godless." As recently as the 1940's, some school districts wrote into their teacher contracts the requirement that the teacher agree to attend church in the local community.

The issue of religion in education will probably persist for many years to come, and the long standing suspicion of education as a threat to established religions is still in evidence in some segments of U.S. society. What, then, is the implication for the social education of children and youth? Let us consider several viewpoints.

Why Consider Religion at All?

There is a variety of positions on this question, positions which range from demands for released time for religious instruction to demands that nothing at all that suggests religion be expressed in the public school. James Panoch and David Barr have insisted that religion is part and parcel of the school experience, whether by choice or otherwise. It is their thinking that the issue is *how* religion should be considered, not *whether* it should be.[1]

Members of the American Association of School Administrators have expressed themselves as follows, "A curriculum which ignored religion would itself have serious religious implications. It would seem to proclaim that religion has not been as real in men's lives as health or politics or economics. By omission it would appear to deny that religion has been and is important in man's history—a denial of the obvious."[2]

A rational approach to the question of religious instruction in the schools would conclude that when the spiritual nature of man is considered, when the purpose of human life and its relation to supernatural forces is contemplated, when beliefs and practices relating to man's spiritual nature are proposed, we are dealing with religious matters. Religion is highly personal, dogmatic, and traditional; its sources of knowledge and truth lie in mysticism and revelation. The phenomenon of religious experience is, of course, universally expressed in human beings, and the variety of religious practices and beliefs may be studied in an orderly and reasonable way. The validity of a religious system— its internal consistencies and its comparative worth to people—these things cannot be studied rationally in the public schools because the facts are not tenable to public test.

As a matter of social necessity, children should become aware of the private and mystical nature of human religious experience in order that they may have a foundation upon which to build respect for the *right* of others to believe and practice in different ways. The nature of U.S. society, it seems, requires this much, if personal freedom is to be meaningful at all. Not until the secondary school level should students look into the ways in which religion has been misused by people to further their political and economic goals. Some communities may not allow even this much, but the professional educator is obliged to make the attempt.

That a teacher's first responsibility is to provide educational experiences that are compatible with dominant community preferences would be a practical approach to the religious question. If the community

---

[1] James V. Panoch and David L. Barr, "Should We Teach About Religion in Our Public Schools?" *Social Education* 33, no. 8 (December 1969): p. 910.
[2] American Association of School Administrators, *Religion in the Public Schools* (New York: Harper and Row, 1964), p. 56.

wanted opening prayers, I would call for them in my class, but I wouldn't fuss with children who did not pray. The individual pupil who becomes skilled in reading and critical thinking will have the freedom to form his own questions, to develop his own answers. The school prepares the child to inquire; it should not force feed him on specific items that are as private and subjective as religion.

A person's religious beliefs and practices do not seem to have much to do with his success in life, as long as he holds certain values about human dignity, democracy and social responsibility. Consequently, what the school does or does not do about religion will have little or no effect on his accomplishments in later life.

    1. *Which of the above four views is nearest your own? What would you estimate to be a predominant view today?*

    2. *After examining the four positions set forth here, develop your own individual or small group position. Keep in mind the need to set forth a position that would likely be given consideration in most school communities.*

How Does Religious Experience Relate to the Human Condition?

Man's ability to inquire, to organize his thoughts, to remember, and to anticipate the future gives rise to the phenomenon known as religious experience. Man's age old concern with perplexing questions about the purpose of human life, or any life form, about the origins of the universe, man's condition after death, and the awesome forces of nature have led to a variety of beliefs and practices which deal with man and the supernatural or man and the unknown. Religions have a number of common characteristics, most of which are related to the concerns mentioned above. At first glance, it would appear that these common concerns would draw men together in recognition of their condition of innocence or ignorance. As you know, that has not been the case historically, although recent ecumenical movements may portend changes.

Although most religions are concerned with universal questions, their differences have arisen from a variety of sources, and these differences have been used as excuses or reasons for violent actions against other religious groups. One of the most common and important differences is found in the conflicting views about revealed truth and major prophets. Islam regards Mohammed as the true prophet, Christianity calls for recognition and faith in Jesus Christ, and the Hebrew faith calls for obedience to one god, Yahweh, doubting that the Messiah has yet appeared.

From such fundamental differences with respect to the sources and prophesies of revealed truth, further differences arise within the literature which presents the "divine truth to mortal man." Accordingly, various tests of faith and obligatory acts of faith have served to set religious groups apart as each sought to reassure itself and convince all doubters. It is possible to take a cynical view of religion generally, based upon

"Now, boys and girls, it's time for our voluntary group prayer. Does anyone not want to pray today?"

some of the more tragic ways in which people have used religious persuasion to justify political actions—witness The Spanish Inquisition; The Holy Wars of Islam; and the imperialism of the nineteenth century, which moved under the guise of bringing salvation to the heathen people of Asia and Africa. In such instances, it would seem that one might call for religion to be saved from man, rather than vice versa.

The point remains that the human quest for the meaning and purpose of existence and man's proper relationship to all of creation will continue. In the face of nonscientific evidence on these matters, it is unlikely that religious "facts" will soon be proper subjects for public investigation and testing, nor in our multi-ethnic, conglomerate society will we see consensus on one approach to religion in the public schools.

Is There a Place for Teaching About Religion?

By this time you may have made up your mind on this matter. The authors have found themselves constantly rethinking the entire problem, and occasionally they have changed their positions. The last word has certainly not been said on this, so it is suggested that you need not feel inadequate if you find yourself undecided on this matter.

If we are to attempt to continue a way of life which guarantees individual freedom in religious matters, then it seems that the school must provide the basis for respect and concern for that right. Such a base can be developed as pupils become aware of the many different religious systems that exist in their own community and throughout the world. As children and youth gain understanding about man's attempts to comprehend himself and the world about him, the realm of the unknown should be included. Where information is not to be had, man will act on belief, if indeed he must act. In the extract immediately following is an example of one school's approach to religious study at the elementary level:

A Fifth-Grade Unit, Wheaton, Illinois, District 36

Special Note: In your study of religion, you may wish to notify parents. This can be effective public relations and may also bring you further assistance in the area of books and materials. Here is a sample note which could be used:

Dear Parents:

In order that you may be aware of what we are doing in social studies, I am sending this outline of our present unit. Perhaps you will be able to offer suggestions and opportunities for enrichment. I am hoping this will also prevent last minute work on assignments which were given earlier. Please sign and return this form. Thank you.

Sincerely,
(Teacher's Name)

Generalization; Each civilization has certain significant values, beliefs, and religious ideas that influence its growth and development.

Content

A. All religions have some things in common—they all have beliefs about:
   1. The relationship of man to the universe
   2. The nature of supernatural power
   3. The nature of good and evil

B. Judaism
   1. Brief history
   2. Basic Jewish beliefs
      a. Monotheism: belief in a unique personal Supreme Being
      b. Israel's people are divinely chosen among the people of the world
      c. Salvation is consequent upon observance of the Mosaic Law which includes the Ten Commandments
   3. Religious groups
      a. Orthodox: Oldest and strictest
         1. Strict observance of Jewish Law
         2. Complex liturgy including ceremonies for worship, thanksgiving, atonement, and commemoration of events in its history
      b. Reform
         1. Stands opposite Orthodoxy as a liberalizing force
         2. Maintains that Divine revelation was intended for all peoples in the world
      c. Conservative
         1. Seeks a middle course between Orthodox and Reform
         2. More adaptable than Orthodoxy and more stable than Reform
   4. Basic documents
      a. Old Testament
         1. Torah (Ten Commandments)
         2. Prophets
         3. Writings

b. Talmud (an attempt to clarify the Mosaic Law)
   5. Number and location of followers
      a. 13 million Jews
      b. About 50% in U.S. and 50% in Israel

C. Christianity
   1. Branches
      a. Roman Catholic
      b. Protestant
      c. Eastern Orthodox
   2. History
      a. Church in Jerusalem (first and second centuries)
      b. Church divides into two groups: Catholic and Orthodox (eleventh century)
      c. Catholic Church split by the Protestant Reformation (sixteenth century)
      d. Many religious groups settle in New World (seventeenth century)
   3. Basic Christian beliefs
      a. Divinity of Christ
      b. Life after death
      c. Worth of the individual
   4. Basic Christian document: Bible
   5. Number and location of followers

D. Major religions not prominent in Western World (These will be studied in depth in sixth grade. It should suffice to mention where the religion is practiced and how many followers it has.)
   1. Buddhism
   2. Islam
   3. Hinduism
   4. Shintoism
   5. Confucianism
   6. Taoism

E. Minor philosophies practiced in Western culture (You might wish to investigate these, but they should not be considered mandatory.)
   1. Theosophism
   2. Baha'i
   3. Atheism
   4. Indian religions

Materials

A. Filmstrips—the following filmstrips with their accompanying booklets should prove very helpful in giving you and the class a summary of the beliefs and practices of each major religion:

1. "Protestant Christianity Today"
2. "Roman Catholic Church Today"
3. "Judaism Today"

B. Books
   1. *World's Great Religions* by the Editors of Life. New York: Golden Press.
   2. *Passover* by Norma Simon. New York: Thomas Y. Crowell Co., 1965.
   3. *The Children's Bible* (Illustrated). New York: Golden Press.
   4. *Bible Story Library*, edited by T. Hodges and E. MacLean, Indianapolis, Indiana: Bobbs-Merrill Co., Inc.

C. Organizations
   1. Anti-Defamation League (will furnish materials in kit form for teaching about Judaism), 222 West Adams, Chicago, Illinois 60606.
   2. American Bible Society, 310 Michigan Avenue, North Chicago, Illinois 60601.

Map and Globe Skill

A. Make a map showing the location of western religions.
B. Make a map to show the spread of the Reformation.

Activities

A. Show filmstrips after discussing vocabulary given at the front of filmstrip booklets. Have the children take notes and write their notes into a summary.
B. Have children conduct religious services in one of the major religions. Use as many different religious objects as possible (Torah, Cross, prayer wheels, hymn books, prayer books).
C. Make a mural or draw illustrations depicting celebrations of various religious holidays.
D. Visit a Catholic cathedral, a Jewish synagogue, or a Protestant church for comparison of emphasis and tradition.
E. Have each child write a report on his own religion or denomination and present it to the class. Several people belonging to one group could make a joint presentation.
F. Make a chart showing the world religions, number of followers, and location.
G. Collect and read news clippings that deal with religion.
H. Have groups give presentations on the major Western religions. The following points might be included:

Religion and Social Science Education 281

    1. Brief history
    2. Beliefs and practices
    3. Documents
    4. Worship form
    5. Special holidays

I. Make a chart showing likenesses and differences between the major Western religions. (This is a good spot to emphasize: people are more alike than different.)

J. Discuss reasons for separation of church and state in the United States. Have children find evidence in the Constitution for separation.

K. Find out what countries have state churches and what relationship the church and state have. State Churches: England, Norway, Sweden, and Denmark.

L. Have someone make or draw the Christian Year Calendar. For example, March—Lent, April—Easter, Pentecost, etc.

M. Dramatize some events which took place during the Reformation.

Field Trips

Western Suburban Temple, River Forest, Illinois; Queen of Heaven Mausoleum, Hillside, Illinois; Baha'i National Center, Wilmette, Illinois.[3]

Suggested Scope and Sequence

The early religious experiences of children are of an attitudinal and emotional type, and for some persons, religious experience is never raised to the cognitive level. Because of the sensitive and private nature of religion in our society and because young children usually are not disturbed by the nonscientific nature of religious knowledge, the writers recommend that no more than an *attitudinal* and *awareness* concern for religious experience be developed in the primary years. We do not consider this to be a simple or easy matter, however, since it depends so much upon the sensitivity of the teacher to the diversity of religion and upon the origins of bigotry, which appear to grow from early perceptions and experiences.

Primary levels

Develop awareness of the different religious groups in the community and throughout the world. Use the occasions of religious holidays of

---

[3] Used by permission of Wheaton, Illinois, Elementary District 36. This unit was prepared by Edward Storke.

many faiths to acquaint children with the fact that there are many religions which observe different important events or celebrate the same event in differing ways. This *awareness activity* may be promoted by teacher comment concerning interesting occasions of note. The use of pictures may direct attention to a religious event, and the planned treatment of religions may be tied to a story about people of other lands or other times.

The teacher's attitude and behavior are of a critical nature here if children are to perceive differences in a nonjudgmental light. It is, of course, intellectually dishonest for the teacher to support the impression that any one religious group has a more reliable set of truths than any other. A casual comment by the teacher about the backward, primitive or peculiar religions of other people is damaging to the building of respect for the *right* of people in our type of society to enjoy religious freedom.

Develop an attitude of respect (reverence or compassion) for the world in which we live. Thus, the bases will be laid for effective relationships between the child and the physical and social forces of his environment. Whatever may be the eventual decision of the individual concerning the relationship between self and the totality of existence, whatever he may finally believe about the sources and purposes of all life on this planet, the writers believe that early school experiences should build feelings of respect and security in the face of the many mysteries of life which man's intellect has not unlocked.

The day to day experiences in the classroom must carry this aspect of human religious experience. The attitude of the adult toward plant and animal life can provide models for later behavior. The care of plants in the school and the treatment of living things in the school area (including stray dogs) sets the stage. Why and in what manner do we keep animals caged in our classrooms? Does the teacher propose that our own selfish purposes are not the only concerns? Does the teacher permit children to express amazement, mystery, and speculation about the sprouting of bean seeds, the hatching of eggs, and about the other "whys" of various natural phenomena? Does the teacher project an attitude of interest and concern for the big questions that children ask? Does she let the children know that adults do not know everything; that part of the human experience is the effort to understand and to respect the efforts of others to do so?

Middle levels

Learning about religious experiences may be appropriately approached from a sociological viewpoint. The growing acquaintance with various human groups around the world provides the setting for consideration of the religious systems and how they have helped man deal with the problems of existence.

A beginning awareness of the differences between religious and scientific knowledge. Religious and scientific knowledge are parts of the human effort to understand human existence, but they use different types of "input." The child should begin, at this level, to consider the limitations of scientific knowledge in areas that do not provide objective data and the limitations of religious knowledge to resolve public problems in a free and open society. This should be approached by a factual introduction to the major religions of the world, including the effect of religious systems upon aspects of daily living, the common elements in all religions, and the ways in which man has satisfied his need to be secure in his perceptions of natural forces and their origins.

The consideration of "ways of knowing" in connection with religious truth may be more than some communities will accept. However, it cannot be disputed that the "personal, private, mystical nature of religious truth and belief" is the key reason why young people in an open society need to appreciate the right to religious freedom and to respect this right without feeling obliged to cast other beliefs in an inferior light. The use of scientific knowledge to resolve issues in the public domain can be properly developed.

Teacher attitude and behavior are, as always, critical factors that affect pupil perceptions of adult-model responses to such matters. The noncritical, nonjudgmental approach of the teacher is a difficult goal, and some teachers will argue that they have a right or a moral obligation to *persuade* youngsters on religious matters, conveniently assuming that the children will be otherwise bereft of religious experience. Unless the schools can manage the task of teaching about religion and the place of religious knowledge in the public arena, freedom of religion itself will be a myth and the social maturity necessary to the protection and respect for individual, private, religious experience will not be fostered.

Upper levels

The historical dimension may be added to the sociological approach to the study of religion. Ways in which religious beliefs have led men to migrate, to revolt, and to missionize may be included. Some aspects of contemporary problems, as they are influenced by religious interests, may offer factual bases for viewing the use of religion in political and economic matters. The Arab-Israeli conflict, the Pakistani-Indian situation, the Catholic-Protestant conflict in Ireland—these are recent occurrences which can be examined in the classroom. Religious content is not the subject, rather the place of religion in human experience and conflict is the social science concern.

Suggested Guidelines for the Study of Religion

It is the position of the writers that elementary school children should be involved in awareness, attitudinal, and informational activities dealing with human religious experience and organization. The requirements for mature conceptions of religion and for the protection of the personal and private nature of religion are far more demanding in an open society than in a theocracy or in a mono-religious society, and they cannot be properly disregarded in the school experience.

The elementary school is not the appropriate place to introduce the matter of comparative religious systems nor to carry out analyses of the various local religious groups. This position is realistic, we believe, in terms of child maturity factors, parental desires, and community views.

The school should not be hostile to religion, nor should it take up a proselytizing position for a particular religion. Some persons may object to the definition of religion to denote those areas of question and concern where meaning and truth cannot be obtained through rational inquiry, where the consideration deals with man, life, and the meaning and purpose of creation. From psychological and sociological perspectives, we would conclude that all men are religious, though not necessarily in the conventional sense. We would not argue that a neo-religious position should be advanced by the school, but we do believe that evidence drawn from human experience supports our recommendation that religion is a phenomenon which is universally human and that its effects historically and its implications currently make it an appropriate item for study.

We further believe that the place and treatment of human religious experiences in the schools are just on the verge of careful attention and development. The future of our free society will depend largely upon the adequate conceptualization by our citizens of the nature of religion and their protection of it as a private individual freedom. The public school is the proper institution in our society to concern itself with the public attitude toward religion. The home and the churches are properly concerned with belief, theology, doctrine, and practice. The school is properly concerned with those aspects of the study of religion which will lead to respect for individual belief and practice and to value for this freedom to the end that neither church nor any other institution will prevail against the exercise of this personal freedom.

Other Aspects of Religion

In this approach to religion in education, we have purposely omitted any emphasis upon the political and economic aspects of religious interests. The political forces, which have been generated by specific religious organizations, we view as appropriate for study at secondary and college levels. In this we may have erred in our judgment regarding the readiness of the 10-to-12-year-old to encounter the concept of religion as political. There has been no intention to protect or to hide religious-political realities from scrutiny. Certainly, the prospective teacher must be aware of and informed about the nonpersonal elements of the activities of religious organizations.

In recent years, the positions of the Roman Catholic Church on birth control and overpopulation, celibacy of the priesthood, and divorce have come into public view as issues. The interest and activities of certain American Jewish organizations in support of the state of Israel in its contentions with the Arab states is an example of the political thrust of a religious organization. The fact that a nationalistic identity is present cannot obviate the religious factors that serve as organizing elements.

The social implications of the dogma of the Latter Day Saints concerning the limited status of the Negro in its organization has emerged as a public issue in a number of communities. In a similar vein, the problem of tax exemptions for religious organizations which operate profit generating businesses ought not be obscured because of fear of offending religious bodies. Those activities of religious groups which project into the public domain as political, social or economic issues must be subject to public test. We believe such matters are usually beyond the scope of the elementary program, but we certainly urge you to challenge this position and to consider alternatives.

Suggested Problems and Projects

1. A group of students who believe that a common core of religious beliefs should be included in the school experiences of all children may wish to work out a plan that will include content and a way of teaching. This should

not be attempted unless there are students who have strong ideas about this. Care should be given to the matter of keeping any such common core approach within the requirements of the U.S. Supreme Court rulings on the subject.

2. A simple survey of various individuals on the topic of religion in the public school should be helpful in providing information about commonly held views. The student committee may wish to select a survey population including professional persons, skilled and nonskilled workers and urban and rural residents. The interview should be uncomplicated and might involve the following:
- A. Should the public schools teach religion?
- B. What are the two or three most important religious ideas that you want taught?
- C. Why should (should not) the school teach religion?
- D. If the school's approach to religion is contrary to U.S. Supreme Court rulings, what should be done?

3. The authors support a social science approach to the study of religion as a universal function of human beings which aids them in understanding and coping with various life situations. As you read this chapter, make a list of weaknesses and strengths you find in this approach.

4. Consider the following position: A teacher has a first responsibility to the supreme law of the land, in religious matters as in others. Hence, the individual teacher and the local and state professional education organizations are obliged to refrain from participating in illegal religious activities in the public school. Just as members of the medical profession would not be party to illegal practices in a local hospital, even if many people approved, so members of the teaching profession must accept responsibility for permitting only legal educational practices in any given school.

5. Arrange for a group of students in your class to write a critique of the Wheaton Unit for grade five. Have the students use an outline for analysis which includes such items as interest to 12-year-olds, accuracy of statements in the Unit, etc.

Related Readings

Dillon, J. D. "Introducing Religion to Public School Curriculum." *Religious Education* 64 (March 1969): 83–90.

Gerard, B. S. "Teaching About Religion: When and Where to Begin." *Religious Education* 63 (May 1968): 215–18.

Little, L. C. "Religion in Public School Social Curricula." *Religious Education* 64 (March 1969): 99–104.

Noss, John B. *Man's Religions,* 3rd edition. New York: The Macmillan Company, 1963.

Pilch, J. "Teaching About the Meaning of Religion." *Religious Education* 64 (March 1969): 90–96.

Rice, A. H. "Why Don't Schools Act Responsibly About Religion?" *Nations Schools* 81 (January 1968): 8.

Smith, Huston. *The Religions of Man.* New York: Harper and Row, 1958.

"Units, Courses, and Projects for Teaching About Religions." *Social Education* 33 (December 1969): 917–30.

Warshaw, T. S. "Teaching About Religion in Public School: 8 Questions." *Phi Delta Kappan* 49 (November 1967): 127–33.

11

WHAT ARE SOME SPECIFIC PROBLEMS?
    Generalizing from limited data
    Covering too much
    Confusing practices with values
    Social maturity factors
    Looking at ourselves and others

INTERNATIONAL RESOURCE PERSONS

WHAT ARE THE PROSPECTS FOR IMPROVING INTERNATIONAL STUDIES?
    The Glens Falls story

WHAT IS THE PLACE OF MINORITY GROUP STUDIES?

SUGGESTED PROBLEMS AND PROJECTS

RELATED READINGS

Cross-Cultural Studies

The study of people in lands other than our own is not a strange and novel undertaking to be included in the curriculum because it is interesting to learn about human oddities. In the study of other cultures, children make use of the same inquiry processes that they use in the study of any ethnic and racial group in their own society. Social science education is concerned with the careful and orderly study of the human condition, and the location of a particular group of people on the earth does not automatically make them different and unusual.

You may want to object to the opening paragraph inasmuch as most human beings seem to be inclined to view *normal* and *acceptable* behavior as that behavior to which they have become accustomed in their own social environment. Simply saying that the study of different human groups is really no different from the study of the group to which we belong does not cancel the cultural biases and ethno-centric tendencies which are known to exist. We would agree that cultural bias and nationalistic loyalties are factors which we must take into account when we attempt to view another cultural group in an objective manner. However, when we study ethnic and racial subgroups in our own society, do we not encounter the same problems caused by bias and loyalty to our own group? To this extent, it appears that any time we study *other* people, here or abroad, we must begin with the awareness that our perceptions of good and bad, civilized and primitive, and right and wrong are influenced by the value orientations implanted during early, firsthand contacts with our own cultural subsystem.

What Are Some Specific Problems?

We have just discussed problems of bias and prejudice, which may be produced by our perceptual blinders. Let us now consider other problems that actually arise from the careless use of inquiry.

Generalizing from limited data

This is a common error which is made by people in many situations where it is particularly difficult to obtain pertinent data about a problem or concern. When children are attempting to increase their understanding of other nations and people, they often work with limited data. If you examine several intermediate level social studies textbooks, you will likely discover that the information about an entire nation may be limited to two or three pages. The study of ways of living in other lands will lead to many misconceptions and erroneous generalizations when the information is limited and spotty.

A photograph of a Fulani cattle herder which appears in a textbook selection may support a concept of Nigeria that is inaccurate and weak if the growing industrialization and urbanization of Nigeria is not adequately treated. Likewise, a geography book which concludes a one and a half page treatment of a small African country with the statement, "Cows are still used in trading for wives," *may* lead children to generalize that all Africans have similar marriage practices and that such people hold important human values in low esteem.

Children examine miniature tools and carvings from Nigeria to gain understandings of another way of life.

Covering too much

The problem of generalizing from insufficient data is part and parcel of a common classroom ailment known as "covering the ground." Efficient inquiry, hence sound conceptualization, is aborted when teachers feel the need to go through a book with little time for reflection and development of understandings. In the study of other lands, it has been a traditional practice to survey the lands of the Eastern World or the Western World. A geography oriented teacher may desire that the pupils recognize and recall names and places, and although this is not respectable geography, it does get the class over a lot of territory and through a book in good time. The opportunity to study in depth the ways of life, the environment, and the heritage of any one group of people is limited or completely ruled out when covering ground is the driving concern.

Confusing practices with values

Those things which we view as very different from what we accept as normal and proper are apt to attract our interest and attention. We are inclined to make judgments about the values that people hold on the basis of unusual practices and life patterns.

Can we properly conclude that education is not highly valued in a nation where only 20 per cent of the school age children go to school? What other information do we need? Can we correctly conclude that the people do not value cleanliness and good health in a nation where indoor and outdoor toilets are provided in fewer than 30 per cent of the households? What else would you like to know? A rural Lesotho bridegroom presents money and gifts to the bride's family as part of a traditional bride price. Should we conclude that this man and his people do not value mutual respect in marriage?

> A Nigerian educator once remarked that he could not understand why visitors from the United States were prone to stare at the sight of a person relieving himself by the side of the road. Upon being informed that such public toilet habits appeared to be indecent, immodest, and unsanitary, the Nigerian asserted that sanitation was the only real problem here; that people who stared were inconsiderate of the others and indeed, probably indecent for their curiosity about a very natural function of all humans.

Social maturity factors

There are legitimate questions to raise with respect to the most appropriate time to involve youngsters in the comparative study of cultures. Our children are expected to adopt the dominant value orientations of our society and to behave in accord with normative practices. Individuality is valued only to the degree to which it does not place great strain and present a threat to the normative patterns. A so-called valueless approach to the study of other cultures is not only impossible, but with elementary children it may be confusing and threatening. It may be unduly threatening even to adults.

"Now we will read about the strange people who live in the country of _____."

There is some reason to believe that the young child has the need to experience success and security in coming to grips with the behavioral demands of his own social group before he can deal effectively with the variant characteristics of other human groups. Either from ignorance or by clever design, human groups have historically viewed other tribes, races, nations, etc., as being basically inferior. This may have been a culture preserving response, which was necessary for group identification. The young in every cultural group need to value their own way

Cross-Cultural Studies

of life and to understand that this cultural attachment is a universal human phenomenon.

> *Survey a local newspaper or a news magazine for expressions of cultural, racial or national superiority. Analyze elementary social studies textbooks for examples of cultural bias.*
>
> *What very real obstacles do you see in our nation and in other nations to the early development of a "one world—one people" view? Are the problems mainly economic and political?*

Looking at ourselves and others

There is a growing number of interesting studies which deal with children's perceptions of people who are different or are thought to be different. No attempt is made here to present an extensive summary of such studies, but it is generally true that children consider themselves more intelligent, more clever, more industrious and energetic, more peaceful, more honest, and kinder than children in other groups.

Before meeting with several young students from South Vietnam, a group of rural New York pupils were asked to indicate, on a checklist, what they expected the visitors to be like. The majority of students expected the South Vietnamese to possess generally negative characteristics, such as, cruelty, cunning, dishonesty, and the like. After three days of being with the South Vietnamese students throughout the school day and in activities after school, the New York youngsters were asked to use the checklist again. Significant shifts had occurred in all categories, and the South Vietnamese were generally viewed as being just about "as good as our fellow Americans."

What does the preceding account suggest with respect to involving visiting international students in your studies of other cultures? How do you account for the great shift in the way the New York students perceived the South Vietnamese? Is this reassuring or potentially dangerous?

Here is a tabulation of the perceptions of a group of students in Liberty, New York before and after the visit of young South Vietnamese students: [1]

---

[1] Milton E. Ploghoft et al., "International Studies: A National Concern" (Athens, Ohio: Ohio University, 1967). A monograph of the Cooperative Center for Social Science Education.

	Phrase or Word	Before visit of Vietnamese	of Self	After visit of Vietnamese
1.	Hard-working	438	117	320
2.	Efficient	37	53	100
3.	Quick-tempered	48	206	90
4.	Dirty	126	8	50
5.	Not reliable	39	28	20
6.	Intelligent	57	120	180
7.	Clever	101	67	210
8.	Without ambition	35	46	30
9.	Religious	204	76	100
10.	Lazy	9	144	10
11.	Superstitious	193	30	55
12.	Ignorant	164	15	70
13.	Ambitious	153	142	155
14.	Honest	67	284	120
15.	Quiet	158	132	130
16.	Trustful	47	168	90
17.	Dependable	55	220	75
18.	Cruel	56	13	40
19.	Fighter	218	75	136
20.	Good sense of humor	11	335	70
21.	Weak	73	21	50
22.	Loyal to family	314	177	161
23.	Artistic	12	70	16
24.	Deceitful	36	18	30
25.	Kind	32	155	50
26.	Helpful	66	194	60
27.	Obedient	115	92	75
28.	Brave	255	60	163

Barry Beyer and Perry Hicks reported, "American students possess a very clear-cut and strongly stereotyped image of Africa south of the Sahara—an image that can best be described as Tarzan-like." Among a number of 12- and 13-year-old students sampled, the following terms were used by over 75 per cent of the group in referring to Sub-Sahara Africa:

wild animals	daktari	elephants
witch doctors	jungles	tigers
spears	tribe	natives
poison darts	drums	black
savage		

The same researchers reported that twelfth-grade pupils in their study

Cross-Cultural Studies 295

seemed to know more about Africa than did the seventh graders, but the stereotypes that were held did not differ between groups.[2]

If the situation is not good with seventh and twelfth graders in respect to the dearth of knowledge about sub-Sahara Africa, what has been happening in the elementary program? Is the situation equally gloomy with respect to the knowledge and attitudes our young have toward other nations and cultural groups?

When teachers, children, and parents take an inventory of the community, they will find learning resources, such as, those displayed here. The increase in travel at home and abroad makes such resources more common than ever before.

Of particular interest to prospective elementary teachers are the reports of the Wallace Lambert and Otto Klineberg studies of children's views of foreign peoples. With reference to differences among children of various age groups, it appears that six-year-olds do not see themselves as being similar to foreign people, and they do not readily express affection for foreign people, whereas ten-year-old children express affection more readily and tend to view others as similar to themselves.[3]

---

[2] Barry K. Beyer and E. Perry Hicks, "Final Report of Project Africa" (June 1970). Sponsored by U.S. Dept. of Health, Education, and Welfare, project no. 7-0724, Office of Education Contract −3-7-070724-2970.

[3] Wallace E. Lambert and Otto Klineberg, *Children's Views of Foreign Peoples* (New York: Appleton-Century-Crofts, 1967), p. 188.

If we were to act on the basis of the generalization made by Lambert and Klineberg, the middle levels of the elementary school would be the logical starting point for extensive cross-cultural studies, especially of those components that deal with prevailing customs and beliefs as they relate to the ways of life of other peoples. The research information is not sufficiently complete to suggest *why* the ten-year-old holds friendlier attitudes toward people of other countries, but we may speculate that a growing sense of security in dealing with his culture outside of the home contributes to his curiosity, or perhaps it is a desire to explore what common ground exists among the various people of the world.

Other observations made by Lambert and Klineberg indicated that:

1. U.S. children tended to view British, Italian, Canadian, and French as similar peoples; they tended to view Chinese, African Negroes, Japanese, and Russians as different.
2. The early teaching of children with respect to the concept of their "own group" apparently exaggerates their view of their own people and supports the early formation of stereotypes about "different" people in their own country.
3. Emphasis upon differences among people is stressed from earliest years of childhood and this probably leaves a durable impression on the individual. Higher intellectual functioning is required to identify the similarities among people than to identify differences.
4. The pattern of reaction to different ethnic and racial groups in one's own society appears to have transfer strength when peoples of other nations are considered.[4]

International Resource Persons

There is a general inclination to limit our search for learning resources in this area to the books, magazines, films, and records that we can locate. Frequently overlooked is the presence of more than 100,000 international students and teachers who are in our schools and universities each year. Not every international visitor to our nation is interested in being, nor perhaps qualified to act as, a resource person in the elementary classroom. The experience at Ohio University with an International Studies Advisory Council, which works with interested schools through the College of Education, has proven that large numbers of international students are eager to be of assistance in extending accurate understanding of their respective nations.

---

[4] *Ibid.*, pp. 216–227.

International resource persons are most effectively involved when some careful planning goes on before the visit to the classroom. The international resource person should be informed of the age levels of the groups with which he will work. He should know, at least generally, the nature and extent of the study which has been done on his country. Special care should be taken to provide the equipment which he may need in his presentation. He should know beforehand just what is expected of him.

Elementary children should be prepared to welcome the international visitor to their classroom. If any language difficulties are anticipated, the children should be prepared to listen carefully and to question politely. They are the hosts and the first responsibility for communication is theirs. Unless we are willing to speak the language of the visitor, we should be most grateful that he is making an effort to communicate with us.

"Canned questions" may seem undesirable to many of you, but it is advisable for the children to be prepared with questions to ask. With most international resource persons, the canned questions serve to generate other questions and comments, and soon a natural exchange will occur.

It has been our experience that international resource persons will accept, without offense, the honest questions that children ask. As a matter of politeness, the very personal questions should be avoided, just as it would be in our own public groups. A rather common curiosity of adults in the U.S. seems to concern "how many wives a male visitor has or plans to have," although we would not ask such a question in our own public meetings. Fortunately, children have other questions which relate to the kinds of schools, who goes to school, the kinds of recreational opportunities, the wildlife, and the kinds of homes, villages, and cities there are in a given nation.

If at all possible, the international visitor should have the opportunity to mingle with the children in an informal setting in order that such firsthand contacts will make the experience much more personal to the children. Visitors who travel a considerable distance to the school gain much and give much from being welcomed as guests in homes in the district. Colleges and universities in your area may not be organized to provide the coordinating services which bring teachers, children, and international resource persons together. Usually, if a school district or a few teachers will plan carefully for effective use of such resources, then an inquiry to the Dean of the College of Education or to the foreign student's advisor will bring results, often at no cost beyond travel arrangements.

Remember, *build background before the visit of a resource person; do not treat the occasion as a novel affair or the person as a curiosity.*

Small group discussions with persons from other lands are intended to diminish levels of hostility and suspicion toward people from different cultures.

What Are the Prospects for Improving International Studies?

The television medium would seem to be a boon to the improvement of international studies in the elementary schools. Few children can escape an awareness of many people and places, but unfortunately, so much of this intake is of the crisis variety. The youngster could readily conclude that the world would be a good place if there were not so many foreign places where we get into difficulty. Although television brings the world to the living room, the task of the school in helping the child deal with and interpret the total context of the television message is a greater one than ever before. More data is being presented and more stereotypes will be initiated and supported than before unless analysis and evaluation is provided.

An increasing variety of children's books, visual aids, and realia which deal with aspects of life in other lands is available. In most communities there are *informed* persons who have had extended experience in other countries and may be helpful. The emphasis here should be upon the use of sources and materials that are reliable and objective. There is no need to add error and bias through haphazard use of related resources.

The Glens Falls story

The City School District of Glens Falls, New York, has provided one of the more interesting examples of an intensive, carefully calculated effort to improve the teaching of world affairs throughout the entire system. For more than a decade, the Glens Falls schools have tried a variety of activities and materials designed to make "world awareness" a normal part of classroom life. A report and compilation of teaching ideas have been made available by the National Council for the Social Studies, and you may find this a useful resource. Here, however, as in any other material, it is necessary to be sensitive to erroneous conceptualization and bias which may weaken or detract from the effort. Inasmuch as there is much to be gained from the Glens Falls gleanings, we are obligated to point out some of the misconceptions and stereotype reinforcing items in the material. Consider the following:

1. Japanese are little people—one must be little to live in such a little country.

2. Great man Commodore Perry from America Knocked on Japan's door so loud Ruler finally said Come In! Japan was very fortunate.... Soon Japan is most eager to be like America.

3. From a "Jungle Conversation—"
   Mother: "Is this a barn?"
   Pupil: "No, that's a big house. Many families can live in it. Each has his [sic] own corner."
   Mother: "Where's the furniture?"
   Pupil: "We don't use much furniture. You see we move about often, and we don't want a lot to carry."
   Mother: "Why is that house up so high?"
   Pupil: "See this big river?"
   Mother: "Yes."
   Pupil: "Well, sometimes the water gets very deep and wide.... so we put our houses up on stilts...."
   Mother: "What a fine idea! Why is that tall fence around this house?"
   Pupil: "That's to keep lions and tigers from getting into our house while we sleep." [5]

In a mystery person game designed to interest children in current world happenings, one clue to the identity of Mao Tse-Tung was, "I get rid of some people who don't like me."

---

[5] *Bringing the World into Your Classroom* (Washington: The National Council for the Social Studies, 1968), pp. 30, 106–110.

In the inquiry-oriented classroom, there will be opportunities to examine statements and generalizations in the examples above. Are the people of the jungle nomadic, moving their stilt-houses about or constantly building new ones? Do highly mobile people generally use little furniture? Are the people of the U.S. regarded as mobile? If the Japanese were so eager to be like Americans, why did these two nations engage in a war in 1941? How did Commodore Perry make a big knock on Japan's door?

What Is the Place of Minority Group Studies?

The question of whether to include special units of study of American Negroes, American Indians, and Mexican-Americans should be resolved by the same decision-making processes that are applied generally. What are the objectives for the study of any particular groups? What do we hope to understand? What relevance is to be found in the study of any given group?

In most recent years there has been a rapid growth of black studies centers and courses in black history and culture. William Sutton has viewed the situation of the 1960's as one that required special programs and courses to reverse the long standing tendency to overlook the Negro in American history. An additional concern was expressed for the identity confusion which the black American experienced as he attended schools with lily white curricula, based on the assumption that few, if any, notable contributions had come to modern humanity from either black African or black American cultural sources.[6] In Sutton's judgment, the specialized courses and institutes should be unnecessary once the social science curriculum has become mankind oriented rather than white oriented.

Criticisms have emerged from some quarters to the effect that we should include Polish studies, Irish studies, Syrian studies, Jewish studies, and so on, if we are to consider black studies separately. This is a question that calls for judgment-making with overriding purposes in view. Has the justification for black studies been one of political expedience? Should curriculum be influenced by black pressure groups? Has curriculum been influenced by white pressure groups? From the viewpoint of educational objectives for elementary children, what do you believe to be the proper role for black studies? What reasons can

---

[6] From an address by Dr. William Sutton, director of the Black Studies Institute, Ohio University, to a Black Studies—African Studies Conference, Cleveland Heights Schools (February 27, 1970).

you give for having white youngsters study black history or black literature?

At this point, the relationships between the study of other cultures, foreign and domestic, should begin to emerge quite clearly. The same basic questions and strategies apply to the study of all cultures and subcultures. Each question which you raise with respect to the place and relevance of any one minority group studies should be raised of all. If the black myths and heroes are to be rigorously questioned, will we do likewise with Anglo-Saxon, European, and American figures? (If not, do you know why?)

Certain school districts have made progress in the development of balanced programs to include minority or intergroup studies for teachers and children. The Clark County, Nevada school district has organized a Division of Intergroup Education to initiate and support desired developments in that area of social education.[7] Additional references and sources are available in the bibliography at the end of this book.

Suggested Problems and Projects

1. Prepare a plan for developing learning experiences that will help overcome the erroneous generalizations and stereotypes mentioned by Lambert and Klineberg.
2. What kind of learning experience could you plan that would use the celebration of certain holidays to develop the generalization that "different cultures attach particular meaning and significance to an event and differ in their ways of dealing with it?"
3. Working in teams of three or four, develop a plan using one aspect of life patterns in two different cultures to develop the idea of cultural variety in response to basic human needs.
4. A West African visitor objected to a classroom display that depicted an African village with crocodiles, lions, and elephants in the scene. He maintained that such erroneous presentations would give children the idea that only foolish people would live in the midst of such a situation. What do you think?
5. What implications are there for teaching human understanding in this statement, "I believe we should teach that the world is one big, brotherly place. We should feel kindly toward the Hindus, Buddhists, and Moslems. They are good guys. They don't bother us much. In fact, I wish that some of our people here at home would be as easy to get along with."

---

[7] Claude Perkins, "The Role of Black Studies" (Las Vegas, Nevada: Office for Intergroup Education, Clark County Public Schools, 1969).

Related Readings

Coles, Robert. "When I Draw the Lord He'll Be a Real Big Man." *The Atlantic* 214 (May 1966): 69–75.

Kenworthy, Leonard. "Studying Other Countries." *Social Education* 23 (April 1959): 59–162.

Larrick, Nancy. "The All-White World of Children's Books." *Saturday Review,* September 11, 1965.

Oliva, Peter F. "Essential Understandings for the World Citizen." *Social Education* 23 (October 1959): 266–268.

Ploghoft, Milton E., et al. *International Studies: A National Concern.* Athens, Ohio: Cooperative Center for Social Science Education, Ohio University, 1967.

Social Education vol. 33 (April 1969). Issue devoted to "Black Americans and Social Studies" and to "Minority Groups in American Society."

Spock, Benjamin. "Children and Discrimination." *Redbook Magazine* (October 1964). Reprints available from the Anti-Defamation League of B'nai B'rith, 315 Lexington Avenue, New York.

12

WHAT IS A STRUCTURAL APPROACH TO CONTEMPORARY AFFAIRS?
    Common difficulties
    Other factors

LEARNING ABOUT THE MEDIA
    Newspaper study
    The development of receiver skills—television

SUGGESTED PROBLEMS AND PROJECTS

RELATED READINGS

Contemporary Affairs in Social Science Education: An Emerging Role

The introduction and careful study of contemporary affairs in the social science education experiences of children is predicated on two assumptions: 1) early experiences with contemporary affairs will provide the attitudinal and interest bases which will support continuing concern and participation in public affairs; 2) the study of and response to contemporary issues and problems are of critical importance in a democratic society. The pertinent attitudes and skills must be developed in the educational program.

What are the objectives here? In accord with the central concern of social science education, the following objectives are set forth for the inclusion of contemporary affairs:

1. The pupil will develop and extend social science concepts and skills into the "here and now world" of human activities through experiences with contemporary affairs.
2. The pupil will develop his skills to deal with the mass media and their various techniques of persuasion.

Contemporary affairs are viewed here as adding another dimension to the content and process of social science education, and the basic concern of helping children understand human affairs and their relation to them applies here, as in other aspects of the learning program. Concept development and skill application, especially the inquiry process, can be attended to by using contemporary affairs as a vehicle to the attainment of those ends.

It is our intent to propose these two objectives as being major concerns of social science education that will not normally be dealt with in other school activities. Both objectives can be evaluated in terms of pupil growth.

The first objective is very much social science oriented. If indeed the child is to develop his abilities and skills in understanding human events, the content of current affairs should be used as the raw material for extending *concepts*. Why should the child develop concepts about *social groups* and *political power* if these concepts are not brought into operation in the treatment of current affairs? The events of the here and now are used because they are more than interesting; they provide opportunities for continual application of concepts and the use of inquiry in non-textbook settings.

The second objective is derived from the fact that the majority of adults in the United States receive more than 50 per cent of their formal information messages via television, a medium that is being used with considerable sophistication to persuade the viewer toward a particular position. This is the case with many news casts and special events features. Newspapers, which at one time were expected to do their editorializing on the editorial page, now include interpretive comments within the body of factual accounts. So, at the very outset, a social science education approach to current affairs requires that the individual concern himself with the nature of the media, processes, techniques, and motivations. The tentative acceptance of any information should have a reasonable basis, which comes with an understanding of communications media and the development of the skills needed to identify, analyze, and interpret messages.

What Is a Structural Approach to Contemporary Affairs?

In keeping with our concern for the development and extension of concepts, we suggest a structural approach to the study of contemporary affairs. The structure that we have in mind is closely tied to that of the social sciences. Human activities have been more or less arbitrarily classified as economic, political, sociological, and so on. We recommend that children be introduced to simple analytical schemes as they deal with contemporary affairs, thus, their sensitivity to structure will be developed inductively. We do not propose that teachers ask children to identify a news story as being economic or political; rather that they consider the kinds of human problems and activities that are reported and accorded importance by the media.

An example of an analytical scheme may be helpful in clarifying what we are talking about. This scheme may be used, even in the primary levels, to introduce children to a systematic way of thinking about news items:

    A.   What is the news story about?
          1.   New stores, factories, businesses for our town
          2.   Problems of running our town or school

3. People and problems dealing with nature
4. Activities of a particular group of people in our community: church, club, etc.
5. Problems between people or groups of people
6. People from other places who have come to our town for a special reason

B. Why is the news story important to us?
1. Will it affect people in our family or town?
2. Is it about an old problem?
3. Will we need to do something about it?
4. Should we keep track of further news on this item?

You can see that this analytical scheme includes attention to the content and to the more personal aspect of what it means to us. Numerous approaches can be used to develop the child's awareness of the recurring content of news stories, an awareness that should lead the individual to organize his own thinking. Later, hopefully at upper elementary levels, children will be ready to consider which social science tools and study methods would be most useful in studying the kinds of human problems that are reported by the media.

Children should not be pressed for responses, nor should they be urged to arrive at consensus on the importance of any news item. The major concern here is to provide an opportunity for children to think about contemporary affairs and to provide a working setting in which children and adults talk about the kind of situation that is involved.

In the middle levels of elementary school, the model for analysis can become much more oriented to the identification of social science concepts in reports of contemporary affairs. Although one of the major concerns here is for the development of pupil awareness of the social science aspects of current happenings, we do not suggest that children be urged to classify news stories as being political, economic, or historical. The interdisciplinary nature of human events may be seen through an analysis that does not insist on air tight categories for each happening. Economic matters are usually political also. Intergroup conflicts often involve political and economic elements, and it is expected that the child will come to see this through his ever widening contacts with reality.

Beginning in the middle grades, the following analytical scheme can be effective in helping children develop their abilities to classify news content, to consider its importance to themselves and other people, and to become sensitive to the element of persuasion:

A. What is the main topic of the news story?
1. The control or use of resources
2. Use and control of transportation and communication
3. Distribution of wealth; labor management
4. Problems of an ethnic or racial group
5. Men in government, actions by government
6. Unusual problems in human behavior
7. Man's progress or problems in science
8. Citizens, law, and justice
9. Relations between nations

B. Why is the news story important?
1. Will it affect us, our family and acquaintances?
2. Does it affect certain groups in our nation?
3. Will it have long lasting effect on us or other groups?
4. What, if anything, should be done about the situation?

C. What was the quality of the news story?
1. Who wrote it; where did it come from, does it seem factual?
2. Is the source to be trusted? Why or why not?
3. Would anyone have reason to want us to think in a certain way about the topic of the story?
4. What words were used to arouse our feelings?

In using this analytical guide, most teachers have encouraged the children to consider categories of content that need to be added, since the model given here is open for development. Each child should have his own mimeographed copy of the analytical guide so he can refer to it as the class discusses a particular news story. As the pupil gains experience in using the guide, he will approach his news reading or television news viewing with a critical attitude and a useful frame of reference for thinking about media content.

There are numerous variations that the teacher may use in dealing with contemporary affairs in the classroom. A few are suggested here:

1. Organize pupil committees to present the major news story(ies) of the week. The news items should be presented on a bulletin board so the class may become familiar with content before oral discussions are held.
2. Reaction and analysis may be carried out as small group activities or as a total class activity. The analytical guides should be used.

3. If the class has a television set, the group may watch an open newscast at regular times. (A formal daily discussion session is not suggested for middle grade youngsters.)
4. At least one copy of a daily newspaper should be present in the classroom for pupil use.

Common difficulties

A frequent shortcoming is that the contemporary affairs session becomes a perfunctory activity where several pupils read accounts of "important events" and the rest of the class is then asked, "Do you have any questions?" Usually, they do not. In those cases where pupil questions are raised, the pupil reporter usually can offer no further enlightenment or interpretation, so the teacher bails him out.

If children are to grapple with the news, they need the help of an analytical guide. If they are to grow toward maturity, they do not need an adult to *conclude* for them. In too many classrooms, the teacher has decided upon the importance of news items—here we suggest that pupils consider the importance of news items. The contemporary affairs activity should strive for sharp focus on a limited number of items—one or two —rather than a hodgepodge. If a classroom news bulletin board is used, it should be kept up to date, again with only two or three items displayed.

Other factors

The persuasive aspects of accounts of contemporary affairs are similar to those of propaganda. It can be argued that children of elementary school age are intellectually and emotionally unprepared for serious attention to the psychological factors involved in persuasion. It is true that a complete distrust of all sources of information presents an unhappy prospect, although an equally dismal reality is the situation where people accept, with little or no question, much information that has no more credence than that afforded by a printing press or a television camera.

The use of information about current happenings has been plagued by some chronic problems. As a required weekly assignment, the current events sessions frequently result in a mish-mash of unrelated reports of varying degrees of social concern. A common occurrence in U.S. homes on "current events day" is the rapid rustling through the newspaper in search of an article that can be quickly clipped for classroom reading. At least part of the difficulty has come about because of the numerous purposes for the study of current events. Michaelis reported that it was customary for curriculum guides and teacher textbooks to recommend current events as a means "to develop wholesome attitudes toward others." [1]

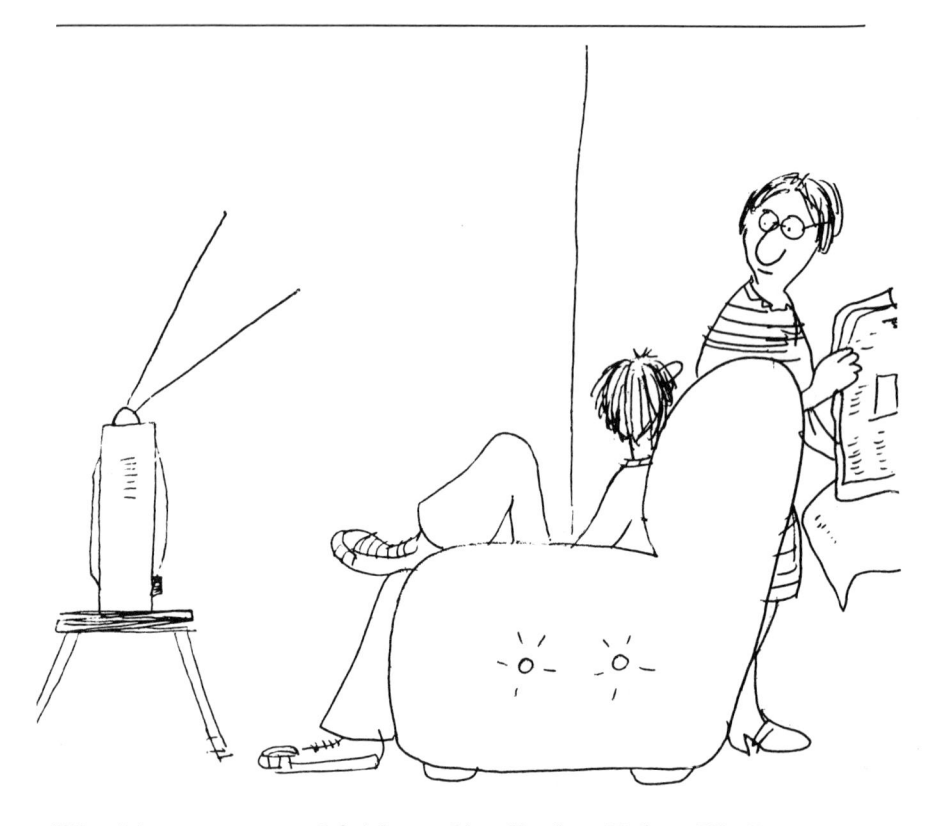

"Yes, Mom, as soon as I finish watching Hunkey-Binkey, I'll clip out my current event for tomorrow."

Jarolimek has narrowed the specific purposes for including current events and issues in the social studies program to three:

1. To promote interest in current affairs and news developments
2. Promoting skills needed to read newspapers, to discriminate between important and less important news items, to take and support a position, and to predict consequences of developments

---

[1] John U. Michaelis, *Social Studies for Children in a Democracy* (Englewood Cliffs, N.J.: Prentice-Hall, 1968), pp. 168–169.

3. To help the child relate school learning to life outside the school [2]

Learning About the Media

There is considerable evidence to support the idea that people are rather easily impressed by the printed word. Religious systems often refer to writings on sacred tablets or in the particular books that contain holy scripture. The expression, "It has been written..." continues to carry ominous power in various human situations, and the printed matter in books, magazines, and newspapers carries a measure of credibility and influence that is not actually justified.

The advent of television has introduced into the lives of children new dimensions for persuasion that far exceed those of the printed page. Recent information indicates that more than 50 per cent of the adults in the U.S. depend upon the television for the majority of their news and that more than 30 per cent continue to depend primarily upon the newspaper. Both newspaper and television require attention in the social science education of our young people. Inquiry and critical-thinking processes should be extended beyond the textbooks and other materials of the classroom, although the skills that will be used will be common to all situations.

Newspaper study

This activity is usually meaningful to pupils in the intermediate levels; it is essential that all children, whether they are considered slow or rapid learners, have experience in this aspect of newspaper study. This activity should be carried out several times during the school year, and evaluative effort should be made to determine pupil progress. The working outline for a plan for newspaper study may be as simple as this:

    A. What are the main parts of a daily newspaper? Children may work together in groups of two or three to determine this. Findings can be compared with other groups. Differences between large city and small town newspaper content sections may be noted.

    B. Which parts of a newspaper are more important than other parts? This draws the pupils into subjective judgments, and

---

[2] John Jarolimek, *Social Studies in Elementary Education* (New York: The Macmillan Company, 1965), pp. 342–343.

it will lead them, hopefully, to see that a newspaper will appeal to different people for different reasons. Some subscribers prefer the crossword puzzle, others like Dear Abby, and still others want the stock market report or the ad sections. This should lead to the next item.

C. Why are newspapers important to our nations? Informed citizens, economic reasons, entertainment—children should be urged to give their ideas.

D. How does a newspaper company make a profit? This introduces the idea of the newspaper being a profit-making business, and this will help children understand that the newspaper publisher must consider the ideas of many people.

The following information can be obtained from a small daily newspaper publisher. You may use this with your class; it will add excitement to use the data for a newspaper that is read by the class.

1. Income: subscriptions
advertising
classifieds
official notices
2. Costs: salaries
equipment and repair
3. Who provides most of the income to the newspaper? Advertisers or subscribers? Could this affect news policy?

E. Do newspapers inform you, try to make you think a certain way, or both? The elements of persuasion and slanting will enter here as you ask children to locate and cite evidence of this in a newspaper. They may decide that persuasion is on the editorial page and that information is in the news items.

Examples of newspaper content. Front page items of a large metropolitan newspaper: *The New York Times,* June 28, 1970:

1. City Council passes rent control law
2. Federal computers organize information on interesting citizens
3. Shortage of summer jobs for young people
4. Riots flare in Northern Ireland
5. U.S. planes to support Cambodia
6. Saigon urged to revalue money
7. Plan to train firemen and policemen as nurses

8. Basque stir Bishop to action
9. A photograph of Syrian soldiers surrendering to Israelis

The items listed were identified from the headings and without further reading; the adult reader will likely gain a fair estimate concerning the nature of the problem being reported. The middle elementary student can identify the news articles that deal with *conflicts between nations, conflicts between groups within a nation,* and the *problems in rentals* and in *job scarcities.* At an early stage of becoming aware of the social science content of the newspaper, this crude problem identification from examining headlines is enough. It helps to answer the question, "What kinds of people problems are reported on the front page?"

An area newspaper in southeastern Ohio presented the following topics on its front page on July 1, 1970:

1. Nixon on television
2. Draft lottery held
3. President's veto is overridden
4. American Nazis threaten peace senators
5. Helicopters shot down in Cambodia
6. Mrs. Nixon in Peru on good will trip
7. Violence in Ireland between Catholics, Protestants
8. Kent students favor ROTC

The approach to an analysis of the newspaper to determine the various people problems is the same for any newspaper, large or small. Middle elementary youngsters may observe the differences in the depth and breadth of news coverage as they examine metropolitan and local publications. The target of the experience remains that of building student awareness of the news media as the focal lens through which human problems of a contemporary nature are projected on the newspaper's front page (or on the television's screen). Beyond this first awareness is the task of developing a frame of reference or an organized set of expectancies which the child brings to the newspaper. This approach is planned to increase the child's efficiency in his use of the newspaper as a means of understanding human events and the relationships between reported events and his own life conditions.

The School Times, a bi-weekly student newspaper geared to the reading levels of the intermediate elementary child, bases its appeal on an imaginative combination of news photographs and diverse topics. In the May 25, 1970 issue of *The School Times,* the following subjects were presented:

1. The new marker for the geographic South Pole
2. The S.S. Manhattan's second voyage to the Canadian Arctic
3. An experiment in living under the sea
4. Efforts to save a magnolia tree in Brooklyn from being cut down
5. Forecast of major league baseball winners for 1970
6. TV specials on the Rocky Mountains and Washington, D.C.
7. Duke Ellington honored at White House
8. Recent records released
9. Dr. Barry Commoner and his environmental concerns
10. Yellowstone: a place in the news
11. Map Talk—a feature showing locations of national parks, seashores and monuments

Again, it is worth noting that the student newspaper can be viewed in terms of the kinds of human activities and problems it includes. Comparison of regular daily newspapers and student newspapers can be carried out periodically to aid the upper intermediate student in appreciating that publications direct their products toward specific customers, a fact that can be noted also by examination of specialty magazines.

The development of receiver skills—television

The emphasis upon the development of skills needed in analyzing and evaluating informational messages has been limited for the most part to printed media. Until the advent of television, the tendency was to regard the newspaper as the major purveyor of information and persuasion on topics that were of great interest and concern. Now, more than twenty years after the television medium penetrated the households of the majority of our citizens, education has not taken into account the fact that young people need to be well prepared to receive in a critical fashion the messages that come via the tube. Suggested teaching procedures and instructional materials are not yet generally available for use in activities that would develop the child's skill to critically receive and respond to a variety of television messages.

James Anderson, director of media research at Ohio University, has proposed that the child's awareness of the persuasive capabilities and motivation of commercial television can be increased through involving children in "behind the scenes" studies of television.[3] Anderson recommends introducing children to the *selection processes* whereby

---

[3] James Anderson and Milton E. Ploghoft, "The Development of Receiver Skills Appropriate to Effective Use of Television" (mimeograph, Cooperative Center for Social Science Education, Ohio University, 1969).

the news that we see on television is selected from a large number of events, all of which could not be shown due to time factors, viewer interest, and relative importance of various happenings.

The involvement of middle level pupils in *selection processes* need not be highly complicated and can be carried out in several ways. If your classroom has television receivers readily accessible, the pupils can be scheduled to view a live news telecast and asked to select only two or three items which they would show on a news *spot* if they were television news editors. The discussion which follows as the children compare and support their selections will introduce the key factors that are involved. Will the news items capture the interest of the viewer? Are the news items that you selected high in interest and low in importance to people? How will we choose when faced with interesting, unimportant items and unexciting, but important items? If the child plays the role of the businessman who is paying for a newscast in order to show his "ads," what kind of news items would he prefer? Will he have anything to say about this?

The introduction to selection processes can be carried out through the use of the front page of a newspaper where children are asked to select five items that they would use for a television newscast. Working with the pictorial and aural media presents problems and possibilities, however, that printed media do not, hence the use of live or taped newscasts is preferable. Because the concern here is with contemporary affairs and the influence of the television medium on that which we see, other aspects of receiver skills will not be dealt with here. As you continue to teach for effective inquiry, you will undoubtedly be alert to the development of guidelines and materials that will be helpful.

In addition to selection processes, it is recommended that you involve children, at both primary and intermediate levels, in viewing television commercials (at home, if unavailable in school). Two key questions form the frame of reference; "Why do I think that I want to get the thing they are advertising?" (identifying with the sales appeal) and "How do I know that the product will be 'good' for me?" (objective analysis). Such viewing activities are most effectively carried out in the group setting where immediate discussion follows. Obviously, the aim here is to condition the individual to assume a critical, questioning attitude when viewing television and to provide at least an elementary analytical scheme for the child to use.

For the very energetic and imaginative 11- or 12-year-old children in the classroom, an inquiry venture into the television industry can be exciting and informative. Such questions as, "How much does it cost to produce a 30 minute network show?" "Who pays for the costs of a television program (first and then finally)?" "Why is it necessary for television commercials to cause people to *want* things that they may not *need?*" "What techniques does television use to lead us to think in a certain way so we will act the way that an advertiser wants us to act?" "What dangers are there in systems that are able to control the thoughts of the people?" "What are the alternatives?" and "What can we do?" stimulate interest.

Suggested Problems and Projects

1. Divide your class into groups of four or five students and have each group prepare a contemporary affairs display that would be appropriate for use with elementary children at various levels. Follow the suggestions provided in the chapter.

2. Develop a simple plan for analyzing the "persuaders" that are used in television. Then arrange for each student to view a specific type of television program and report back to the entire class on the types of persuaders that were used in the program and in the commercials. From this experience, develop a plan that you believe could be used with middle elementary school children.

3. The matter of reliability of information is of great importance in a nation that makes use of mass media. What kinds of activities can you create that will develop pupil sensitivity to this problem? Can you devise any ways to build pupil skill in checking for reliability of sources?

Related Readings

Endres, Raymond J. "Criticism of Current Events." *Social Studies* 57 (January 1966): 8–16.

McLendon, Jonathan C. "Using Daily Newspapers More Effectively." *Social Education* 23 (October 1959): 263–265.

Preston, Ralph C. "Children's Reactions to Harsh Social Realities." *Social Education* 23 (March 1959): 116–120.

"TV and Your Child." A series from 1969 issues of *TV Guide* (Radnor, Pennsylvania: Triangle Publishers, Inc.).

Wass, Philmore B. "Improving Current Events Instruction." *Social Education* 25 (February 1961): 79–81.

Wilson, Richard C. "Using News to Teach Geography." *Social Education* 24 (February 1960): 56–57.

SECTION IV

The behavior of the teacher is viewed in a new light in chapter thirteen as the role requirements and society's conventional expectations of teachers are examined. Teaching social science education is fraught with more potential pitfalls than is the teaching of grammar, and the thoughtful teacher will be aware of the impact of her behavior and in control of her actions. The problem of evaluation of pupil progress toward the goals of social science education is dealt with in chapter fourteen. Some interesting examples of "model" items are presented for evaluating pupil use of inquiry.

13

WE DON'T WANT NO BOAT ROCKERS, *Dr. Willard F. Reese*

ABOUT YOU AND TEACHING

    How do you view education?
    How do you view human potential?
    How does self-awareness help?

TEACHER MOBILITY

CLASSROOM CLIMATE

    The teacher and the child's perceptions
    Do teachers hold democratic attitudes?

HOW TEACHERS LEARN TO HELP CHILDREN FAIL, *Estelle Fuchs*

SUGGESTED PROBLEMS AND PROJECTS

RELATED READINGS

Teachers and Social Science Education

Dr. Willard F. Reese

The extent to which a teacher may be effective in her work with young people is determined by the interaction of many forces in the school-community setting. Strong agreement does not always exist with respect to the various perceptions of the teacher's role, and serious conflicts may develop when teachers, board members, administrators, and parents take up inflexible positions.

Dr. Willard F. Reese of the Department of Elementary Education at The University of Alberta, has illuminated some very real aspects of the role perception problem. As you read "We Don't Want No Boat Rockers," reflect upon your perceptions of your role as a teacher and speculate as to the way you would respond if you were Miss Johnson.

This article provides an excellent vehicle for role playing a situation in which Mr. Petic, Mr. Adams, and Miss Johnson have come together in a conference to decide whether to employ Miss Johnson for another year. We believe that Dr. Reese's article is an appropriate entree to your consideration of your role as a teacher of social science education.

Dr. Willard F. Reese, "We Don't Want No Boat Rockers," *Phi Delta Kappan* (December 1968).

We Don't Want No Boat Rockers

Chester Petic, recently elected to the local school board, had made a special point of encountering his neighbor, Ralph Adams, during the noon hour. The neighbor, mild-mannered principal of the town's only elementary school, realized that this was no chance encounter.

"No siree Bob! We don't want no boat rockers teaching our kids." The double negative, affected to further his political ambitions, now came naturally into Petic's conversation—even with educated people. "Lord knows we're payin' teachers enough—oughta be willin' to do what we tell 'em, Right?"

Adams, only two years from his retirement pension, hesitated momentarily, then nodded in the affirmative. His mind raced through his list of teachers and tried to pinpoint the object of Petic's concern.

"This is a pretty good town, Adams, and it's up to guys like us to keep it that way. Hell, that's the only reason I'm on the school board—thankless task, but somebody's got to do it. This town's been good to me, so I figured I should repay it."

A weak "Commendable," followed by a more convincing "Yes, very commendable attitude." He wished that he knew what Petic was driving at. He didn't get a chance to speculate.

"Don't like to see teachers downtown during school hours. Hard enough gettin' folks to go along with the high salaries we've got to pay 'em without the damn teachers goofin' off when they should be working."

"Oh, ah, yes." Mr. Adams recalled having reluctantly given a new teacher permission to go downtown to find some materials she needed for a class activity. "Miss Johnson was on school business during her free period...."

"Free? None of her periods are free to us taxpayers," Petic interrupted. "You hadn't better let these young fillies pull the wool over your eyes. They can pick up some queer ideas in college these days." He gave Adams a friendly shove on the shoulder but there was an element of warning as he concluded the conversation. "Remember—no boat rockers."

All the way back to the school Adams worried about the school board member's remarks. "Maybe he has a point," he thought. "If any of my teachers could be considered different it would certainly be that Johnson girl." He resolved to see what else she might be up to. "She's made some pretty far-out suggestions at the staff meetings," he recalled. However, in all honesty, he had to admit that her children seemed to love her and the parents hadn't had any complaints—so far at least. "On the other hand," he continued his mental investigation, "there have been several occasions when I almost went into her room to quiet the buzz I heard from the hall." He made up his mind to go in that very afternoon during her last-period science lesson. "That's the time it seems worse than usual," he reasoned.

He'd often indicated at staff meetings his intention of visiting each classroom, but so far he'd settled for simply listening outside each door. "Less disturbing," he reasoned. Besides, he was convinced that most of his teachers were top-drawer; he seldom heard any unusual noises from the corridor.

Therefore it was an unusual procedure for him to be knocking on the grade five classroom door at 3:15 that afternoon. However, Miss Johnson seemed pleased to see him and invited him in. He noted the room with a degree of distaste. He made a mental note to recommend to her that she take down a lot of the stuff the children had made and use more commercially prepared materials for decorating her classroom. He also was going to suggest that she get rid of the other junk which was cluttering up her room. "The other teachers' rooms don't look like this," he thought.

It was time for science, but instead of introducing the lesson Miss Johnson was taking some jugs out of a big cardboard box. Adams noted that the children didn't even have their textbooks out but were getting ready to take notes.

"Why isn't she talking?" he thought. "She should at least be scolding those boys in the back who are standing up to watch her." Three or four children had their hands raised but the teacher continued to take out the jugs and line them up across the front of her desk. Finally she acknowledged one of the children, whose question, naturally enough, was, "What are you doing?"

"I'm placing these jugs on my desk," she replied.

"Why?" a child countered.

"Because I want them to be there," she smiled.

Realizing the apparent fruitlessness of this line of questioning, the next child wanted to know what the jugs were for.

"I need them." This evasive answer shocked Mr. Adams, but it only seemed to whet the children's curiosity. Now almost all hands were raised and each child had almost the same question—"Why?"

"Why don't you try to guess?" Miss Johnson challenged in her cheerful voice.

"Here it comes," thought Mr. Adams. The buzzing he'd heard from the halls was now going on right in front of him. Each child seemed to be conferring with his neighbor about this problem.

After a few moments of "near bedlam," as Mr. Adams was later to recall it, the teacher asked for the children with guesses to raise their hands. Almost every hand went up again. Calling on several children resulted in similar responses; each thought that she would pour something into the jugs. But after each response Miss Johnson only smiled and shook her head.

Finally Jack, one of the best science students, said, "Wait a minute. This isn't how we learned to solve a science problem."

"This isn't a science problem," Judy interjected.

"Well, it's a science class, ain't it?" Jack rebutted.

Mr. Adams made note of the fact that Miss Johnson failed to correct this poor grammar and that some children were even talking out of turn without having been called upon.

The teacher asked the children please to put their hands down for a moment. Then she informed them that even if this wasn't a science problem, it didn't follow that they couldn't use a scientific approach in their guessing.

Poor Mr. Adams mentally shook his head and muttered to himself, "Scientists don't guess—they know."

When questioning was resumed, Judy, who obviously had missed the whole point of what Miss Johnson had been saying, asked, "Well, are you going to pour something into the jugs?"

"Let's pretend that I'm not here to answer your questions. How then would you go about making a scientific guess?"

"Collect data," Dick said confidently.

"Yes, let's look at the jugs," Bobby agreed.

Miss Johnson passed a jug down each row for the children to examine. When it got to Billy he blew across the top and made a funny noise, causing everyone but Mr. Adams to have a good laugh. When this activity was finished Barbara had her hand up. "I don't think we've really identified the problem yet."

"Good thinking, Barbara." Miss Johnson was obviously pleased and invited Barbara to write the problem on the chalkboard.

As Barbara was writing, the principal was thinking, "She's evidently not prepared for this class and is trying to get the children to help her kill time." He admired her intestinal fortitude, attempting to pull this off right in front of him. "Petic warned me that they might try stuff like this," he thought. Adams had taught long enough to realize that even a good teacher occasionally has a period for which he is not prepared. "But a smart one would at least read from the textbook so it wouldn't be a total loss!"

Barbara had written: *What are the jugs for?* Several hands came up. The teacher called on Suzy. This surprised Mr. Adams because he recalled that her last two teachers had said that Suzy was too shy even to volunteer.

"Shouldn't we say that they are plastic?"

"Good thinking, Suzy." The excitement level (noise level, according to Adams) rose as the children discussed and agreed on modifications of their problem.

The final wording was as follows: *How will Miss Johnson use these seven, white, plastic, gallon jugs?* The children, without being told, copied the problem at the top of a fresh page of notebook paper. Mr. Adams couldn't help thinking that there would be all hell to pay if any of the parents ever took the time to look at their children's science notebooks. He especially shuddered to think what would happen if little Tommy Petic took his home to his dad.

"Now that we've decided on the problem, let's hear Dick's suggestion again."

"Collect data," Dick repeated. He was a boy of few words.

"Data on what? We've already looked at the jugs and we've listed their characteristics in the problem," Judy said.

"Not all of 'em. Don't forget you can cut them," Betty said.

"Yeah, and they melt," George added.

"Also they're empty," someone said. "No they're not—each one's full of air!" And so it went until much data on the jugs had been collected and recorded.

"Now what?" asked the teacher.

Teachers and Social Science Education

"Is it important that you are going to be the one who uses them?" Another contribution from Suzy, Mr. Adams noted.

"Let's make another list of data about Miss Johnson," Jack said.

This listing of Miss Johnson's characteristics was more embarrassing for the principal than it was for his teacher. It included the following pertinent (?) information: teaches fifth grade; has lots of good ideas ("There's an apple polisher," thought Adams; he also got some twisted pleasure out of noting the fact that it was Tommy Petic's contribution): likes most everything; raises tropical fish; plays the piano; comes from Denver; went to school at Colorado State College; is pretty (this observation caused a few snickers from the children and a wince from Adams); good figure (another titter, especially from the boys, as Adams cringed in his seat); is lots of fun; lives in an apartment house; isn't too old. Adams expected them to say something about the bachelor biology teacher from the high school who had been dating her pretty steadily. Certainly the children knew about it. Perhaps it was out of deference to his presence in the room, they omitted reference to it.

Following this, George suggested that there might be other things involved. When pressed by his classmates he replied that the time of year might make a difference, because this is the right time to make birdhouses for the spring and that's what he thought she might like to do.

When all pertinent data had at last been written on the board and in the notebooks, Miss Johnson beamed proudly on the lists and congratulated the children on the first stage of their investigation. Adams checked his watch and was relieved to learn that it was almost time for the bell. He mentally began compiling the points he would make in an attempt to straighten out this poor teacher.

"Over the weekend you are to use the information in your notebooks to help you form a good hypothesis. Each of you will make at least one guess as to what you think the answer to your problem could be." The children buzzed excitedly as they left the room.

When the last child was gone, Mr. Adams began his talk to Miss Johnson. It was to her rather than with her, because he failed to listen to her explanation of the unorthodox science lesson. "This isn't the way we teach science in our school," he kept repeating. It ended where it began, with a total lack of communication. But Mr. Adams did promise, albeit reluctantly, to return again on Monday to witness the culmination of this "time-wasting nonsense."

For the eager children it was a long wait until Monday's science period. Each child had one guess and many, like Jack, had several.

Jane wrote them on the board. Some of the children's guesses and their reasons for each guess were as follows:

1. To make a musical scale (because there were seven jugs and you could blow into them—as Billy did—and get different notes if they held different amounts of water). You could make your own scale or play a tune. Someone else had a similar idea—tapping them—but he'd tried it at home and it didn't work very well.

2. Making decorative light fixtures (because plastic is translucent and you could paint it).

3. Making an outdoor sign with "Johnson" on it for her apartment. (There were seven jugs and seven letters in her name.)

4. Wear one on each of her shoes, so that she could reach the top shelf in the supply cupboard. The other five jugs were dismissed as "spares."

5. Cut the top half off for cheerleaders' megaphones (maybe she was going to a basketball game or something).

6. Use the top half for funnels and the bottom for pencil boxes.

7. Make bird houses. (Fred still insisted that this was a good idea, and besides, "She likes birds.")

8. Containers for poster paint (this from the class artist, who thought the other jars were too small).

9. Making aquariums. ("She raises tropical fish, doesn't she?")

10. Planting flower bulbs. (She brought some to school last week and they're still wrapped in moss in the back cupboard.)

All the unduplicated guesses were listed on the board. There was a brief buzz session as the children speculated on who had the right guess.

Finally Miss Johnson hushed the class and again complimented them on their creative efforts and investigative skills. "But," she reminded them, "these guesses are now hypotheses. What do we do in science with hypotheses?"

"Test them," came the choral response. But they weren't sure how to go about it.

"We could wait and see how you do use them," Evelyn suggested.

"Good idea," agreed Bob. "How soon will you use them?"

"I already have," Miss Johnson replied with an enigmatic smile at the puzzled faces of her pupils.

"Now we'll never know unless you tell us," Judy said with discouragement in her voice.

"Look at your data list and see if the first trait after my name doesn't give you a clue." Everyone reread *Teaches fifth grade.*

"You're going to teach us something with them," Billy concluded.

"But she's already used them," Barbara replied.

After a long silence it was Jack who came up with the right answer. "If you've already taught us something and the only thing we've done is to think—then you used them to help us learn how to think."

A happy Miss Johnson retraced the inquiry activity from its inception to the final conclusion.

After the children left she took stock of the experience. She knew that she had succeeded with the children, but she feared she had failed with the principal. Mr. Adams had sent in a note just after lunch explaining that he couldn't make it today because of the press of other business.

Yes, Mr. Adams was busy that afternoon. He had to make certain that the janitors removed all the black scuff marks from the gymnasium floor before the PTA meeting that night. Anyway, he'd made up his mind about Miss Johnson. Petic was right, this was no place for boat rockers, especially not now with his pension coming in a couple of years. "Anyway," he rationalized, "she's a pretty girl and will probably get married before I have to fire her. Odd that those little devils didn't kid her about her boyfriend when she was wasting time with them last Friday."

About You and Teaching

It has been a truism in education that "we teach the whole child." At first glance, the statement seems too obvious for comment, since it is apparent that each child brings all of himself into the school, whether the situation deals with mathematics, music or quoits. The degree to which the teacher accepts the whole child within the context of any specific learning task is something else. The child may "let it all hang out," but the teacher may choose to "see" only that which she believes to be relevant to the given situation.

We have decided to include this chapter because, it seems to us, the social education of the child is an area where the sum total of the child's behavior must be considered. It would be nice if the child were to develop positive civic attitudes in mathematics, along with knowledge and skills, but if such is not the case, there may be no great problem posed to mathematics. Information and constructive attitudes toward the concerns and problems of human societies are, indeed, quite as critical as the skills of social inquiry, and in these matters, the teacher has no desirable alternative to involvement with the whole child. In our judgment, a school-wide approach to the social education of the child is desirable, but whatever the conditions that exist, the teacher in social science education has a major individual responsibility. The failure to help the child move from his socio-psychological realm toward understanding and effective participation in the larger social units of the school, community, and world, will, indeed, contribute to naive adult social behavior, alienation, and social lethargy.

It is unrealistic to expect that the experiences in mathematics, physical education, literature, music, and art will somehow contribute equally with social science education to the development of an individual who is informed about the social dimensions of man and is skillful in approaching issues and questions that deal with human values, perceptions, and actions. A rather traditional view has been that the social studies would teach geographical and historical information and the entire school would conduct social education. The position of the writers is that we would take nothing away from other learning areas, but we would place specific responsibility for social education upon the field of social science education.

How do you view education?

Education, whether institutional or informal, is defined as a process of behavior change. The individual will be different as an outcome of a specific learning experience. The function of the school in every society is to bring about behavior change in the young members of the society, and the nature and extent of the change is prescribed narrowly or broadly according to the dominant values and needs of the adult society.

For many years, it was customary to state in courses of study that the major aim of education was to perpetuate the existing society. Gradually, such openers were changed to say "... to transmit and improve the social order." A few persons have seen a contradiction in this statement, but it is still found in many state curriculum guides, perhaps as a political expression rather than as an educational aim.

In more recent years, the teacher has been called a "change agent," a "manipulator of human beings," and a "human engineer." You may not like these labels, but even if they are displeasing, it may be enlightening to consider their implications.

Is it the primary function of the teacher to prepare children to fit into society as it is now? Let us consider the positions of two teachers. Which position is nearer to your own?

> Miss Adams, teacher of 11-year-old children, likes the idea of preparing pupils to fit into a stable society, and she bases her preference on the assumption that young people need to know that there are some important values, customs, and institutions that really change very little. Children need the security that comes from knowing some things for sure. Most children, Miss Adams reasons, will grow up to be followers, since only a few can become leaders. Very few people will be involved with social change, so it is far more important that they be good followers and stable citizens in a peaceful society. From the beginning, we cannot hope to make every person his own king or we would have chaos.

> Mrs. Elliott is also a teacher of 11-year-olds. She points to the changes that have come about as a result of technology, social evolution, and world involvement. She doubts that it is honest to teach children that society is basically unchanging in its values, customs, and institutions. Young children live in the midst of change in man's relation to man and to his environment. The moon landing was accepted more calmly by youngsters than by adults, Mrs. Elliott believes. As adults react to changes, children are living in change. The job of the teacher is to prepare children to understand and manage the forces and processes of change in society.

How do you view human potential?

The concept that a teacher has of human potential will determine, to a considerable extent, the way she works with children and the kinds of experiences that she will include in the classroom program. The ethnologist, Levi-Strauss, has observed that modern man sees himself as living within a powerful, irreversible, oneway stream of history in which human potentials have been determined. Insofar as every man is deeply encased within his own cultural shell, it is difficult for the teacher to conceptualize new human possibilities, particularly those of a social nature that have not been demonstrated before. The historical perspective may divert us from even considering new dimensions in human behavior, or it may be used to counsel us with respect to the difficulties which have been experienced in the study and attempted modifications of human behavior.

With the accomplishment of nuclear fission, Einstein called for a "new way of thinking" which would enable men to control the new sources of energy that their science had given them. In the face of such overwhelming forces, it would appear that all men would strive to make a corresponding breakthrough in the resolution of human conflicts which continue to be ever more destructive and brutal. A population explosion, if unchecked, will have the world in a dire situation by the year 2000. New environments in sea and space promise new frontiers and new problems of a social nature. This is all familiar information to most people in the United States, and yet there are many teachers who ask, "What does this have to do with my job with children?"

In this matter, it is difficult for the writers to assume a neutral position before the prospective teachers who use this book. It is our belief that teachers must hold an optimistic view of human potential to understand and cope with the social problems which relate to, or result from, the developments of science and technology. A pessimistic outlook by the teacher can do no more than support a fatalistic acceptance of whatever befalls us.

There is evidence that suggests that children build their "life views" and their "world views" as a result of many subtle interactions and that the parents and other selected models have a strong impact on the view that finally becomes part of the personality. No elaborate claims are made here with respect to the capability of the school to replace or undo home-neighborhood influences, but there is evidence which indicates that the school environment and the teacher-pupil relationship can modify the child's self-concept and his perceptions of what is real and of value.

In this matter, it is important that teachers not behave as though all of the big human accomplishments have been realized, that our age old problems will always be with us. The idea of "human history repeating itself" gives rise to the acceptance of inevitable events. No teacher has the right to shut off at the source the potentials of new conceptualizations about man and what he can do.

The school in America should be a place where children are not catalogued by teachers' judgments or by standardized tests into a slot which will determine the extent of their realization of their potential. Again, the self-image that the child possesses is built from looking into the many human mirrors of the people around him. The school and its teachers offer only one composite of reflections, but if the home and neighborhood reflection is negative, the school should not provide reinforcement for this negative self-image.

> Dr. L., now academic vice-president of a college, related that his guidance counsellor had suggested that he pursue a life career in a service occupation, such as, waiter, bell hop or taxi driver. Dr. L. is an American Negro who grew up in the Hill District of Pittsburgh in the 1930's. His parents were poorly educated, but they supported their son's efforts to get through high school. Why did Dr. L. decide to try to get a college degree? He isn't sure, but he recalls that his high school principal invited him to lunch at his home and that he talked about the many opportunities open to boys, both black and white.

> Billie Davis, the hobo kid, travelled the western part of the country in the 30's in the model T which carried her migrant-worker parents from one orchard to another. All of her possessions were in a shoe box. For whatever reason, Billie always found the local school and always there was a "Desk for Billie," always a teacher who said, "we're pretty full but we have room for you." Billie Davis has recounted the impact that she thinks the schools had on her life. "My parents didn't encourage me, but they never discouraged me either." "Schools," Billie Davis said in later years, "make you better than you were." [1]

It is the job of the entire school staff to do the things necessary to help children "become better than they were." It is the particular responsibility of the teacher who helps children come to understand the meaning of the American vision of human potential, for it is a vision that moves away from the historical notions that children are limited by family, place of birth, and socio-economic class.

---

[1] "A Desk for Billie," film, a moving biographical account of Billie Davis' experiences as a traveling pupil in America's schools (Washington, D.C.: National Education Association, 1955).

The task is not easy. The children who come to school with meager aspirations often present personality characteristics that make them undesirable in the eyes of some teachers. The disadvantaged come from big city ghettos, hill communities of Appalachia, and the absentee-parent homes of wealthy suburbia. In such young people, a variety of factors has already produced a barren concept of the human condition and of their own potentials. In such situations, if the experiences in social science education are not supported by an optimistic teacher, the matter is purely academic.

How does self-awareness help?

There is the familiar story about the education professor who spent much of the term lecturing about the limitations of the lecture as a way of teaching. Occasionally, a professor who urges the students to be critical of all they hear and read is dismayed when the criticism is turned upon him. During your student life you may encounter a professor who has written a book in which the recommended teaching strategies bear no resemblance to his own. So, we are reminded of Robert Burns' plea for the gift to see ourselves as others see us.

A strong consistency between what the teacher says and what she does is desirable in all teaching behavior; it becomes a crucial factor in social science education, where the inquiry into the social behavior of man must finally be applied to the inquiry class. There is considerable agreement on this point, but the difficulties in extending it to classroom teacher behavior still persist.

The teacher as an adult "model." In recent years there has been a tendency for teachers to resist the idea that they provide working models for the children. It has been argued that the teacher is an ordinary human being, subject to the same shortcomings as other people in society, and it is only honest to show children the real person that is the teacher. Usually, the bone of contention has centered upon topics, such as, smoking, drinking, obtaining divorces, and other "moral" issues. In most urban areas these are no longer seen as issues, but in some rural areas they still persist as very real issues.

It is difficult to insist that the teacher's personal habits be impeccable lest they have a negative influence upon the eventual choices of the child, in view of the fact that the mass media have brought before the child a host of "successful" public figures who seem to be likable and yet, may present controversial behavior models. Witness Zsa Zsa Gabor as she chats casually about her many discarded husbands, while speculating about her next one. Arthur Godfrey "confides" on a television talk show that he has been sterilized. A Joe Pyne television show, broadcast on a Sunday afternoon into Pacific coast living rooms, presented an engineer and his school teacher wife who related their mate swapping experiences. You may wonder why we bother to raise the point of teacher effect at all.

Whatever the situation may be in the larger society, it remains a fact that teachers are the adults who work most closely with children for long periods of time for the specific purposes of modifying behavior patterns. In the realm of responsible and effective human relationships, the teacher is in a position to provide a working model to young people. *The teacher's style in dealing with the life activities in the school provide a genuine model of an adult authority figure functioning as an agent of social control.* Whether the teacher smokes or not seems less critical than the image she projects in the situation just cited.

The manner in which the teacher relates to the total social structure of the school is another concern. Her perceptions of the other authority figures in the school, particularly the principal, provide "models" for children of the "big" authority figures in their school life. The ancient game of "feigned compliance" to the regulations can be well taught by the teacher who confides her own evasions to the children. In this way, the teacher seems to play the same weak role as the citizen who blames "the big shots in charge," although he cannot be bothered with expressing his opinion at the polls or supporting the political candidates of his choice; he just complains to the fellows at the neighborhood tavern.

Teachers, and other humans, have struggles with their egos once they become sensitive to the impact of their day to day behavior on the children. It makes us feel better when we let the pupils know that the principal has flubbed—then they know that we are bright, too, even though we are just teachers. It is satisfying to smirk at the backside of a domineering colleague as she exits from your classroom after telling you, "Your kids have been causing trouble in the toilets." The effects of these very human aspects of teaching may not be serious if the predominant pattern of the teacher's behavior is oriented toward understanding the other person's problems and responsibilities. Items of major proportions require professional consideration and action, not subversion and ridicule displayed before children.

The teacher as team member. Much has been written and said about the school as a cooperative endeavor which calls for participation by a variety of people both within, and outside of, the school. Group action, committee work, team effort—these terms have been the subject of professional cynicism and dubious humor. But, the matter cannot be left at that.

As a member in a team teaching or coordinated teaching arrangement, the teacher again projects a model of adult behavior in a situation which involves shared decision making and joint responsibilities for action. In such situations, it is necessary that each teacher examine her behavior in realistic terms. Inasmuch as a major tenet of her work with boys and girls deals with their ability to "get along with others," to assume responsibility for the welfare of the total group or activity, to respect the views of others, and to support consensus positions, the extent to which the teacher's behavior is compatible with her verbalizing may well determine her overall effectiveness.

Another dimension of the teacher's team involvement has to do with the use of district wide curriculum guides and participation in cooperative curriculum development projects. Several examples of actual positions are provided for your analysis and discussion:

> Mrs. Elbert has been a teacher of sixth grade social studies for ten years, and she is generally recognized by her colleagues and by parents as being a "good" teacher. Mrs. Elbert makes no bones about her contempt for the district guide in social studies and for any other guide. She has refused to serve as a member of any of the committees in social studies, maintaining that her time is better spent in preparing interesting activities for her classes. No pressures have been placed upon Mrs. Elbert because, it is felt, she does her job well.

> Fox Run school is in a well-to-do neighborhood in a school district which serves 20,000 youngsters. The principal of the school contends that the instructional concerns of Fox Run are not typical of most other schools in the district, and he prefers to have his teachers build and gear their social studies programs to fit the youngsters, many of whom have travelled widely. For this reason, the teachers at Fox Run are seldom involved in district wide projects in the social studies area.

> The Pine Ridge District has adopted a new social science education curriculum which was developed after two years of "task force" activity. According to school board policy, curriculum development is the responsibility of the professional and once accepted by the board, a curriculum guide is an official part of the district's program. A considerable number of teachers have confided that they plan to go on teaching social studies in their usual manner, expressing doubts about "inquiry" by children and "concepts" instead of facts.

Some typical college student reactions to these examples include the following:

1. It is better to have a "good" teacher who is a loner than a cooperative teacher who is ineffective.

2. A teacher who thinks she doesn't need the benefit of other people's ideas and criticism has a problem.
3. Principals like to think that they know what is best for their school, but they don't want a district wide committee to decide what is best for the district nor a teacher to decide what is best for her own individual classroom.
4. When teachers are hired they should be told what the ground rules for cooperative action are.
5. Why does a principal have the right to cut off the teachers from activities and programs that are planned for the whole district?
6. Mrs. Elbert should share her techniques if they are so good.

Which of these responses is nearest to your own? What other factors do you believe may be behind the three positions? Compare your reactions with your colleagues.

Teacher Mobility

Traditionally, people in the United States have held considerable reservations about teachers. The teacher's formal education has been valued for the extent of success it could help one realize. But, beyond the practical applications of education, there continue to be doubts, and the term "intellectual" does not generally carry a good implication.

Teachers are mobile; their preparation allows them to move quite freely from one place to another in the practice of their profession. Contrary to other professionals, who often set up practice and remain in one place for a long time, the tenure of teachers as a total group is short. Contributing to this mobility is the fact that the large majority of elementary teachers are females, and many of them marry after a brief career in teaching. The constant occurrence of vacancies creates a demand for new teachers.

Most teachers come from home situations of modest economic means. A college education and a career in teaching provide a readily available route to an improved level of living, at least for some. The common practice is for the new teacher to begin her career away from her home community and school; she goes as a stranger to work with the children of parents who do not know her. At this point, you may observe that in the United States, we are brought into contact with doctors, mechanics, delivery men, and merchants whom we hardly know, if at all. How different is the strange teacher to the community?

1. In most communities, the teacher has attained a higher level of formal education than the average person.
2. The teacher, in contrast to other professional persons, will have a long term relationship with children, a relationship in which she supplants the parents.
3. The teacher is commonly perceived as the adult who transmits cultural values to children.
4. Most people have an idea, gained from their own school days, concerning good and poor teaching, and they feel free to judge their child's teacher.

Since you plan to work with young people in an effort to help them gain understanding about man's behavior as a social creature, you will find it valuable to become a student of the school-community to which you come as a stranger. Conditions in a particular school or community may appear to be quite primitive and unenlightened to the new teacher, and things may indeed be in a bad way. Nonetheless, a community's values are projected in the school through the support given to it and through the state of development which exists. All situations have their histories, and local school matters are not exceptions.

In any effort to be an effective teacher, it is necessary to consider existing values, goals, and customs, not in order to succumb to them, but in order to build channels for communication and cooperative relationships based upon mutual human respect.

Occasionally, the young teacher may be overwhelmed with the apparent futility of his efforts to improve the educational opportunities amid the lethargy of the community and the smug satisfaction of a faculty that has dried up. The urge to test the community with a few radical ventures may result in a showdown involving patrons, school administrators, and professional associations. If the objective of the teacher is to promote "change for the better," it is important that his efforts not actually delay progress through the overt provocation of incidents. Self-discipline and ego control may be forgotten in the most well-intentioned efforts of idealistic teachers. Consider this example:

> During the period of the Vietnam War Moratorium activities, a sixth grade group expressed the idea that war was indeed bad, and when they grew up they would work to end the use of war as a way to settle problems. Mr. O., their teacher, asked why they should wait to begin their efforts to end wars. He pointed out that there were several examples of war-like monuments in their own community, such as, the old cannon in the city park. A community that is really dedicated to Christian ideals and peaceful motives should hardly display their war hardware in the town square, according to Mr. O. As an outcome, the sixth grade group drew up a request which they sent

to the city council and to the American Legion Post, asking that the cannon be removed in favor of a symbol of peace.

Very shortly, Mr. O. was visited by the commander of the local Legion Post who warned Mr. O. to "cool it," and said that Mr. O. was being closely watched as a potential Communist. Mr. O. was visited by the superintendent who observed that it was better to stick to the textbook than to get children involved in issues that were beyond their maturity levels. The Local Teachers Association, when asked by Mr. O. to consider the matter, decided that this was not a proper concern for the Association since it did not yet involve the question of firing Mr. O.

In small groups, consider this actual case. Had Mr. O. behaved in an unwise manner?

Did the learning experience promise worthwhile results for the children?

How would you have proceeded? What would you say to the Legion Commander, to the superintendent, to the local Association?

Classroom Climate

The role of the teacher with respect to her influence upon the social and emotional climate of the classroom has been the subject of considerable study by several researchers.[2] The results of such investigations indicate that the relationships between pupils are affected by individual pupil-teacher relationships as well as by the interaction among the children themselves. There seems to be a positive relationship between the emotional-social climate of the learning environment and the performance of the learners, although it must be pointed out that for such comparisons pupil performance should not be confined to academics only.

It is evident that the orientation of the child in the classroom is of an individual nature, for what disturbs one child may not necessarily disturb other children. However, it seems that some conditions are more conducive to learning than others. A situation in which the teacher is sincerely interested in the child as an individual, in which the child

---

[2] Ned A. Flanders, "Personal Social Anxiety as a Factor in Experimental Learning Situations," *Journal of Educational Research* 45 (October, 1951): 100–10; John Withall, "The Development of the Climate Index," *Journal of Educational Research* 45 (October, 1951): 93–100.

finds success and growth within his reach, and in which children enjoy the security of a friendly atmosphere is a situation that provides a milieu for social interaction and for personal and mental growth.

Withall has made some important contributions to the study of classroom climate as affected by the teacher.[3] It is the position of Withall that the prevailing types of statements and questions which are used by the teacher may be classified as to their apparent aim in direction of the learner, and that this aim exerts an influence upon the classroom climate. Chart 13-1 presents the different types of statements and questions and their purposes, as proposed by Withall.[4]

Generally, it seems that the teacher must assess her classroom

CHART 13-1. Types of Teacher Statements and Questions

Type	*Aim*
Learner supportive	To encourage the learner
Accepting or clarifying	To help the learner move toward the solution of a problem by removing confusing or extraneous obstacles
Problem structuring	Neither pupil centered nor teacher centered, it helps sustain the pupil as he attempts to isolate and identify the nature of his problem
Neutral (such as repeating a thought to one's self)	
Directive statements	To have the pupil take the teacher's point of view and follow the course of action proposed by the teacher.
Reproving, disparaging statements	To cite behavior that is socially or morally undesirable, in terms of the prevailing cultural patterns
Teacher supportive	To defend the teacher; to support the teacher's position in the fact of contradictory evidence

[3] J. Withall, "Assessment of the Social-Emotional Climates Experienced by a Group of Seventh Graders as they Moved from Class to Class," *Educational and Psychological Measurements* 12 (Autumn, 1952): 440-51.
[4] *Ibid.*

conversation in terms of the kind of responses which she believes are desired. Pupil responses may not always be immediate and may involve far more than mere verbalization insofar as emotional health, personality development, and mental growth are jointly concerned. With this in mind, the teacher will study the situation and select the course of action which is most likely to bring about pupil responses which indicate the children accept responsibility, feel at home in the classroom, and feel free to move with considerable independence toward the solution of their learning and total behavior problems.

Occasionally, one reads of a teacher who has won local acclaim for her sharp wit and her success in using it to keep youngsters on guard or even on the defensive. Lest there be misunderstanding of the use of the sarcastic rejoinder by the teacher, it should be pointed out that such verbal jabbing is genuinely appreciated only when used with persons who understand and accept one another, either socially, professionally or intellectually. Its use in the elementary school classroom must be questioned severely. As a general procedure, the teacher will do much toward the creation of a favorable climate for learning by using statements and questions that are pupil-centered and problem-oriented.

The teacher who is informed with respect to the factors and forces which affect learning may assess his classroom setting in terms of the following characteristics of situations which are favorable to efficient learning:

1. Consideration is given to the mental maturity and learning capacity of the child.
2. Basic life needs of children are recognized in planning the classroom program for learning.
3. Motivation and incentive for learning are fostered.
4. Drill and practice are provided when necessary to maintain skills and to provide readiness for further learnings.
5. Meaningful applications of the skills learned are provided.
6. Evaluation of the learning environment is looked upon as a continuous concern of the teacher.

The teacher and the child's perceptions

There is humor and sadness in the examples of teacher behavior and its effect on the way the child perceives himself and his situation. Several such examples are provided to focus our attention upon the importance of the teacher being extremely aware of the impact that his feelings and actions can have upon children. Self-control and self-discipline appear to take on unusual value as we consider these situations.

Teachers and Social Science Education

> Eight-year-old Michelle had asked the teacher for permission to go to the restroom. It was 3:10, and Mrs. Wilson thought that Michelle could wait five minutes until dismissal. Michelle could not. She had what some teachers call an "accident." Embarrassed before her classmates, frustrated and angry, Michelle tearfully cried out her disgust at this peculiar use of teacher authority. "Why do you think that you can tell when kids have to go to the toilet? Teachers don't know everything."

It has been observed that elementary school teachers are kidney conscious, that an uncommon amount of attention is given to the management of the toilet habits of children. One can speculate about the reasons for making the restrooms a focal concern, but it is more helpful to consider the value of permitting children to manage their own needs. Teachers who project continuing concern about what goes on in the restrooms generate certain expectations in the children. Something, it follows, ought to happen in the restrooms, if the teacher implies that mysterious and forbidden things occur there. Beyond these implications is, of course, the problem of allowing children to develop the ability to manage themselves and their personal needs, to accord to children a measure of self-respect and privacy, and the need to represent the school environment as something better than a totalitarian Big Brother operation.

Consider the following incidents. In the first two examples the teachers reveal their attitudes toward specific human differences. How can such actions by teachers have negative effects on a child's perceptions? In the third situation, the teacher avoids reinforcing negative perceptions and simultaneously broadens her students' perceptions. How would you handle these situations?

> I was visiting a student teacher in a large midwestern city school. During playground period, the student teacher and I were talking about various topics when we observed a tearful girl of eight or nine complain to a teacher, "Sue said I was as dumb as a nigger." "Well, don't you cry about that," the teacher soothed, "you know you aren't a dumb nigger, so why are you upset?"

> As the five-year-olds were entering the kindergarten room one morning, I stopped to chat a moment with Mrs. J., the rotund motherly-type teacher. As the only Mexican child in the group passed by I was attracted by his sparkling black eyes and rich tan skin. "Gracious, he is a handsome boy, isn't he?" I remarked. "Oh, I suppose he is," Mrs. J. replied, "but, you know I just can't bring myself to touch him."

The sixth grade pupils were anticipating the visit of Mr. Chamnong, a graduate student from Thailand who had agreed to talk with the group about life and schools in his country. Some of the children recalled an earlier visit by a person from France, and they expressed concern about the "poor English" that foreigners speak.

Their teacher replied, "Yes. I guess it isn't easy to understand a person to whom our language and country are strange. But, until we can speak his language, I think we should appreciate the effort he is making to communicate with us in English. You remember when Monsieur Chasson visited us, even those of you who have been taking French for two years did not feel comfortable talking to him in French."

Do teachers hold democratic attitudes?

In concluding an article which dealt with the democratic attitudes of teachers and prospective teachers, John Weiser and James Hayes asked, "How many teachers are there who really understand and practice democracy?" [5] Information which had been presented in their research report included the following items:

1. Sixty-four per cent of a sampling of elementary teachers believed that newspapers should *not* be allowed to print anything they want except military secrets.
2. Twenty-five per cent of the same group believed that the government should prohibit some people from making public speeches.
3. Seventy-four per cent of these teachers believed that a foreign visitor to our country should not be allowed to criticize the government.
4. Fifty-two per cent of a sample of prospective elementary teachers believed that police may be right in using "third degree" methods to make a man talk.
5. Forty-seven per cent of the prospective elementary teachers believed that the large mass of people are not capable of deciding what is good or bad for them.
6. Eighty-seven per cent of the experienced elementary teachers believed that communism in the Soviet system and our democracy should be compared and contrasted in the schools.
7. Ninety-one per cent of the prospective teacher group and seventy-four per cent of the experienced teacher group believed that we should *not* firmly resist any efforts to change the American way of life.[6]

---

[5] John C. Weiser and James E. Hayes, "Democratic Attitudes of Teachers and Prospective Teachers," *Phi Delta Kappan* (May 1966).
[6] *Ibid.*

Teachers and Social Science Education

> Before you discuss this section, plan to sample the opinions of your class on these items. Does the class hold positions very close to those reported by Weiser and Hayes?
>
> Turn to the appendix to examine an opinion test that was used in 1970. Mark your own responses on a sheet of paper, then tabulate the results for the entire class.

The Opinions of Young Americans Test was developed for use with students in both secondary schools and colleges to obtain responses to situations that involved either a democratic principle, a nationalistic position or both. The initial form of the test is presented in Appendix D in order that you may use and discuss the implications of your responses. In brief, the responses of more than 3000 high school seniors, who took the test in 1970, indicated that:

1. The idea of a separate black nation within the U.S. was not accepted, but the idea of a separate Biafra in Nigeria was viewed as reasonable.
2. One out of four respondents supported the actions of the Chicago police in moving against the Black Panthers' apartment in late 1969, during which action two people were killed; however, very few students agreed that the Nazis were justified in using Gestapo methods to subdue potential threats to the Third Reich.
3. A board of education should not abolish magazines from the school library just because they were published in the Soviet Union or Mainland China.

We will conclude this chapter by requesting that you develop your own set of tentative conclusions concerning the role of the teacher and the prospects for changes that you decide are in order. As we pointed out in chapter six, attitudes and life views are firmly structured during the early years, and the modification brought about by the experiences of high school and college may be minimal and transitory. Curriculum change that depends upon teacher change has more to take into account than mere textbook adoptions and new resource centers. The following selection by Estelle Fuchs should provide the fuel for your discussions of the entire chapter.

Estelle Fuchs

This selection deals with a very real aspect of the shaping of teacher attitudes, a process that has great impact during a teacher's first year on a job. In this selection, Professor Fuchs considers the problems of the disadvantaged inner-urban child in the classroom. You may find it helpful to consider the way in which the school seeks to modify or change the attitudes and behavior of the young teacher in order to make her more compliant and less critical of the system's view of educational "success."

How Teachers Learn to Help Children Fail

When a new teacher enters the classroom, she must learn the behavior, attitudes, and skills required in the new situation. Much of this learning is conscious. Some of it is not. What is significant is that, while on the job, the teacher is socialized to her new role—she is integrated into the society of the school, and learns the values, beliefs, and attitudes that govern its functioning.

The saga of class 1–5 shows the subtle ways in which one new teacher is socialized to her job. In just a few months, she accepts the demands of the school organization and its prevailing rationale for student failure.

The new teacher of class 1–5 in a slum school begins her career with a warm, friendly attitude toward her students. She respects and admires their abilities and is troubled by what the future holds for them: by the sixth grade in her school, educational failure is very common.

Estelle Fuchs, "How Teachers Learn To Help Children Fail," *Trans-Action* (September 1968).

Very early in her teaching career, however, a more experienced teacher exposes the new teacher to the belief, widely held, that the children come from inferior backgrounds and that the deficits in their homes—expressed here as lack of newspapers and parental care—prevent educational achievement. That the teachers and the school as an institution contribute to the failure of the children is never even considered as a possible cause. The beginning teacher, in her description of what happens to class 1–5, then provides us with a graphic account of the ways in which this attitude can promote failure.

First, let us examine the actual instruction of the children. Early in her career, this new, very sincere teacher is painfully aware of her own deficiencies. Unsure about her teaching of so fundamental a subject as reading, she raises serious questions about her own effectiveness. As yet, she has not unconsciously accepted the notion that the failure of children stems from gaps in their backgrounds. Although no consensus exists about reading methodology, the teacher tells us that there are serious weaknesses in feedback evaluation—and that she is unable to find out what the children have been taught or what they have really learned.

By the end of the term, all this has changed. By that time, the eventual failure of most of class 1–5 has been virtually assured. And the teacher has come to rationalize this failure in terms of pupil inadequacy.

In the particular case of class 1–5, the cycle of failure begins with a drop in the number of students registered in the school. The principal loses a teacher, which in turn means dissolving a class and subsequently distributing its children among other classes. The principal and the teachers have no control over this event. In the inner-city schools, education budgets, tables of organization, and directions from headquarters create conditions beyond the control of the administrators and teachers who are in closest touch with the children.

A drop in pupil registers would seemingly provide the opportunity for a higher adult-pupil ratio and, consequently, more individualized instruction and pedagogical supports for both youngsters and teachers. In a suburban school, this is probably what would have occurred. But in this slum school, the register drop leads to the loss of a teacher, larger classes, and—perhaps most important—increased time spent by the administrator and his staff on the mechanics of administration rather than on the supervision of instruction. (Why *this* particular teacher is released is unclear, though her substitute status and low rank in the staff hierarchy probably contribute to her release.) As a result many classes are disrupted, several first-grade class registers grow larger, time for instruction is lost, and concern is felt by teachers and pupils alike.

An even more significant clue to the possible eventual failure of the children is described in poignant detail—when the teacher tells how the youngsters in her class are to be distributed among the other first-grade classes. Educators now know that children mature at different rates; that they have different rates of learning readiness; and the developmental differences between boys and girls are relevant to learning. To forecast the educational outcome of youngsters at this early stage of their development, without due provision for these normal growth variations, is a travesty of the educational process. Yet here, in the first half of the first grade, a relatively inexperienced young teacher, herself keenly aware of her own deficiencies as an educator, is placed in the position of literally deciding the educational future of her charges.

A few are selected for success—"I felt that once you're in a '1' class, unless you really don't belong, you have a better chance. The '1' class is really the only class that you would term a 'good' class." Several children are placed in a class labeled "slow." And the remaining youngsters are relegated to a state of limbo, a middle range that does not carry the hope of providing a "better chance."

Early tracking of children's futures

Thus, before these youngsters have completed a full four months of schooling, their educational futures have been "tracked": All through the grades, the labels of their class placement will follow them, accompanied by teacher attitudes about their abilities. Some youngsters are selected very early for success, others written off as slow. Because differential teaching occurs and helps to widen the gap between children, the opportunity to move from one category is limited. In addition, the children too become aware of the labels placed upon them. And their pattern for achievement in later years is influenced by their feelings of success or failure in early school experiences.

The teacher, as she reflects upon what a "good" or "bad" school is, continues to include how well the children learn as a significant criterion, together with good relations between staff and administration. But the children in her school do not achieve very well academically, so when describing her school as "good," she stresses the good relations between the administration and the teachers. The fact that the children do not learn does not seem so important now: "the children are not as ready and willing to learn as in schools in middle-class neighborhoods."

How well our teacher has internalized the attitude that deficits of the children themselves explain their failure in school! How normal she now considers the administrative upheaval and their effects upon teachers and children! How perfectly ordinary she considers the "tracking" of youngsters so early in their school years!

The teacher of class 1–5 has been socialized by the school to accept its structure and values. Despite her sincerity and warmth and obvious concern for the children, this teacher is not likely to change the forecast of failure for most of these children—because she has come to accept the very structural and attitudinal factors that make failure nearly certain. In addition, with all her good intentions, she has come to operate as an agent determining the life chances of the children in her class—by distributing them among the ranked classes on the grade.

This teacher came to her job with very positive impulses. She thought highly of her youngsters and was disturbed that, with what appeared to be good potential, there was so much failure in the school in the upper grades. She looked inward for ways in which she might improve her efforts to forestall retardation. She was not repelled by the neighborhood in which she worked. There is every indication that she had the potential to become a very effective teacher of disadvantaged youngsters.

Her good impulses, however, were not enough. This young teacher, unarmed with the strength that understanding the social processes involved might have given her and having little power within the school hierarchy, was socialized by the attitudes of those around her, by the administration, and by the availability of a suitable rationale to explain her and the school's failure to fulfill their ideal roles. As a result she came to accept traditional slum-school attitudes toward the children—and traditional attitudes toward school organization as the way things have to be. This teacher is a pleasant, flexible, cooperative young woman to have on one's staff. But she has learned to behave and think in a way that perpetuates a process by which disadvantaged children continue to be disadvantaged.

The organizational structure of the large inner-city school and the attitudes of the administrators and teachers within it clearly affect the development of the children attending. No theory proposed to explain the academic failure of poor and minority-group children can ignore the impact of the actual school experience and the context in which it occurs.

Suggested Problems and Projects

"There are many things that we must do in life without asking or thinking about them. Things that we have always done, things that we are just expected to do. This is true in teaching, too. Neither teachers nor pupils have the time and background information to raise questions about the purposes of the many day to day activities of the school. Most of the school program is a product of accepted conventions and habits. The remainder is a mix of individual teacher innovation and application of curriculum guidelines."

1. Organize four investigative teams in your class for the purpose of obtaining reactions to the foregoing statement from the following groups:
    a. 30 teachers
    b. 30 parents who have children in school
    c. 30 school administrators
    d. 30 professors, not limited to education

Reproduce the statement and ask the subjects of your investigation to generally agree or generally disagree with the statement. Ask how they would like to change the statement.

2. Compare the results with the dominant position of your class. Identify major implications for the teacher of social science education.

Related Readings

Alden, V. R. and Hodges, J. A. "When Classrooms Fail." *Teachers College Record* 66 (1965): 305–309.
Ausubel, D. P. "A New Look at Classroom Discipline." *Phi Delta Kappan* 43 (1961): 25–30.
Cartwright, W. H. "The Teacher in 2065." *Teachers College Record* 66 (1965): 295–304.
Dunfee, Maxine. *Elementary School Social Studies: A Guide to Current Research.* Washington, D.C.: Association for Supervision and Curriculum Development, 1970.
Flanders, Ned A. "Teacher Influence in the Classroom." *Theory and Research in Teaching.* Edited by Arno A. Bellack. New York: Teachers College, Columbia University, 1963.
Hunter, E. C. "Changes in Teachers' Attitudes Toward Children's Behavior Over the Last Thirty Years." *Mental Hygiene* 41 (1957): 3–11.
Leeds, C. H. "Teacher Behavior Liked and Disliked by Pupils." *Education* 75 (1954): 29–36.
Loukes, H. "Passport to Maturity." *Phi Delta Kappan* 46 (1964): 54–57.
"The Problem: Teacher Supply and Demand." *NEA Research Bulletin* 42 (1964): 118–123.
Rich, J. M. "How Social Class Values Affect Teacher-Pupil Relations." *Journal of Educational Sociology* 33 (1960): 355–359.
Robinson, D. W. "Here the Teachers Treat You With Respect." *Phi Delta Kappan* 43 (1961): 40–42.
Teachers for the Real World. Publication of the American Association of Colleges for Teacher Education under grant by the U.S. Office of Education, 1969.
Weiser, John C. and Hayes, James E. "Democratic Attitudes of Teachers and Prospective Teachers." *Phi Delta Kappan* 66 (May 1966).

14

GROWTH IN THE ACQUISITION OF KNOWLEDGE OR INFORMATION
    Evaluating pupil growth in reading charts, graphs, and tables

EVALUATING DEVELOPMENT OF ATTITUDES AND VALUES SUPPORTIVE OF EFFECTIVE CITIZENSHIP
    Evaluating attitudes or values

EVALUATING INQUIRY
    Importance of defining a task

MODEL FOR GRADES 4 TO 6 IN EVALUATING THE PUPILS' USE OF THE ELEMENTS OF INQUIRY

A PATTERN OF EVALUATION TO GUIDE THE TEACHER
    Establishing criteria
    Collecting data
    Interpreting data
    Planning a course of action

SUMMARY

SUGGESTED PROBLEMS AND PROJECTS

RELATED READINGS

Evaluating Progress in Social Science Education

We have been faced with a number of seemingly unresolvable problems in trying to evaluate social studies learnings. The community and school have often not agreed upon common objectives for the traditional social studies program. In addition, much of what is taught in the traditional social studies program either requires rote memory in the fashion of assign-recite-test or a lifetime to determine its effectiveness. The new social science education program, organized around concepts and generalizations, is based upon long-and-short-range behavioral objectives which can be evaluated during the time the child is under the influence of the teacher and/or the school. To accomplish this, each teacher must understand her role in the evaluation process.

Evaluation, simply defined, is a comprehensive process of inquiry, which, through the utilization of many data-collecting techniques, analyzes the extent to which the learner has achieved the stated objectives as determined by change in his behavior. We have often assumed learning by the outcome of an activity based upon teacher judgment, frequently without being aware of any specific objectives to guide our judgments. If the experience seemed satisfactory, it was judged "good." For example, a mural which is being painted by the children may turn out to be an excellent piece of work depicting the routes through the Appalachian Mountains to the West. But, how do we evaluate this? Is the mural or the final product evidence that certain attitudes, skills, knowledge, and behaviors have been acquired?

Children must know the bases of evaluation. If the teacher is teaching for facts, then the child needs to know this. On the other hand, if the application of the facts to the development of generalizations is important, then he needs this information. The new social science education brings with it the need to assess the child's progress in the acquisition of knowledge or information, development of attitudes and values, growth in using the inquiry process, and development in conceptualizing and generalizing. It also assesses the child's ability to make inferences applicable to other situations among other learnings. This chapter is concerned with presenting certain guides or procedures which will facilitate the teacher's approach to pupil evaluation in the new social science program. This chapter will not deal with all the testing instruments and devices found in educational measurement courses, but will serve as a practical base for teachers to appraise pupil progress in the modern social science program.

Growth in the Acquisition of Knowledge or Information

In the modern elementary social science program, information takes on a different meaning than it has in traditional programs of read, memorize, and recite. In the latter type of program the child must be able to display or in some way give back to the teacher the evidence that he now possesses the desired information (knowledge); whereas, the new program calls for the ability to select relative or pertinent information, to analyze this information, and to arrive at some conclusion. However, this whole process might be less satisfying to some persons because it calls for solutions or answers which are never more than tentative. As new information comes to light, the conclusion or answer might be altered. When information is used in this process, the learner must be able to act on the basis of the information he has acquired and analyzed, but he must also be flexible enough to change his behavior should new information become available. He, therefore, acquires knowledge from his inquiry into what others have found out and from new and better ways of attacking a problem. Of importance here is the fact that he must learn that there are not many hard and fast truths which exist for all time—knowledge and truth are relative.[1]

The task is to evaluate the extent of growth in the acquisition of information (knowledge). Obviously, this objective cannot be handled in the traditional test of memorized facts. Let us examine a behavioral objective related to the acquisition of information. Keep in mind that, as we said in chapter five, an objective tells us what a successful learner is capable of doing when that objective has been achieved. We are interested in eleven-year-old Cindy being able to locate information pertinent to the problem she is seeking to solve. She wants to know why it is necessary for a state park to charge persons to swim in the lake. As she analyzes her problem, Cindy has to identify a number of questions, the answers to which she will need in her search for knowledge. Such questions as, "How much does it cost to operate the park each year?" "What

---

[1] Benjamin S. Bloom, ed., *Taxonomy of Educational Objectives: The Classification of Educational Goals, Handbook I: The Cognitive Domain* (New York: David McKay Company, Inc., 1964), p. 32.

Evaluation is concerned with pupil growth in group processes.

does it cost for maintenance of the park?" "How widespread is the practice of charging for swimming in other parks in the state?" "How many people swim in the lake?" "What size families swim in the lake?" "Are there families who don't visit the state park because they can't afford to pay for their children to swim?" "Where does the money come from to operate the state park?" "Should public-owned lands be free for all to use?" These and many other questions will confront Cindy as she seeks a solution to her question. Her ability to seek out information or facts concerning the problem will be evaluated. But, an effective evaluation can only be started when the teacher knows the information the child possesses before beginning the search for the solution to the problem. Thus, the teacher needs to determine the amount of prior knowledge possessed by the pupil. The teacher might use some of the following guides in this endeavor:

1. What is the pupil's aptitude for learning concepts?
2. At what level of abstraction is the student capable of dealing with issues?
3. What is the student's attitude toward the problem he is trying to solve?

4. What does he know about sources of information available to him?
5. What evidence is in his record which supports his ability to proceed on his own in problem solving?
6. Can he arrive at a solution to the problem in a reasonable amount of time?
7. Does he work better alone or with other students?

As these guides are used, the teacher and Cindy can establish specific behavioral objectives to be achieved within the limits of her school time. Then, Cindy and the teacher can determine the extent to which Cindy has achieved the specified objectives. For example, the following guides to Cindy's progress might be used:

1. How many new resources did Cindy learn about while investigating this problem?
2. Was she able to determine the pertinent facts related to the problem?
3. Did she learn to use human as well as material resources in seeking the solution to the problem?
4. What new technique did she master in seeking knowledge (interviews, state records and reports, questionnaires, etc.)?
5. Did her behavior change when she completed her study?
6. Did she acquire new attitudes about the responsibility of the state to the people?
7. What knowledge did she acquire concerning why it was necessary for the state to charge for swimming at state parks?

The teacher's role is one of varied positions in the learning process. For example, the teacher must continually focus on the student and his learning style. The teacher in this role is concerned with methodology. She must determine whether the student needs more concrete materials or whether the materials used are too difficult for the learner. The teacher must be cognizant of the student behaviors which are trying to be achieved to the extent that alternatives might be suggested if it appears that the behaviors are not going to be measurable or observable.

The teacher needs to become a partner with the student in learning, to share the opportunity of exploring new learning experiences with him. Thus, the teacher's perception of his own pedagogical philosophy becomes an important aspect of the evaluation process. Because evaluation processes are related to the teacher's own perceptions of himself as a teacher, the way he perceives both his role and the teaching process will, in fact, dictate the kind of evaluation used. When the teacher views his role as an authority behind the desk, he obviously will reflect this same strategy in evaluation. The teacher then might make the decision that one source of data is more acceptable than another. Such a decision could "turn off" the learner and result in decisions by opinion instead of decisions based upon examination of all pertinent data, inasmuch as the student will no doubt want to please the teacher.

Evaluating pupil growth in reading charts, graphs, and tables

The modern social science program requires the pupil to be able to collect and interpret data found in various forms. The reading program, for the most part, has not taught the skills essential for this learning activity, nor has it provided reading material of this nature. Yet, these skills are essential if the child is to become an active, informed participant in the decision-making processes of everyday life. To learn to see relationships between one thing and another, between one trend and another trend, for example, requires the ability to first examine relevant data. The following chart [2] might be used to determine a trend by fifth-grade children involved in studying population shifts:

CHART 14–1. Households, by Residence: 1910 to 1957
(In thousands)

Year	Total	Nonfarm	Farm
1957	49,543	44,325	5,218
1950	43,554	37,279	6,275
1940	35,153	28,001	7,152
1930	29,997	23,268	6,729
1910	20,183	13,984	6,194

Students might be asked to make a graph showing the decline in farm families. They might further be questioned concerning why there was a decline in farm families and what effect this shift in population from an agrarian life to an industrialized society has on a country. Of course, the quality of the questions will have much to do with whether the students will be encouraged to ask other questions, as well as to seek solutions to problems which emerge. It is not difficult to determine if the children can read the chart and if they understand it. Questions, such as, the following examples, might be asked to determine the ability of the pupils to understand the chart as well as the amount of knowledge learned from it:

---

[2] "Cleveland Heights Social Science Program, Grade Five" (Cleveland Heights–University Heights City School District, 1965), p. 55.

What do we mean by households?

How many years does the chart cover?

What is a nonfarm household?

How many farm households were there in 1930?

What per cent of households in America were nonfarm in 1950?

The important point is that we do need to evaluate the acquisition of skills, concepts, and knowledge from such sources of data as various kinds of charts, graphs, pictures, and tables, since these are basic to learning in the modern social science program. Similarly, map and globe skills must be evaluated. These skills can be demonstrated, and as competency is achieved, the pupil can move on to learning to use more sophisticated skills. The seeking of data in self-directed learning provides constant reinforcement of the skills learned.

Evaluating Development of Attitudes and Values Supportive of Effective Citizenship

The abundance of cultural alternatives which citizens in the modern United States face presents the teacher of social sciences with a series of dilemmas which she must resolve. The society, which once held that the public school was responsible for the transmission of its culture to its children, now finds itself confronted with numerous doubts about the school's being the basic source of cultural transmission. Clearly, however, the school, with the support of the public, must utilize its position as a center where all children may develop the values and attitudes essential to bringing harmony out of the social conflict which has permeated U.S. society for the past several decades. Not that such upheavals did not occur in the early days of our nation, but, at this time, world tensions and confrontations on the international scene have brought us to the crossroads of civilization vested with few alternatives—either men must learn to live with men in harmony, or society, itself, may be faced with extinction.

The cultural changes taking place, both in our nation and throughout the world, demand that individuals examine values and readjust their habits and patterns of conduct. If the time-honored system of values is being challenged on all fronts in terms of the best ways to rear children, the content of subject matter being taught, the kinds of personal relationships established, the economic controls of production and distribution, the rights of all persons to an annual income, and so on, then some system of values must be considered in giving some direction to all schools in our democracy. Teachers may become bewildered by their role and confused as to the direction they should follow in directing the learning of values. Behavior grows out of the system of values held by the individual. His philosophy of life is acquired from these values, and, whether consciously or deliberately spelled out in his thinking or poorly defined and operating in a vague, subconscious fashion, it nevertheless is the basis for his actions. For the elementary school child, *values mean his way of believing in, and responding to, situations and guiding his behavior in such a way that his actions bespeak one who has the facts and knows the "rules" of his culture.*

Growth in citizenship skills and attitudes or values is one of the most difficult areas to evaluate. We can't wait for two decades to determine the extent to which children, who would then be adults, have developed desirable social behavior. Perhaps we need to look at short-range objectives which relate to "appropriate" citizenship behavior. That is, specific behavior objectives which can be evaluated during the time the child is with any given teacher. Such an objective might be, "Does he have respect for other people's ideas, experiences, and interests?" While observation on the part of the teacher will be the best means of providing data concerning the extent to which certain children achieve this objective, checklists developed with the children and used by them might also contribute to collecting evidence of their growth or lack of growth. A simple checklist for use by either the teacher or the children is presented here as an illustration. The checklist is an attempt to objectify observations, but it will still involve value judgments.

CHART 14–2. Growth in Respect for Ideas of Others

Name   Grade 5

Behavior to be Checked	Always	Nearly Always	Sometimes	Never
1. Considers ideas contrary to his own.		X		
2. Listens while others speak.			X	
3. Does not ridicule persons who present ideas different from his own.		X		
4. Supports the rights of each person to suggest ideas.	X			
5. Suggests alternative ideas for consideration.		X		
6. Shows no signs of rejecting persons who do not accept his ideas.	X			

Can you develop a checklist which you could use as a teacher for your own guidance in evaluating an attitude or value?

Such a checklist might be extended and used by each child. Of importance, however, is that the appropriate behavior be evaluated in terms of the age and maturity level of the learner. The checklist might be used by the children at least three different times during the year, then the progressive results compared so that the children can determine how they feel about their own growth. The teacher might also want to keep a checklist for selected children to compare with those kept by the children. Conferences could then be held to discuss differences and to work out behavioral objectives.

Additional objectives dealing with citizenship might also be evaluated by the teacher through using observation, checklists, interviews, and other techniques. But, the point is that if objectives are to be valuable, they must be such that the learner and the teacher can determine some degree of progress achieved within the time the teacher is in contact with the child. Some objectives which deal with democratic values might be:

1. To what extent does the pupil respect private and public property?
2. Does the pupil obey necessary school regulations?
3. What evidence is there that the pupil is working to improve health conditions in the school?
4. Does the pupil respect the rights of all races and religious groups?
5. What is the pupil's behavior during a fire drill?

Needless to say, you can extend this list and even differentiate the objectives for primary, intermediate, and upper elementary children. The important point is, if you are trying to find out if a child is progressing in certain behavior, you must establish with him what that behavior is, ask him to do it or place him in a situation where this behavior becomes evident, and then carefully observe his behavior. If you want to know if he respects school regulations, then you will need to observe how often he breaks the regulations. If you are concerned about his behavior during a fire drill or emergency situation, then observe his specific behavior at these times. But, develop guides to the specific types of desirable behavior you are fostering. These guides can be used over the period of time that you have influence over the child's learning.

Evaluating attitudes or values

To determine the values children hold concerning certain aspects of human living is one of the more difficult tasks for teachers. Nevertheless, there are ways of going about this. One group of teachers was interested in testing the hypothesis, "A person is irresponsible when he causes unnecessary problems for other people." The idea used was to develop a series of slides or pictures that showed examples of behavior by pupils or adults in the following categories: responsible, irresponsible, and irrelevant to the notion of responsibility. The following suggested pictures or scenes were used; the numbers in parentheses indicate the order in which the slides were shown.

Series No. 1 (Irresponsible)

(1) 1. A child leaving a messy room for his mother to clean up
(7) 2. A child leaving toys on a stairway
(4) 3. A child spilling some soft drink on the floor, walking away and not cleaning up after himself
(8) 4. A child walking on flowers in another family's garden

Series No. 2 (Responsible)

(9) 1. A child helping a smaller child across the street
(5) 2. A child helping Mother with the dishes
(11) 3. A child helping an animal in distress
(2) 4. A child going to the end of a lunch line

Series No. 3 (Irrelevant)

(12) 1. A child walking down a sidewalk
(6) 2. A child looking out on the countryside for the top of a mountain
(10) 3. A child riding in a car
(3) 4. A child reading a comic book

Data would be gathered from the results of pupils arranging the twelve pictures or slides into these categories.

Responsible	Irresponsible	Irrelevant
2,5,9,11	1,7,4,8	3,6,10,12

When evaluating the data, after the children have arranged the slides or pictures into the three categories, you could have them develop a hierarchy for each category. Have them briefly explain how they arrived at their particular arrangement.[3]

The above practical suggestion for determining pupils' attitudes or values can be carried into many other areas of values. The teacher should take the initiative in working to perfect her own ideas which might grow out of the one suggested above. Team efforts at developing this type of instrument, with continuous attention at refinement, could produce some very useful devices for evaluating pupil values and attitudes.

Evaluating Inquiry

Inquiry is essentially finding out for oneself, and thus it is the application of purpose to data in order to develop useful knowledge in solving a problem, satisfying a curiosity, answering a question,[4] and so on. The elements of the process oif inquiry must be continually evaluated by both the users of the process and the teacher. The users of the process need to learn to check themselves against falling into following the path of least resistance. The teacher needs to help the learners to improve on the techniques they are using. The elements of inquiry are:

Defining a task—purpose

Developing a tentative answer—hypothesis

Testing tentative answer—testing

Developing a conclusion

Applying a conclusion (to new situations, new data)

Generalizing [5]

Importance of defining a task

The first step in evaluating the pupil's use of the inquiry process is to determine if the problem or purpose is real and meaningful to the learner. Inquiry-oriented experiences cannot be superimposed on problems isolated from the real world of the pupils. Teachers must become skillful in guiding children to the identification of the problem. Regardless of the

---

[3] Developed at a two week summer institute sponsored by the Cooperative Center for Social Science Education, College of Education, Ohio University, Athens (June 1970).

[4] Barry K. Beyer, "Using Inquiry in the Social Sciences: Guidelines for Teaching" (Athens, Ohio: Ohio University, The Cooperative Center for Social Science Education, 1967).

[5] *Ibid.,* p. 7.

age level with which the teacher is working, it is not sufficient for her to tell the individual or the group what his or its purpose is in any inquiry experience. Success will come when the teacher uses the internal motivation of the individual to pursue a problem. Persons in real life try to inquire when they are moved by a problem or conflict which means something important to them. It behooves the teacher not to overlook the importance of the problem to the individual child, recognizing his level of maturity as he identifies the task in his own language.

Inasmuch as evaluation is an ongoing process, it is a better teaching principle to seek out the pitfalls of inquiry as the children move from one element to another in using the process for problem solving. Little value can be found from the traditional method of presenting possible pitfalls before the children even try the process. The following model illustrates how some teachers set up patterns for evaluating whether pupils can successfully recognize a problem as well as whether they can carry out or use the elements of inquiry:

Model for Grades 4 to 6 in Evaluating the Pupils' Use of the Elements of Inquiry

Defining a task—purpose. Dick's father worked at the cannery. He planned to buy Dick a new bicycle before school started. Dick and his father went to Mr. Finney's shop to select the one Dick wanted most. Mr. Finney promised to hold the bike until Father paid for it at the end of summer. However, the bean harvest was poor, and the cannery closed in midsummer. Some workers lost their jobs, but a crew was employed to install new machinery. Farmers were hopeful that the beet and carrot yields would be heavy. Dick was worried that Father would not be able to buy the shiny, red bike before school started.

Scoring has three parts: 1) one point for each correct response in the probably true—probably false section; 2) three points for selecting problem 4 as most important, two points for selecting problem 2, and one point for selecting problem 5; 3) two points for each response which is consistent with the sequential problem solving, regardless of which one of the three probably true problems the pupil selects as most important.

Based on this story, which of the following problems are probably true and which are probably false?

1. Mr. Finney must close his bicycle shop.
   Probably true _____ Probably false _____
2. Some workers lost their jobs when the cannery closed.
   Probably true _____ Probably false _____
3. Dick's father did not plan to buy him a shiny, red bike.
   Probably true _____ Probably false _____

4. Dick was afraid his father could not afford the bicycle.
   Probably true _____   Probably false _____
5. Dick's father worked at the cannery and lost his job.
   Probably true _____   Probably false _____
   (4, 2, 5)

Reread *carefully* each of the problems which is probably true. Then choose the one which seems most important to you. Write the number of that problem here: _____

Hypothesize. What do you think is most likely to happen?

1. Father will work with the crew to install machinery.
2. Mr. Finney will give the bicycle to Dick.
3. Dick will decide to buy a blue bicycle.
4. The cannery will re-open to process beets and carrots.
5. Mr. Finney will hold the bicycle for Dick.
   (1, 4, 5)

Gather Data. Where would you go to get information about a possible solution to the problem which you selected as being most important?

1. Check with the cannery to find out when it will re-open.
2. Check with Father to find out if he still has a job.
3. Check with Mr. Finney to find out if he will hold the bicycle longer than he first agreed.
4. Check with Dick's friends to find out if they are buying new bicycle.
5. Check with Mr. Finney to find out if he also sells bows and arrows.
   (2, 1, 3)

Test Your Hypothesis. Which of these sentences from the story agrees with your hypothesis?

1. Some workers lost their jobs, but a crew was employed to install new machinery.
2. He planned to buy Dick a new bicycle before school started.
3. Dick was worried that Father would not be able to buy the shiny, red bike before school started.
4. Mr. Finney promised to hold the bike until Father paid for it at the end of the summer.
5. Farmers were hopeful that the beet and carrot yields would be heavy.
   (1, 5, 4)

Analyze/Evaluate Data. What information will help you find an answer to the problem you chose?

1. Dick can buy a bike from Mr. Finney later.
2. Mr. Finney agreed to hold the bicycle until the end of the summer.
3. Father was hired to install new machinery.
4. Dick can buy a used bike for less money.
5. Farmers expect good beet and carrot harvests.

(3, 5, 2)

State Your Conclusion. Relate your hypothesis to the story and to the problem you selected. Then choose the conclusion which makes sense to you:

1. Dick will decide he wants a bow and arrow.
2. Father will work with the crew to install new machinery and will buy the shiny, red bike for Dick.
3. Farmers will have heavy harvests of beets and carrots, and the cannery will re-open to process them.
4. Dick's grandparents will come to see him.
5. Mr. Finney will hold the bike until Dick's father can pay for it.

(2, 3, 5)

State a Generalization. Think carefully back over the entire story and the steps you have worked through to this point. Then choose the sentence which best fits your idea about everything that happened.

1. Storekeepers are kind-hearted men who hold bicycles until parents can pay for them.
2. When fathers have jobs, they can buy many of the things their families need and want.
3. All boys like bow and arrow sets.
4. When the cannery closed, Dick thought he would not get his bicycle.
5. Canneries depend on good crops from farms in order to keep operating.

(2, 5, 1)[6]

Developing a tentative answer or forming the hypothesis. After the task has been identified, then it becomes important for children to learn to develop possible solutions to the problem. For example, in the preceding model there were several possible hypotheses cited. Children need to learn to examine critically the problem so that they can delineate those factors which are not logically tenable. As logical deductions and

---

[6] Summer Institute, Ohio University, Athens (June 1970).

implications are explicated, then the hypotheses can be narrowed down to those which have implications for which evidence will be sought to support the hypothesis. For example, the second hypothesis in the model, "Mr. Finney will give the bicycle to Dick," seems to have no logical support from any statement in the problem. But the first hypothesis does have some logical basis. Some men will be employed to install the new equipment, but further evidence is needed to determine if Dick's father will be employed. Thus, the hypothesis gives implications for the types of evidence or facts which must be gathered to support the hypothesis. The point to be made here is that the teacher can set up models of the type presented here to help children to become proficient in forming hypotheses.

Testing tentative answers. Here the children must learn to gather data and test it to see if it supports the hypothesis. Of major importance here is whether the children can learn to get information pertinent to the problem and identify relevant sources of information, as well as distinguish between authoritative and nonauthoritative sources of knowledge. A checklist can be prepared from which the children can make certain decisions in testing the data collected against the hypothesis. The model cited above provides some alternatives to information which might lead to possible solutions to the problem. As the information collected is tested through various processes, irrelevant information can be eliminated; pupils can thus learn to test for tentative answers.

Developing a conclusion. The conclusion represents the most tenable solution to the problem based on the best evidence available. The children should learn to write an explanatory statement in the form of a generalization. In the model, possible conclusions are stated, and the child can determine which statement best meets the criteria of the hypothesis. But, he needs to determine if sufficient evidence is given and if it provides irrefutable support for the conclusion. However, if the conclusion, based upon the evidence, is true only under certain conditions, then the conclusion needs to be rewritten, including the conditions under which the conclusion or generalization is justified.

Application. Once the conclusion has been stated, then children should experience trying to apply the conclusion to new situations. By forming further generalizations which have broader implications, we are able to generalize from Dick's father's experience, "When fathers have jobs they can buy many of the things their families need and want." Children, however, need to know that the generalization does not represent a final truth; the conclusion does not represent an absolute, even though all possible data collected support the conclusion. Inquiry at its best is a never ending process. The learner must be cognizant that new data may become available which will lead to altering the conclusions, and thus, an open mind is essential for citizens of the future so that the phenomena of social change can be more readily accepted without causing frustration and mental conflict. Children must, therefore, learn to accept the tentative nature of a generalization.

A Pattern of Evaluation to Guide the Teacher

The nature and philosophy of evaluation has suggested some ways of working with children in the classroom. Four points [7] are now suggested which might help to crystallize the thinking of the teacher and to suggest possible approaches following the previous discussion.

Establishing criteria

The teacher must establish criteria. The beginning point of evaluation is realistic in that one must know what the child needs and what behavior patterns are most desirable for him. The criteria may then be specifically described in terms of certain behavior patterns, skills of inquiry, desirable habits that can be attained, attitudes and understandings which can be achieved, and so on. As the new social science program emerges, there is every reason to believe that a wiser selection of learning experiences for each child is possible. Finally, the evaluation of progress begins to take on new meaning as both the teacher and pupil become better acquainted with what the *child* actually does.

Collecting data

It is not the purpose here to elaborate upon all the instruments and devices discussed in educational measurements, but to call attention to the value to the teacher of using these instruments and devices for important information about the child. Through testing and behavior observation, the teacher obtains a better idea of what is happening to the child and whether or not the best results are being achieved.

Interpreting data

Perhaps the most difficult task in the evaluation process is analyzing data to decide how well the child is progressing. At this point, many questions are raised to cause the teacher to make and alter decisions concerning the child. Does the information on hand support the value judgment? Is the direction of behavioral change the most desirable and so on?

---

[7] Albert H. Shuster and Milton E. Ploghoft, *The Emerging Elementary Curriculum,* 2nd edition (Columbus, Ohio: Charles Merrill Publishing Company, 1970), p. 472.

Planning a course of action

In light of the collected data and cooperative interpretations about the child, that final important step of deciding upon achievement of desirable results by a pattern must now follow. Changes in the teaching and/or learning style may be needed. Before a new course of action is taken, additional data might be needed. New insights might result from new data, and the use of specialized personnel or resource persons may be needed.

Evaluation procedures and how they are used have a definite relationship to the effectiveness of the modern social science program.

Summary

Evaluating modern social science instruction requires some creative techniques and devices yet to be discovered. However, sufficient beginnings have been made, by building on past contributions, which can aid the teacher in her efforts to more objectively determine pupil growth. Objectives, both individual and group, should be established in behavioral terms in order to record progress about pupil growth as it occurs. This means that objectives must be giving direction to programs built around the maturity level of children and not judged by adult standards. The proof of achieving a behavioral objective is when a child applies the skill or understanding, or when he possesses the knowledge to move ahead with the activity identified by the objective.

Teacher-made devices are useful in helping to make teacher judgments more objective. Standardized and teacher-made tests should be used respectively when the teacher's purpose calls for the information which such tests reveal. Although future citizenship behavior cannot at this time be predicted from such tests, there are ways for the teacher to use such tests in beginning to evaluate attitudes and values and to determine immediate citizenship behaviors. Observation seems to be the most important technique in assisting the teacher to evaluate whether an objective has been achieved. But, it is essential that criteria be established for the total evaluation program.

Suggested Problems and Projects

1. Form several teams of three or four members each and investigate the evaluative approaches used by various social science teachers in the

surrounding elementary schools. Use discretion in planning your visits; preplan what you are looking for; contact the principal and review your plans with him; and make appointments with teachers, ask to see sample copies of several different tests teachers have used, and seek other evaluative devices they have used. Compare your results with suggestions in this chapter and in chapter five. Have your team discuss with the class the systems now being used as determined by your school visit. Make clear the differences which exist between the information in chapter fourteen and the devices you found teachers to be using.

2. Ask your instructor to permit each of you to evaluate yourself for at least half a semester (quarter). Ask him to evaluate you simultaneously; at the end of the time, compare your results. What are the pros and cons of each form of evaluation? After completing this experience, ask a team of teachers from a local school to come to your class to discuss self-evaluation and its functional values in the elementary classroom.

3. Form two teams and debate the problem of determining pupil attitudes and values. What are the pitfalls that teachers must guard against in recording judgmental results about attitudes and values?

Related Readings

Berg, Harry, ed. *Evaluation in Social Studies, 35th Yearbook.* Washington, D.C.: The National Council for the Social Studies, 1965.

Bloom, Benjamin S., ed. *Taxonomy of Education Objectives: The Classification of Educational Goals, Handbook I: Cognitive Domain,* chapter 6. New York: David McKay Company, 1961.

Fraser, Dorothy McClure, ed. *Social Studies Curriculum Development: Prospects and Problems, 39th Yearbook,* chapters 7, 8. Washington, D.C.: The National Council for the Social Studies, 1969.

Green, John A. *Teacher-Made Tests.* New York: Harper & Row Company, 1963.

Joyce, Bruce R. *Strategies for Elementary Social Science Education.* Chicago: Science Research Associates, 1965.

Krathwohi, David R., Bloom, Benjamin S., and Masia, Bertram B. *Taxonomy of Educational Objectives: The Classification of Educational Goals, Handbook II: Effective Domain,* Part II. New York: David McKay Company, 1964.

Massialas, Byron G. and Cox, Benjamin C. *Inquiry in Social Studies,* chapter 11. New York: McGraw-Hill Book Company, 1966.

Our Conclusion—Your Beginning

There are additional materials in the appendixes which are designed to be useful to you as you prepare to teach and when you begin your work in the classroom, but for all intents and purposes we will take our leave at this point. We hope that your consideration of the issues, purposes, and directions of the social education of the children of our society has provided you with information and skills that are essential to teaching social science education. You should be ready to begin the process of self-development that will enable you to become an exceptional teacher.

Several chapters of this book will provide a working guide for you during your first years of teaching. The chapter on Inquiring Processes will afford you the organizing and implementing ideas for inquiring experiences with children. The chapters on Concepts, Methods, and Learning Resources will give valuable guidance as you put together your teaching plans. You will be able to enrich the social education of children by drawing on the suggestions contained in the chapters on Cross-Cultural Studies, Contemporary Affairs, and Religion. Finally, you will find model items which will help you in writing your own evaluation instruments for growth in social science knowledge and skill.

So, at the point of your beginning, we urge you to take this effort at communication with you. We believe it will be a valuable resource in the years ahead, although at times you may want to talk back to us! In such an event, your suggestions and criticisms are invited and welcomed. We assure you that they will be carefully considered, if not always enjoyed, and the second edition of this book will be made better.

Appendix A

The Taba Social Studies Curriculum Project

Some examples of grade level units from the Taba Project materials were included in chapter four. At this point, a brief statement of the major characteristics of the Taba Curriculum will be provided. The basic assumptions upon which the Taba Curriculum was developed include the following:

Thinking skills can be taught.

Thinking involves an active transaction between an individual and the data with which he is working.

How well an individual thinks depends on the richness and significance of the content with which he works, as well as the processes which he uses.

Teaching strategies that are emphasized involve concept development, inferring and generalizing, and applying generalizations.

Eleven key concepts are developed throughout the Taba Curriculum. As you consider them, you may want to refer to the Syracuse concepts which are presented in chapter four. The Taba concepts are:

Causality	Conflict	Cooperation
Cultural change	Differences	Interdependence
Modification	Power	Societal control
Tradition	Values	

The Taba Project report presents an extensive and highly integrated program which is envisioned as the outcome of teacher involvement and preparation in using this curriculum. If you desire to become more completely informed, you are referred to the report which should be available in your library.

Appendix B

The Social Sciences: Concepts and Values

This textbook series,[1] which is by Paul F. Brandwein et al, is based on a conceptual schemes approach that is designed to reduce random encounter by selected, planned experiences in search of meaning. The concepts of man as a social being and the values that make him human are the substance of the program.

The chart which follows provides an overview of the behavioral themes and cognitive schemes that are developed at the seven levels of the textbook series. As was the case with the information in Appendix A, the intent here is to provide an opportunity for the prospective teacher to gain firsthand familiarity with selected materials, rather than to recommend any particular program.

---

[1] © 1970 by Harcourt Brace Jovanovich, Inc., and reproduced with their permission.

Beginning Level
CHART B–1. Children interact with the physical and social environment

Behavioral Themes	Cognitive Scheme A	Cognitive Scheme B
	Man is the product of heredity and environment.	Human behavior is shaped by the social environment.
6. Responsibility for man and his environment—through development of systems of behavor.	6. Biological and cultural inheritance results in variation in the people of the Earth.	6. Social systems are shaped by the values of interacting groups.
5. Responsibility for man and his environment—through cultural patterns of behavior.	5. The interaction of biological and cultural inheritance results in the adaptation of man to his environment.	5. Cultures in varying environments have similar components.
4. Responsibility for man and his environment—through adaptive patterns of behavior.	4. Man inherits and learns patterns of behavior.	4. Man learns social behavior from groups with which he interacts.
3. Responsibility for man and his environment—through adaptive behavior of the larger group.	3. Community groups adapt to the environment.	3. The characteristics of a community are the results of interactions between individuals and other groups in a specific environment.
2. Responsibility for man and his environment—through adaptive behavior of the basic group.	2. Members of the family group are alike because of heredity and environment.	2. The family group teaches the child the social behavior of his culture.
1. Responsibility for man and his environment—through adaptive behavior of the individual within the group.	1. Individuals resemble each other.	1. Individuals learn from each other.

Appendix B

Beginning Level
CHART B–1. Children interact with the physical and social environment

Cognitive Scheme C	Cognitive Scheme D	Cognitive Scheme E
The geographic features of the Earth affect man's behavior.	Economic behavior depends upon the utilization of resources.	Political organization (government) resolves conflicts and makes interactions easier among people.
6. Political organization alters the map.	6. Economic systems are shaped by the values of the culture.	6. Political systems are developed, changed, or maintained through the interaction of individuals and governments.
5. Man modifies the environment in order to utilize his resources and increase them.	5. The patterns of buying and selling depend upon choices people make.	5. Regional and national governments cooperate.
4. Man utilizes his environment to secure basic needs.	4. Man interacts to utilize available resources.	4. Man's peaceful interaction depends on social controls.
3. Communities develop different modes of adaptation to different environments.	3. The culture of the community determines the use of resources.	3. Community groups are governed through leadership and authority.
2. Family groups throughout the world live in different environments.	2. Family groups utilize resources to satisfy their needs.	2. Members of family groups are governed by rules and law.
1. Individuals live in different environments on the Earth.	1. Individuals use the resources available to them.	1. The behavior of individuals is governed by commonly accepted rules.

Appendix C

Sample Teaching Units

Three examples of teaching units are included here. The first example deals with only selected objectives, questions, and activities of a unit on The Airport, since the total unit plan is too comprehensive and lengthy to include here. It is intended that this portion of the airport unit will provide you with an idea of a traditional unit. Notice the broad sweep of the objectives, especially the inclusion of many general education objectives.

The study plans provided in parts two and three of this appendix reflect different approaches to concept development.

Excerpt of Sample Unit I—The Public Airport

I. Objectives

    A. Knowledge

        1. Broad Generalizations

            a. Individuals and groups tend to act according to standards expressed in laws, rules, and other social controls.
            b. The work of society is carried on through various groups in which individuals have responsibilities and opportunities, to either lead or follow and contribute to individual and group welfare.
            c. Interdependence is a persistent factor in person-to-person, institutional, and international relationships.
            d. Environment influences man's ways of living; man adapts to certain features of the environment and modifies others.
            e. The level of technology of a nation, which is directly related to its level of education, affects production, transportation, communication, and other basic activities.

Appendix C 371

2. Basic Understandings
   a. Laws and regulations apply to the airport's many activities and employees and serve to better insure the safety of the public. (a) [2]
   b. Many airport workers must have special training for their jobs to be better qualified to serve the public. (a)
   c. Because of the importance of the flight plan in keeping track of an airplane's location, a pilot is required to file his flight plan with the control tower before each flight. (a)
   d. Groups, such as, the Federal Aviation Agency, have been set up to provide safety regulations for all. (a, b)
   e. People work at many different jobs at the airport—pilot, mechanic, and waitress—to better serve members of the community when they are traveling, waiting, departing or arriving. (b)
   f. The airport is an organization of groups of people working together to provide services to and for the community. (b)
   g. The need for an airport has increased its value to aviation and the community.
   h. Faster shipment of perishable products from other communities enables our community to enjoy fresh food. (c)
   i. The community depends upon the airport to provide transportation services and employment for its residents, while the airport depends upon the community for appropriations and business. (c)
   j. Airport workers are dependent upon each other for the completion and success of their respective jobs. (c)
   k. Pilots depend upon special facilities, such as, runway light and tower control, to aid them in their jobs. (c)
   l. With the use of lights, radio beams, and radar, the airport remains open all night. (c)
   m. Since the terminal building is so large (and because it is), it offers many different types of services and goods to the public. (c)
   n. Because of the fast transportation facilities, airports help to "tie" communities together. (c)
   o. The airport is an important part of the community because it provides a terminal and approved landing area for airplanes carrying goods and people. (c, d)
   p. The airport's physical location, size, and services are de-

---

[2] The letters following each basic understanding refer to the applicable broad generalizations.

pendent upon the size of the surrounding community and the topography of the land. (d)
q. The growing proximity of the airport's and community's location has caused problems, such as, noise, runway length, and safety. (d)
r. Because of the airport's contribution to mail service, mail delivery is now much faster. (e)
s. Man is able to visit friends, see other lands, and fulfill business plans much faster and more conveniently through the use of air transportation. (e)
t. Because of the hangars' size, they are able to store planes, as well as provide space for mechanics to work on them. (Not related directly to any of the above generalizations, but considered to be important.)
u. Because of the development of the commercial jet airliner, air transportation has become much faster. (e)
v. Due to the increased runway length needed for jet airliners, many airports have had to buy land closer to the community in order to extend their runway length. (e)
w. Due to new airport and airplane innovations, such as radar and instrument landing equipment, air transportation is now available in weather which would have previously been considered unsuitable for flying. (e)

B. Attitudes and Appreciations

1. An appreciation of the contributions made by men interested in aviation in order to make our lives easier.

2. Respect for the dignity and responsibility of certain jobs at the airport.

3. An appreciation of the importance of the airport to the community.

4. An appreciation of the services provided by the airport.

5. An attitude of responsibility, cooperation, and concern for others is necessary in interdependent relationships.

6. A willingness to act in ways conducive to the general welfare and human progress.

7. A clearer understanding of the airport's problems in relation to the community and aviation.

8. An understanding of the economic interrelationships between the airport and the community.

Appendix C 373

        9. An understanding and appreciation of the effects of the forces of nature on air technology and transportation.

C. Skills

1. Adhere to group standards of safety and behavior.
2. Apply problem-solving and critical-thinking methods.
3. Work as members of a group.
4. Make and use simple aeronautical maps to learn directions and locations and to gather information about the airways.
5. Organize information about airports and present it in written, oral or display form.
6. Identify and define issues, standards, and problems about the airport.
7. Formulate hypotheses and generalizations and make tentative conclusions in discovering airport problem situations.
8. Detect errors of thinking, unstated assumptions, and unwarranted assertions in evaluating gathered information.
9. Learn to make plans for the group.
10. Share, plan, discuss, carry out, and evaluate learning experiences related to airport interdependency.
11. Improve the ability to listen, report, take turns, speak, and write with accuracy.
12. Locate, appraise, and select information on the airport.
13. Interpret airway maps and the reasons for airport locations.
14. Evaluate your own progress in learning group cooperation and acquired information.

II. Problem Questions

A. Since there are many types and sizes of aircraft using the airport's facilities, how does this affect the type and size of the airport?

1. What are the types of public airports?
2. What types of planes provide the transportation?
3. What new services and procedures at the airport have resulted from the use of commercial jet transportation?

Appendix C

      4. What effect does the size of the airplane have on the runway length?

      5. What planes are allowed to land at a public airport?

  B. Since the beginnings of public air transportation, a terminal building has been needed. Why?

      1. What facilities for the aircraft are located in the terminal building?

      2. What public facilities necessary for flight are found in the terminal building?

      3. Why are the provided facilities located in one building?

      4. What has been the terminal building's importance to aviation?
         a. It is the center of what?
         b. What regulations in the terminal building are necessary for better airport safety?

  C. The airport personnel and the community's business and general population are, by the very nature of their jobs, interdependent. Why?

      1. What services does the community provide for the airport?

      2. What services does the airport and its personnel perform for the community?

      3. Why is airmail service so important to the community?

      4. Why do people use airplanes for transportation?

      5. What new jobs does the airport provide for the community population?

  D. Science questions

      1. What is a windsock?

      2. Why are lights necessary?

      3. Why are there so many different colors of lights?
         a. What color are the runway lights?
         b. What color are the taxi strip lights?

      4. What does a rotating beacon tell the pilot?

      5. What is an "apron?"
         a. What is the purpose of it?
         b. Where is it?

Appendix C 375

III. Experiences and Activities

    A. Opening Activities

        1. Discussion of pupils' trips by airplane—what they did when they were in the terminal, where they went, how long the trip took, and what the ground looked like from the air.

        2. Show the film, *Airport-Passenger Flight.*

        3. Discussion of what the students would like to learn about the airport and put their decision on an experience chart.

        4. Read the story, *Ride on the Wind,* by Alice Dalgliesh.

    B. Developmental Activities

        1. Planning ways to solve problems.

            a. Display books, pictures, and pamphlets of planes, airport facilities and airport workers to stimulate thinking.
            b. Plan a trip to the airport.
            c. Write a letter to an airport worker and ask him to come and speak to the class.
            d. Organize committees to report on certain jobs at the airport.
            e. Organize committees to discover the uses of an airplane.
            f. Read several stories about airport workers and their jobs.
            g. List needs for materials, steps to take to solve questions the children have about airports and the problems of individual responsibility.
            h. Sing songs about flying to further stimulate interest.

        2. Locating, gathering, and appraising information.

            a. Take a guided tour of the community airport.
            b. Hear reports from student committees which were established to gather information pertaining to various appropriate topics.
            c. Science demonstrations on:
                1. Effects of rain and weight on a sod runway.
                2. How a plane flies.
                3. How a jet engine works.
                4. How clouds are formed.
                5. Wind effects on flying.
                6. How lights work.
            d. Show the films and filmstrips, *Airport America, Airport Activities,* and *Air Around Us.*

- e. Use reading lists, indexes, and tables of contents to find information about airport workers and airplanes.
- f. Set up small group projects to:
  1. Draw a floor plan of a terminal.
  2. Draw an airport including buildings, runways, and parking spaces.
  3. Find information on the different types of airplanes.
  4. Build airplane models.
  5. Find the shortest distances and fastest means of travel between a few designated places.
- g. Read stories—both teacher and children.
- h. Learn to read and interpret air sectionals.

Sample Unit Excerpt II—A Social Science Education Approach to the Primary Level Study of Human Groups

During a recent workshop sponsored by the Cooperative Center for Social Science Education at Ohio University, participating classroom teachers developed plans which would be used later with children. Two excerpts from those plans are presented here to show how emphasis is placed upon the involvement of children in inquiring into data which has been selected to develop a major idea or concept in the social sciences.

Bear in mind that these sample units represent the preplanning of teachers and that these plans will be modified and extended as a result of experiences with children in the classroom. It is suggested that you develop a plan for teaching a specific concept using these samples for guidance. Use your own plan with a group of children or in a peer teaching situation.

Sample Lesson Plan—Primary Level

Major Question:

How do individuals interact within various groups and how are they dependent upon the individuals with these groups to satisfy their basic needs?

Implementing Question:

To what groups do we belong?

Objectives:
1. To identify the family as one of the groups to which the child belongs.
2. To identify a family as people who live together.
3. To construct a family group with the use of pictures.
4. To identify families as being different in size and structure.
5. To construct and interpret a histogram.

Appendix C

Generalizations:
1. A family is made up of people who live together in a home.
2. The family size may differ from family to family.
3. A family may include people who do not live together.

Vehicle Media:
1. Picture of a family group including mother, father and children.
2. Pictures showing individuals who differ in size, age, sex and race. Mount these on oaktag cards approximately 6" x 8".

Data:
1. Show a picture of one type of a family group. Possible questions:
    a. What do you see in this picture?
    b. What do you think is happening?
    c. What name would you give to these people?
    d. Where are these people?

Probable Hypothesis:

These people make a family group.

Data:
2. Place mounted pictures on the chalkboard ledge. Have children, one at a time, come up and choose pictures to represent the various members in their family group and tell about them. Note the different sizes of families and the people within the family group.

Data:
3. Make a histogram, charting the sizes of family groups. Example:

CHART C-1. Family Sizes

				X			
	X			X			
	X	X		X	X		
	X	X		X	X		
members	3	4	5	6	7	8	9

Have the child place his X in the column showing the number of members in his family.

Lesson Plan

(This will probably cover several days work.)

Implementing Questions:

   To what groups do we belong?

Behavioral objectives:

1. Child will use words, such as, groups, family, and relative.
2. He will identify some groups to which he belongs.
3. He will describe the family as one of these groups.
4. He will discover that all individuals do not belong to the same groups.
5. He will be able to identify the formal names of some of the groups in his community.

Strategy and Vehicles:

   Teacher has pictures on display and shows some slides depicting families in various cultures similar to and somewhat unlike that of the community. She reads a story about a child in a family situation. (Example: "Big Brother," by Charlotte Zolotow, Harper & Bros., 1960.) Teacher asks,

Teacher's Questions	Child's Possible Answers
What do we notice about the people in these pictures, slides, and story?	1. All are happy (or sad). 2. All are busy or resting. 3. All belong to a family.
What is a family?	1. A family is people. 2. A family is our people. 3. A family is people who are related. 4. A family lives together.
Can a family be animals such as cats or dogs?	1. Yes, animals have families. 2. Animals are not really part of our family. 3. You can't have animals and people in one family.
What people live in a family?	1. Most families are mother, father, brothers, and sisters. 2. Not all families have all those and some have more.

Appendix C 379

Can a family have any other members? What do we call them?	Sometimes grandmothers, grandfathers, aunts, uncles, and cousins are members of a family. We call people in our family relatives or relations, etc.
Have you ever heard of another name for people when they are together?	1. They are a group. 2. They are a team. 3. They are a gang.
To what groups do you belong? Teacher might write the names of these groups on the board. Then, "How many of you belong to this group, this one, etc.?" YMCA? Sunday School class? A church group? A school? Cub Scouts? Dramatics club? Girl Scouts? Brownies? Junior church choir? Swim class? Jewish Center groups? Ballet class? Little League team? Reading group?	Child indicates to which group he belongs.
What can we say then about the groups to which we belong?	1. All of us belong to more than one group. 2. None of us belongs to all of the groups.

Evaluation:

This might take the following forms:

1. Teacher presents a chart showing various pictures including mothers, fathers, children, dogs, cats, goldfishes, a house, a car, etc. "Pick out the members of a family." Any family would be accepted as correct, providing it did not mix people and animals and did not include inanimate objects.

2. The child might be asked to draw a picture or to tell about a group to which he belongs.

Bibliography and Subvehicles:

1. Pictures of family life may be collected or obtained as collections from the school or public library.

2. The audio-visual department of the school will have slides on life among the American Indians, in foreign lands, and in a community in the U.S., showing family life.

3. The following are some books which have pictures of family life in the U.S. and in other lands:

   North Africa: Economakis, Olga. *Oasis of the Stars.* New York: Coward-McCann, Inc., 1965.

   School groups: Engeman, Jack. *My First Days at School.* New York: Bobbs-Merrill Co., 1960.

   Mexico: Garrett, Helen. *Angelo, the Naughty One.* New York: Viking Press, 1944.

   Caucasian U.S.: Greene, Carla. *I Want to Be a Homemaker.* Chicago, Illinois: Children's Press, 1961.

   Israel: Pinney, Roy. *Young Israel.* New York: Dodd Mead, 1963.

   American Negro: Scott, Ann Herbert. *Big Cowboy Western.* New York: Lothrop, Lee & Shepard Co., Inc., 1965.

Sample Unit Excerpt III—A Social Science Education Plan for Developing Concept of Adaptation

The teachers who developed this plan of study chose to relate several topics that have been included in conventional social studies programs. As you analyze this plan, what evidence do you find of a concern for the development of inquiry skills, for concept centered experiences? Are the purposes set forth in the rationale reflected in the questions and activities?

What use could you make of this study plan if you decided to involve children in an investigation of adaptation in your own community? How can adaptation take on personal characteristics that are within the experiences of children?

Level 3

Developed by: Ron Gaydosh, Eleanor Nonemaker

Major Concept: Adaptation

Relating Topics:

  Indians (of New Jersey and others)

  Early Colonization

Appendix C 381

Traders

Colonizers

Generalizations:

Early man tended to adapt his way of life to the resources supplied by the area (climate) in which he lived.

Basic *needs* remain the same but *wants* may be added as new factors are introduced.

Adaptation to or modification of an environment is tempered both by the environment and the people.

Man's use of land depends up climate and what the land offers (forests, mountains, plains, water supply, etc.).

What man *needs* to survive differs from what he *wants*.

Each member of the community (family, organization) has his own contribution (work) to do upon which the others are dependent.

People satisfy their wants and needs in different ways (related to the first generalization, "haves" and "have-nots").

People have basic desires to obtain what they need and protect what they have.

Knowing about people is basic to understanding them.

There are ways of communicating even though different languages are spoken.

Wants may become almost as basic as *needs* in terms of the society in which one lives.

Skills:

1. Listening
2. Discussing
3. Drawing inferences (from experience, pictures, maps, stories, information, etc.)
4. Observing
5. Differentiating between fact and opinion
6. Map reading (directions, differentiation between land and water, topography, legend of a map)
7. Appreciation of a legend (story) (different meanings of "legend")
8. Applying to other situations

9. Relating own experiences
10. Organizing information
11. Evaluating in terms of: importance (pertinence), reliability, etc.

Questions to stimulate inquiry, interest, and give direction:

1. What does everyone, no matter who he is or where he lives, need if he is to survive?

2. Have you ever driven into the country where practically no one lives? What is it like? What would . . . ? Glen Ridge? . . . ? be like if we took away all the things that people have made? Where would you start, what would you have to work with if you had none of the tools that we know and use today? What would you have to start with?

3. Who were the first people who came to live here and had these problems to start? Why do you suppose they settled here? What did this area have to offer them? How do you think they used these resources? Why do you think that they built houses and not tents (tepees)? Why were they able to grow some of their own vegetables? What food was available that they would not have to grow for themselves? What did they wear? Why? Why do you suppose that they were peaceable (unwarlike)?

Culmination of first area of study of New Jersey (local) Indians and those from representative areas of the country (comparison of Indian cultures).

Objectives:

1. Preparation for field trip to museum.
2. Organize information.
3. Draw tentative conclusions in terms of the following generalizations:

   Early man tended to adapt his way of life to the resources supplied by the area (climate in which he lived).

   Man's use of land depends upon climate and what the land offers (forests, plains, etc.).

   Each member of the community (family, organization) has his own contribution (work) to do upon which the others are dependent.

   People satisfy their wants and needs in different ways (related to generalization).

   Knowing about people is basic to understanding them.

   There are ways of communicating even though different languages are spoken.

Appendix C

Skills:

1. Discussing
2. Organizing
3. Drawing inferences and supporting them
4. Differentiating between fact (actuality) and stereotype
5. Appreciation of legend, custom, ingenuity, and creativity in manipulating environment

Visual materials:

1. Pictures from books, collections.
2. Maps
3. Artifacts and reproductions of them
4. Materials brought in, contributed or made by children

Guiding questions: (suggested)

1. What did we decide were the basic needs of *all* people?
2. Did all Indians have homes? Were they all the same? Why? (or why not?) In what ways did they differ?
3. Did all Indians wear the same kind of clothing? Why? (or why not?)
4. Did they all eat the same kinds of food? Why or why not?
5. Why were there differences in costume, ceremonies, ceremonial dress?
6. How did they obtain other things that they wanted or needed? (trade, wampum, etc.)
7. Why did some Indians settle in one place and others move from place to place?
8. In what ways were all of these Indians the same? Why?
9. What might you expect to see at the museum?
10. Do you think that we know all there is to know about Indians or do you think we will learn more? Ideas? (might list some of these)

Second day:

Trip to local museum where there is a good representative collection of artifacts of the Indians of different geographic areas of the country. Children sit on Indian rugs, handle various tools, bowls, masks, etc. Trained docent leads them in discussion, discrimination of the different displays (clothing, utensils, ceremonial dress, etc.). Materials used and reasons for, etc.

Third day:

Evaluation:

1. Were there things that you learned that you had not understood or known before?
2. Did what you have seen support the ideas we have had? How? In what ways?
3. Did anything give you other ideas or information that would reject or alter your conclusions?
4. What did you like best? Why?
5. Do you think the Indians did a pretty good job of making use of the things they had? ("things" meaning resources, etc.)
6. Have you changed your ideas about Indians, how they acted, what they were really like, etc., now that we have studied about them?
7. In what ways?
8. What do you think has been the reason for this change? * (* assumption on part of teacher)

Bibliography—used in building unit for review:

1. Grant, Bruce. *American Indians Yesterday and Today.* E. P. Dutton & Co., Inc., New York, 1958. An elementary encyclopedia of Indian tribes and related items arranged in alphabetical order—pictured, simply written.
2. Leavitt, Dr. Jerome E. *America and the Indians.* Children's Press, Chicago, 1962. Indians of each area considered and representative tribes including those of the eastern woodlands.
3. (Discovery book) *The Delawares.* Garrard, New York, 1960's. Very simply written story of life of the Delaware Indians of which Lenni-Lenape were a branch—well illustrated.
4. Bleeker, Sonia. *Delaware Indians.* Morrow, New York, 1953. Complete consideration of way of living, life, customs—written for children (better readers—4th grade level). Pertinent line drawing illustrations. Other tribes in series (Iroquois, etc.).
5. Martini, Teri. *True Book of Indians.* Children's Press, Chicago, 1954. Most significant and demonstrable differences of ways of life of a few characteristic tribes. Pictures, simply written.
6. McNeer, May and Ward, Lynd. *The American Indian Story.* Ariel Book, New York, 1963. Way of life based on legends, use for pictures, reading to children, or for precocious readers.

Appendix C

7. Brewster, Benjamin. *First Book of Indians.* Franklin Watts, Inc., New York, 1950. Sign language, legends, illustrations, comparison of Indian cultures, simply written.
8. Holling C. Holling. *Book of Indians.* Platt and Munk Co., Inc., New York. Pictures, stories, characteristic cultures, glossary, excellent introduction.
9. Israel, Marion. *Apaches.* Melmort Publishers, Inc., Chicago, 1959. People, customs, pictures, simply written.

Rationale for Study of Indian Cultures:

We realize that in many communities the study of Indian cultures is considered passé, outmoded, old hat—whichever term may apply. We defend and champion the role in our curriculum which this study plays (or should play).

1. The topic in itself is not the goal but lends itself well toward engendering the basic understandings we are trying to develop. That development of these concepts is confined or contained only within selected, "modern," or "sophisticated" subject matters is both an unrealistic and false assumption.
2. The Indian culture is basic to that of the white man. He provided the tools and adaptations necessary to sustain life in a strange environment. White man rightly utilized the experiences of these earlier settlers in their initial habitation of a strange land to which they added refinements from their own background of experience. This has been a continuing process throughout the history of the country.
3. The idea that we can deny the Indian cultures which have been so basic to our own and which, in some parts of the country, are still existent is both unrealistic and unperceptive.
4. A finer example of fact vs. stereotype in actuality is difficult to find. And we have it in terms that children will understand.
5. Children enjoy this study which relates so directly to their conceptual growth and understanding of peoples.

To reiterate, it is not the topic, tool, or vehicle (whichever terminology we use). It is the end toward which we are striving that determines the true value of an area of study.

Appendix D

Opinions of Young Americans

Prepared by Milton E. Ploghoft and Albert G. Leep for The Cooperative Center for Social Science Education, Ohio University, 1970.

1. An official of the Black Panther party wanted to speak on a local radio station to answer charges made against his group. The radio station, and later, the local newspaper, refused to carry the Black Panther position, saying that the Panthers were not interested in the general welfare of the nation.

    (a) Agree with the action of radio and newspaper
    (u) Undecided
    (d) Disagree

2. Gov. Rhodes of Ohio, on February 3, 1970, called for strong police action to remove "hippies" and other undesirable persons from areas near universities where they seem to live.

    (a) Agree with the governor's suggestion
    (u) Undecided
    (d) Disagree

3. A philosophy professor in a California University was relieved of her position when she acknowledged that she advocated communist economic ideas.

    (a) Agree with the dismissal action
    (u) Undecided
    (d) Disagree

4. In the 1960's, a group of black separatists demanded that American Negroes be allowed to form their own black Nation in the United States. They pointed out that Negroes were in the majority in Alabama and that would be a good place to form a black Nation where they could live in their own way.

Appendix D 387

    (a) Agree with the black Nation idea
    (u) Undecided
    (d) Disagree

5. Chicago police, in the winter of 1969, broke into the apartment of several Black Panther leaders and killed two persons. The police reported that they found guns and ammunition there and stated that the Panthers were a threat to the United States.

    (a) Agree with the police action
    (u) Undecided
    (d) Disagree

6. In a traditionally Democratic stronghold in Alabama, a progressive Republican candidate found it impossible to buy radio time or newspaper space for his campaign messages. When the Republican complained that he should have the chance to present his views, he was ignored by the owners of radio and newspaper.

    (a) Agree with the radio and newspaper owners
    (u) Undecided
    (d) Disagree

7. A local police chief glanced through the book *Tropic of Cancer* and ordered bookstores to stop selling it.

    (a) Agree that a police chief may need to do this
    (u) Undecided
    (d) Disagree

8. The press secretary for a United States President said that he was concerned about the television coverage and commentary following presidential speeches. So the press secretary asked the major networks to inform him beforehand of the way they planned to handle future presidential addresses. The television officials complained that this was unfair interference by the government.

    (a) Agree with the press secretary's request
    (u) Undecided
    (d) Disagree

9. The police believed that three college students (roommates) possessed marijuana. When the police went to the room they found only two of the students so they held the two students in the room for five hours waiting for the other roommate to return, believing that he might have the marijuana on him. The students protested that they were illegally held since they were not arrested or charged.

(a) Agree with the police action
(u) Undecided
(d) Disagree

10. When Sharon Tate was murdered in 1969, her gardener was immediately arrested as a suspect. He claimed that he was beaten and otherwise abused by police before he was released. The police claimed that it is sometimes necessary to use harsh measures to get suspects to tell the truth.

(a) Agree with the police
(u) Undecided
(d) Disagree

11. A local high school library received copies of English language magazines from the Soviet Union and Mainland China. A few parents protested and several organizations asked the school board to order the magazines removed. The board agreed.

(a) Agree with the school board action
(u) Undecided
(d) Disagree

12. A member of a school board recently called for a curriculum that stressed basic skills of reading, writing, and arithmetic at all levels. "Most people will never become capable of helping decide what is good for them and society so we should emphasize job preparation and leave leadership to the few who will be able to handle it."

(a) Agree with the board member
(u) Undecided
(d) Disagree

13. In the spring of 1968 a Pennsylvania school board took action to require all pupils to join in an opening prayer each day, the prayer to be led by the teacher. The board acknowledged that its action was contrary to U.S. Supreme Court rulings on the matter, but the board wanted the pupils to become law abiding citizens and they thought that a required daily prayer would help.

(a) Agree with the school board action
(u) Undecided
(d) Disagree

14. Mr. Wilson, a social studies teacher, stated that his main purpose is to help the pupils realize that the American way of life is superior to that of any other country.

Appendix D 389

    (a)   Agree
    (u)   Undecided
    (d)   Disagree

15. In Nazi Germany it was common for the secret police to break into the homes of persons suspected of being disloyal to the Third Reich. Accused persons were often given the "third degree" to obtain information, but the Nazis argued that they did these things to protect their country.
    - (a) Agree that the secret police actions were justified
    - (u) Undecided
    - (d) Disagree

16. A visitor from Yugoslavia was invited to talk to a high school class about life in the communist system of his nation. The talk was later cancelled by the principal who said that it was dangerous to expose young students to such ideas.
    - (a) Agree with the principal
    - (u) Undecided
    - (d) Disagree

17. The Soviet Union announced in June 1969, that an American professor was asked to leave that country because he had been spreading false information about the superior way of life in the United States.
    - (a) Agree with the Soviet action
    - (u) Undecided
    - (d) Disagree

18. Since the arrival of white men in North America, the Indians have been forced off of the land that they once occupied. Reservations were set up for the Indians to live on and the U.S. government gave them living allowances. This treatment of the Indians was right since it made it possible to build a modern, democratic nation here.
    - (a) Agree
    - (u) Undecided
    - (d) Disagree

19. In a recent civil war in Nigeria, the Ibo tribesmen tried to form the nation of Biafra, claiming that they should be allowed to have their own government and live in their own way. Many Americans felt that the Nigerian government should have allowed the Biafrans to form their own country.
    - (a) Agree with the Biafrans
    - (u) Undecided
    - (d) Disagree

20. In an effort to end the War Between the States (U.S. Civil War) General Sherman led his Union troops on the famous "March through Georgia." The soldiers tore up railroad tracks, burned barns, killed cattle and destroyed supplies of grain. This caused much suffering to the people in Georgia, but it was a good idea since it helped to end the war.

    (a) Agree that it was all right
    (u) Undecided
    (d) Disagree

21. Several hundred college students were peacefully protesting the presence of naval recruiters on the campus. The local draft board noticed that some men holding student deferments were shown in pictures of the protest activity. The deferments for these men were cancelled and they were drafted immediately.

    (a) Agree with the draft board action
    (u) Undecided
    (d) Disagree

22. In South Africa, the native Africans have been forced to live on reservations (Bantustans) by the Europeans who have developed the country, built cities, and created jobs. The European settlers say that everyone is better off now, that progress has been brought to an area that was underdeveloped.

    (a) Agree with the European settlers
    (u) Undecided
    (d) Disagree

23. In the closing months of the Biafran rebellion, the Nigerian government tried to stop shipments of food and other supplies into Biafra. Many Biafrans died of starvation and disease, but the Nigerian government said this helped to end the war, so its actions were right.

    (a) Agree
    (u) Undecided
    (d) Disagree

24. There is some danger in studying opinions of people on the topics included here since it may lead some persons to lose faith in ideas they have held for a long time.

    (a) Agree
    (u) Undecided
    (d) Disagree

Appendix D

25. In the spring of 1970, many citizens and some public officials of St. Clair County in Alabama refused to assist the workers on a Black Muslim owned farm in the investigation of suspected poisoning of many cattle on the farm. The citizens who refused to assist indicated that the Black Muslims had purchased a farm in an area in which they were not wanted, therefore, the community had a right to drive them out by poisoning the cattle.

    (a) Agree with the citizens and public officials who refused to assist in the investigation
    (u) Undecided
    (d) Disagree

26. Some protestors of the war in Vietnam have refused to pay Federal income taxes because the taxes are used to support the fighting, and as citizens, they feel they have the right to determine when they should pay taxes and how the tax they pay should be spent.

    (a) Agree with the citizens refusing to pay tax
    (u) Undecided
    (d) Disagree

27. Mr. Jones was called for jury duty in a controversial civil case involving an important industry in the community. Although Mr. Jones' salary would continue to be paid during his participation on the jury, he asked to be released from the duty because he did not want to get involved in making a court decision that might offend some of the influential people in the community.

    (a) Agree with Mr. Jones' decision
    (u) Undecided
    (d) Disagree

28. In a recent protest meeting on a college campus, 400 of a student body of 14,000 presented a statement of demands for curricular change. The President of the University suggested that the total student body and faculty be allowed to vote on the desirability of each of the demands. The student protest group indicated that the students and faculty who were not at the meeting had forfeited their rights and the demands should stand as presented.

    (a) Agree with the protest group
    (u) Undecided
    (d) Disagree

29. The Business Man's Association in a town in Indiana recently organized its forces to prevent a clothing chain from establishing a store in the community because the clothing stores in town could not financially

stand the competition of a chain owned store. The President of the Business Man's Association said that the group felt that they had a right to decide what new businesses should be allowed to enter the town.

(a) Agree with the Business Man's Association
(u) Undecided
(d) Disagree

30. In Columbus, Ohio, during the winter of 1969, a woman was attacked and robbed in front of a supermarket. Many observers of this incident refused to assist the woman or to assist the police in identifying the suspects. One observer indicated that it was none of his business so he stayed out of it, besides if one reported the crime or identified the suspect he had to testify in court and that took a lot of time and bother.

(a) Agree with the observers of the crime
(u) Undecided
(d) Disagree

Recent Opinions of Young Americans on Selected Issues

In the spring of 1970, more than 2,000 graduating high school seniors in four widely separated regions of the United States responded to the items in the OPINIONS OF YOUNG AMERICANS instrument. The results are presented here with some discussion in order that you may compare these responses with those of your own class.

Nine of the items dealt in some manner with censorship and control of ideas. These were items 1, 3, 6, 7, 8, 11, 16, 17 and 24. In all of these items except 3, 8 and 17, the students strongly rejected the idea of censorship or limiting the access that people should have to a variety of ideas.

You will notice that there were other items that dealt with the right of due process for persons accused or suspected of criminal behavior, and again the students indicated a strong support for the constitutional guarantees. With respect to the right of dissent, you will notice that the students did not believe that war dissenters had the right to withhold payment of taxes which would be used to support a war. However, the students disapproved of draft boards reclassifying for immediate call those students who were seen in a crowd of people which was objecting to the presence of military recruiters on campus.

An item by item summary is given here in percentages, and it is suggested that you and your colleagues compare your own positions with those of the high school seniors. It should be pointed out that the responding seniors from these four widely separated regions of the United States did not differ significantly in major positions on most of the items. How would you account for such strong agreement? What other information would you like to have? How will you explain the agreement or disagreement that your class may demonstrate on the OPINIONS TEST?

Appendix D

CHART D-1.

Question	% Agree	% Undecided	% Disagree	Question	% Agree	% Undecided	% Disagree
1.	25	14	61	16.	4	9	87
2.	23	20	57	17.	20	34	46
3.	44	22	34	18.	10	13	77
4.	14	17	69	19.	53	31	16
5.	24	23	53	20.	24	28	48
6.	5	8	87	21.	18	11	71
7.	6	16	78	22.	13	23	64
8.	30	27	43	23.	12	16	72
9.	15	10	75	24.	12	17	71
10.	7	8	85	25.	6	12	82
11.	15	16	69	26.	27	22	51
12.	20	25	55	27.	16	17	67
13.	15	17	68	28.	13	18	69
14.	21	20	59	29.	17	24	59
15.	6	12	82	30.	2	7	91

How might you use similar opinion samplers with elementary school children? What purposes might be served?

Appendix E

Recent Projects in Social Science Education

Introduction

Since the Sputnik achievement by the Soviets, a rash of federally supported research projects and developmental institutes have contributed to the curriculum areas, including, most recently, the social studies. We will attempt to present a brief overview of the scope and nature of the curriculum research and development projects in social studies inasmuch as the programs in the schools are beginning to incorporate ideas generated by the projects.

Textbooks and other commercially produced instructional materials are beginning to reflect the changes suggested by various projects and, accordingly, we will include excerpts from selected materials in order that you may gain familiarity with their major elements.

What was the nature of the projects?

A number of the social studies curriculum projects incorporated comprehensive features in an effort to attain an interdisciplinary approach that would be particularly suited to the elementary school. Examples of this type were the activities of the Concepts and Inquiry Project of the Educational Research Council of America, the Minnesota Social Studies Project, The Elkhart Project, and the Taba Curriculum Project.

Other projects centered their efforts upon single discipline approaches. The Georgia Anthropology Project, the Developmental Economic Education Project (DEEP), The Minority History and Culture Project, and the Lincoln-Filene Center Project in Citizenship and Public Affairs are examples.

Georgia Anthropology Project. The scope of the Georgia Project is revealed by the student materials which have been developed. The Concept of Culture is introduced and developed in the levels K-4, and topics, such as, race, caste and prejudice, life cycle, urban community, and the Indian in American culture, indicate areas of study. The materials produced by the Georgia Anthropology Project focus upon the cognitive learning of the "concept system" of Anthropology. A programmed text for the fifth grade deals with archeological methods.

Appendix E 395

Committee on Civic Education. Materials from this project, based at the School of Law at the University of California at Los Angeles, attend to the principles of democratic processes, and stress is placed upon skills of critical analysis rather than the mastery of bodies of information. A casebook for students constitutes the primary instructional unit.

Lincoln-Filene Center Project. For the elementary level, the materials consist of two volumes dealing with the intergroup relations dimension of citizenship. Volume II includes learning activities, instructional units, and bibliographies for pupil and teachers.

ERC Social Science Project. Once known as the Greater Cleveland Social Science Program, the Concepts and Inquiry materials were finally developed by The Educational Research Council of America. The scope of this program is suggested by grade level topics which range as follows:

> Kindergarten—"Learning about the World" and "Children in other Lands."
> Grade I—"Learning about our Country" and "Explorers and Discoverers."
> Grade II—"Communities at Home and Abroad."
> Grade IV—"The Story of Agriculture" and "The Story of Industry."
> Grade V—"The Human Adventure" and "The Middle East."
> Grade VI—"The Human Adventure" and "Latin America."

The emphasis is upon a sequential development of concepts and generalizations drawn from the several social science disciplines.

The Elkhart Project. Professor Lawrence Senesh, an economic educator, initiated this project as a primary level economic education activity. It was expanded into a K-12 activity which attempted to integrate all of the social sciences.

The primary level materials, now commercially available, appear to be economically oriented, the titles being *Families at Work, Neighbors at Work,* and *Cities at Work.*

Grade four materials deal with the study of regions of the state, the U.S. as a political, economic, and cultural unit is dealt with in grade five, and in grade six, the regions of the world are viewed from the standpoint of economic development.

MATCH Program. The units of this program involve multi-media kits which are designed to support learning through the use of real objects. Units deal with "The Japanese Family," "A House of Ancient Greece," "The City," and others now in planning or production stages. The MATCH Box kits contain films, pictures, games, recordings, and a teacher's guide.

Minnesota Social Studies Project. This project has attempted to present an integrated program drawn from the several disciplines although the concept of culture is the basic theme which runs throughout. The Kindergarten – Sixth Grade sequence is as follows:

K—The Earth As the Home of Man
1 —Families Around the World   Cultural Diversity
2 —Families Around the World
3 —Communities Around the World—Schools, Churches, Government
4 —Communities Around the World—Economics
5 —Regional Studies—U.S., Canada, Latin America
6 —The Formulation of American Society

Appendix F

Bibliography

Readings for Teachers

In addition to a carefully chosen list of books which provide reliable background on social studies and social science education, every teacher should keep in touch with the "other side" of the social world through continuing contact with the following periodicals:

Atlas, 1180 Avenue of the Americas, New York 10036 (a periodical publication of articles drawn from all over the world).

Childhood Education, by the Association for Childhood Education, Washington, D.C. (Published monthly October–May, especially concerned with children ages 2–12.)

Commentary, 165 East 56th Street, New York. (A journal that provides broad coverage and analysis of current issues and affairs.)

Educational Leadership, by the Association for Supervision and Curriculum Development, Washington, D.C. (Published monthly, October–May, devoted to curriculum and staff development areas.)

Phi Delta Kappan, by Phi Delta Kappa, Bloomington, Indiana (the official publication of this professional fraternity covers research areas of interest to all educators).

Saturday Review, 380 Madison Avenue, New York. (Published weekly, a magazine of general interest. Sections on Education and Communications are of interest to teachers.)

Social Education, by the National Council for the Social Studies, Washington, D.C. (eight issues per year).

The Center Magazine, The Center for the Study of Democratic Institutions, Santa Barbara, California. (Contains articles written by the resident scholars of the Center, often providing different views of common concerns.)

Trans-Action, Rutgers University, New Brunswick, New Jersey. (A periodical that focuses upon the contemporary dimensions of the social and behavioral sciences.)

Books for the Teacher's Professional Shelf

Berelson, Bernard, ed. *The Behavioral Sciences Today.* New York: Harper and Row, 1963.

Brookover, Wilbur B. and Gottlieb, David. *A Sociology of Education.* New York: American Book Co., 1964.

Eiseley, Loren. *The Immense Journey.* New York: Vintage Books, 1957. A fascinating, non-technical book by an imaginative anthropologist, helps man find his place along a grand route.

Hanna, Paul R.; Sabaroff, Rose E.; Davies, Gordon F.; and Farrar, Charles R. *Geography in the Social Studies.* Boston: Houghton Mifflin Co., 1966.

Joyce, Bruce. *Strategies for Elementary Social Science Education.* Chicago: Science Research Associates, 1965.

Preston, Ralph. *Teaching Social Studies in the Elementary Schools.* New York: Holt, Rinehart and Winston, 1968.

Servey, Richard E. *Social-Studies Instruction in the Elementary School.* San Francisco: Chandler Publishing Co., 1967.

Social Science Seminar Series. Muessig, Raymond H. and Rogers, Vincent R., ed. Columbus, Ohio: The Charles E. Merrill Publishing Co., 1965. A series of inexpensive paperbacks dealing with the content and methodologies of anthropology, geography, political science, sociology, history, and economics.

Resources for Children

Almedingen, E. M. *A Candle at Dusk.* New York: Farrar, Straus & Giroux, 1969.

Archer, Jules. *Red Rebel: Tito of Yugoslavia.* New York: Messner, 1968.

Asimov, Isaac. *The Near East. 10,000 Years of History.* Boston: Houghton Mifflin, 1968.

Baumann, Hans. *Alexander's Great March.* New York: Walck, 1968.

Berna, Paul. *The Mule on the Expressway.* New York: Pantheon, 1968.

Boucher, Alan. *The Land Seekers.* New York: Farrar, Straus & Giroux, 1968.

Brown, Roy. *A Saturday in Pudney.* New York: Macmillan, 1968.

Chapin, Henry. *The Search for Atlantis.* New York: Macmillan, 1968.

Chubb, Thomas Caldecot. *The Venetians: Merchant Princes.* New York: Viking, 1968.

Cohen, Robert C. *The Color of Man.* New York: Random House, 1968.

Collins, Robert. *East to Cathay: The Silk Road.* New York: McGraw-Hill, 1968.

Appendix F

Coolidge, Olivia. *The Golden Days of Greece.* New York: Thomas Y. Crowell, 1968.

Daudet, Alphonse. *The Brave Little Goat of Monsieur Seguin; a Picture Story from Provence.* Cleveland, Ohio: World, 1968.

Doherty, C. H. *Tunnels.* New York: Meredith, 1968.

Dorbrin, Arnold. *Italy: Modern Renaissance.* Camden, N.J.: Thomas Nelson, 1968.

Epstein, Sam and Beryl. *A Holiday Book: European Folk Festivals.* Champaign, Ill.: Garrard, 1968.

Feigenbaum, Lawrence H. and Kalman Seigel, *Israel: Crossroads of Conflict.* Chicago: Rand McNally, 1968.

Fisher, Aileen. *Easter.* New York: Thomas Y. Crowell, 1968.

Garfield, Nancy. *The Tuesday Elephant.* New York: Thomas Y. Crowell, 1968.

Glubok, Shirley. *Discovering Tut-ankh-Amen's Tomb.* New York: Macmillan, 1968.

Glubok, Shirley. *Knights in Armor.* New York: Harper & Row, 1969.

Green, Roger Lancelyn. *Tales of Ancient Egypt.* New York: Walck, 1968.

Havrevold, Finn. *Undertow.* New York: Atheneum, 1968.

Heady, Eleanor B. *Coat of the Earth: The Story of Grass.* New York: W. W. Norton, 1968.

Heady, Eleanor B. *When the Stones Were Soft; East African Fireside Tales.* New York: Watts, 1968.

Heintze, Carl. *The Circle of Fire: The Great Chain of Volcanoes and Earth Faults.* New York: Meredith, 1968.

Helfman, Elizabeth S. *Wheels, Scoops, and Buckets; How People Lift Water for Their Fields.* New York: Lothrop, Lee & Shepard, 1968.

Hitin Aung, U. and Traeger, Helen G. *A Kingdom Lost for a Drop of Honey, and Other Burmese Folktales.* New York: Parents' Magazine Press, 1968.

Hoag, Edwin. *The Road of Man.* New York: Putnam, 1968.

Hodges, Cyril W. *The Spanish Armada.* New York: Coward-McCann, 1968.

Household, Geoffrey. *Prisoner of the Indies.* Boston: Little, Brown, 1968.

Howard, Cecil. *Pizarro and the Conquest of Peru.* New York: American Heritage, 1968.

Jonsson, Runer. *Viki Viking.* Cleveland, Ohio: World, 1968.

Kannik, Preben, *Military Uniforms in Color.* New York: Macmillan, 1968.

Kaula, Edna Mason. *The Bantu Africans.* New York: Watts, 1968.

Klagsbrun, Francine. *The First Book of Speces.* New York: Watts, 1968.

Landry, Lionel. *The Land and People of Burma.* Philadelphia: Lippincott, 1968.

Lang, Robert. *The Land and People of Pakistan.* Philadelphia: Lippincott, 1968.

Laurence. *A Village in Normandy.* Indianapolis, Ind.: Bobbs-Merrill, 1968.

Leskov, Nikolai. *The Wild Beast.* New York: Funk & Wagnalls, 1968.

Liston, Robert A. *Downtown: Our Challenging Urban Problems.* New York: Delacorte, 1968.

Luhrmann, Winifred B. *The First Book of Gold.* New York: Watts, 1968.

McGiffen, Lee. *Yankee of the Yalu: Philo Norton McGiffin, American Captain in the Chinese Navy (1885–1895).* New York: Dutton, 1968.

McGuire, Edna. *The Maoris of New Zealand.* New York: Macmillan, 1968.

Macfarlane, Iris. *The Children of Baird God Hill.* McGraw-Hill, 1968.

Maddock, Reginald. *The Great Bow.* Chicago: Rand McNally, 1968.

Masey, Mary L. *Stories of the Steppes: Kazakh Folktales.* New York: McKay, 1968.

Mosel, Arlene. *Tikki Tikki Tembo, retold.* New York: Holt, Rinehart & Winston, 1968.

Mother Goose. *Hurrah, We're Outward Bound.* New York: Doubleday, 1968.

Peterson, Harold L. *A History of Body Armor.* New York: Scribner, 1968.

Ransome, Arthur. *The Fool of the World and the Flying Ship: A Russian Tale.* New York: Farrar, Straus & Giroux, 1968.

Rice, Tamara Talbot. *Czars and Czarinas of Russia.* New York: Lothrop, Lee & Shepard, 1968.

Riwkin-Brick, Anna. *Gennet Lives in Ethiopia.* New York: Macmillan, 1968.

Rockwell, Anne. *Glass, Stones & Crown; the Abbe Suger and the Building of St. Denis.* New York: Atheneum.

Rose, Ronald. *Ngari, the Hunter.* New York: Harcourt, Brace & World, 1968.

Ross, Frank, Jr. *Transportation of Tomorrow.* New York: Lothrop, Lee & Shepard, 1968.

Schatz, Letta. *The Extraordinary Tug-of-War, retold.* Chicago: Follett, 1968.

Smith, Datus C., Jr. *The Land and People of Indonesia.* Philadelphia: Lippincott, 1968.

Spicer, Dorothy G., comp. *The Owl's Nest: Folktales from Friesland.* New York: Coward-McCann, 1968.

Appendix F 401

Stein, M. L. *Under Fire: The Story of American War Correspondents.* New York: Nessner, 1968.

Syme, Ronald. *Bolivar the Liberator.* New York: Morrow, 1968.

Tooze, Ruth. *Three Tales of Turtle.* New York: John Day, 1968.

Walker, Barbara. *The Dancing Palm Tree and Other Nigerian Folktales.* New York: Parents' Magazine Press, 1968.

Webb, Robert N. *Hannibal: Invader From Carthage.* New York: Watts, 1968.

Weiss, David A. *The Great Fire of London.* New York: Crown, 1968.

Wibberley, Leonard. *Attar of the Ice Valley.* New York: Farrar, Straus & Giroux, 1968.

Games and Simulations

This is a suggested list, only. It is intended to be of assistance to you in getting started in the use of a variety of learning resources. If possible, your class should arrange to obtain and use several of these games during the course.

GAME	DESCRIPTION	NO. OF PLAYERS	TIME INVOLVED	WHERE TO PURCHASE
Community Response	A simulation of a community hit by a localized natural disaster.	6–16	2–6 hours	Western Publishing School & Library Department 830 Third Ave. New York, N.Y. 10022
Consumer	A model of the consumer buying process involving players in the problems and economics of installment buying. Consumers compete to maximize their utility points for specific purchases	11–34	6 hours	Western Publishing School & Library Department 830 Third Ave. New York, N.Y. 10022
Credibility Gap	A board game of political lie detection based on possibility of administration's shielding citizens from truth by screen of lies.	2–4	30–90 minutes	Most large department or toy stores.
Crisis	Simulation of international conflict in which students form teams to manage the affairs of six fictional nations.	18–36	4 or more hours	Western Behavioral Science Institute 1121 Torrey Pines Rd. La Jolla, Calif. 60618
Democracy	A composite of eight different games which simulate the legislative process.	6–11	1–2½ hours	Bookstore National 4-H Center 7100 Connecticut Ave. Washington, D.C.

GAME	DESCRIPTION	NO. OF PLAYERS	TIME INVOLVED	WHERE TO PURCHASE
Economic System	Simulation of the interrelationship of a competitive economic system. Mine owners, manufacturers, workers and farmers market, produce and consume goods while trying to make a profit and maintain a high standard of living.	7–13	2–4 hours	Western Publishing School & Library Dept. 850 Third Avenue New York, N.Y. 10022
Election	A board game with map of the United States, and alternative routes in passing through states to compete for a majority of electoral votes.	2–6	1–4 hours	Most large department or toys stores.
Ghetto	Simulates the pressures that the urban poor live under and the choices that face them as they seek to improve their life situation.	7–10	2 or more hours	Western Publishing School & Library Dept. 850 Third Ave. New York, N.Y. 10022
Neighborhood	To stimulate development of an urban area. Teams of players plan an urban area. Students learn about social classes, segregation and integration.	4–12		Wellesley School Curriculum Center Wellesley, Mass.

GAME	DESCRIPTION	NO. OF PLAYERS	TIME INVOLVED	WHERE TO PURCHASE
Parent-Child	Simulates the relationship between a parent and an adolescent in respect to five issues differently important to both.	4–10	½ hour or more	Western Publishing School & Library Dept. 850 Third Ave. New York, N.Y. 10022
Pollution	Pupils take various community roles such as those of a chemical company owner or farmer. Each player seeks to maximize his profits even though his business may be polluting the streams and air.			Center for Collaborative Learning Wellesley Public School Phillips School Wellesley, Mass.

Name Index

Agnew, Spiro, 20
Alden, V. R., 345
Alpenfels, Ethel, 8
Anderson, James, 314
Anderson, Robert H., 246
Arendt, Hannah, 20
Armstrong, H. C., 49
Ausubel, D. P., 204, 345

Barr, David L., 273, 274
Barth, Alan, 34, 101, 102
Battle, H. J., 53
Beck, R., 54
Beiser, Morton, 204
Berelson, Bernard, 19
Berg, Harry, 363
Beyer, Barry K., 294, 295, 356
Billings, Neal A., 159
Black, H. C., 44
Blake, Paul, 8
Bleeker, Sonia, 384
Bloom, Benjamin S., 179, 181, 186, 187, 188, 226, 227, 246, 348, 363
Blumer, Herbert, 156
Bowerman, C. E., 204
Brandwein, Paul, 245
Breckenridge, Marian E., 196
Brewster, Benjamin, 385
Broek, Jan O. M., 137, 138, 139
Brookover, Wilbur, 201
Brown, B., 205
Brown, Edmund G., 124
Brown, James W., 270
Brownfain, J. J., 47
Brownell, W. A., 173

Bruner, Jerome S., 165, 191, 192, 193, 246
Buchanan, Scott, 207
Burns, Robert, 329
Burt, Cyril, 226

Cantril, H., 53
Carls, Norman, 241, 242
Carmichael, Stokeley, 34, 91, 92
Carpenter, Helen McCracken, 28
Carroll, John B., 173
Cartwright, William H., 5, 16, 345
Chessman, Caryl, 34, 123, 124, 125, 127, 128, 131
Clarke, Wentworth, 193, 210
Commager, Henry Steele, 134, 135
Commoner, Barry, 314
Connell, Joseph, 34, 73, 74
Cox, Benjamin C., 363
Crabtree, Charlotte, 228

Dalgliesh, Alice, 375
Davie, J. S., 205
Davis, Billie, 328
Dennis, Jack, 205
Deutsch, M., 205
Dewey, John, 6, 226, 235, 237
Dillon, J. D., 286
Dimond, Stanley, 173
Dixon, Jeanne, 23
Douglass, Malcolm P., 188
Doxsee, Gifford, 5

Easton, David, 149, 151, 205
Economakis, Olga, 380
Edgerton, Stephanie G., 229

Elkin, Frederick, 205
Ellington, Duke, 314
Ellsworth, Ruth, 229
Endres, Raymond J., 316
Engeman, Jack, 380

Fancett, Verna S., 173
Farson, Richard E., 34, 67
Fenton, Edwin, 8
Flanders, Ned A., 334, 345
Flattery, Sister M. J., 251
Fraser, Dorothy McClure, 8, 32, 176, 183, 188, 263, 268, 363
Frederick the Great, 10
Friedman, K. C., 205
Froebel, Friedrich, 235
Fromm, Erich, 34, 81, 82, 114
Fuchs, Estelle, 339, 341

Gabor, Zsa Zsa, 329
Galbraith, John K., 22
Garrett, Helen, 380
Gaydosh, Ron, 380
Gerard, B. S., 286
Getzel, J. W., 45, 229
Girvetz, Harry, 124
Godfrey, Arthur, 329
Gordon, I. J., 205
Grant, Bruce, 384
Gray, John, 226
Green, Carla, 380
Green, John A.
Griffin, Alan, 32

Hagerman, Neva, 246
Hamilton, Charles V., 34, 91, 92
Hanna, LaVonne A., 246
Hanna, Paul R., 32, 160
Harceleroad, Fred F., 270
Hartley E. L., 205
Hayes, James E., 338, 345
Hendrickson, G., 173
Herman, Wayne L. Jr., 17
Hickman, Warren, 157
Hicks, E. Perry, 294, 295
Hilgard, Ernest R., 264

Hodges, J. A., 345
Hodges, T., 280
Holling, C., 385
Horowitz, F. D., 205
Hunter, E. C., 345
Hutchins, Robert M., 19, 20

Israel, Marion, 385

Jarolimek, John, 310, 311
Jesus Christ, 276
Joyce, Bruce, 34, 117, 122, 156, 188, 229, 363

Kahn, Herman, 17
Kazamias, Andreas, 32
Keith, Lowell; Blake, Paul; and Tiedt, Sydney, 8
Keller, Charles R., 32
Kennedy, President, 137
Kenworthy, Leonard, 302
Kidd, John W., 32
Kilpatrick, William, 235
Kinch, J. W., 204
Kirk, Samuel, 48, 49
Klineberg, Otto, 295, 296
Koehl, Robert, 169, 302
Krothwohl, David R., 181, 186, 188, 363
Krug, Mark, 32

Lambert, Wallace E., 295, 296
Larrick, Nancy, 302
Lasswell, Harold, 149
Leavitt, Jerome, 384
Leeds, C. H., 345
Leep, Albert G., 386
Lerner, Max, 34, 111
Levin, H., 205
Lewis, Richard B., 270
Little, L. C., 286
Loukes, H., 345
Lowe, Olympia P., 202, 204

MacLean, E., 280
MacLuhan, Marshall, 4, 69

Name Index

Mager, Robert F., 175, 184, 187, 188
Mallan, John T., 156, 157
Mao-Tse Tung, 23, 299
Martini, Teri, 384
Martin, Richard J., 146, 148
Martin, W. E., 44
Masia, Bertram B., 181, 186, 188, 363
Massialas, Byron, 32, 222, 363
Mayer, Martin, 17
McAuley, John, 241, 242
McLendon, Jonathan C., 316
McNeer, May, 384
Mead, Margaret, 69, 209
Michaelis, John U., 6, 246, 310
Miller, Reuben G., 146, 148
Moore, B. M., 53
Muessig, Raymond H., 134, 143, 145, 147, 148, 150, 151, 167
Muller, Philip, 195, 196, 198, 204
Murdoch, William, 34, 73, 74

Nass, John B., 286
Nixon, Mrs. Richard, 313
Nixon, Richard, 313
Nonemaker, Eleanor, 380
North, Robert C., 17

Oliva, Peter F., 302

Panock, James V., 273, 274
Parker, Francis, 231
Parten, M. B., 205
Pelto, Pertti J., 144, 145
Perkins, Claude, 301
Perkins, F. T., 46
Perry, Commodore, 299, 300
Pestalozzi, Johann, 235
Phillips, Lewis, 270
Piaget, Jean, 195, 196
Pilch, J., 287
Pinney, Roy, 380
Ploghoft, Milton E., 7, 235, 247, 265, 293, 302, 314, 361, 386
Potter, Gladys L., 246

Preston, Ralph C., 7, 173, 188, 316
Price, Roy, 157, 158
Pyne, Joe, 329

Quillen, I. James, 173

Reese, Willard F., 318, 319
Rice, A. H., 287
Rich, J. M., 345
Robbins, Lionel, 146
Robinson, D. W., 345
Rogers, Vincent R., 134, 143, 145, 147, 148, 150, 151, 167
Rose, Caroline B., 141, 142, 143
Rosenbaum, M., 205
Russell, David H., 158, 195, 196, 227, 229

Saint Christopher, 22
Sands, Lester B., 270
Schultz, Morton J., 252, 270
Schwartz, S., 205
Scott, Ann Herbert, 380
Sears, P. S., 205
Senesh, Lawrence, 9, 158, 168, 395
Servey, Richard, 188
Shane, H. G., 50
Sherif, M., 53
Shumsky, Abram, 247
Shuster, Albert, 235, 247, 265, 361
Simon, Norma, 280
Skinner, B. J., 270
Smith, F. J., 32
Smith, Gerald, 157
Smith, Huston, 287
Sondergaard, A., 53
Sorauf, Francis J., 148, 149, 167
Sorenson, Frank, 241, 242
Spock, Benjamin, 27, 302
Storke, Edward, 281
Sutton, William, 300

Taba, Hilda, 7, 152, 160, 163, 366, 394
Tate, Sharon, 388

Thomas, George I., 247
Thorpe, Louis P., 192, 197, 198
Tiedt, Sydney, 8

Vinacke, William, 226, 227
Vincent, E. Lee, 196

Wallbank, Walter, 26
Ward, Lynd, 384
Warshaw, T. S., 287
Washington, George, 156
Wass, Philmore B., 316
Weiner, Anthony J., 17

Weiser, John C., 338, 345
Weller, Jack, 73
Welton, David A., 15, 28, 240
Wesley, Edgar, 16, 17
Williams, Robin J., 39, 41
Wilson, Richard C., 316
Wise, W. M., 53
Withall, John, 334, 335
Woodruff, A. D., 54

Zachary, C. B., 46
Zolotow, Charlotte, 378

Subject Index

Affective Domain, 180–81
  goals, 180
  teacher's role in identifying, 184
Africa
  student images, 294
Aims
  see Objectives
American history, 6
American Legion, 6
Anthropology, 6
  children discover, 145
  main ideas, 145
  social science disciplines, 144
Application, 178
Appraisal
  see Evaluation
Attitudes, 55–57
  changing, 55
  changing children's, 55
  and inquiry, 209
  teacher, 337–39
  toward evaluation, 355–57
Audio-visual Aids, 256 ff
  graphs, 256
  guidepost for using, 265–66
  maps, 256
  motion pictures, 255
  overhead projector, 251
  radio and television, 251–53
  still pictures, 251

Behavioral Objectives, 181
  for this course, 186–87
  selection of, 184
  in social science education, 12
  teacher's use of, 184–85

Black People
  and electoral power, 93
  migration of, 93–95
  power of, 93
  students, 70
Black Studies, 300–01
Bloom's Taxonomy, 186
B'nai B'rith, 302
Books
  professional references, 398
  resources for children, 398–401

Center for the Study of Democratic Institutions, 207
Change
  obstacles to, 9
  in social studies, 9, 15
Characteristics of New Programs, 394–96
Charts, 351
Checklist
  development of, 253–54
Child Development
  developmental tasks, 198–99
  intellectual development, 195–96
  language development, 202–03
  principles of learning, 197–98
  social development, 191–92
  social education, 195
Children
  concept of group, 296
  developmental tasks, 198–99
  disadvantaged, 200–02
  failing, 341–42
  individuality of, 83
  language development, 202–03

Children (cont.)
  reasoning of, 195–96
  social concerns of, 193–94
  and thinking, 24
Christianity, 279
Citizenship Education
  evaluating, 352–54
Clark County, Nevada
  curriculum guide, 163
  guide to generalizations, 163–64
  intergroup education, 301
Classroom Climate, 334–35
Cleveland Heights District, 300
Cognitive Domain, 176–79
  goals, 176
  teacher's role in identifying, 184
Community Resources, 264–65
  see Instructional Resources
Comprehension, 178
Concept Development, 13
  and content, 155
  learning activities of, 240–45
Concepts
  Contra Costa list, 160–61
  development of, 155
  inquiry as concept, 221
  levels of, 165
  in map use, 169–70
  perception of, 155
  of political science, 167
  relationship to behavior, 154
  relationship to content, 155
  Syracuse list, 157–58
  teaching for, 160–61
  a teaching plan for, 240–41
  types of, 156–57
Conflicts
  adult society, 59–60
  daily affairs, 60
  early childhood, 45–8, 59, 61
  values, 38
Confucianism, 23
Contemporary Affairs
  analysis of, 304–06
  newspaper study, 311
  objectives, 305, 310–11

social science concepts, 306–07
structural approach to, 306–10
Crisis
  in values, 118
Critical Thinking
  hypothesizing, 215–16, 359–60
  methods of, 179
  problem identification, 214
  use of information, 217–18
Cross-cultural
  bias in, 289
  specific problems, 289–91
  studies, 292
  understanding, 289–93
Curriculum
  change in, 15–16
  projects, 366, 395–96
  reform, 9
  religious scope and sequence, 281
  three R's, 4

Democracy
  and inquiry, 208
Developmental Tasks
  child development, 198–99
Disadvantaged
  alienation of, 200
  characteristics, 200
  children, 200–01
  and reward system, 202
  self-concept, 201
Disciplines
  orchestration of, 8
  sources of concepts and structure, 134–50
Discussion Method, 234

Ecology, 74
  and growth, 78
  misconceptions, 74
  pollution, 76
  technology, 76
Economics, 145–48
  concepts, 166
  social science disciplines, 145

Educational Objectives
  and social education, 238
  in the U.S. and U.S.S.R., 11
Emerging Programs, 12
  characteristics of, 12–15
  examples of, 161–64
Environments
  expanding approach of, 192–93
  improvement of, 71
Eugene, Oregon
  guide to generalizations, 163–64
Evaluation
  of attitudes, 355–57
  attitudes and values, 352–55
  citizenship education, 352–54
  growth and knowledge, 348
  guide for the teacher, 361
  of inquiry, 212, 356
  of materials, 268–69
  model for pupil evaluation, 357–59
  pupil growth, 349–52
  of skills, 351
  teacher's role in, 212
Experience Units
  see Units

Fascism, 90
Field Trips, 264
Films, 255
Filmstrips, 251
First Amendment, 273
Flat Pictures, 254–55

Games
  descriptions, 261–62
  levels of, 165
  of political science, 167
  simulations, 260
  suggested lists, 401–04
Generalizations
  as focal points, 160
  guide: Clark County, Nevada and Eugene, Oregon, 163–64
  using, 158–59
Geography, 137–38
  early study of, 26
  generalizations, 139
  social science disciplines, 137
Ghettoes, 97
Glen Falls Story, 299
Globes, 257
Goals
  affective, 180
  cognitive, 176
Goals of Education
  of social science education, 238
Graphs, 351, 356–59

Hebrew, 276
History
  children discover, 136
  early experiences, 168–69
  limitations of, 134
  social science disciplines, 134
  of social studies, 5
Hobo Kid, 328

Imperialism, 276
Individuality, 82
Individualization
  individually, guided education, 238
  of inquiry, 212
Instructional Resources
  charts, 351
  community, 264–65
  evaluation of, 268
  films, 255
  filmstrips, 251
  flat pictures, 254–55
  globes, 257
  for independent study, 252
  international resource persons, 296–98
  library, 266
  programmed, 264
  radio, 253
  reading materials, 249–50
  still pictures, 251
  tapes and records, 255

Instructional Resources (cont.)
  television, 253
  textbook procedures, 249–51
Integration, 99
Intellectual Development, 195–96
Interdependence, 240–41
International Studies Council, 296
  improving studies in, 298–300
Inquiry
  analysis, 178
  attitudes and, 209
  concept of, 221
  criticisms of, 8
  definition, 3
  elements of, 208–09, 238
  evaluation of, 212
  hypothesizing, 215–16, 359–60
  individualization of, 212
  limits on, 11–12
  place of, 13
  problem identification, 214
  problem solving, 207, 227
  in schools, 208
  strategies, 222–23
  teacher's role in, 210
  use of information developmental approach, 219
Islam, 276
Israel, 285
Issues
  continuing, 63–64
  and values, 65

Knowledge
  changing, 19
  claims, 27
  and perceptions, 23
  in public transactions, 25
  pupils' concept of, 24–25
  types of, 23, 283
  ways of knowing, 19, 21–24

Language
  and concept development, 203
  of disadvantaged, 201
Latter Day Saints, 285

Laws, 244
Learning
  principles of, 197–98
  problems of, 231
Lesson Planning
  teacher's role, 210
  textbook procedures, 249–51
  see Units
Library
  skills, 266–67
  use of in social science, 266–67
Loyalty
  and freedom, 101
  and patriotism, 109
  and the schools, 101

Maps, 139, 169, 256
  concepts of, 169–70
  graphic representations, 256
  skills, 169–70
  special considerations for, 171
Marriage, 67–68
Methods
  developmental approach, 233
  discussion, 234
  early methods of teaching social studies, 231–32
  individually guided education, 238–39
  levels of self-evaluation, 236
  plan for teaching a concept, 240–41
  pupil-centered, 235–36
  recitation, 232
  teacher-centered, 232–33
  teacher-pupil planning, 235–36
Migration, 242
Minority Group Studies, 300
Motivation, 197

National Council for the Social Studies, 7–8, 176, 253, 263, 268

Objectives
  behavioral, 181ff

Subject Index

Objectives (cont.)
  historical perspectives, 176
  place of, 29
  selection of, 183–84
  teacher's role in defining, 184
  types of, 176–79
  uses of, 29–30
Opinions of Young Americans, 339
Oregon Maps, 257–59
Organic-experimental Approach
  in social science education, 193

Personality, 85
Political Science, 149
  and children, 150
  concepts, 167–68
  generalizations, 167
  scope of study, 149
  social science disciplines, 148
Population, 78
Prayer in Schools, 273
Problem Solving, 207, 227
  hypothesizing, 215–16
  processes, 179
  use of information, 217–18
Programmed Materials, 263–64
Projects in Social Studies, 394–96

Questions
  use of, 222–23

Radio
  see Instructional Resources
Readiness
  for cross-cultural studies, 292
Reasoning in Children, 195–96
Religion and Education
  A.A.S.A. position, 274
  B'nai B'rith, 302
  Christianity, 279
  comparative studies, 284
  fifth grade unit, 277–78
  freedom of, 276
  guidelines for study of, 284
  Hebrew, 276

Latter Day Saints, 285
prayers in school, 273
Roman Catholic Church, 285
school's role, 283
scope and sequence, 281
teacher's role, 283
universal nature, 275
U.S. Supreme Court, 273
Resource Unit
  see Unit, 237
Resources
  see Instructional Resources
Roman Catholic Church, 22, 285

Self-Evaluation
  levels of instructional, 236–37
Simulation, 260–63
  games, 260
Skills
  of inquiry, 207
  of maps, 169–70
  of social science education, 28–29
Social Concerns of Children, 193–94
Social Content
  of child's life, 194
  as structure for education, 194
Social Education
  child development, 195
  and educational objectives, 238
Social Science Disciplines
  anthropology, 144
  economics, 145
  geography, 137
  history, 134
  political science, 148
  sociology, 140
Social Science Education
  aims of, 133
  behavioral objectives, 12
  characteristics, 12–15
  content of, 14
  definition of, 10
  emerging programs, 12
  explained, 3

Social Science Education (cont.)
  goals of, 237–40
  major objectives, 30
  organic-experimental approach, 193
  place of conceptualization, 13
  place of inquiry, 13
  purposes of, 30–31
  religious scope and sequence, 281
  skills of, 28–29
  study of social man, 20
  use of school library, 266
  value base of, 40
Social Studies
  appearance in curriculum, 5
  changes in, 9
  confusion in, 6
  criticisms of, 8
  definition, 6
  early methods of teaching, 231–32
  history of, 5
  obstacles to change, 9–10
  role of, 8
  and social sciences, 16
  unified approach, 6
Socialization of Teachers, 343
Sociology, 140–43
  social science disciplines, 140
South Vietnamese
  students' views of, 293–94
Student Protests, 68
Study of Man, 26
Surveys, 286
Synthesis, 178

Taba Curriculum, 160–64, 366
Teacher
  adult authority model, 329–30
  attitudes, 337–39
  child perceptions, 336–38
  readings for, 397–98
  role in evaluation, 212
  role in inquiry, 210
  self-awareness, 329
  self-evaluation, 236

  socialization of, 343
  society's view of, 326
  values, 49–50
  view of children, 342
Teaching
  developmental approach, 233
  machines, 263–64
  methods, 234–36
  organic-experimental approach, 193
  team, 330–31
Teaching Machines, 263–64
Team Teaching, 330–31
Television
  receiver skills, 314–15
  see Instructional Resources
Textbooks
  improving use of, 250
  procedures for using, 249–51
  as resources, 242–43, 249–51
Thinking, 86
  children's, 24
Time line, 136
Transactions and Knowledge, 25

Units
  concept-centered learning:
    interdependence, 240
    migration, 242
    social control, 243
  examples of, 370–85
  grade one, 161
  grade two, 161–62
  grade five, 277–78
  grade six, 162–63
  of learning, 236–38
  organization of, 237
Universal Developmental Tasks, 198–99
Universal Values, 36–38

Values
  American, 39–40, 111
  changing, 54
  conflicts, 38, 61–62
  confusion, 36
  crisis, 118

Values (cont.)
  in education, 35
  meaning of, 43
  myths of, 118–19
  parents and, 57–58
  pupil achievement, 51
  relation of teacher and achievement, 52
  school's role in, 41–42, 48, 291
  in social science education, 40
  sources of, 38, 53
  structure of, 39–41, 59–60
  teaching, 36, 39
  universal, 36–38
  value guides, 50–51
  varying views, 42
  verbalism, 119
Virginia State Board's Guide, 267
Voluntary Prayer, 277

Wheaton, Illinois, Unit, 277–81